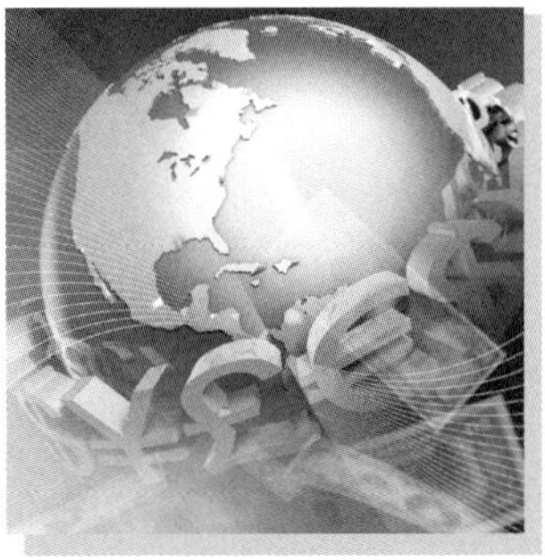

HANDBOOK ON INTERNATIONAL POLITICAL ECONOMY

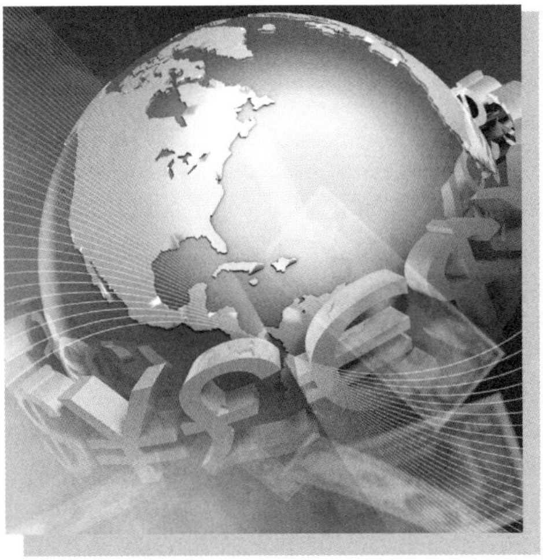

HANDBOOK ON INTERNATIONAL POLITICAL ECONOMY

editor

Ralph Pettman

University of Melbourne, Australia

World Scientific

NEW JERSEY • LONDON • SINGAPORE • BEIJING • SHANGHAI • HONG KONG • TAIPEI • CHENNAI

Published by

World Scientific Publishing Co. Pte. Ltd.
5 Toh Tuck Link, Singapore 596224
USA office: 27 Warren Street, Suite 401-402, Hackensack, NJ 07601
UK office: 57 Shelton Street, Covent Garden, London WC2H 9HE

British Library Cataloguing-in-Publication Data
A catalogue record for this book is available from the British Library.

HANDBOOK ON INTERNATIONAL POLITICAL ECONOMY

ISBN-13 978-981-4366-97-7
ISBN-10 981-4366-97-8

In-house Editors: Agnes Ng and Samantha Yong

Typeset by Stallion Press
Email: enquiries@stallionpress.com

Printed in Singapore by B & Jo Enterprise Pte Ltd

Foreword

More than four decades have passed since the publication of Susan Strange's germinal article "International Relations and International Economics", which launched the contemporary study of international political economy (IPE). Much progress has been made in the field in the intervening decades. We have a good understanding of the role of interests, ideas and institutions in the making of economic policy. We know the circumstances that make it more likely that states will comply with their international obligations and the reasons that some international institutions are more effective than others. An enormous literature on globalisation has aided our comprehension of this multi-faceted phenomenon and its impact on peoples' lives across the globe. Even for those most important yet most difficult questions on what makes for successful economic development and what strategies are most effective in alleviating poverty, our knowledge is much more sophisticated than it was when Susan Strange's article was published.

These achievements notwithstanding, long-standing contributors to the field have increasingly voiced their anxiety about the directions in which it is heading. Such concerns have been expressed not only by those outside of the 'mainstream' but also by many of those, such as Benjamin J. Cohen, Peter Katzenstein and Robert Keohane, whose work was central to the establishment of IPE as one of the leading sub-fields of international relations in universities in the United States. The principal concern is the manner in which the contemporary study of IPE has become little more than a sub-field of economics.

Not only do we see the worst sort of reductionism — with attempts to explain everything political by reference to some underlying economic characteristic — but also a dogged assertion that the application of certain statistical methods are the only means for achieving analytic rigor. Large *N* statistical studies have indeed contributed to our understanding of some dimensions of IPE. But to equate analytic rigor with this single set of methodologies has substantial drawbacks. It is often the case that adequate statistical measures of various dimensions of causal factors in IPE are not available. The consequence is either that the analyst searches for 'proxy' indicators that seldom capture the relationships under investigation or a whole range of questions is left entirely unexplored because they are not easily susceptible to econometric modeling. The obsession with statistical analysis — a recent report notes that ninety percent of all articles in IPE in the last decade relied on quantitative analysis — has left the contemporary field unable to address 'big' questions and relegated to a position of little interest to policy makers.

The subordination of contemporary IPE to the discipline of economics is particularly ironic because it was precisely the narrowness of the range of issues that economic theory addresses that was at the heart of the concerns that Susan Strange expressed in her 1970 article. Her argument then was that economics lacked a political theory of analysis and explanation and that the contributions of economists to the study of international economic relations were naïve. Economics alone was an insufficient grounding for understanding the multi-dimensionality of power and how structures systematically discriminate against weaker actors. For Strange and many other pioneers in IPE, it was not just a question of 'bringing politics back in' but of creating a field that drew on insights from multiple disciplines — including history, geography and law. While the application of insights from economic theory was something that Strange believed to be important to IPE (hence the subtitle to her article which expressed concern at the 'mutual neglect' between the two fields), it was but one of several potential sources of insight on which analysts should draw.

In her article, Strange was also critical of the tendency of the economics discipline to exaggerate human rationality. The preoccupation of contemporary IPE with simple rational choice models is particularly ironic when the global economy has just experienced the most severe financial crisis for three quarters of a century, a crisis that demonstrated vividly how inadequate models based on expectations of 'rational' behaviour really were. Indeed, contemporary IPE is lagging behind the discipline of economics itself, where the sub-field of behavioural economics, with its challenges to the conventional assumptions of what underlies rational behaviour, is gaining increasing influence.

The depressing narrowness of much of the contemporary study of IPE makes this comprehensive *Handbook* particularly welcome. What follows addresses big questions — the changing role of global institutions, the consequences of the rise of China and India, the impact of changes in the global economy on the environment. It includes chapters on gender and labour, subjects seldom examined in any depth in much of the contemporary scholarship on IPE. And it does all these things from a multi-disciplinary perspective. It thus points the way to a welcome return to a conceptualisation of the field that is akin to that envisioned by its pioneers.

John Ravenhill
Head, School of Politics and International Relations,
Australian National University;
Fellow, Academy of Social Sciences, Australia

Contents

List of Contributors

Hans A. Baer is a Senior Lecturer in the School of Political and Social Sciences at the University of Melbourne. He is currently developing a critical anthropology of climate change. His books include (with Merrill Singer) *Global Warming and the Political Ecology of Health* (Left Coast Press, 2008).

Geoffrey Blainey held the Chair of Economic History at the University of Melbourne from 1968 to 1977 and of History from 1977 to 1988. He has served as Chairman of governing bodies of national institutions like the Australian Council for the Arts and the National Council for the Centenary of Federation. His *Short History of the World* has been translated into many foreign languages. He has written more than thirty other books.

Verity Burgmann is Professor of Political Science at the University of Melbourne, a Fellow of the Academy of Social Sciences and a former President of the Australasian Political Studies Association. Her books include studies of labour, syndicalist and socialist movements, environmental protests in the 1970s, new social movements and anti-corporate mobilisations. Her current research interests are international labour movements' opposition to globalisation, contemporary protest movements, utopianism, autonomist marxism and other radical political ideologies.

Loren R. Cass is Associate Professor of Political Science and Director of the Environmental Studies Programme at the College of the Holy Cross. He is author of *The Failures of American and European Climate Policy: International Norms, Domestic Politics, and Unachievable Commitments* (SUNY Press, 2006).

Thomas W. D. Davis is a Fellow of the School of Social and Political Sciences at the University of Melbourne. His most recent publications include *Human Rights in Asia* (Edward Elgar, 2011), which he edited with Brian Galligan, and "Foreign Aid in Australia's Relationship with the South: Institutional Narratives", *Round Table*, August 2011.

Nidhi Dutt is a Masters student at the University of Melbourne. Her thesis explores the impact of armed rule on the governance of Pakistan. She has a Bachelor of

Communication from Bond University and has focused for several years on emerging markets, particularly those in South Asia. She is currently a foreign correspondent in Mumbai, India.

Shaun Fitzgerald studied at the University of Melbourne and the University of London, gaining a Master of International Politics, a Bachelor of Laws (Hons) and a Bachelor of Arts. He won the McMahon Ball and Janette Kosky Prizes at the University of Melbourne in 2009 for outstanding scholarship in the field of international relations. He is joint author with John Langmore of "Global Governance: Addressing the Economic Deficit", *Development*, 53(3), 2010.

Leslie Holmes is Professor of Political Science at the University of Melbourne and a Recurrent Visiting Professor at both the Graduate School for Social Research (Warsaw) and the University of Bologna. He specialises in comparative corruption studies and post-communism.

Lance Hoovestal has an MBA from the University of College, Cork, an MA from the University of New South Wales, and a PhD from the University of Melbourne. Lance has also worked extensively for Greenway Enterprises Inc., a US-based international contractor.

Sheila Jeffreys is Professor of Feminist Politics in the School of Social and Political Sciences at the University of Melbourne. She is the author of eight books including *Man's Dominion: The Rise of Religion and the Eclipse of Women's Rights* (Routledge, 2011).

John Langmore is a Professorial Fellow in the School of Social and Political Sciences at the University of Melbourne. Formerly Economic Advisor to the Australian Treasurer, he has also served as an MP in the Australian House of Representatives, Director of the UN Division for Social Policy and Development, and Director of the ILO Office at the UN. His most recent publications include *Dealing with America: The UN, US and Australia* (2005) and *To Firmer Ground: Restoring Hope in Australia* (2007), both published by the UNSW Press.

Kate Macdonald is a Lecturer at the University of Melbourne, having held previous positions at the London School of Economics and Political Science, the Australian National University, and Oxford University. Her research focuses on the politics of transnational production and business, with a particular focus on social labour and the human rights regulation of global business.

John Mikler is a Senior Lecturer in the Department of Government and International Relations at the University of Sydney. His research interests are primarily focused on the role of transnational economic actors, particularly multinational corporations, and the interaction between them and states, international organisations, and civil society. He has had his research published in leading journals such as *Business and Politics* and *New Political Economy* and is the author of *Greening the Car Industry: Varieties of Capitalism and Climate Change* (Edward Elgar, 2009).

Philomena Murray is Associate Professor in the School of Social and Political Sciences at the University of Melbourne. She holds Australia's only Personal Jean Monnet Chair. She is a Research Associate of the Institute for International Integration Studies at Trinity College Dublin; a Visiting Professor at the College of Europe; a Research Associate at the United Nations University — Comparative Regional Integration Studies; and an Adjunct Senior Fellow, NCRE, University of Canterbury. Her most recent books include *Australia and the European Superpower* (Melbourne University Press, 2005) and P. Murray (ed.) *Europe and Asia: Regions in Flux* (Palgrave Macmillan, 2008).

Gerry Nagtzaam is a Lecturer in the Law School at Monash University where he specialises in international environmental law. His main areas of research include climate change, whaling, nuclear waste and eco-terrorism. He is currently writing a book on the concept of environmental exploitation.

Ralph Pettman is Professor of International Relations at the University of Melbourne. He has held teaching and research positions at the Australian National University, the University of Tokyo, Princeton University, Cambridge University, the New School for Social Research, the London School of Economics, the Frankfurt Peace Research Institute, and Sciences Po, Paris. His most recent book is *Psychopathology and World Politics* (World Scientific, 2011). He is also the author of *Understanding International Political Economy, With Readings for the Fatigued* (Lynne Rienner, 1996).

José Pablo Zambrano Ramírez studied journalism and history at Universidad Finis Terrae, Chile. Since he graduated, he has been writing freelance for different magazines and newspapers. He also works as an outdoor tour guide, leading treks and hikes in the Patagonian Andes and the Atacama Desert. He is currently a Masters student by research at the University of Melbourne, focusing on climate change and environmental security.

Hana Sabanovic (B. Arts/Sciences; Master of International Politics) is a Research Fellow in the School of Population Health at the University of Melbourne. Hana has a background in political science and is currently studying towards a Master of Public Health at Monash University.

Susan K. Sell is Professor of Political Science and International Affairs and Director of the Institute for Global and International Studies at the George Washington University in Washington, DC. She is the co-editor (with Deborah Avant and Martha Finnemore) of *Who Governs the Globe?* (Cambridge University Press, 2010); author of *Private Power, Public Law: The Globalisation of Intellectual Property Rights* (Cambridge University Press, 2003); and numerous other books, articles and book chapters on globalisation, development, international trade and intellectual property. Her work has been translated into Chinese, Korean and Japanese.

Pradeep Taneja works on Chinese politics, political economy and international relations in Asia at the University of Melbourne, where he is also a Fellow of the Australia-India Institute. Pradeep lived and worked in China for a number of years and is a fluent Mandarin speaker.

Sally Trethewie is a Senior Analyst in the food security, environmental security and climate change programmes at the Centre for Non-Traditional Security Studies, S. Rajaratnam School of International Studies, Singapore. She was previously Public Affairs Officer at the Australian High Commission in Singapore. She holds a Master of International Politics from the University of Melbourne and a Bachelor of Music Studies (Performance) from the Sydney Conservatorium of Music at the University of Sydney.

Mark Triffitt is a former journalist, political advisor and corporate executive. Over the past decade and a half he has advised Australian premiers, senior ministers and corporate leaders on political strategy. He is currently writing a PhD on China and democracy at the University of Melbourne.

Meagan Tyler is a Lecturer in the School of Social Sciences and Psychology at Victoria University, Melbourne. She has a PhD from the University of Melbourne where she taught in the areas of International Relations and Gender Politics. Her research has been published in *Women's Studies International Forum* and *Women and Therapy*, and her first published book is *Selling Sex Short: The Pornographic and Sexological Construction of Women's Sexuality in the West* (Cambridge Scholars Press, 2011).

Stephen Woolcock is a Lecturer in International Relations at the London School of Economics. He is Head of the School International Trade Policy Unit and has worked for many years on a range of trade issues including multilateral trade, European trade policy and free trade agreements.

Introduction

CHAPTER 1

International Political Economy: Competing Analyses

Ralph Pettman

University of Melbourne

International political economy (IPE) is a very diverse discipline. It covers a wide range of issues not only to do with the analytical discourses currently used to describe and explain (and prescribe policy for) its many and varied concerns, but also to do with the history of the discipline *per se*. The most significant aspect of contemporary IPE is the way it exemplifies the industrial/scientific revolution and its technological consequences. This revolution has made — and continues to make — radical changes to global production and consumption, finance and trade, management and work, overdevelopment and underdevelopment, global gender balances and imbalances, and environmental sustainability and distress.

The table of contents of this *Handbook* clearly reflects this diversity. As such it highlights the disciplinary concerns that contemporary scholars and practitioners find most compelling.

It provides a comprehensive coverage of what IPE involves. It flags out in the process, the issues that most analysts think of as being central to the discipline.

A HANDBOOK

The contributors to this book/volume were invited to write as they saw fit about the general or specific topics they agreed to discuss. In some cases those working on a particular part met to share their ideas about the approaches they thought they would take. By so doing they tried to maximise the degree of coherence between the general account of what was involved and the applied discussions of it. In other cases they did not meet, usually because this was not feasible. They made the contribution they considered most appropriate, whether general or applied, and they submitted that, relying on the editor's account of the structure of the work as a whole to place their piece within the context the *Handbook* sought to provide.

They were chosen because of their expertise. They were also known to the editor to be analysts able to provide contributions that would be stimulating and up-to-date.

To be of maximum benefit to the reader, however, this *Handbook* had first and foremost to include all the key topics that dominate the discipline today. This is what is meant by comprehensive coverage, and this is what this work strives to provide.

AN ANALYTICAL OVERVIEW

Before going any further it is important to confront the fact that it is impossible to talk about any part of this discipline without using an analytical language of some kind. Moreover, talking in analytical languages also means talking in analytical dialects. The latter provide much of the nuance with which each analytical language presents itself.

To talk about IPE without using an analytical language or dialect at all would require the talker to be so intellectually detached and socially alienated that he or she would have to be divine or insane or both. Most people are not divine or insane. Though imbued with the modernist/rationalist culture that is hegemonic today, they never achieve total detachment or alienation.

In practice, while analysts and practitioners may reach in the direction of detachment, they continuously fall short, smuggling back in to their understanding of IPE one or more underlying assumptions. It is these assumptions which underpin the various articulations of modernist/rationalism that are used to describe and explain (and prescribe for) mainstream accounts of the subject. It is these assumptions that result in the various analytical languages and dialects that characterise the diverse discourses that dominate the discipline today.

Noteworthy too is the way the most radical assumptions about objectivity result in the meta-discourse of modernist/rationalism itself. These assumptions have already been flagged. They are two-fold, namely, epistemological detachment and ontological individuation.

These radical assumptions result in the marginalisation of those deemed insufficiently rationalistic. Modernist/rationalists, that is, consign to the periphery of IPE those they deem incapable of prioritising reason as an end in itself. They tend to include in this regard women, environmentalists, post-colonials, indigenous peoples and the poor. Members of these groups respond in turn by pointing out why they are central rather than peripheral to IPE and what the implications of their centrality happen to be.

These radical assumptions are also manifested now in a range of auto-critiques. Many of those who prioritise reason as an end in itself have come to see how this limits and distorts their understanding of the world. As a result they now try, by various means, to compensate for these limits and distortions; hence such approaches as postmodernism, poststructuralism, psychopathology, emotivism, phenomenology, and sacralism.

There is a great deal of information in the preceding paragraphs. They are so compressed that what they say could hardly be called engaging. As a consequence the rest of this Introduction will discuss what is said above in a more expansive and hopefully more engaging way.

To reiterate however: the question of competing of analytical approaches is so basic that in this *Handbook* it is placed upfront. It attempts to show what these approaches are, how they relate to each other, and how they inform any attempt to discuss IPE.

To begin with it is worth considering IPE in context of world affairs as a whole (for a more extended discussion see Pettman, 2010). It is worth considering, that is, what the main ways in which world affairs is described and explained might be.

IPE AS ONE OF THREE DIMENSIONS TO WORLD AFFAIRS

Most obviously there is the strategic dimension to world affairs. This is often called the political dimension but that is to confine the political to the strategic. Politics is about politicking, that is, the process of getting one's own way, whether individually or collectively. As such it pertains to every aspect of human experience. It is about much more than strategic affairs.

The strategic dimension to world politics is mostly to do with the politics of state affairs, that is, politics of affairs of the diplomatic and military kind. This dimension is the anarchic one of security dilemmas and the competitive, so-called 'realist' attempt to survive and prevail in a self-help environment where human nature is seen in the worst possible light and peace is deemed to be only ever a lull between wars.

It is also characterised by calculative behaviour, however. As such it is one where a more optimistic sense of human nature is manifested in the form of state-makers creating international regimes, organisations and laws and where, in the process, they bring about tit-for-tat outcomes that state competitiveness alone would never allow.

It is characterised as well by an even more optimistic sense of human nature that highlights the capacity for cooperative, hail-fellow-well-met behaviour. It is this sense that sees in world affairs the rudimentary possibilities of global governance.

The politico-strategic dimension to world affairs is well represented by the sort of map most commonly on display, usually in its Mercator projection, on schoolroom walls across the world. A map like this highlights the world's sovereign states. It shows their borders and their capital cities.

Less obvious but no less significant is the dimension to world affairs that lies behind this sort of map, namely, the map of the politics of global market affairs, that is, global production and consumption, finance and investment, work and trade. This is the international political economy. Like the strategic dimension to world affairs there is one account of IPE that highlights human competitiveness. This account highlights how economic nationalism (or economic protectionism) continues to prevail. Like the strategic dimension to world affairs there is also an approach that highlights the human penchant for calculation. In the case of the politics of the market dimension to world affairs this is seen to be what makes it possible to promote economic liberalism. And like the strategic dimension to world affairs there is a third account that highlights human nature in the most positive of terms. This throws into clear analytic relief people's cooperative capacity to administer equal outcomes, that is, to promote economic socialism.

The least obvious dimension to world affairs lies behind both the politico-strategic and the politico-economic ones. It is the dimension to do with the politics of the world's social or civic affairs. As with the strategic and market dimensions there is one account of it that highlights human competitiveness. This account highlights the significance of nationalism and how, in a world of several thousand nations and only two hundred sovereign states, the legitimacy accorded by the doctrine of national self-determination is the basis for considerable global strife. Like the strategic and market dimensions there is also an approach that highlights human nature as essentially calculating. This account highlights how individuals have arrived at doctrines of human rights and democratic rule. The third account of the civic dimension to world affairs highlights the human capacity for cooperation. It highlights global social movements that promote common causes.

All three dimensions cited above are part of world affairs. Moreover, all of the analytical languages that articulate these dimensions do so in the light of the assumptions about human nature that those who speak these languages see as being significant.

IPE WITH REGARD TO HUMAN NATURE

The international political economy is the marketeering dimension to world affairs. As such it can be compared with the strategic and socio-civil ones and as such it is articulated in terms of the same assumptions that are articulated by strategic and socio-civil analysts, that is, in terms of assumptions to do with people as being by nature bad, calculating or good.

IPE is articulated in both proximal and distal forms. The proximal form is typically the classical one and the distal form is typically a more contemporary one.

For example, the account of economic nationalism provided by Thomas Mun, an early English trader and one-time director of the East India Company, in his book on *England's Treasure by Forraign Trade, or the Balance of Our Forraign Trade is the Rule of Our Treasure* (Mun, 1664 [1630]), is a proximal/classical one. Mun was a practitioner and his account of foreign trade was that of someone involved in trade himself. Not surprisingly, he identified foreign trade as the way a state might increase its wealth. By astute foreign dealings, he said, a state could sell more each year than it buys. It could maximise its worth by combining an increase in exports with import substitution, that is, by enacting laws that prohibited imports and compelled the use of local goods it could undercut other suppliers, use national transport, and add value to its primary products.

Mun's concept of economic nationalism was the dominant doctrine of IPE in the early stages of European capitalism, that is, from the sixteenth to the eighteenth centuries. It remained so until economic liberalism took its place. That said, economic nationalism did not disappear. It remained a key approach and it does so to this day, informing not only individual state policies but regional policies like those of the European Union.

Relatively more contemporary and distal dialects of the same analytical language talk similarly about protecting sovereign autonomy by promoting exports, inhibiting imports, controlling capital flows, and keeping currency and foreign reserves in state hands. They talk about self-sufficiency in terms of tariffs, quotas and other restrictions, protected secondary and agricultural industries, and state growth in an otherwise adversarial economic world. Taken to voluntary extremes an approach like this can result in autarky (like Myanmar). It can also be involuntary, that is, it can be imposed by other states in the form of economic sanctions (like Cuba).

A representative example of such an account is Frederick List's *National System of Political Economy* (1856 [1841]). List argued that states that were united would be more prosperous. Like a strategic realist or a socio-civic nationalist, however, he saw states as "victims of each other" and their self-referential policies and as failing to promote their collective potential for economic development (List, 1856 [1841], pp. 70–71). What was to be done? According to List, a state was likely to become more rich and powerful the more it exported manufactured products and imported raw ones (List, 1856 [1841], p. 77). It had to seize the day in this regard, he said, since states that did not were likely to be left behind.

States like Japan responded almost immediately to List's advice. They used it as the basis for one of the most dramatic development projects ever seen. More recently China has found in List's neoprotectionism an important key to its own politico-economic growth.

In positing self-reliance as the basic source of state wealth List was specifically critiquing Adam Smith. As a classical economic liberal, Smith advocated opening every state market to the world market. He assumed that the world would be peaceful enough to make such openness possible. List was a pessimist, however, and as such he did not see people as capable of sustaining a system of interstate law that would be sufficiently compelling to allow for interstate confederacy. With the spread of industry he did admit that war might be made "improbable, if not impossible" (List, 1856 [1841], p. 191). In his reading of the historical record, however, he saw "political" or strategic union as invariably preceding the commercial variety. In practice, he believed that free trade results not in a "community of nations" but in the "universal subjection of nations to the supremacy of the greater powers in manufactures, commerce, and navigation" (List, 1856 [1841], p. 200). In practice, he saw economic protection as the "only system" by which "less advanced" states could achieve the same level as those that dominate global manufacturing. In practice, he advocated excluding foreign products so that states could defend their own interests and not fall victim to foreign ones. It was, after all, a "vulgar rule of prudence", he said, for those who had reached the "pinnacle of power" to "cast down the ladder" by which they had climbed so that others might not follow. A state which by "protective duties …" had built up a "manufacturing industry … to such a point of … power as not to fear the competition of any other", he said, could pursue "no safer policy than to thrust aside the means of elevation, [and] to preach to others … the advantages of free trade …" (List, 1856 [1841], pp. 440, 488).

Adam Smith saw human beings as essentially calculating. It was this assumption that informed his account of economic liberalism, an account that became the classical/proximal liberalist one and the foundation for the discipline of modern economics.

Adam Smith was a prominent member of the Scottish Enlightenment and as such he promoted the prioritisation of the use of reason as an end in itself. It was a short step from promoting this perspective to one that saw human beings as being by nature essentially self-referential and rationalistic and Smith used that assumption to describe and explain IPE.

His key work was entitled *An Inquiry into the Nature and Causes of the Wealth of Nations* (Smith, 1993 [1776]). In this work Smith began by highlighting the significance of the division of labour. A workman's woollen coat, however "course and rough", could not exist, he said, without the "joint labour of a great multitude" of others (Smith, 1993 [1776], p. 19). Any economy relies on reciprocity, he said, with each individual in it supplying others and the resulting "general plenty" trickling through "all the different ranks of the society" (Smith, 1993 [1776], p. 18). This reciprocity was not the result of a wise assessment, however, of what was achievable in this way, but rather of the human tendency to "truck, barter, and exchange one thing for another". It was the result of people saying "[g]ive me that which I want, and you shall have this which you want ... [Thus i]t is not from the benevolence of the butcher, the brewer, or the baker", Smith concluded "that we expect our dinner, but from their regard to their own interest ..." (Smith, 1993 [1776], p. 22).

Smith was highly critical of economic nationalism, basically because of the way it exalted the significance of a favourable balance of trade. He did not believe that restricting imports by using duties and tariffs, and fostering exports using subsidies for infant industries and the like, could make a state wealthy.

He did not, in short, see one state's gain as another state's loss. Granted, everybody strives to use their capital to their advantage, he said. However, "the study of ... [that] advantage naturally, or rather necessarily" led to "... that employment" which was the "most advantageous to the society" (Smith, 1993 [1776], p. 289). Thus while individuals did pursue their own interests, they were also prompted "by an invisible hand" to promote interests they did not intend. Moreover they were prompted to do so "more effectually" with regard to the social good than any plan could possibly provide (Smith, 1993 [1776], p. 292). A liberal and free trade system between states was in his view, therefore, the most effective way to pursue wealth.

Smith's idea of absolute advantage was carried a step forward in the nineteenth century by David Ricardo and his concept of comparative advantage. It was Ricardo's abstract conclusion — that those states that were more productive in every way still had an incentive to trade — that became the cornerstone of the contemporary liberalist account of the global system of trade (Ricardo, 1951 [1817]).

In the twentieth century Smith's ideas were made the basis of a more contemporary/distal account of market behaviour. This analytic dialect not only promoted Smith's concept that human beings were by nature calculating. It was even more convinced that government control over markets distorts them.

The so-called neoliberalists involved articulated what by the 1990's had come to be called the 'Washington Consensus'. They advocated balanced budgets and small or no budget deficits, reduced state expenditure of all kinds as a way of achieving such a balance (even where this required less spending on education, health and public infrastructure), tax reforms that broadened the tax base and reduced the tax burden on the well-off, interest rates and exchange rates determined by the market and not by bureaucrats, the liberalisation of imports and in particular no import licensing, the liberalisation of foreign financial flows, more privatised commerce and industry in general (that is, more deregulation of the economy) and more secure property rights. Neoliberalism was the fruit of what came to be called the Chicago school. Milton Friedman was one of this school's most eminent exponents. Trained originally as a mathematician, Friedman preferred analyses that were highly abstract. He endorsed what he saw as social science and the distinction between positive and normative knowledge. Despite his detachment he was also part of a movement that began in Switzerland in 1947 to promote the principles of the free market in the face of those of Soviet state-planned socialism, a movement whose leader was an equally eminent neoliberalist: Friedrich A. von Hayek. However, it was Friedman who advised American Presidents like Richard Nixon and Ronald Reagan. It was Friedman who received the Nobel Prize for economics in 1976. And it was Friedman who in his book *Capitalism and Freedom* (1962) wrote about the need to maximise personal freedom and minimise state interference. Governments were necessary in a market-centred society, he said, to act as umpires and to maintain the integrity of the system. He agreed with Smith on that. But control of foreign exchange, of imports, and of domestic production was the best way, he believed, to convert a market-centred society into an authoritarian one. "Concentrated power", he said, "is not rendered harmless by the good intentions of those who create it"(Friedman, 1962, p. 201).

In marked contrast to all liberalists were those who saw human beings as basically good enough to envisage distributing the largesse of the industrial revolution in an equitable fashion so that everyone's fundamental needs for food, shelter, clothing, education and healthcare would be met. With the industrial revolution the species now has this capacity. Economic socialists are those who see no reason why planning to realise this capacity should not succeed.

This sort of socialism is *reformist* and as such is not the *revolutionary* socialism associated with Karl Marx, for whom socialism was the next stage in humanity's history. Marx saw socialism in terms of the proletariat rising up to overthrow the bourgeoisie and dismantle the apparatus of the state in order to establish advanced communism.

To reformist socialists Marx gave socialism a bad name. Marx, in turn, saw reformist socialists as utopian and ineffectual.

There is a fundamental difference between these two approaches in that economic socialists articulate an optimistic assumption about human nature ('people are basically good') while Marx saw human nature as only manifesting once the process of historical materialism was at an end, that is, once humanity's "species being" had ceased to be distorted by ruling class exploitation. Marx highlighted the material nature of human nurturing practices.

Examples of proximal/classical socialism include nineteenth-century British and French optimists like Robert Owen and Henri de Saint-Simon. Owen, for example, instituted reforms in workers' pay, participation and education. He sought to make self-reliant collectives of the manufacturing enterprises that he owned. In his work *A New View of Society, or, Essays on the Principle of the Formation of the Human Character, and the Application of the Principle to Practice* (1817 [1813–1816]), for example, he flagged his belief in the human capacity for personal improvement where rulers put the interests of the ruled before their own. The result of this for his fellow manufacturers (Owen was a cotton miller) was increased production, since a well-managed enterprise, he said, like a well-maintained machine, responded favourably to proper maintenance. This meant providing workers with training, food, comfortable conditions and humane control. Owen expressed not only a high degree of optimism about human nature in this regard but also a high degree of optimism about what the appropriate forms of human nurture could achieve. Because people are basically good, he said, if they were treated well that goodness would reveal itself and there would be greater prosperity and less aggression. People actually preferred, he said, useful and rewarding work, while children responded positively to the sort of instruction that taught consideration and the well-being of others. Economic nationalists saw such conclusions as unrealistic. Economic liberals saw them as falling foul of the human capacity for calculation. Owen thought that regardless of what we were born to be, we could learn to be generous and kind and that ideas of inherent human superiority were wrong. This suggests that Owen did not in the end subscribe to any fundamental assumption about human nature. Why, however, do good qualities manifest themselves if given the chance to do so — as Owen argued they would — unless these were not the most basic forms of human being? Socialism like Owen's is underpinned by optimism in this regard. Pessimists tend to be protectionists, as indicated above, while those who see human beings as calculating tend to be economic liberalists.

Like the other analytical languages, there are diverse analytical dialects of economic socialism too, one of the more contemporary and distal being Hugh Stretton's *Economics: A New Introduction* (1999). Like a classical socialist Stretton highlights how rich states do less than they might to help the poor and how as their wealth increases so does poverty. He argues, in the face of this fact, that the benefits of economic growth ought to be distributed collectively. States should use their capacity to make their product available to all so that everyone might have a sustainable quality of life regardless of the wage they earn. He wants greater equality, in other words, and less inequality. He wants economic collectivism to take precedence over economic growth and public power to be used to help the poor, both within states and between them.

In practice, Stretton sees the hegemony of neoliberalism as resulting in the underestimation of "social commitments" and the overestimation of what is possible on the basis of "universal selfishness ..." (Stretton, 1999, pp. 61–63). He sees neoliberal policies resulting in "absolute poverty and death in some poor countries, and relative poverty and insecurity in rich countries, on a scale to rival any effects of poor doctoring or engineering"(Stretton, 1999, p. 61). He sees neoliberalists, and indeed, all economic liberalists, as promoting arguments like public enterprise is inefficient and ineffective and as much market activity as possible should be moved into the private domain where it is subject to the discipline of competitive calculation. He himself, by contrast, wants "good performance by a well-designed public sector". For this he sees no alternative but "good government"(Stretton, 1999, pp. 468–470, 484).

Stretton's economically socialistic proclivities are also evident with regard to international money and banking. The "price of credit", he says, "cannot equilibrate the supply and demand for it …". Nor can it ration bank lending "either to its most productive or … most socially desirable uses". Indeed, Stretton sees opening state borders as guaranteed to take from their inhabitants their "best means" of controlling their rates of "investment, employment, and inflation"(Stretton, 1999, p. 722).

IPE WITH REGARD TO HUMAN NURTURE

In discussing Robert Owen's work, mention was made of approaches that articulate assumptions about the essential nature of human nurturing practices as opposed to approaches that articulate assumptions about the essential nature of human beings. These approaches do not focus on human nature. They focus on how human beings learn to be.

There are three key approaches in this regard, one that highlights the material nature of human nurturing practices, one that highlights the mental nature of human nurturing practices, and one that highlights a mixture of the two. The general point to note here is that not all analysts and practitioners think human beings are by nature essentially anything. They think that what matters most is what dominates people's educative environment. There is a particular point to note too, which is that the nature/nurture dichotomy is a conceptual one. In practice people are both one and the other, though this does not stop analysts and policy-makers from dichotomising the two and using this dichotomy to inform their descriptions and explanations of (and policy prescriptions with regard to) IPE. There is another particular point which is that the results of articulating the material, mental and mixed assumptions about human nurturing practices cuts across the three dimensions to world affairs highlighted above. They do not highlight the strategic, marketeering and socio-civic aspects of the larger discipline. As such they tend to be critical of those who do. They do not talk of IPE, hence their reputation as 'critical' approaches (with a small 'c').

While the first such approach can be articulated in politico-geographic terms, the best known materialist approach is marxism. In its classical/distal form this analytical language describes and explains how changes in the material means of production cause changes in the overall mode of production, that is, the social superstructure or class system.

The best known articulation of marxism is Karl Marx and Friedrich Engels' *Manifesto of the Communist Party* (1975 [1848]). The *Manifesto* provides a brief account of the class struggles that have historically informed the relationships between "freeman and slave, patrician and plebeian, lord and serf, guild-master and journeyman ...". It describes the way all these struggles have ended either in the "revolutionary reconstitution of society at large" or in the "common ruin of the contending classes"(Marx and Engels, 1975 [1848], pp. 32–33).

The *Manifesto* sees the contemporary world as split between the owners and managers of the means of industrial production and those who sell their labour for a wage. As a mode of production Marx and Engels call this capitalism and like its predecessors they see it as exploitative and destined for revolutionary overthrow, that is, they see the workers as eventually rising up against those who exploit them and their state system.

The bourgeois world, as Marx and Engels describe it, is one of "naked self-interest ... [and] callous 'cash payment'". Moreover, in the place of "numberless ... chartered freedoms", they say, it has put "one unconscionable freedom — Free Trade".

It is also highly expansionist, in short, it has established connections all over the world, creating in the process a global market that has provided a "cosmopolitan character to production and consumption in every country ... In place of ... old wants [that is], satisfied by the production of the country, we find new wants, requiring for their satisfaction the products of distant lands and climes. In place of the old local and national seclusion and self-sufficiency, we have ... universal inter-dependence ..."(Marx and Engels, 1975 [1848], pp. 35–38).

More contemporary and distal analysts have taken this approach further to highlight how local elites in poor countries have become comprador allies of corporate interests in rich ones and have ceased in the process to serve the interests of their own populations. They highlight how bourgeois states produce too much, seeking new markets and new ways of more radically exploiting old ones. Some of these analysts articulate a neo-marxist approach called *dependencia.* Others highlight the structural features of the capitalist world economy and the way it has a centre, a periphery, and a semi-periphery. It is the uneven nature of the development of this system that accounts, they say, for the "multiple forms" of class conflict (Wallerstein, 1979, p. 36).

Marx and Engels did not think the revolution they envisaged would take place until the class struggle was a worldwide one. This is why they would not have countenanced attempts to reconcile marxism with local circumstances the way communist revolutionaries did in Russia and China. Revolutionaries wanted to jump over capitalism in order to go straight to revolutionary socialism. Marx and Engels did not think this was possible and, indeed, it was not. It was entirely predictable that China and Russia would have to go back and have capitalism, which is what is happening today.

The opposite to marxism as a materialist approach to IPE is a 'mentalist' one. This, too, highlights the essential nature of human nurturing practices but rather than the material nature of those practices it emphasises their mental aspect.

The best known mentalist approach is that of constructivism. To a constructivist, how people think about IPE is what they get. IPE is a result of norms, ideals and values. It has a self-fulfilling quality to it in that what people see as being significant about IPE is what becomes significant there.

Constructivism completely contradicts the marxist approach. Where Marx inverted Hegel to see the means of production determining everything else, including norms, ideals and values, constructivism inverts Marx to adopt a neo-Hegelian perspective that make ideals analytically central.

Like every other analytical language constructivism is replete with diverse dialects. Some are determined to defend a scientific understanding of IPE. Some are prepared to be less rigorous in this respect. Others are highly abstract, emphasising how rules result in rule. Others again are much more applied, emphasising how a mental awareness of the world is built from the ground up.

Some analysts and practitioners approach IPE on the basis of a combination of both materialism and mentalism. This sounds like a contradiction in terms. For those aware of how intimately they are entwined, however, and how difficult it is to disentangle the doctrines they articulate, this is the only approach that makes much sense.

Marx and Engels themselves saw materialist assumptions impinging upon mentalist ones and the ruling class that is defined in material terms as being the ruling class that defined what obtains in mental terms too. Other analysts highlight how advertising and popular culture are part of a 'culture industry' which hides from wage workers the full significance of their exploitation using values, norms, ideas and ideals.

THOSE MARGINALISED BY MAINSTREAM IPE

The analytical languages and dialects discussed so far are all mainstream ones in that they all articulate the modernist/rationalist project. This is the Enlightenment project that prioritises the use of reason as an end in itself.

Modernist rationalism was devised in the main by white, middle-aged, Western, environmentally-indifferent, males. In turn, they characterised large swathes of humankind as insufficiently rationalistic or as not capable of prioritising reason. These swathes included women, environmentalists, post-colonials, indigenous peoples, and the poor.

By asking where the women are in IPE it is possible to draw attention to the radically gendered nature of the whole discipline and the way its seemingly conventional practices are radically loaded in terms of their gender outcomes (Enloe, 1989). What is made to seem normal and natural in this regard is anything but, in part because of the worldwide use of a public/private distinction that successfully hides the extent of gender discrimination. Those determined to draw attention to this discrimination have a wide choice of analytical dialects with which to do so. They can opt, for example, for a liberalist approach that argues for human rights regardless of secondary qualities like gender ones. They can opt for a marxist approach that sees women as the world's last colony and women's liberation as requiring the overthrow of global capitalism. Or they can make alliances with others similarly marginalised by the modernist/rationalist project (like environmentalists) or those from that project who currently critique it for being limited and distorting (like postmodernists or poststructuralists).

By asking why environmentalists are seen as too subjective to deserve consideration in modernist/rationalist terms it is possible to draw attention to the way IPE marginalises this issue too, that is, the treatment of the global eco-sphere and what the contemporary generation will leave behind for following ones. Are current forms of development sustainable, for example? If so, how can this be so in the light of scientific evidence of widespread and increasing human damage to the atmosphere and the biosphere? What might sustainability mean in the light of a population that continues to grow and continues to put increasing pressure on the planet's resources and its capacity to cope with human pollution?

Post-colonials and indigenous peoples are well placed, despite being marginalised by the modernist/rationalist project, to highlight the racist nature of IPE. Both are aware of the way patterns of imperialism persist as a continuing fact of life. And they fight back. Post-colonials, for example, highlight how 'orientalism' makes all Middle-Eastern and Asian peoples appear to be exotic 'others', thus rendering central to the discipline all US and European 'selves'. Indigenous peoples, meanwhile, highlight their own forms of IPE and how these provide constructive alternatives to those imposed upon them.

The poor also bear witness to the highly skewed nature of contemporary IPE. The agricultural/industrial largesse provided by the scientific and technological revolutions that began in the seventeenth century means that no one need go without life's fundamental necessities anymore. That so many still do reflects a lack of political will. It does not reflect a shortage of the requisite global product. The poor are marginalised since they are depicted by modernists/rationalists as not knowing how to prioritise reason. If they did, modernists think, they would demand the kind of education that would allow them to do so. This is to trap the poor in a self-defeating spiral. They tend not to be heard because of their illiteracy and lack of advocacy and because a radical lack of resources prohibits them from getting these skills. Nonetheless, there are those who speak on their behalf and who highlight how poverty is no longer a human necessity.

THE MODERNIST MAINSTREAM AND ITS AUTO-CRITIQUES

The modernist/rationalist project is now under siege from within as well as without. This has consequences for IPE too.

By turning reason back upon itself, for example, it is possible to ask what the reasons are for prioritising reason. This is to unsettle the certainty of modernist/rationalism as a meta-discourse, to unsettle the certainty of all the attempts to articulate IPE provided by mainstream analysts and practitioners, and at the same time to open up thinking and speaking spaces for marginalised accounts of IPE like those of women and environmentalists. This is postmodernism as generally understood.

By highlighting the way language determines the conclusions rationalists come to, it is possible to do the same. This unsettles the modernist/rationalist sense of identity and all that flows therefrom. This is poststructuralism as generally understood.

Modernist/rationalist truths are similarly challenged by other auto-critiques. Psycho-pathologists see reason as resulting from unconscious needs and drives. Romantics prefer to describe and explain IPE in emotivist terms, that is, in terms of their gut feelings. Phenomenologists prefer to bracket off rationalism in order to see things-in-themselves in intuitive terms, that is, in terms of their gut thinking. Sacralists prefer to opt for the spiritual context that modernist/rationalism was originally set up in opposition to, choosing instead to meditate or pray. This allows them to arrive at very different approaches to IPE, for example, economics as construed in Buddhist terms.

CONCLUSION

So there it is: an introduction to all the ways in which IPE is analysed. Recognising the assumptions a particular analyst or practitioner is making immediately reveals the approach that he or she is taking. It reveals what he or she wants to say and more importantly, what he or she does *not* want to say. However: to know what is not being said requires a comprehensive and coherent account of all the ways in which IPE can be accounted for. Hence the systematic summary of these ways provided above. Hence the hope that the reader never gets lost again in the swamps of what is a highly complex subject, where so many competing part-truths masquerade as the whole-truth, and where the use of modernist/rationalism leaves so much to be desired itself in terms of those it marginalises and what its own limits and distortions entail.

REFERENCES

Enloe, C (1989). *Bananas, Beaches and Bases: Making Feminist Sense of International Politics.* Berkeley: University of California Press.

Friedman, M (1962). *Capitalism and Freedom.* Chicago: The University of Chicago Press.

List, F (1856 [1841]). *The National System of Political Economy*, translated by GA Matile. Philadelphia: J.B.Lippincott and Co.

Marx, K and F Engels (1975 [1848]). *The Communist Manifesto.* Peking: Foreign Languages Press.

Mun, T (1664 [1630]). *England's Treasure by Forraign Trade, or the Balance of our Forraign Trade is the Rule of our Treasure.* London: Thomas Clark. http://socserv.mcmaster.ca/econ/ugcm/3ll3/mun/treasure.txt [16 December 2011].

Owen, R (1817 [1813–1816]). *A New View of Society, or, Essays on the Principle of the Formation of the Human Character and the Application of the Principle to Practice.* London: Longman, Hurst, Rees, Orme and Brown. http://socserv.mcmaster.ca/econ/ugcm/3ll3/owen/newview.txt [16 December 2011].

Pettman, R (2010). *World Affairs: An Analytical Overview.* Singapore: World Scientific.

Ricardo, D (1951 [1817]). On the Principles of Political Economy and Taxation. In *The Works and Correspondence of David Ricardo,* Vol. 1, P Sraffa (ed.). Cambridge: Cambridge University Press.

Smith, A (1993 [1776]). *An Inquiry into the Nature and Causes of the Wealth of Nations.* Oxford: Oxford University Press.

Stretton, H (1999). *Economics: A New Introduction.* Sydney: University of New South Wales.

Wallerstein, I (1979). *The Capitalist World-Economy.* Cambridge: Cambridge University Press.

CHAPTER 2

From Political Economy to International Political Economics

Hana Sabanovic and Sally Trethewie

University of Melbourne

As noted in the first chapter, international political economics (IPE) is a highly complex discipline, drawing not only from the fields of politics and economics, but also those as varied as philosophy, history and anthropology. This makes the task of producing a brief and yet coherent history of it an extremely challenging one.

If IPE is taken to mean quite literally the nexus between politics and economics it would be possible to draw upon the writings of the great philosophers of antiquity. It would also be possible to draw on the great thinkers of the Middle Ages and the experiences of the merchant traders of the great European empires — to just name a few.

As with all historical documentations of events and ideas, however, it is also important to enquire about the untold stories. There are many undocumented episodes that have shaped the political economy of today. Whole groups of people crucial to the story of production and trade (women in particular) are almost completely absent from most texts on the history of wealth acquisition and its interrelationship with state-making.

To make the task more manageable this chapter will document the public history of IPE as an academic discipline. It will also consider the subject as a field of enquiry in its own right.

As such IPE is extremely young. It can be said to have emerged in Europe during the 1970s.

This said, its roots go back much further, indeed, to the seventeenth, eighteenth and nineteenth centuries. In the beginning politics and economics were considered as one, under the heading of 'political economy'. Only later did the concepts used today within IPE develop and only later were the political and economic spheres of social life turned into separate entities. This separation was the result of a renaissance in thinking about the individual's place in society, spurred on by a revolution in science and technology. The great changes in consumption, production and lifestyle that these events brought about led to a need to reconsider the relationship between the state and citizen internally and the state as an entity in world affairs externally.

By the 1970s a range of factors, including the dismantling of the Bretton Woods institutions, lingering memories of World War Two and of the Great Depression, plus the challenges brought about by the OPEC oil crisis, inspired pioneering scholars and practitioners of world affairs to reconsider the linkages between two. The initiatives of those political scientists, who pushed for the inclusion of economics in the sphere of politics, were initially dismissed. Economists took just as much convincing, generally perceiving political, social and cultural factors as background noise (Cameron *et al.*, 2008).

Once it was accepted that IPE was a discipline of value, a decade-long struggle ensued between political scientists, economists and IPE scholars to determine where it was to be placed within the pantheon of world affairs. For some it was a sub-discipline of international relations (IR). Others argued that IR and economics should be considered sub-disciplines of IPE. This debate remains unresolved.

As may be expected from the above, histories of IPE as a discipline are as disparate and varied as the field itself. Generally speaking, most of the literature is structured in two main ways.

Firstly, IPE approaches and perspectives are categorised as falling under one or the other of three distinct analytic camps, namely, mercantilism (or economic nationalism), economic liberalism or economic socialism. Each one of these camps takes its starting point from an assumption about the intrinsic nature of humankind. This point is important because any description, explanation or policy formulation these perspectives espouse will be tempered by how it perceives human nature.

Whilst this kind of categorisation is useful and works well for economic nationalism and liberalism in their various guises, alternative approaches tend to be lumped together into a third or 'other' category. This results in an awkward grouping that contains economic socialists (who regard human nature as intrinsically good); marxists and constructivists (who see human nature in nurturist terms); as well as critical accounts of IPE such as feminism, environmentalism, post-colonialism, developmentalism, Fourth Worldism and sacralism (Pettman, 2010).

The second most common way to portray the history of IPE (from the 1970s onwards) is to differentiate between the US and British schools of thought. The division of perspectives and analysts along this socio-geographic line works well given the two schools' distinctive approaches and assumptions. Care needs to be taken, however, not to take this division as absolute so as to avoid the danger of either exaggerating the differences involved or perceiving this to be the only contemporary division in IPE thought. Continental European, Canadian and Australian scholars are often considered to be loosely aligned with the British School, while those from the 'rest of the world' are often perceived as being aligned with the

US School. Both make significant contributions in their own right, however. One of the problems with this categorisation is that the work of these other scholars is not credited as such.

This chapter will begin with an overview of the historical context within which IPE arose. Particular attention will be paid to the origins of the three key assumptions constructed and developed between the seventeenth and nineteenth centuries, which shaped the discipline as it is now known and which are integral to the study and practice of IPE (as well as to politics and economics as separate fields in their own right).

The penchant for the quantitative numerical measurement of socio-economic phenomena will also be noted. This was first developed during the Age of Reason by Sir William Petty, who pioneered this methodology.

This will be followed by an overview of Adam Smith's application of rationalist/individualist thought to IPE. It will also provide an assessment of William Jevons' influential argument that economics and politics need to be considered apart.

In order to avoid duplicating Pettman's introductory discourse above, where he describes the historical foundations of economic protectionism, liberalism and socialism, this chapter will focus on the development of the discipline of IPE as it emerged in the 1970s under the aegis of two relatively distinct (US and British) schools. It will conclude with an overview of IPE under the influence of globalisation since the 1970s.

It should be noted that whatever structure the history of IPE is given, the story is one that is necessary to tell. After decades of working and teaching in the field, for example, Cohen said there were three reasons for an intellectual history of it (Cohen, 2008). Firstly, there were reasons of practical importance that relate to the subject matter of IPE. Secondly, there was the ability of IPE to interpret world affairs. Thirdly, there was the fact that the development of IPE as a discipline was in no way complete. Cohen also highlighted how important it was to tell the story of IPE as the multi-faceted discipline that it is. This stemmed from his observation that the majority of IPE students he came into contact with were only exposed to one dominant narrative, namely, that of the hegemonic US School. Whilst this chapter may lack the comprehensiveness and depth of insight of a scholar like Cohen, who has taught and researched in the field for several decades, it is a determined attempt nonetheless to provide a broad and systematic account of IPE's history as a discipline.

THE CONCEPTUAL ORIGINS OF IPE

Contemporary world affairs are a product of, and a continuation of, the conceptual realisations that emerged during the period called the Enlightenment. For many reasons IPE today can be seen as part of the Enlightenment project still; as a product of modernity. The intellectual era that IPE operates in today is one that considers reason to be virtuous and absolute. Whilst this may appear so self-evident that it can pass without mention, it deserves noting here because this contextualisation of current streams of thought provides the analyst with a unique perspective on the history of the discipline.

The term 'political economy' was coined by Sir William Petty in a work he wrote on Ireland around 1671 (Hull, 1899, p. 181). Petty's life deserves description in its own right. He was an extraordinary man who rose from relative poverty and a life on the Irish seas at fourteen to a professorship of anatomy at Oxford University. This posting gave Petty access to many of the great minds of the Enlightenment period including René Descartes and Thomas Hobbes, with whom he forged close friendships. It was Hobbes in particular, and his attitude to reason and the idea that numbers and statistics could be used as tools for deciphering complex political and economic events, that most influenced Petty's methodological convictions. As Tony Aspromourgos says, "Petty imbibed deeply of the Hobbesian conviction that mathematics is the appropriate model for all rational inquiry" (Aspromourgos, 1988, p. 346). It led to his conviction that "the purpose of theory is to determine the rational requirements for civil peace and material plenty" (Aspromourgos, 1988, p. 347).

Working alongside Hobbes as his personal secretary, Petty devoted himself to determining the conditions necessary for wealth. He admired and studied the work of Francis Bacon and his use of mathematics as the basis for rationalistic thought. Given the precision that equations and statistics allowed, Petty developed what he called 'political arithmetik', which was the foundation of modern-day statistics. Whilst the principles of Petty's 'political arithmetik' may no longer be applied today with the same hope he had for it, the impact he had in this regard can be clearly seen in contemporary economics and IPE.

Writing a century after Petty, Adam Smith led a shift away from the Enlightenment era's penchant for numbers. His germinal work written in 1776, *The Wealth of Nations*, rebelled against mercantilism and relied very little on statistics. Smith's valuable legacy in the field of classical economics and as a founder of economic liberalism is well documented but perhaps his most powerful yet understated influence was his starting point: the assumption that human beings are by nature inherently rationalistic and calculating. Much in the same way that Enlightenment scholars took to numbers, Smith's contemporaries adopted 'rational choice' as an assumption. Despite the limitations of such an approach, it continues to be promoted and protected as the basis of all the mainstream schools of contemporary IPE thought.

Perhaps less well known than Smith and his work on rational choice, William Jevons sparked a debate that can be seen today all over the world in academia, literature, international organisations, and government decision-making bodies (though more so in the US and less so in Europe). Jevons was an economist who worked at the height of the late industrial revolution. He was a man of the natural sciences who made the transition to what was termed the 'moral sciences', or the scientific study of human behaviour. Jevons' work was revolutionary in the sense that prior to the publication of *The Theory of Political Economy* in 1871 (Jevons, 1970 [1871]), economics and politics were considered inseparable. He is credited as having introduced a deep structural rift into this intellectual equation and to have instigated the gulf that exists today between politics and economics as separate fields of enquiry and practice. Jevons also introduced the concept of 'diminishing marginal utility' as the basis for a theory of exchange. This in turn helped launch the 'marginalist revolution' that established the theory of neoclassical economics that was to replace the classical theory of Smith and his contemporaries.

Since the marginalist revolution of the 1870s and the split of economics and politics, all the way through to the socio-political upheavals of the first half of the twentieth century, mainstream scholarship required that political scientists work on politics and economists on economics. The two fields developed separately from and yet parallel to each other, influencing and being influenced by the events that shaped world affairs during this time.

Despite this division between the narratives of economics and politics, thinkers on the 'left' continued to pursue political analysis within the heuristic structure of political economy. Most notably it was their work that gave rise to dependency theory and the concept of uneven development. These critical analyses of mainstream thought highlighted the interwoven nature of politics and economics, both nationally and internationally, thus placing pressure on the orthodoxy that mainstream scholarship espoused. Pressure was also slowly building from radical factions within both economics and international relations for the inclusion of issues and actors outside the confines of their respective disciplines.

THE CONSTRUCTION OF IPE

Despite the aforementioned anticipation of change, within mainstream scholarship the practitioners of politics and economics continued to guard their respective territories. It took bold insight, speed and determination by the intellectual entrepreneurs of the time to break through the confines of the mainstream which firmly cemented both the methodologies and the analytical frameworks that determined the actors and issues under scrutiny for each respective discipline.

Today's IPE practitioners owe much to the groundbreaking work of the late Susan Strange and the publication in 1970 of her germinal article "International Economics and International Politics: A Case of Mutual Neglect". It was this article that paved the way for the marriage of politics and economics in international relations. Though received with staunch opposition in some quarters and not as widely read as it deserved to be at the time, on hindsight it can be seen as a "manifesto" for cooperation between the disciplines (Cohen, 2008).

Strange was a graduate of the prestigious London School of Economics. She made a career for herself writing for *The Economist* and *Observer* prior to becoming an academic and teaching at University College, London. There she began to specialise in the politics of international currency. She also became a fierce advocate for cooperation between the disciplines.

In 1971 she founded the International Political Economy Group (IPEG). This consisted of researchers, policy makers and journalists at the Royal Institute of International Affairs at Chatham House. Today IPEG continues to be considered one of the key foundation stones towards IPE as a contemporary discipline.

In 1972 she organised a ten-day conference at Cumberland Lodge that brought together forty economists and political scientists to discuss ways in which they could better cooperate (Cohen, 2008). This was by no means an easy task. The economists criticised the political scientists for their lack of methodological and theoretical rigor. In return, the political scientists chastised the economists for their narrow focus on the pursuit of wealth. The conference was a success nonetheless and resulted in mutual respect and communication between the disciplines, that is, a new shared understanding and a commitment to making the new approach work.

Meanwhile across the Atlantic, Joseph Nye (a scholar-statesman) and Robert Keohane (a well-respected academic) joined forces as editors of *International Organisation* (a journal established a quarter of a century earlier with the brief to analyse the workings of international institutions). During their time at the journal the duo produced a special issue called *Transnational Relations and World Politics* (1970; see Keohane and Nye, 1972). This was a response to calls by those behind the journal for the pair to better elucidate their push towards a more theoretical approach and one that was more inclusive of economic issues. The approach they sought was inspired by the work of Strange (and others). It also reflected all the disparities between the issues and actors they knew about in government and in academia (and particularly at Harvard University where Nye is still professor). This special issue is now considered one of the key publications in the birth of contemporary IPE.

Keohane and Nye's contributions to IPE did not begin and end there. In 1977 the pair published an influential book entitled *Power and Interdependence: World Politics in Transition* in which they introduced a concept that was fundamental to the early days of the discipline, namely, "complex interdependence". Whilst not considered to be a complete explanation of reality or theory, "complex interdependence" was intended as a new way to discuss world affairs (Cohen, 2008). "Complex interdependence" had three main facets, namely, multiple channels of communication, a lack of hierarchy amongst issues, and a diminished role for military force. It shifted the focal point of analysis from the centrality of the state as the key political actor to recognition of other emerging global entities as agents capable of affecting change in their own right. Drawing upon the work of the classical economists Keohane and Nye paved the way for a new form of strategic liberalism, that is, neoliberal institutionalism (as it came to be known).

Though many in the field were slow to accept the new approach, it was becoming increasingly difficult to ignore the pressing political consequences of market turmoil, such as those brought about by the oil crisis in 1973. The system set up by the post-World War Two Bretton Woods institutions to promote free trade and to protect against economic protectionism was being challenged by the collapse of pegged exchange rates. Meanwhile, state economies were becoming increasingly interdependent. An acute need was developing for systems and theories capable of governing this interdependence in order to avoid the challenges it posed to state sovereignty and the danger that states would revert to economic protectionism.

The *zeitgeist* of the time also suggested that the dominant analytical approach to world affairs, realism, was ill-equipped to explain international events. This was the case particularly following the thawing of tensions between the two nuclear superpowers in the 1970s (before they resumed in the 1980s) and a shift towards demilitarisation in the developed economies, especially in Europe. With the exception of the Cold War (which was what — according to some accounts — made this very shift possible), the Vietnam war, and other proxy hot wars, the threat of such violence in the West seemed by this stage unlikely.

Some scholars did not believe that "complex interdependence" was sufficient to explain these new circumstances. Gilpin, for one, argued that realism had not lost its place in world affairs and was as relevant as ever as an analytic language. Gilpin argued that "complex interdependence" could only be seen and understood in the context of a state-centric system. Like Nye and Keohane, Gilpin, a political scientist by profession, never set out to work in the field of IPE but could not help but notice changes in world affairs that necessitated the inclusion of economic issues in the discourse of world affairs. His work on nuclear weapons policy in particular highlighted the interwoven nature of technological development and international politics (Cohen, 2008).

Early on, Gilpin identified three main schools of thought which he believed characterised the analysis of the emerging field of IPE, namely, mercantilism, liberalism and marxism. Each one of these he saw as being related to international relations. Gilpin's classification is arguably his strongest legacy to the birth of the new field (Cohen, 2008). It continues to be used in textbooks to this day.

US AND BRITISH SCHOOLS OF IPE

To tell the history of IPE it is necessary to attempt a heuristic classification of the field by identifying commonalities beyond those that Gilpin highlights. In terms of methodology and approach, IPE as a discipline can be seen in terms of two distinct schools of thought, the 'British' and the 'US' (Murphy and Nelson, 2001; Cohen, 2008). Such a simplification has its drawbacks but if it is not interpreted too literally, it is a useful way to distinguish two approaches that are different with respect to the actors included in the respective discussions and what are seen to be the principal problems and issues deserving of analysis. If this system of classification is followed it is safe to say that the US school dominates the mainstream internationally while the British approach is clearly appreciated in Australia and Canada (as well as other countries). Between the two schools a gulf continues to exist in terms of understanding, appreciation and cooperation (Cohen, 2008).

In the US, those driving the field were initially a number of economists, as well as political scientists like Keohane, Nye and Gilpin. Over time, however, the "custody" of IPE was left predominantly to political scientists (Cohen, 2008). Cohen says that this occurred for a number of reasons. Firstly, during a period of conscious anti-communism economists were uncomfortable with IPE's links to leftist ideologies, particularly so since its agenda prior to the 1970s could be said to be centred on dependency theory and studies of inequality. Secondly, critical analyses of the origins of government policy and behaviour did not sit neatly within the economic lexicon given that their focus was directed towards studying outcomes. Thirdly, economists were not at ease with tackling complex qualitative issues that could be exhausted without appeal to quantitative modes of analysis.

This left the task of developing IPE in the US predominantly to political scientists. They in turn took a positivist approach, that is, one influenced by the scientific rigor of their economic counterparts. Ironically, it is this reductionist methodology that continues to dominate analysis within the US school of IPE today. This is clearly evidenced by the proportion of articles published in leading IPE journals. Those adopting this method have skyrocketed from six percent in 1970–1974 to forty-seven percent in 2000–2004 (Cohen, 2008). Cohen refers to this as "creeping economism" (Cohen, 2008, p. 43). He says that the US school is "self-consciously limited to what can be learned from rational, empirical enquiry" and that its adherents tend to focus on "key relationships isolated within broader structures whose characteristics are assumed, normally, to be given and unchanging" (Cohen, 2008, p. 4). As such the scholars concerned are notorious for preferring to sit in the realm of mid-level positivist theory. Whilst the quantified, empirical research they conduct may be useful and precise it is nonetheless based on mathematical assumptions that cannot always be translated into the socio-political sphere, thus narrowing their field of view.

What we can loosely call the British school has taken a distinctively different approach, no doubt due to such different circumstances as the characters involved and Britain's own geopolitical history and experience. Again, by considering the concept of a school not as a mandated approach to issues or methodology, but as a grouping of loose similarities, the British school of IPE is generally characterised as having embraced a normative approach that is inclusive of non-state actors, preferring to answer the big questions at a meta-theoretical level. It is known to be multi-disciplinary and draws upon studies in human geography, law, philosophy, anthropology and business, amongst others.

Questions relating to 'who gets what and how' are prioritised within the British school and there is a lesser focus on policy. Politics of identity are also of importance in British IPE scholarship. Social norms and aspirations are perceived as influencing factors in response to which individual identity is forged (Watson, 2008). This is in contrast to the US school, which often only goes so far as to assume that individuals will act in a calculating, rationalistic manner, as decreed by Adam Smith.

The direction taken by British IPE is largely indebted to Strange, who not only advocated the birth of the discipline but actively encouraged collaborative, multi-disciplinary research and discussion. As a mentor she inspired many of the school's leading thinkers. She questioned authority at every opportunity, often reminding colleagues of earlier days when moral philosophy was linked to the study of political economy. Strange saw scholarship as "inseparable" from values and encouraged others in the field to make moral judgments (Cohen, 2008, p. 56). Cohen identifies five key themes in Strange's scholarship which are reflected in the direction that the British school took: an emphasis on structural power and on the role of agency; a deeply rooted scepticism about international organisations and regimes; competition amongst authorities; and ambivalence towards the US, both intellectually and geopolitically (Cohen, 2008).

Canadian scholar Cox, best known for the critical approach he took to IPE (an approach informed in turn by his background in historical studies), was another strong influence on the British school. Like Strange, challenging orthodoxy was central to Cox's work. Unsurprisingly the US IPE school did not warm to Cox's historical materialism, nor to his intellectually eclectic and so-called unscientific approach to scholarship (Cohen, 2008). Cox's approach to IPE became influential nonetheless in the area of systemic transformation, up to and including current accounts of globalisation.

GLOBALISATION AND IPE

An explosion of literature on the concept of globalisation has emerged in recent decades. One of the key challenges in giving an overview of the field of globalisation studies, much like providing an account of the study of IPE itself, is its multidisciplinary nature and the lack of an agreed definition of what the term means.

Rosamond (2003) suggests that contemporary IPE itself might be considered the study of globalisation, highlighting at the same time three observations that make the concept problematic. Firstly, as also noted by Scholte (2002), there is lack of agreement over what globalisation is, which makes the study of globalisation equally ambiguous. Without clearly defined parameters scholars are hard pressed to develop meaningful explanatory statements. Secondly, as Rosenberg (2001) says, social scientists have yet to explain whether the experience of regional integration, such as the contemporary European experience, is a result of globalisation or an example of resistance to its effects. Lastly, as Shin (2000) says, there is the problem of sourcing data relevant to globalisation and its effects. As O'Rourke (2002) argues, based on such measures as commodity market integration, capital market integration, and labour mobility, the nineteenth century period demonstrated greater economic integration than the late twentieth century one.

Rosamund says that there have been three waves of literature on globalisation. The first wave either took globalisation for granted or exaggerated it (Hay and Marsh, 2001). The second wave — that he terms "refutionist" — developed in reaction to the first (Rosamund, 2003). The third wave critiques the hype of globalisation by testing for its effects. It argues that globalisation is anything but a new phenomenon. It sees globalisation as being as old as trade itself.

Cox and the British school more generally have remained focused on the overarching theoretical questions of IPE which they tackle from a sociological perspective. For example, they focus on issues such as how to manage the social inequality propagated by unregulated markets that function according to principles that have their origins in entrenched systems of privilege and marginalisation. The British school generally argues that the system is currently going through a period of major structural change and it incorporates a multidisciplinary approach in order to understand this system. Not so much the US school.

In keeping with the "creeping economism" referred to earlier in the US school (Cohen, 2008), US scholars tend to be sceptical of globalisation. They avoid overarching theories and downplay the significance of globalisation and its effects. Keohane and Nye, for example, see globalisation merely as an extension of interdependence. Those who tend towards realism still see markets as being controlled by the state. Of the US school, Katzenstein is the exception to this rule, but he tends to research particular aspects of globalisation rather than globalisation as an overarching phenomenon.

Others, particularly contemporary marxists, understand globalisation as having the characteristics of late industrial hyper-capitalism. For them the commodification of culture is a key signal. Marx himself predicted globalisation in *The Communist Manifesto* when he referred to the battering down of the walls of China. For those who sympathise with this view, and for those influenced by the work of Gramsci and his conceptualisation of hegemony, globalisation represents a "movement towards convergence" (Cox, 2004, p. 308) spurred on by the neoliberal economics that creates, and needs to create, new markets where none previously existed before. Globalisation uses a subtle mix of soft and hard power, as exercised by the international institutions dominated by the powerful states in IPE, to effect this convergence. Others have gone further to conceptualise globalisation as *Empire* (Hardt and Negri, 2000), thereby referring to the hegemonic power of the United States in the international system.

CONCLUSION

The evolution of IPE has not been straightforward or linear (Amawi and Crane, 1997). In reality it has been much more nuanced than the categorisation of the discipline into three broad analytical approaches (mercantilism, liberalism, and marxism) and two loose schools of thought (the US and the British) allows for. Cohen sees a great irony in the fact that even though bridges have now been firmly established between politics and economics, a new "dialogue of the deaf" appears to have developed between the diverse approaches to the discipline (Cohen, 2008). Though there are examples of approaches borrowing from each other, further cooperation and more ambitious analyses are called for. These can only be of benefit to what, after all, is a relatively young field of enquiry.

REFERENCES

Amawi, A and G Crane (eds.) (1997). *The Theoretical Evolution of International Political Economy*: A Reader. New York: Oxford University Press.

Aspromourgos, T (1988). The life of William Petty in relation to his economics: A tercentenary interpretation, *History of International Political Economy*, 20(3), 337–356.

Cameron A, A Nesvetailova and R Palan (2008). Introduction: Histories and Theories of International Political Economy. In *International Political Economy*, Vol. 1, pp. xxx–xxxvii. Los Angeles: Sage Publications.

Cohen, B (2008). *International Political Economy: An Intellectual History*. Princeton: Princeton University Press.

Cox, R (2004). Beyond empire and terror: Critical reflections on the political economy of world order, *New Political Economy*, 9(3), 307–323.

Hay, C and D Marsh (2001). Introduction: Demystifying Globalisation. In *Demystifying Globalisation*, C Hay and D Marsh (eds.). Basingstoke and New York: Palgrave.

Hardt, M and A Negri (2000). *Empire*, Cambridge: Harvard University Press.
Hull, C (ed.) (1899). *The Economic Writings of Sir William Petty*. Volume 1. Cambridge: Cambridge University Press.
Jevons, W (1970 [1871]). *The Theory of Political Economy*. Harmondsworth: Penguin.
Keohane, R and J Nye (1977). *Power and Interdependence: World Politics in Transition*. Boston: Little, Brown.
Keohane, R and J Nye (eds.) (1972). *Transnational Relations and World Politics*. Cambridge, MA: Harvard University Press.
Marx, K and F Engels (1967 [1848]). *The Communist Manifesto*. London: Penguin.
Murphy, C and D Nelson (2001). International political economy: A tale of two heterodoxies, *British Journal of Politics and International Relations*, 3(3), 393–412.
O'Rourke, K (2002). Europe and the Causes of Globalisation. In *Europe and Globalisation*, H Kierzkowski (ed.). Basingstoke and New York: Palgrave.
Pettman, R (2010). *World Affairs: An Analytical Overview*. Singapore: World Scientific Publishing.
Rosamund, B (2003). Babylon and on? Globalisation and international political economy, *Review of International Political Economy*, 10(4), 661–671.
Rosenberg, J (2001). *The Follies of Globalisation Theory*. London: Verso.
Scholte, J (2002). What is Globalisation? The Definitional Issue Again. *CSGR Working Paper* No. 109/02, University of Warwick, ESRC Centre for the Study of Globalisation and Regionalisation.
Shin, M (2000). Measuring economic globalisation: Spatial hierarchies and market topologies, *Environment and Planning*, A(34), 417–428.
Smith, A (1892 [1776]). *An Inquiry into the Nature and Causes of the Wealth of Nations*. London: George Routledge and Sons.
Strange, S (1970). International economics and international relations: A case of mutual neglect, *International Affairs*, 46(2), 304–315.
Watson, M (2003). Theoretical Traditions in Global Political Economy. In *Global Political Economy*, J Ravenhill (ed.). Oxford: Oxford University Press.

CHAPTER 3

The Industrial "Revolution" and its Aftermath: The British, US and Japanese Empires

Geoffrey Blainey

University of Melbourne

The industrial revolution was both a shattering and a creative event. It is still shattering and recreating our lives. It is also relatively recent.

In 1800 the economic life of the most advanced countries of the world was very simple, even compared with most of the poorer African lands of today. In Europe most people still earned their living from farming, forestry, mining and the other primary industries. At least seventy percent of the workforce was in primary industry: today it is rare for an advanced country to have ten percent of its workforce in primary industry. In most economies today there is a swing towards secondary industry as a massive employer (China) and a swing away again (the USA). Now tertiary industry, small in 1800, is the dominant employer in Western Europe, the USA and Japan. It will eventually happen in China and India too. Here is one of the simplest effects of the industrial revolution as it proceeds: wide fluctuations in the workplace, both within nations and between them.

Two centuries ago in Europe and North America the dominant event of each year was the collection of the grain harvest. If the harvest was abundant for two years in succession, the marriage rate usually increased. If the harvest was lean for two successive years, the death rate could soar. Even France, rich and productive by the standard of the times, had experienced major famines in the preceding one hundred years. In 1800 a typical European family on the bottom half of the income ladder ate mainly bread. A rise in the price of flour and bread could spur riots in the cities. In 1800 the proportion of the population living in cities was small whereas today many nations are eighty percent urban and a few such as Singapore are ninety-nine percent. London, then the biggest city in the world, held just over one million people. All kinds of industries which are now massive employers were then small. In 1800 all the full-time bankers and financiers of Europe could probably be assembled in St Peter's in Rome with maybe three quarters of the seats empty. The health industry was tiny by today's standards.

In 1800 most adults in Europe had probably never visited a doctor. More than half of the European children under the age of twelve could neither read nor write. How could a country run a compulsory education system without either a strong economy to finance it or willingness on the part of people to endure a lower standard of living in order to pay for schools and teachers? Even if schooling was made compulsory, the doors would have had to close for say, three months of the summer, so that all the children could rejoin the labour force for the busiest time of the year.

In short, in 1800 the industrial revolution had barely begun. This is sometimes called the age of steam but steam was still rare and steam engines in factories were still few. Textile mills were using the newly invented machines but most were driven by waterwheels, which is why the big, modern factories stood on the banks of rivers. The horse was still a vital part of economic life, especially for transport and farming. In 1765 the young Scot, James Watt, had invented the separate condenser. This made possible an effective steam engine. Thirty-five years later, however, the steam train and steam ship had still not yet been invented (Rosen, 2010).

The transformation of the more advanced economies in Europe, North America and a few other favoured lands occurred over the next one hundred years. This became the first age of fast machines. Driven by steam power or compressed air or gas or electricity, these machines did almost everything from sawing timber to breaking rocks, from printing newspapers to making shoes and flour, and finally to propelling trains and ships. Coal was the vital source of their energy. That Italy owned no valuable deposits of black coal was one reason for its economic backwardness.

Machines did more than anything else to lift the standard of living of the average breadwinner in the two centuries between 1800 and 2000. In essence two people were now able to produce what ten or twenty or even forty people had once produced, using simpler tools. Another set of machines revolutionised farming in the richer, more innovative nations. Even by 1900, in many nations, the bringing in of crops of ripe grains was no longer the central and most labour-consuming economic event of the year. Manufacturing was now challenging farming as the main employer of labour in Britain, North Germany and the more successful economies.

Machines also revolutionised transport and the fighting of wars. It was very difficult to predict how innovative machines would affect each different activity in the space of, say, the following thirty or forty years, and this will probably prove to be true with regard to the present revolution in communications as well. The failure of predictions by outstanding thinkers in the nineteenth century offers us a warning. Nobody was more impressed with the power of the new factory machines to reshape the world than the theorists of modern socialism, Marx and Engels, but a key part of their prediction — that the new factories would lead to workers' uprisings — failed.

Machines transformed warfare. Most military experts on the eve of the First World War expected it to be a short war, however, the latest technology, including machine guns, heavy artillery, and quickly-dug fortifications, turned it into a long and terrible war. The war of 1914–1918 being so long, emotionally embittering, and dislocating for both the national economies concerned and the world economy, was an important cause of the communist revolutions in Russia in 1917, the world economic depression of the early 1930s, and the rise of Hitler and the Nazi Party in Germany.

Sight and sound occurs as the result of eyes and ears. The growing speed with which advances in computing technology make statistics and projections available renders it tempting to jump to premature conclusions about what is happening to the international political economy in the longer term. This effect is arguably increasing. The role of unexpected or unpredicted economic trends and events arguably grew over the last half century. Even when the industrial revolution was in its first stages, it was difficult to predict where it would be the most dynamic. It still did not have a generally accepted name until the 1840s and in Britain — the real home of the revolution — the name did not catch on widely until a lecture on industrial change given by Arnold Toynbee Sr. in 1881. Even then it was seen as primarily an industrial event though it could be said at that time that its strongest as well as its longest lasting influence would likely be on transport rather than production.

James Watts' stationary engine led to the steam engine which — by a series of innovatory leaps — resulted in the portable petrol engine and those profoundly stirring events: the advent of the motor car, the propeller, the jet aircraft, and the spacecraft. In 1881 Toynbee had not yet seen a motor car, which is why it could be said that the name 'industrial revolution', while intensely useful, is not quite right. That conceptual label was based largely on the first generation of changes in production, with their blinding clouds of factory smoke and their grim-looking textile mills. This said, it does seem that 'industrial revolution' is now common parlance.

The startling and momentous 'communications revolution' (CR), to use another popular phrase, also needs a new name. Perhaps any naming is premature because of the cluster of innovations now exciting us and the way in which they might veer unpredictably, exerting their main effects in unexpected directions. Incidentally, the CR is regarded as recent and in one sense it is, but there was an earlier communications revolution in the period 1810–1850. It was driven by steamships, railways and the electric telegraph. The telegraph, which sent messages by wires laid on land and the seabed, linked all the main continents by 1872. It was succeeded by the telephone, the radio (first called wireless telegraphy), the internet, the mobile phone and other innovations; the point being that, even as late as 1900, who could confidently have predicted anything of the sort (Blainey, 2005)?

By 1950, then, the industrial revolution, in both industry and transport, had transformed much of the world. It had manifested all the advantages of the new forms of energy.

Moreover, many of the key components of the industrial revolution were transferable. They were easily copied and disseminated.

Britain led the first wave of innovations in industry and transport and communications (Ferguson, 2003). In the second wave of innovations, beginning in about 1860, the United States and Germany were probably ahead of Britain, however. In the twentieth century the US was most frequently the leader (More, 2000). In the twenty-first century it is impossible to tell whether it will be Asia that takes the lead in terms of the international capacity to innovate and propagate (Kennedy, 1989).

In terms of the general process of industrialisation, the first of the Asian nations to 'catch up' was Japan. Its devastating naval victory over Russia during the war of 1904–1905 awakened the world to the fact that Japanese technicians and naval officers and shipyards belonged to the twentieth century. Indeed Japan was the first navy to use wireless telegraphy in a war. Many of the Japanese warships had been built at home, while others were bought from British and French shipyards. After 1913 the Japanese ceased to buy foreign warships and by 1920 they owned the third largest navy in the world. The remarkable industrialisation of China, especially in the last twenty years, is often seen as a unique achievement for an Asian nation but Japan showed the way. Its high rate of economic growth foreshadowed China's by several decades.

The Western world was generally slow to appreciate Japan's sprint along the road to industrialisation and it became common in the 1960s to attribute its economic miracle largely to American aid. 'It pays to lose a war' was a popular saying. In fact, Japan was conducting its own economic miracle before the Second World War. That helped it, in December 1941, to surprise the Americans at Pearl Harbor and in the Philippines.

The 'industrial revolution' and the swing in employment from farms to factories helped create a new financial system in which credit was mobilised as never before. Banking became a major industry both nationally and globally.

Economic fluctuations became ever more important. At one time a boom year was largely determined by a bumper harvest but now its causes were far more complex. By the 1840s a hallmark of the new system was the tendency for advanced countries to experience booms followed by slumps.

Something cyclical was at work. Every seven to eleven years the economy passed from a high to a low and back again.

Called the trade cycle, this puzzled economists. The world depression of the 1930s was the worst period ever experienced as a result of these incessant fluctuations. The global financial crisis starting in 2008 was another such downturn, though not one so dislocating. Significantly, it was made all the more damaging by the fact that a crisis of such severity had not been expected any more.

The industrial revolution that began in Britain in the eighteenth century succeeded not only because of a score or scores of major inventions and a few hundred middling inventions but also because the supplies of new sources of fossil fuel proved to be huge. In 1800 the known reserves of fossil fuel (coal, oil and natural gas) were tiny and mostly in England. Even if it was assumed that half of the known and workable deposits of black coal went down to a depth of one hundred metres — a brave assumption at the time — nobody seems to have tried to compute what those reserves were and how many years they would last. The proven reserves of coal were very small. They were not larger in total than that which the world today consumes in twenty-four hours. Even in 1900 many of the world's great fuel reserves — for example the oil and natural gas of the Middle East — were completely unknown. Since then prodigious quantities of fossil fuel have been discovered; albeit more coal than oil.

The finding of huge reserves of fossil fuel across the globe's lands and seabeds certainly proved to be as important for the industrialising nations as the technology devised by James Watt and his nineteenth century circle of ingenious inventors and entrepreneurs. If Watt had been asked on the eve of his death, at the age of eighty-three, "will the world be able to mine enough coal to sustain your fast-multiplying steam engines, for another sixty years?", he would probably have replied, "I don't know". Some coal experts were very pessimistic in the nineteenth century. The great English economist W. S. Jevons thought England would soon cease to be a great power because it would run out of first-class black coal. This shows how difficult it is to provide reliable predictions with regard to what can be obtained in the future!

CONCLUSION

Every technology has its reverse effects, large or small. The whole question of global warming is a case in point. Complex and uncertain as many of its facets are, global warming has to be placed potentially on the red side of the ledger. Whether it will be a significant or insignificant deficit we do not yet know: indeed we cannot yet know. On the other hand, adversity can turn events around: it can stimulate ingenuity. The last period of global warming, far more severe than anything predicted for our world's near future, set in motion an earlier economic revolution. It probably led to the domestication of plants and animals and spurred the invention of agriculture, which was in some ways an invention even more important than the industrial revolution. It certainly had key consequences that are still with us today.

This highlights a key theme of this chapter, namely, how hard it is to forecast the effects of a new technology. It also highlights how hard it is to forecast the effectiveness of policies designed to tame or eliminate the effects flowing from new technologies.

REFERENCES

Blainey, G (2005). *A Short History of the 20th Century.* Melbourne: Penguin and Vintage.
Ferguson, N (2003). *Empire: How Britain Made the Modern World.* London: Allen Lane.
Kennedy, P (1989). *The Rise and Fall of the Great Powers.* New York: Vintage.
More, C (2000). *Understanding the Industrial Revolution.* London: Routledge.
Rosen, W (2010). *The Most Powerful Idea in the World: A Story of Steam, Industry, and Invention.* London: Jonathan Cape.

CHAPTER 4

Global Economic Governance

John Langmore and Shaun Fitzgerald

University of Melbourne

The remarkable growth in the extent of international economic integration in recent decades has far outpaced the existing capacity for global economic governance. The intensification of globalisation has increased the inadequacy of the institutions of global economic governance and their policies. This became especially apparent during the Global Financial Crisis, also known as the Great Recession, which began most notably in 2008 and from which the destructive effects still continue. The crisis showed that contemporary national and international economic institutions could not achieve stability let alone other goals. In fact, some of the policies that multilateral economic institutions have been promoting over the last thirty years contributed to the contagion which spread globally from the US where the crisis began. The frequency and speed with which economic problems in one country have spilled over into others indicates the need to strengthen international institutions sufficiently to ensure that they are capable of taking swift, effective corrective action.

John Maynard Keynes, the most respected economist of the twentieth century and the principal negotiator for the British at Bretton Woods, would have expected as much. The issues he was attempting to persuade the US and the other countries attending the Bretton Woods conference in 1944 about were much the same as those with which the world wrestles today. For example:

> The challenge ... which ... faced Keynes was to devise a plan to lock the USA into a system which would maintain balance of payments equilibrium between all countries without trade discrimination but also without forcing deflation, unemployment or debt-bondage on the deficit countries (Skidelsky, 2000, p. 182).

Keynes proposed an elaborate plan for an International Clearing Union, the principal purpose of which was to ensure that countries with either current account deficits or surpluses had an incentive to settle their accounts through an International Clearing Bank. This would have removed the deflationary bias of a system which depended on adjustment only by deficit countries. Balances would have been settled through a new form of 'bank money', later called the 'bancor'.

Harry Dexter White, however, the leading American negotiator, also had a plan. He proposed the establishment of two institutions, an International Stabilisation Fund and a Bank for Reconstruction.

The fundamental difference was that White's Stabilisation Fund quotas set the amount of capital to be subscribed to and so the right to buy currencies. The Clearing Bank enabled currencies to be purchased as a claim on an overdraft.

Although Keynes' proposal was intellectually stronger, the US was politically more powerful and it was White who largely prevailed. Skidelsky concludes that the final agreement reflected the views of the US Treasury rather than the British and was shaped by the US desire for an updated gold standard (one that fixed the value of gold against the dollar) as a means to liberalise trade. "If there was an underlying ideology, it was Morgenthau's [the US Treasury Secretary's] determination to concentrate financial power in Washington", writes Skidelsky (Skidelsky, 2000, p. 357). Keynes acquiesced because his greatest concern was to lock the US into a rule-based post-war financial order. The location of the Bretton Woods Institutions (BWIs) in Washington rather than New York, where they would have been closer to the UN Economic and Social Council, symbolised the American determination to control them rather than to allow internationally inclusive governance. The Bretton Woods agreement has determined the institutional framework of global economic governance ever since.

The purpose of this chapter is to discuss the way in which national policies impinge on other countries and how they make the effectiveness of international economic governance a high priority issue. It also discusses the question of the adequacy of the institutions available early in the second decade of the twenty-first century for addressing these spillovers and governance goals and the potential that institutional reforms might have for strengthening the capacity to mutually enhance global economic governance and hence people's wellbeing.

THE IMPERATIVE FOR EFFECTIVE GLOBAL ECONOMIC GOVERNANCE

In an integrated world, economic events in one country — and especially the larger ones — affect others. For example, if a major developed country reduces its interest rate to stimulate domestic demand its attractiveness to foreign capital and its exchange rate will tend to fall. This in turn will discourage imports as their prices rise. It will also increase the competitiveness of exports. The exports of competing countries will therefore tend to fall, damaging not only their balances of payments but also their growth rates and employment levels. Yet externalities like these — to the economy of the initiating government — are often disregarded when reductions in interest rates are made.

The Great Recession is the most spectacular recent example of such interdependence. Many groups in the US and the UK were responsible for the Great Recession. The combination was one of greed, hubris, conformity, extreme individualism, market fundamentalism and passivity. Amongst the powerful actors were greedy, bullying bankers who increasingly lent to borrowers who did not have sufficient savings or the earning capacity to service their loans if anything went wrong. This was the basis of 'subprime' house mortgages. Both bankers and borrowers naively expected that the value of these houses would go on appreciating endlessly. Bank managers thought they had a better understanding of financial risks than ever before, based on highly sophisticated models of risk and return. Their assumptions were unrealistic, however. Hubris-driven financial market dealers in the global financial centers of New York and London massively underestimated the risks. Substantial proportions of this new lending were financed by short-term borrowing. Banks put large numbers of mortgages into packages suitable for selling to other investors. The combination of toxic assets, testosterone, and herd behavior led to a shadow banking system which had no basis in productive economic activity. The misjudgments were compounded by duplicitous credit rating agencies which graded the corporations that were paying them for their ratings.

Naïve or misguided politicians and their official advisors were seduced by the most powerful lobbyists (and by a simplistic neoliberal ideology) into excessively deregulating the financial sector. For example, the repeal of the US Glass-Steagall Act in 1999 allowed commercial banks to run large investment banking businesses. Sleepy regulators failed to rigorously apply even the limited available regulatory framework, thus failing to constrain the reckless activities of the financial markets. Ignorant or unrealistic mortgage borrowers failed to rigorously assess their borrowing capacity and self-indulgent consumers borrowed massively until household debt in some countries grew to be one and a half times the national income. Like the frog in the bowl in which the temperature of the water is rising, the point at which a stop should have been called, the point of clear moral and technical failure, was difficult to detect with clarity. Between 2004–2006, financial services in the US accounted for twenty to twenty-one percent of national income compared with about twelve to thirteen percent for manufacturing (Phillips, 2008, p. viii). In the US in 2007 "the financial sector claimed 41 percent of all corporate profits"(Morris, 2008, p. xviii). In the US the share of national income going to the top one percent grew from nine percent in 1980 to twenty percent in 2006, and by far the largest proportion of that went to the top 0.1 percent—nine percent of the total national income (Morris, 2008, pp. 152–153). Never before in human history had so many people become so rich so quickly.

The rationale for these activities was the ideology of economic neoliberalism. Neoliberalists principally recommend minimising the role of the state by reducing public expenditure and taxation, privatising public enterprises, and deregulating the financial and corporate sectors. At its extreme, neoliberalism becomes market fundamentalism, which often involves making marketisation an end in itself rather than a means to other economic and social goals.

The bankers, regulators and politicians described above were misled by neoliberalist economic theories of 'rational expectations' and 'efficient markets'. Anatol Kaletsky, editor-at-large of *The Times,* writes that with "... those two reassuring adjectives, rational and efficient, the victorious academic economists erected an enormous scaffolding of theoretical models, regulatory prescriptions and computer simulations that allowed the practical bankers and politicians to build ... towers of bad debt and bad policy"(Kaletsky, 2009).

The 'rational expectations' hypothesis sees immutable economic laws governing markets. The theory was developed by disciples of Friedman at the University of Chicago who posited that Keynesian policies would not work because the belief that stimulatory government spending would be inflationary had become general. Whenever public spending was increased, these disciples argued, business would follow 'rational expectations' and raise prices and wages, so preventing an increase in employment. Though the theory could never be proved empirically, belief in it continued because it suited those who opposed active public sector regulation and the provision of services.

Similarly the 'efficient market' hypothesis was based on the belief that financial market participants, who were rationalistic and competitive, would set prices that took account of all available information. It was asserted that because 'the market' knew more than anyone else there was no point to regulators attempting to prevent or control market imperfections. The theory survived, despite repeated large-scale financial turbulence and periodic breakdowns, because it conveniently justified the free market ideology (and allowed executives to pay themselves huge salaries and bonuses). It survived, that is, despite the diversity and ubiquity of market failure, often despite distorting externalities which were not reflected in market prices.

The relevance of this to global economic governance is that the Great Recession was the most destructive economic catastrophe for nearly eighty years. Yet the assumptions and models underlying it were those that were not only being commended by the most powerful international economic institutions and their dominant member states but were also the basis for the conditionality which countries borrowing from the International Monetary Fund (IMF) and World Bank are required to accept. At the same time some countries which had steadily maintained their own models and resisted the pressure from the Anglophone states and institutions to conform (and were even mocked when they refused to do so) continued their steady growth paths — China being the most outstanding example. One result was that the IMF predicted China's real economic output would overtake that of the US in 2016, long before the equivalent predictions made before the Great Recession (IMF, 2011).

The consequences of the Great Recession have been unevenly destructive. Tens of millions of people were made unemployed; poverty increased; many developed and some developing countries' economies contracted; most countries experienced trade shocks; there were large and volatile movements in exchange rates; tax revenues declined causing growing budget deficits and consequent constraints on public services; remittances to some developing countries declined; and confidence in financial institutions fell. A collapse of trust in the banking system led to reluctance on the part of financial institutions to lend to each other, so that the availability of credit became restricted. There were also major social effects. These are likely to last much longer, including as they do, loss of dignity and of the capacity for self-reliance because of the rise in unemployment rates, as well as the disruptions to family and community relationships. One of the most striking consequences was the way the global balance of economic power between countries shifted significantly away from the US and some other developed countries towards the larger developing countries. This could eventually lead to changes in the pattern of global economic governance.

So: there are major lessons from the Great Recession. One is about the importance of the political accountability and transparency of economic institutions, both public and private. If the international financial institutions (IFIs) had been more rigorous in assessing the impact of their policies they would have recognised more quickly the potentially destructive consequences of the undifferentiated application of contractionary structural adjustment policies as well as the pro-cyclical impact of their macroeconomic policy recommendations. Major damage was caused to many economies before the IMF and World Bank began systematically and empirically to examine the consequences of their policies and to apply the lessons learned.

There are two kinds of representational problem here: one, that major global economic and financial institutions — the IMF, World Bank, World Trade Organisation and Bank for International Settlements, for example — are still controlled by the industrialised countries; and two, that the poorest half of humankind and the smaller one hundred and seventy countries are marginalised. A rule-based international system is vital for economic and social development. A necessary condition is that the rules be equitable and inclusive, however.

Another kind of lesson is that there are still major sources of instability within international economic arrangements. Whenever the US relaxes its monetary policy and reduces its interest rates to stimulate domestic economic activity, as it did after the Great Recession, confidence in the dollar declines causing global exchange rate instability. After the Asian financial crisis in the late nineties such instability motivated those developing countries which could do so to accumulate enormous foreign exchange reserves, totalling 3700 billion US dollars by 2007 (UN, 2009, p.113). Since those reserves were held in developed countries, and principally the US, this caused a transfer of financial resources from developing to developed countries, the total of which is far greater than all overseas development assistance (ODA). Pressure on current account deficit countries to reduce their imports, rather than on those with a surplus, also caused global deflation.

The Third World debt crisis is another issue that remains unresolved. It has been three decades since the Third World debt crisis began, yet there is still no adequate mechanism for enabling indebted countries to work out their debts. Arrangements negotiated through the Paris Club often require that indebted countries adopt an IMF-approved structural adjustment strategy. They are obliged to base their projections on excessively optimistic assumptions about growth, however, that give them very little debt relief. This is partly the result of the inadequacy of the resources which poorer developing countries are able to mobilise, either internally or through external, concessional assistance.

Perhaps the most important lesson from the Great Recession was the necessity to be clear about goals, and firm and consistent in the determination to work towards them. Few would disagree that stability is vital: more might dispute that equity between countries and peoples is vital. It is hard to argue convincingly otherwise, however. As Keynes well knew, vigorous disagreement is more commonly about the means of achieving goals than about the goals themselves. As soon as issues of power and sovereignty become involved, conflict is inevitable. The next step, therefore, is to review the existing economic institutions so as to assess more concretely where reforms are necessary.

Institutions

The functions, policies and problems of the IMF and the World Bank (the BWIs) are discussed elsewhere — including in this volume. They have been well-documented (see for example, Buira, 2003). The governance of both institutions suffers from a lack of equity and inclusiveness. In the case of the IMF, this inadequacy can be identified in several areas. Firstly, voting power grossly favours Western nations, especially Europe and the US. The top twenty nations account for seventy-one percent of IMF votes, leaving the remaining one hundred and sixty-six nations with twenty-nine percent of voting power (IMF, 2009). This imbalance marginalises the voices of both large and smaller developing nations. This difficulty is exacerbated by unfair majority rules, which require an affirmative vote from the US to pass major decisions. Without the effective input of developing nations, the BWIs' policies are lopsided in that they favour the wealthier countries of the global North. They do not represent comprehensive strategies that benefit all economies.

Some reforms are underway, such as the intention to end the tradition of selecting the managing director of the Fund from Europe and the president of the World Bank from the US. Marginal changes are also being made in the distribution of quotas so as to take small steps towards greater representational realism. Those ongoing changes will still leave developed countries in a more dominant position than their relative economic or population size warrants, however. Despite the addition of a third African Board member at the Bank there continue to be asymmetries in the structure of the boards, with most member states being members of a group in which developed countries more commonly represent the members than developing countries. The result is that "participants from smaller countries [feel] that there is no role for their authorities in actively contributing to the formulation of their constituency position" (Woods, 2010). With so many countries clamouring for the attention of one director, it is inevitable that many voices are diminished if not drowned out. It is clear that there is a democratic deficit in the operation of these institutions. Yet the BWIs, especially the IMF, have been given an enhanced role by the industrialised powers in response to the Great Recession.

The US was a strong advocate of the establishment of the UN Economic and Social Council (ECOSOC) during the negotiations about the UN at Dumbarton Oaks in 1944, however, it lost interest when its control was eroded because of increasing developing country membership of the UN. ECOSOC was designed to be the principal international forum dealing with global economic coordination. With every state privy to the Council's dealings, it was also the intergovernmental body with the greatest potential to link the 'silos' into which international economic, financial, trade, social and environmental organisations tend to settle. Meetings of ECOSOC are held in public so it is more transparent and accountable than most other international economic and financial forums. Being the most comprehensively representative global economic forum it is also well placed to reflect global economic concerns.

No one would claim that it is even close to fulfilling its functions adequately, however. With fifty-four members it is too large to act swiftly and decisively; its principal session is held once a year during July; high level participation is limited to two or three days; the world's major economies are only episodically engaged with its activities at senior levels; and it has few powers and no resources with which to implement its decisions. There was even debate for some years about whether attempting to reform ECOSOC was worth the effort given the unwieldy size of its membership and its failure to establish the political authority needed for effectiveness. The Commission on Global Governance and other commentators have proposed as a consequence, the establishment of an economic and social security council which would have similar status to the UN Security Council (see below).

Following the 2004 report of the High-Level Panel on Threats, Challenges and Change, Secretary-General Kofi Annan made some modest but valuable suggestions for upgrading the work of ECOSOC by making annual ministerial assessments of progress towards mid-range development goals; by recommending the convening of timely meetings to address crises; and, most importantly, by asserting leadership in driving a global development agenda able to provide direction for the IMF, the World Bank, and other agencies. Kofi Annan's suggestions were accepted by the Global Summit in September 2005. Subsequently, the effectiveness of ECOSOC was improved with the inauguration of Annual Ministerial Reviews able to speed up the implementation of international development goals such as the Millennium Development Goals; to establish biennial Development Cooperation Forums; to convene high level dialogues with the IMF, the World Bank, the WTO and the United Nations Conference on Trade and Development (UNCTAD); to hold more short meetings on high priority issues during the year; and to improve procedures and preparation.

Attempts have also been made to develop systems of global economic governance outside the UN. Amongst the most notable have been the G8, and later, the G20. The G8 was formed in 1975 at the initiative of the French and German governments. Its initial membership of seven (Canada, France, Germany, Italy, Japan, UK, USA) was expanded to eight with the addition of Russia in 1997. The grouping has met annually, at head-of-government level, as a forum for developed economies to discuss and develop common policies in many areas. Although able to meet exclusively for many years, the increasing interdependence of the global economy has led the G8 to broaden both its agenda and its invitees in recent years, with international organisations first being invited in 1996, and non-G8 nations being invited in 2000 (the UN, World Bank, IMF and WTO were first invited in 1996; Mexico, Nigeria, Algeria and Senegal were invited to the 2000 G8 meeting) (Kirton, 2008). Once a powerful club of economically dominant nations, the G8 grouping has become increasingly anachronistic in the twentieth century world, its static membership more reminiscent of "a European dinner club of the rich and decreasingly powerful" (Luce, 2009). Lack of membership of key nations such as China, India and Brazil has caused the G8 to be increasingly irrelevant as a steering committee for the global economy. Its formation more than thirty-five years ago may have seemed like a natural step for its large industrialised members at the time, but its exclusive elitism became a scandal to much of the rest of the world.

The limited nature of its consultations with large developing countries did little to allay this.

The formal downgrading of the G8 took place at the 2009 Pittsburgh G20 Summit, where the Group of 20 Finance Ministers and Central Bank Governors (G20) was anointed by its members as the pre-eminent international economic council. This grouping first met in Berlin in 1999 at the initiative of the then Canadian Prime Minister Paul Martin. It was originally constituted as a meeting at finance minister level with the stated aim of "supporting growth and development across the globe [through] the strengthening of [its] financial architecture and [the] providing [of] opportunities for dialogue" (G20, 2011). The grouping convened at this level until 2008, when it was elevated to a meeting of member heads-of-government.

Selected exclusively by the US and Canadian finance departments, the G20 membership includes both emerging nations and the developed member countries of the G8. The full membership officially consists of Argentina, Australia, Brazil, Canada, China, France, Germany, India, Indonesia, Italy, Japan, Mexico, Russia, Saudi Arabia, South Africa, South Korea, Turkey, the United Kingdom, the United States of America and the European Union. Additionally, the CEOs of a number of international institutions participate in G20 meetings in an official capacity. (These include the CEOs of the IMF, the World Bank, and the International Monetary and Financial Committee.) Whilst this membership does not necessarily include the twenty biggest national economies in the world at any given point, it does account for eighty-five percent of global GDP, eighty percent of international trade, and two-thirds of the world's population. The G20 note that their membership includes "countries and regions of systemic significance for the international financial system, [as well as] geographical balance and population representation" (G20, 2011). Member states' constituent governments are also diverse. They include multi-party democracies, transitioning economies, a monarchy, and a communist one-party state. This diversity of membership and broadened scope are a significant representational improvement over the G20's predecessor body, the G8.

Additionally, the host of each G20 summit invites other states, international institutions, and regional groupings to attend as observers. For example, the South Korean government invited several non-G20 countries (Ethiopia, Malawi, Singapore, Spain and Vietnam); international institutions (the Financial Stability Board, the International Labour Organisation, the International Monetary Fund, the Organisation for Economic Co-operation and Development (OECD), the UN, the World Trade Organisation, the World Bank); and regional forums (ASEAN, the African Union and the New Partnership for Africa's Development); as ad hoc observers to the 2010 Seoul G20 Summit. The presence of these entities broadened the scope of G20 engagement with a range of international economic issues.

Indeed, the elevation of the G20 from a meeting of finance ministers and central bank governors to the level of heads-of-government can be viewed as recognition of the utility of this body across a range of issues and a validation of its composition. The greater prominence afforded to developing nations in the G20 configuration has meant that issues pertinent to the global South have a greater chance of featuring on the agenda of this powerful grouping. Developing economies have used their opportunity to chair G20 meetings to advance their own issues. For example, in 2005 China put on the agenda issues most relevant to developing countries — "demographic challenges, brain-drain, migration and innovative financing mechanisms for development" (Rubio-Marquez, 2009). The broadening of the G20 focus to encompass a broader range of global economic and social issues can only strengthen the legitimacy of the body.

The G20 has also enjoyed a certain degree of success in achieving reform in areas where other forums might have failed. For example, work that had stalled at the OECD on tax havens and transparency was advanced through the G20 after a combined German/Australian initiative that overcame existing roadblocks (Beeson and Bell, 2009). Most notable were the initiatives developed by the forum in response to the Great Recession. G20 member states took concerted, co-ordinated steps to support the global economy. "Massive fiscal stimulus programmes were implemented, central banks injected vast amounts of liquidity into the economy; and the means available to international organisations to assist emerging and developing countries were greatly expanded"(G20, 2011). The G20 developed a Framework for Strong, Sustainable and Balanced Growth and a financial regulation plan to address the root causes of the crisis. G20 meetings also produced agreement on a limited overhaul of the voting and governance structures of the Bretton Woods institutions, actions that demonstrated the G20's capacity to respond effectively to global economic matters of concern.

This is not to say that the G20 is without its problems, however. Issues of accountability and transparency, for example, affect the legitimacy of the G20 as the pre-eminent body in the international economic order. Despite general recognition that this body is an improvement on its G8 predecessor, the autocratically selected and static membership and the lack of transparency undermine the G20's ability to provide representative economic governance. The G20 has a static membership with no provision for change over time, in that member states are chosen through a secretive process by the Canadian, US and now German finance ministries (Martinez-Diaz, 2007). Lacking broader global consultation, this process stamps the G20 with a democratic deficit which is difficult to ignore and ultimately undermines its authority as a representative body. As there is no stipulated process for change or renewal, there is a limited ability to respond to changes in the global dynamic. A similar arrangement diminishes the relevance of the G8 over time.

Whilst the strengths of the G20's current composition have been noted, the grouping lacks formal input from medium and small developing nations, especially low-income countries. As ministers from thirty-four nations have noted, "the G20 must be democratised to include low-income members and ensure that the issues of key concern to them are addressed" (*Australian Financial Times*, 2009). The exclusion of one hundred and seventy nations from critical financial governance decisions is a matter of great concern for G20 effectiveness.

Although it has been noted that non-G20 member entities can and have been invited to participate in G20 summits, several regions do not have adequate representation. Nordic countries are amongst the largest contributors to global development budgets but have not yet been invited to any G20 summit. Former Soviet bloc nations, including the non-Russian transitional economies and western Asian 'stans' are unrepresented. Similarly, regional powerhouses throughout Asia and Africa are denied representation. While debate will continue regarding G20 membership, the non-dynamic constitution of the grouping will undoubtedly call into question its ability to mount a truly global response to critical problems.

Like the G8, the G20 lacks a formal secretariat. There is therefore no international bureaucracy to prepare meetings and develop agendas. This task is performed by the host nation of each summit. Member states are then tasked with the responsibility of implementing decisions arising from these summit meetings. This arrangement has several results that diminish the standing of the G20. Firstly, there are few accountability mechanisms to ensure that meeting outcomes are implemented. Secondly, different hosts afford different issues varying priority. Accordingly, it can be difficult to get traction on any particular issue as agreement at one summit may not be followed up at the next (Rubio-Marquez, 2009). Both of these factors undermine the effectiveness of the G20 as a robust body of international economic governance.

Although G20 governments have lauded the grouping's actions in the face of the Great Recession, certain criticisms can be made of G20 decisions. The reforms enacted by the group have not sufficiently addressed the longer-term structural problems that gave rise to the crisis. Indeed, "the G20's attempt to face the features of the monetary system that give rise to global imbalances can be predicted to lead to more of these imbalances" (Caliari, 2009). Additionally, despite great potential to focus on broader issues of development, the grouping's agenda has become increasingly narrow, focusing solely on financial reform. Two days ahead of the 2010 Seoul summit, former UN Secretary-General Kofi Annan expressed his concern. "Naturally", he said, "it is my profound hope that the principles of fairness, balance and the common good will also inform these discussions – and not only those on issues such as undervalued currencies, lopsided trade statistics or skewed consumption patterns, however important they may be. Unfortunately, the signs are decidedly mixed" (Chaturvedi, 2011). In retrospect, his doubts proved justified.

The G20 also lacks an enforcement mechanism of its own. Its reliance on the IMF to carry out its financial decisions contributes to the group's inadequacies, given the Fund's own issues with skewed policy and accountability. The lack of far-reaching reform in the face of the crisis, its narrow financial focus, and the absence of an implementation structure, all suggest that the G20, as currently constituted, is less effective than required for comprehensive global financial management.

The G20 is undoubtedly an important step in the development of global economic governance. Its enhanced membership and the scope of its capacity to enact reform enhance its potential value. Countering these strengths, however, are its static, undemocratic membership, and accountability issues that diminish this potential. Although a positive step, the G20 ultimately does not adequately resolve the democratic deficit in this area. As a consequence eminent international economist José Antonio Ocampo concludes that "[t]he G20 has been a step forward ... but its representation is inadequate and, particularly, lacks the legitimacy that is required for global consensus building" (Ocampo, 2011, p. 18).

POTENTIAL REFORMS

Since the start of the 1980s, the developed Anglophone world has given much freer reign to the economically powerful to do as they wish. The philosophical justification has been provided by those who regard maximisation of individual income through improvements in competitive efficiency as the preferred economic goal. It is now clear that the sense of entitlement which this generates has established mechanisms for severe financial instability, ecological erosion, growing injustice, and the entrenchment of a global underclass. Radical reform is arguably called for.

The key features of a renewed paradigm of a global economic structure would be of the most general value if they focused on equitable improvements in personal and national wellbeing. These would need to be genuinely broad and more fully inclusive than those that simply seek the maximisation of the incomes of the already privileged and expect the benefits to flow down to the rest. Improving both equity and economic efficiency would involve restoring a better balance between the market and the state. In addition, recognition of the value of diversity in economic strategy would reduce the tendency towards hubris in the centres of capitalist power. Perhaps the rest of the world has lessons to learn from China in this regard, as well as lessons to teach it. It is vital also to acknowledge the necessity of carefully judged regulation in contributing to reducing the risks of economic and financial instability and abuse. In certain areas restoring strong regulatory frameworks are a definite priority.

A particularly clear example of an issue which could only be effectively addressed through international regulation is the tax evasion facilitated by banking secrecy. It has become commonplace to blame tax havens in developing countries for this practice but in practice the principal centres enabling international tax evasion are within developed countries. Any country guaranteeing banking secrecy could be providing the context for tax evasion: for example, it is well known that the states of Delaware and Nevada in the US make establishing anonymous accounts relatively easy. The biggest cases relating to money laundering have involved banks in London, New York and Zurich, and the European Commission has referred four small member states to the European Court of Justice for failing to implement a 2005 anti-money laundering directive (UN, 2009, p. 83). Tax competition undermines the tax policies of developed countries even more than that of developing countries because the former consider that they can afford to make larger concessions. While he was Managing Director of the IMF, Michel Camdessus said (in 1998) that "estimates of the present scale of money laundering transactions are almost beyond imagination — two to five percent of global GDP would probably be a consensus range" (Baker, 2005, p. 162). Applied to global GDP of fifty-eight trillion US dollars in 2009 this indicates international money laundering in the range of US$1.16 trillion to $2.9 trillion annually. Another example of culpable tax evasion is corporate transfer pricing. Raymond Baker estimates that mispricing and abusive transfer pricing alone are worth in the region of US$500–750 billion annually; US$200–250 billion out of developing and transition economies (Baker, 2005, p. 172).

The OECD argues that it should be allowed to continue to control this area of international policy and during the last couple of decades it has been undertaking useful work doing so. The issues are global, however, and the OECD has focused on the interests of its own member states and developing country tax havens rather than the interests of all countries. Demonstrably the current preoccupation with tax evasion through offshore tax havens without simultaneous attempts to tackle the more substantial examples of tax evasion within developed countries is both inequitable and inefficient.

What is required is the establishment of reciprocal international agreements on issues of tax secrecy, the sharing of information, and decisions which are enforceable by international courts. International transparency about cross-border financial flows is currently poor. Agreements like those mooted above would substantially improve the revenues received by both developing and developed nations. The EU has already established such a system. International rules requiring multinational corporations to publish country-by-country reports that show the profits and taxes they have paid in each country in which they operate are also necessary.

This is the case of strengthening global institutional arrangements for international tax cooperation and harmonising regulations. Establishing an international tax organisation would be the most effective step. An obvious way to do this would be to upgrade the UN Committee of Experts on International Cooperation on Tax Matters into an intergovernmental body. Such a body would have an elected governing council, representative of member states, and responsible for drawing up broad objectives and major issues of policy (with the help of a competent staff). This issue is already on the agenda of ECOSOC and it could be usefully discussed by the G20. An agreement to strengthen international tax cooperation would be of value to every country, developing or developed, that is seeking to increase its revenue, to reduce tax evasion, and to strengthen equity.

Enhanced global economic governance would be a key part of reviewing the dominant discourse in international political economy. The most cost-effective national economic policies work partly because they are of benefit to other countries. Many are only possible if other countries adopt them too. If all countries collaboratively introduce expansionary macroeconomic policies, for example, then these become mutually reinforcing without damaging asymmetrical externalities. The most widely recognised example amongst economists is that of 'beggar-thy-neighbour' tariff increases. When introduced to protect national manufacturing or agriculture, they do so at the expense of reduced global trade. The aggregate effect is the retardation of economic recovery everywhere.

Several reforms have been suggested to enhance the effectiveness of the G20. The host nation for the 2011 meetings, France, actively advanced the notion of a G20 Secretariat to oversee the implementation of decisions. This followed the enthusiasm of the previous host nation, South Korea, for such a proposal. Such a secretariat would also provide a more reliable forum for those nations excluded from G20 membership to participate in the grouping's work.

The Global Governance Group (3G), a collection of non-G20 nations, has proposed several modest practical actions that could be taken quickly without significant alteration to current arrangements. These steps aim to consolidate linkages between the G20 and the UN and broaden the representational credentials of the G20 (see Menon, 2010).

The 3G has suggested that the G20 should undertake consultations as widely as possible with non-G20 members before the G20 Summits, through regular and predictable channels. This has increasingly been the case and was made a priority by the French hosts of the 2011 summit. Additionally, there were enhanced efforts to update UN members on the preparations for and the outcomes of G20 meetings. These are positive steps, although further action could be taken to enhance G20 engagement with the UN. Whilst the UN Secretary-General and his staff are regular participants at the G20 meetings, their attendance at the summits and their preparatory meetings respectively could readily be formalised. Additionally, the participation of established regional organisations in G20 Summits could also be regularised. Finally, there is ample flexibility in the G20 process to provide for the participation of non-G20 members in discussions on specialised issues. This would ensure that deliberation on key issues of global concern engage all the relevant parties.

Comprehensively collaborative economic policies cannot be achieved by G20 members alone, however, which is why the Stiglitz Commission on Reform of the International Monetary and Financial System argues that "it is absolutely essential to create better institutional arrangements for coordinating global economic policy". They suggested the establishment of a Panel of Experts and a Global Economic Coordination Council (UN, 2009, p. 137). "There is a need for global collective action to address not only ... issues of global 'externalities' but also the provision of global public goods. Among the global public goods are the stability of the global economic system and fair trading rules ... without coordination, countries do not have sufficient incentives to invest in global and regional public goods ... The same is true for common social objectives such as combating poverty. Among the most important of the global public goods is preservation of the environment"(UN, 2009, p. 88).

The Commission's proposed Panel of Experts could be established quickly, using experts from all continents in order to pool the knowledge and research results of a large number of acknowledged experts, the way the Intergovernmental Panel on Climate Change has done. The Council could also be established "at a level equivalent with the UN General Assembly and the Security Council..." with the purpose of providing "leadership in addressing economic issues requiring global action while taking into account social and ecological factors" (UN, 2009, p. 91). Membership would be by election through a constituency system designed to ensure that all continents and all major economies are represented. It would actively consult with the other institutions of global economic governance.

While this proposal is very attractive there is insufficient concrete detail in the original report for it to be an operational proposal yet. The framework seems sound, however, and the rationale for establishing such a Council is clear.

The Stiglitz Commission makes many other desirable recommendations, amongst them radical reform of the global reserve system. Not only has the current system favoured the US but it has also worsened instability. If the dollar falls it reduces the value of reserves held in dollars by other countries. When exchange rates were floated in the 1970s and 1980s this reduced a number of countries' capacity to achieve full employment. Some leaders, including those of China, suggest that the best method of eliminating these problems would be to do as Keynes proposed and to create a supranational/international reserve currency. The Stiglitz

Commission says that "this is an idea whose time has come". One method would be to steadily increase the number of Special Drawing Rights issued by the IMF, for which the two hundred and fifty billion US dollars which the G20 authorised is an important start. Many issues would have to be worked out and negotiated first, but the initial step would be to decide to start the discussions.

CONCLUSION

To conclude, the Great Recession has clarified the extent of the gaps, distortions, asymmetries and other failures in global economic institutions and policies and the enormity of the costs which they have caused. The imperative for major reform is therefore clear, though some sectional interests argue otherwise. The question is whether there are sufficient wise, disinterested and influential people and countries to be advocates for addressing the challenges of establishing effective global economic governance regardless.

REFERENCES

Baker, R (2005). *Capitalism's Achilles Heel: How to Renew the Free-Market System.* New York: Wiley.

Beeson, M and S Bell (2009). The G20 and international economic governance: Hegemony, collectivism, or both? *Global Governance*, 15(1), 67–86.

Buira, A (ed.) (2003). *Challenges to the World Bank and IMF: Developing Country Perspectives.* London, Athenaeum Press.

Caliari, A (2009). Can the G20 have it Both Ways? Washington, DC: Center of Concern. http://www.coc.org/node/6441 [24 April 2011].

Chaturvedi, S (2011). Mainstream Heiligendamm. Frankfurt-am-Main: Development & Co-operation. http://www.inwent.org/ez/articles/190338/index.en.shtml [25 April 2011].

Developing Nations Seek More Influence (2009). *Australian Financial Times*, 5 October, p. 11.

G20 (2011). What is the G20? Paris: Secretariat-General of the French Presidency of the G8-G20. http://www.g20-g8.com/g8-g20/g20/english/what-is-the-g20-/what-is-the-g20-/what-is-the-g20.70.html [25 April 2011].

IMF (2011). *Regional Economic Outlook: Asia and Pacific: Managing the Next Phase of Growth*, April.

Kaletsky, A (2009). Never Let the Facts Get in the Way of a Good Economic Theory, *Prospect*, April.

Kirton, J (2008). A Summit of Substantial Success: The Performance of the 2008 G8. Toronto: G8 Information Centre. http://www.g8.utoronto.ca/scholar/kirton-performance-080717.pdf [24 April 2011].

Luce, E (2009). New Body Takes on Economic Leadership. *Financial Times*, 26 September. http://www.ft.com/cms/s/0/56934592-a9f5-11de-a3ce-00144feabdc0.html#axzz1glKO6YZZ [14 December 2011].

Martinez-Diaz, L (2007). The G20 after Eight Years: How Effective a Vehicle for Developing Country Influence? Washington, DC: Brookings Institute. http://www.brookings.edu/~/media/Files/rc/papers/2007/1017development/1017development.pdf [24 April 2011].

Menon, V (2010). Strengthening the Framework for G20 Engagement of Non-Members. UN Document A/64/706. New York City: United Nations. http://www.un.org/esa/ffd/events/2010GAWGFC/7/Stmt_Singapore.pdf [25 April 2011].

Morris, C (2008). *The Two Trillion Dollar Meltdown: Easy Money, High Rollers, and the Great Credit Crash*. New York: Public Affairs.

Ocampo, J (2011). Global economic prospects and the developing world, *Global Policy*, 2(1), 10–19.

Phillips, K (2008). *Bad Money: Reckless Finance, Failed Politics, and the Global Crisis of American Capitalism*. New York: Viking.

Rubio-Marquez, V (2009). The G20: A Practitioner's Perspective. In *Networks of Influence? Developing Countries in a Networked Global Order*, L Martinez-Diaz and N Woods (eds.). New York: Oxford University Press.

Skidelsky, R (2000). *John Maynard Keynes: Fighting for Britain 1937–1946*. London: Macmillan.

United Nations (2009). *Report of the Commission of Experts of the President of the UN General Assembly on Reforms of the International Monetary and Financial System*, Professor Joseph E. Stiglitz, Chair, New York, 21 September.

Woods, N (2010). Global governance after the financial crisis: A new multilateralism or the last gasp of the great powers? *Global Policy*, 1(1), 51–63.

Part One

Global Production

CHAPTER 5

Global Production: An Overview

Kate Macdonald

University of Melbourne

Economic production is fundamental to the operation of any economic system, serving to transform economic 'inputs' such as raw materials and labour hours into other more highly valued goods or services. Production is also a dimension of economic life in which most individuals participate directly in the form of paid or unpaid work, with significant and immediate consequences for their quality of life. It is perhaps not surprising then that the social organisation of production is one of the most controversial subjects within the field of international political economy.

Controversies surrounding social systems of production have particular importance within the capitalist economic and socialist domains that dominate contemporary studies of international political economy. (Capitalist systems of economic production, investment and accumulation are the central drivers of the economic growth through which capitalist societies have been able to achieve their much lauded material prosperity and living standards, though capitalist relationships of production are also widely condemned for their exploitation of hired labour, alienation of individuals from more intrinsically rewarding human pursuits, and negative social impacts in the form of widespread poverty, social inequality and environmental destruction.)

'Capitalist' production is typically underpinned by extensive protection systems for private property and a central role for markets in allocating social resources, via setting prices and coordinating market exchange. It also typically involves the dynamics of cumulative investment and the growth of productive output, often referred to as processes of capitalist 'accumulation'.

As capitalist economies have become globalised during recent decades, much debate has focused on the increasingly global organisation of production in many economic sectors. Such debate has been largely social and economic in orientation, focusing on the new global business strategies through which production is coordinated across borders and exploring the implications of changing production patterns for processes of social and economic development (and underdevelopment) in poorer countries. Meanwhile, the significance of global production systems as sites of *political* power and struggle has often been overlooked.

The central aim of this chapter is to highlight the deeply political character of the contemporary reorganisation of global production. It seeks not only to paint a broad picture of globalised production but also to dissect the politics of these changes as they have played out in individual factories, farms and other workplaces around the world. This political orientation entails a focus on both the multiple forms of power involved in shaping new patterns of global production and the consequences of these patterns for the distribution of economic resources.

The discussion begins with a brief review of some important ways in which production is being globalised within the contemporary capitalist political economy. It then surveys several important aspects of the politics of global production: what have been some of the most important political drivers of the globalisation of production; who have been some of the most important winners and losers associated with these changes; and what have been some of the political responses through which the globalisation of production continues to be contested?

The chapter as whole tells a story in which the globalisation of production is being led by transnational businesses, while also being supported and facilitated by governments around the world. These changing patterns of production have important distributional consequences, influencing the way power and resources are shared between governments and businesses, between populations in different parts of the world, and between different occupational and social classes. These shifts in power and profit are giving rise to new forms of cross-border political mobilisation and struggle. A new politics of global production is emerging in which social actors across transnational boundaries attempt to hold powerful companies accountable for the new forms of power and privilege they command within a world of reorganised global production. At the same time, business power remains limited in important ways in the face of complex social and market dynamics and continuing government power. The new politics of global production, therefore, plays out on a complex and shifting terrain, in which neither business nor governments have full control over the social regulation of global production.

THE GLOBALISATION OF PRODUCTION: KEY TRENDS

The changing organisation of global production has been one of the most striking and distinctive features of a globalising political economy over the last few decades. So-called 'globalisation-sceptics', who see contemporary talk about the significance of 'globalisation' as being exaggerated, often point out that extensive flows of trade and investment between countries are nothing new. Yet few doubt that the current organisation of cross-border production through global business networks and supply chains is in many respects unprecedented.

There is much we could say in very general terms about the internationalisation of production during the decades following the Second World War. For most of this post-war period, stocks and flows of foreign investment (measures of which are usually closely linked to the globalisation of production) have grown faster than world income and sometimes faster than world trade. Such changes were particularly pronounced during the 1960s and then again since the mid-1980s. The significance of transnational companies (with operations established in multiple countries around the world) in global production and trade has also increased.

For the purposes of this discussion, three changes in the organisation of production over recent decades are of particular interest: the growth of production within transnational corporations; the growth of production beyond the boundaries of single firms and its coordination through global supply chains; and new geographies of global production.

Increased Production within Transnational Companies

Much global production still takes place within private firms, whose internal organisational systems are deployed to coordinate production and related processes of sourcing inputs, distribution and marketing. To this extent, the globalisation of production has largely mirrored the increased globalisation of transnational business organisation. In recent decades, the importance of transnational business activity organised through transnational corporations has expanded significantly, growing much faster than global trade or income. According to UNCTAD (United Nations Conference on Trade and Development) estimates, there are currently around sixty-four thousand transnational corporations (TNCs), defined as firms that own and operate plants or other facilities in one or more host countries outside their home country base. Together, these have about eight hundred and forty thousand foreign affiliates, accounting for about fifty-four million employees (figures cited by Koenig-Archibugi, 2004). These shifts are reflected in figures describing the increasing role of TNCs in international trade, particularly since the 1970s. About two thirds of international trade now involves TNCs and about one third involves "intra-firm" trade, that is, trade between affiliates of the same transnational company (Walter and Sen, 2009, p. 172).

Increased Production within Global Supply Chains

Since the 1980s, increasing volumes of global production have been organised *beyond* the boundaries of individual firms. In slightly more jargon-laden terms, it is often said that functions that were previously carried out within the organisational boundaries of 'vertically integrated' corporations are now being 'externalised' through an increased reliance on arms-length network and market relationships as a way of coordinating production.

What this means in practical terms is that transnational companies in many agricultural and industrial sectors no longer rely primarily on in-house facilities to organise the production of the goods they sell. Rather, they now source much of their product through chains of contractual, market and network relationships spread across a number of countries. For many companies this has involved a shift toward increased reliance on outsourcing. Sometimes this takes the form of simple, reasonably short-term subcontracting arrangements. In other cases businesses establish longer-term networks of business partners, enabling detailed coordination concerning production processes while retaining some flexibility and responsiveness with regard to changing market conditions (Gereffi, 1996; Gereffi *et al.*, 2005).

The global production strategies adopted by the US mega-corporation Walmart illustrate how these dynamics have played out within many companies in manufacturing and related retail sectors. Increasingly, such firms organise production through complex global supply chains, which powerful buyers such as Walmart largely control. Walmart has been transformed from a company that originally trumpeted its support of US producers to one that now sources up to seventy percent of its product from China. Although Walmart does not own the factories that produce the clothes, toys and other products sold in its stores, it plays an important role in the design and specification of these products, as well as in quality control and other aspects of the production processes involved. These controls are formalised in supplier contracts as well as through a variety of inspection and audit processes.

New Geographies of Global Production

In geographical terms, production in manufacturing sectors has shifted decisively away from the industrialised core economies of the rich world. Two seemingly competing tendencies can be observed. On the one hand, production has been increasingly dispersed across a large number of geographical locations. At the same time there has been significant 'clustering' of production in locations such as East Asia.

The status of China as a central location for global manufacturing production is a familiar story today and is discussed further in the following chapter. China has built up a critical mass of infrastructure and factory capacity that has made it a highly attractive location for manufacturing production. Some refer to it as the new 'workshop of the world'. Geographical clustering dynamics have certainly not been limited to China, however. Low-cost, high-quality manufacturing locations have also been established in other parts of Asia (Singapore, Thailand, Malaysia and Indonesia in particular). Exports of merchandise trade from Asia to the rest of the world have increased substantially — not only for basic goods like clothing but also in more technologically sophisticated products. Trade *within* the Asian region is also important. For example, it is estimated that two thirds of the inputs for China's processing activities come from Hong Kong, Japan, Korea and Taiwan (Ravenhill, 2006). Important regional concentrations of global production sites can also be found in Mexico (whose manufactured exports grew from just ten percent of total exports in 1980 to eighty-five percent by the end of the 1990s), in South America, and in Eastern and Central Europe (Gereffi and Sturgeon, 2004).

Considering these changes overall, the growing use of supply chains together with new geographies of global production have meant that the current patterns of global production are now much more 'chopped up' and 'spread out' — both geographically and organisationally — than used to be the case. In this new environment, firms and countries no longer trade simply in raw materials and final products. Rather, different firms and countries specialise not just in producing different products but in producing different parts of different products, focusing variously on design, assembly and marketing. Because not all production processes are equally amenable to this kind of disaggregation and dispersion, these patterns vary significantly across sectors. The changes involved have been particularly important in manufacturing, though similar forms of restructuring have also been important in some agricultural and horticultural sectors.

The changes involved are reflected in several broader economic trends as well. Trade in manufactured products is increasingly dominating merchandise trade generally, reflecting the dominance of global production chains in manufacturing sectors. Shares of trade in manufactures are also increasingly accounted for by trade in parts and components, again reflecting the tendency for global supply chains to "chop up" production processes and "spread them out" geographically (Gibbon and Ponte, 2005, p. 4).

POLITICAL DRIVERS OF REORGANISED GLOBAL PRODUCTION

In understanding why production has become globalised like this, some consideration of economic drivers is inescapable. Although this chapter aims to analyse global production through a primarily political lens, it is nevertheless important to briefly review some of the most important economic drivers behind these trends.

Firms can decide to reorganise their production activities in increasingly globalised ways for a number of reasons. In some cases, firms establish offshore production locations as a means of positioning themselves close to foreign consumer markets for their products. Global production strategies involving the movement of production facilities between different rich country locations are often motivated in this way.

In other cases, companies decide to pursue global production strategies as a means of lowering their production costs in highly competitive market environments. Global production strategies of this kind have been growing in importance in recent years as many transnational companies have sought new production locations in low-cost emerging markets. The increased competition facing producers in established production locations has played an important role in driving globalised production strategies of this kind. Competitive pressures have been particularly important in labour-intensive, low value-added sectors such as clothing, toys, electronics and other similar manufactured goods. In these sectors, waves of globalised production began in the 1960s and 1970s when many US and European firms found themselves suffering at the hands of emerging Japanese (and subsequently other East Asian) producers. Many such firms sought to reduce costs by relocating production to areas with cheaper labour rather than reorganising production processes at home to increase productivity. In many cases, the falling costs of foreign operations have been influenced not only by relatively cheap labour costs but also by the falling costs of international transport and communications (which are discussed elsewhere in this volume), improved organisational systems within transnational companies, and strengthened productive capacity in some developing country production locations.

These kinds of economic drivers of global production have clearly played a central role in motivating the global production patterns described above. However, excessive focus on economic factors of these kinds can lead to the neglect of the equally important *political* drivers of global production.

One obvious source of political pressure sitting behind these changes was the policy conditions that incentivised or at least enabled many of them. Relevant policy reforms took place in a number of areas as part of international agendas to do with trade and investment liberalisation, as well as to do with broader policy agendas associated with deregulation and liberalisation within many national economies around the world.

At the international level, significant shifts in the international policy environment have occurred over the last two decades. In the first few decades after the Second World War, policy was oriented towards strengthening governments' sovereign rights over national resources and regulating foreign investors in ways that were believed to promote national development. In this environment, transnational businesses seeking global production strategies often faced significant suspicion or hostility from prospective host governments. More recently, extensive international trade and investment liberalisation has played an important role in creating a much more favourable environment for firms pursuing global production strategies. A proliferation of bilateral, regional and multilateral trade and investment treaties between countries has played an important role in facilitating freer trade and investment flows (of critical importance to enabling global production strategies) and providing legal protection for the economic interests of transnational businesses wanting to establish production facilities outside their home country bases. At the multilateral level, the agreements negotiated at the Uruguay Round of the GATT (General Agreement on Tariffs and Trade) negotiations were of particular importance. At the bilateral and regional levels, a wide range of trade and investment agreements have now been signed.

Although these shifts in international policy have been important drivers and enablers of global production, they are only part of the story. Important national policy changes have also been enacted in many countries around the world. Key policy reforms implemented during the period of expansion in global production included increased openness to trade and financial flows and enhanced tax incentives for foreign investors. In some cases, the liberalisation of shipping and other transport markets also played an important role in lowering the business costs of sustaining offshore production activity. Also relevant for some firms were policy shifts that enabled freer currency convertibility. Meanwhile, financial sector liberalisation enabled the growth of a range of financial instruments, making cross border transactions easier to finance and also making it easier to hedge against currency risk. All of these policies played an important role in facilitating the shift towards global production.

This shift was also actively promoted by many local and national governments seeking to fuel industrial development and enhance national competitiveness by attracting foreign investment and technology. In a number of cases, developing country governments established and promoted export processing zones in which offshore production facilities were invited to operate using a range of favourable regulatory and tax policies. The Taiwanese government was one of the first to establish industrial parks where foreign firms could enjoy preferential policy treatment on the condition that their production activities were directed towards export markets (Ravenhill, 2009, p. 351). Incentives of these kinds were subsequently established not only by a large number of national governments but in some cases by provincial or state governments as well, which often invested in infrastructure and other forms of support in their efforts to attract transnational businesses to establish production facilities in their localities.

In a small number of cases, the offshore movement of production facilities was also supported by foreign governments. Highly political motives typically played a key role in cases of this kind. During the 1980s, for example, amidst a climate of

Cold War proxy-wars in Central America, the US government's international development agency USAID played a role in promoting the establishment of export processing zones in a number of Central American countries. One important goal was to bolster links with business interests and business friendly governments. Another was to support the competitiveness of US firms trying to compete with companies from Korea, Taiwan and other emerging industrial economies (Macdonald, 2007).

THE POLITICAL CONSEQUENCES OF REORGANISED GLOBAL PRODUCTION: WINNERS AND LOSERS

These new production and trading arrangements can have profound implications for the capacity of transnational businesses to affect the lives of workers and producers in the countries they source from — particularly those in the developing world. In order to understand the political consequences of changing patterns of global production, it is useful to survey some of the main winners and losers from these changes in terms of the distribution of economic resources and in terms of social and political power.

Consequences for the Distribution of Economic Resources

One of the most direct consequences of new patterns of global production is their impact on the capacity of marginalised workers and producers within global supply chains to protect their material welfare and to exercise meaningful control over the social conditions of their lives.

Many scholars and practitioners studying the dynamics of contemporary global production focus on how reorganised global production influences the distribution of income across differently positioned participants in global production processes. One approach that analysts find helpful for making sense of changing distributions of income is the 'global value chain' framework. Analysing one product at a time, the approach begins by mapping the consecutive stages of the production process and subsequently examining how these stages are distributed across different geographical locations and between different firms. It then maps how income-generating opportunities are distributed across different stages of the chain, identifying those value chain participants who profit from the majority of the 'value-added' generated across the value chain and those who receive very little for their efforts.

Analysts working with this approach attempt not only to map the distribution of income within global production chains, but also to explain why some participants profit so much more than others. The basic explanation offered by this approach is that income-earning opportunities depend on the stage of production undertaken by different participants in global value chains. In general, those functional stages of production such as product design and marketing, in which there are high barriers to entry and correspondingly lower competition, are associated with higher profits. Conversely, those functions with lower technological and other barriers to entry tend to be more competitive, with profit-making opportunities being lower.

Even in highly competitive retail sectors, big corporate buyers such as Walmart are often subject to less intense competition than that encountered by the individual factories producing Walmart's goods in dozens of countries around the world. The latter compete fiercely against one another to receive orders. As a result, large buyers such as Walmart tend to exercise significant power over those directly producing their goods, enabling them to capture the lion's share of profits while pushing down prices, wages and other working conditions for the workers who directly produce these goods.

Researchers working in the value chain tradition have accumulated large bodies of empirical evidence by now, documenting the consequences of these dynamics for the distribution of income between individual workers, producers and firms (Kaplinsky, 2005). The impact of global production arrangements on the distribution of income-earning capacity between countries and regions has also been widely studied (Gereffi, 1996).

On the positive side, integration into global production systems can generate important income-earning opportunities for participating workers, producers and national economies. There are corresponding benefits in terms of poverty reduction, employment creation, and the capacity to pay for imports.

New patterns of global production are also strongly associated with rising global income inequality, however. While some low-income countries have managed to insert themselves competitively into global production systems, others have remained excluded. Of those able to participate, few have successfully moved into higher profit-earning roles within global production systems. These unequalising dynamics are often reproduced at the level of individual workers and producers. Although those workers and producers who successfully participate in global production systems can access new sources of income, those workers or producers who are excluded, or those who remain trapped on the low value-added, bottom rung of global value chains, confront stagnant incomes and limited opportunities to move into more productive forms of employment.

Consequences for Corporate Power

New patterns of global production also have important implications for the power that companies can exercise over workers and communities in the countries where they operate. Such power can be exercised in many ways — both directly via their operations in host countries and indirectly via the channels of transnational organisational and market relationships in which they participate.

By way of example, it is helpful to continue examining the example of Walmart introduced above. Walmart is the second largest corporation in the world in terms of its revenues and the largest in terms of the numbers of people it employs. It is also the largest retailer in the world. It therefore exercises immense influence over the companies to which it subcontracts production. In addition to controlling design and production processes, the company is able to exercise a strong influence over price negotiations thereby indirectly influencing wage rates and other aspects of working conditions in individual factories (and to some extent the wider markets) in which the company operates.

There are, it is true, important limits to these forms of influence, which vary significantly between economic sectors. In the garment industry the line of control from retailers to production sites is generally quite direct. By contrast, distribution and control within supply chains sourcing many agricultural commodities (such as tea, coffee or sugar) are typically much more diffuse. Corporate buyers in these sectors are often separated from producers via lengthy, intermediate trading-chains in which producers sell their products via extensive networks of intermediaries. While such institutional relationships facilitate some forms of indirect control, they also constrain the influence of corporate buyers in important ways. For example, while large retailers are able to exercise a significant influence over factory conditions via the terms of the contracts they set with suppliers, they lack control over day-to-day management practices that play a central role in determining many workplace conditions. In complex, competitive and rapidly changing market environments such as these, corporate power within global production systems therefore remains significantly constrained.

Consequences for the Power of Governments

Despite such constraints, reorganised patterns of global production can also provide companies with new forms of social and political power (albeit indirectly) via their influence over national and local governments in the places where they establish production facilities. Small economies are often particularly vulnerable to the financial strength and private decision-making machinery of individual multinational corporations, whose global budgets often dwarf the national budgets of many such governments.

Corporate influence over the governments of countries in which production facilities are located can be exercised in a number of ways. In some cases, it is exercised via corporate involvement in conventional kinds of lobbying activities. Often this occurs at the national level, where companies seek to influence a range of government policies and regulations. These include environmental and labour regulations, taxation and spending on social infrastructure and services, and broader policy frameworks governing trade and investment liberalisation and protection. Corporate influence over these kinds of policies has also played an important role in shaping regulatory frameworks at the international level, where transnational companies regularly participate in negotiations on international trade and investment rules via industry body representatives or as members of national negotiating delegations. Transnational companies located within politically influential countries such as the United States or major European economies have often been particularly successful at wielding influence of this kind.

Companies can also exercise 'structural' influence over governments as a result of their ability to (re)locate stages of the production process in countries of their choosing. Governments often compete for the jobs, capital, technology, export capacity and managerial expertise that transnational businesses can bring. This enables transnational companies to negotiate with governments using their technological, financial and industrial resources as bargaining chips, strengthening corporate influence over social and economic policies within host countries.

The specific ways in which companies influence governments differs between economic sectors. The policy and regulatory issues at stake can vary widely. In many manufacturing sectors policy issues relating to labour protection, taxation and infrastructure are often central. In agricultural and mining industries, issues concerning environmental protection, the provision of social infrastructure, the cultural rights of indigenous communities, land rights and the like are often especially important. The influence of companies over governments also varies between sectors because of sectoral differences in government dependence on foreign firms. Such dependence can be particularly high when capital- and technology-intensive investments such as large mines or infrastructure projects are concerned, though in some cases governments can in turn wield significant influence over companies as a result of their ability to control access to land and natural resources within their territory.

POLITICAL RESPONSES TO GLOBAL PRODUCTION: NEW FORMS OF POLITICAL MOBILISATION

The changes described above have important implications for the organisation of global political movements, as those who are currently losing out from the globalisation of production — and others concerned about their welfare — have mobilised to try and build new forms of regulation for global production.

Traditionally, the regulation of economic production has been viewed in rather unambiguous terms as the responsibility of national governments. Governments in turn have often worked together to construct international regulatory instruments, designed largely as a way of guiding national regulation towards internationally agreed norms. While international regulation of labour standards has long taken place through the forum of the International Labour Organisation (ILO), for example, efforts to develop intergovernmental codes specifically designed to govern *global* production activity can be traced most importantly to the 1970s when both the Organisation for Economic Cooperation and Development (OECD)'s Guidelines for Multinational Enterprises (MNEs) and the ILO's Tripartite Declaration of principles concerning MNEs were adopted. The development of international standards to govern global production has subsequently continued in the form of the United Nations Norms on Transnational Corporations, labour clauses in some multilateral and regional trading agreements, and other initiatives targeting transnational companies such as the Global Compact.

There have also been attempts in recent years to use the existing instruments of private law as a way to hold transnational companies legally responsible for the harm imposed on workers and communities by global production activities. In some cases it has proven possible to prosecute corporations in their home countries for the harm inflicted in other countries by their subsidiaries. In the US, the Alien Tort Claims Act can be used to hold government officials and corporations liable for wrongs committed against non-US citizens. In one much cited case (Doe v Unocal) Burmese villagers sued the California-based energy giant for complicity in abuses committed by the Burmese military. In other cases, private law instruments relating to unfair business practices or misleading advertising have been deployed within national jurisdictions as a way to hold corporations directly accountable for their impact on extraterritorial populations. Examples of such cross-border regulatory strategies include the Kasky case against Nike and a class action against Walmart in a Californian court.

Increasingly, however, those concerned with the impact of business power upon the communities and workers involved in global production view these state-based international regulatory systems as inadequate. Many regulatory controls over global production have been dismantled at the intergovernmental level since at least the 1990s. Moreover, those existing mechanisms that remain have suffered both from difficulties in negotiation and weaknesses in enforcement. Although private law mechanisms can in theory be binding, their deployment as instruments for regulating the labour and human rights impact of transnational business typically takes them well beyond their original purpose, meaning that they have rarely given rise to successful legal rulings (though favourable out of court settlements have been achieved in some cases).

The significant problems with existing regulatory mechanisms have motivated widespread social demands for powerful businesses to accept responsibility for the social impact of their activities. These demands have in turn given rise to the emergence of a large number of supply-chain governance initiatives. These have taken a number of forms. Many companies have reformed their internal organisation by creating new roles and organisational units focused on compliance with social norms. Contracts regulating the terms of business relationships between buyers and suppliers now commonly incorporate obligations relating to labour and social standards. Many businesses also now participate in a range of standard-setting, auditing and capacity building schemes involving cooperation with governments and non-government organisations (NGOs) in both buyer and supplier countries.

Prominent examples of such supply-chain governance initiatives include corporate, NGO and wider multi-stakeholder schemes that set up private regulatory standards to govern transnational production activities, and they rely on private systems of certification for enforcement. Important multi-stakeholder schemes include the Fair Labour Association, SA-8000 and the Ethical Trading Initiative. Corporate codes of conduct have been particularly common in highly politicised retail sectors such as garments and footwear. Codes developed at the wider industry level have also been established in some countries and sectors. Important examples include the Bangladesh Garments Manufacturers and Exporters Association, the Kenya Flower Council Code, the British Toy and Hobby Association Code, and the Responsible Care Initiative for the Chemical Industry. While many of these schemes tend to focus on issues of social labour and environmental regulation, private governance schemes such as Fairtrade have been particularly important in addressing some of the issues of unequal income distribution within the global production systems discussed above.

These kinds of private regulatory schemes for global production have achieved some improvements in labour and environmental standards within global supply chains. Some have led to material improvements in the enforcement of core standards such as health and safety, and have supported the processes of learning, normative diffusion and capacity building. Such mechanisms suffer from a range of weaknesses, however. Many have limited coverage across sectors and geographical locations, tending to concentrate in certain consumer-oriented and relatively highly politicised sectors such as textiles, chemicals, toys and extractive industries. They also tend to be limited to traded sectors, especially those with links to large and visible corporations in the global North. Such private governance systems are also often limited in the scope of the content they cover, focusing largely on issues Northern consumers or investors are concerned about. For example, labour standards rarely go beyond a small number of core ILO conventions around which

Northern concerns can easily be mobilised, while other issues that are just as important to many workers and producers — such as support for workers' and farmers' political organisation, or the protection of land rights — are often neglected. Moreover, these schemes often contain weak provisions for independent monitoring and enforcement and many have been criticised for being unaccountable to the workers and communities who are the supposed beneficiaries.

Despite the uneven coverage and enforcement of these schemes and their other weaknesses, these instruments nevertheless have potentially important implications for the changing politics of global production. Such initiatives reflect a new supply-chain politics based on the *direct* politicisation of global production activity. Increasingly, regulatory arrangements are being 'hardwired' into the business- and market-oriented institutions of global production systems, rather than being left to the discretion of individual national governments, thereby contributing to a broader reconfiguration of global governance beyond state-centred political institutions.

CONCLUSION

This chapter has painted a picture of a shifting system of global production, in which both transnational businesses and governments around the world have interacted to reshape economic production at a global level. This reconfiguration of production has been reflected in increasingly globalised but also highly uneven geographies of production and also in the new organisational systems through which production is organised. Global production is now organised not only within hierarchically structured companies but also within looser, arms-length business networks in which production processes are chopped up and spread out around different parts of the globe. Economic and technological drivers have played an important role in motivating and facilitating these shifts, however, the chapter has also emphasised the multiple ways in which the relationships of political power and interest centrally underpin these global shifts in production.

This chapter has also emphasised the important distributional consequences of these shifts for individuals, populations and governments around the world. Such consequences are felt not only in relation to the distribution of economic growth and income, but also in relation to the distribution of economic, social and political power. The redistribution of wealth and power can be seen within countries — between social classes and geographical regions — and also between countries, as different countries and regions wrestle for advantage within reconfigured systems of global production.

As reorganised global production engenders gradual shifts of power and wealth, a new politics of global production is emerging, one in which social actors across transnational boundaries attempt to hold companies accountable for the new forms of power and advantage they increasingly wield. Societal actors play an increasingly important role in these politics as they seek to reassert norms of social regulation and equality against the dynamic and yet often highly un-equalising dynamics of contemporary global production.

REFERENCES

Gereffi, G (1996). Global commodity chains: New forms of coordination and control among nations and firms in international industries, *Competition and Change*, 1(4), 427–439.

Gereffi, G, J Humphrey and T Sturgeon (2005). The governance of global value chains, *Review of International Political Economy*, 12(1), 79–104.

Gary, G and T Sturgeon (2004). *Globalisation, Employment and Economic Development: A Briefing Paper.* Cambridge, MA: MIT Industrial Performance Centre Working Paper Series, MIT-IPC-04–007.

Gibbon, P and S Ponte (2005). *Trading Down: Africa, Value Chains and the Global Economy.* Philadelphia: Temple University Press.

Kaplinsky, R (2005). *Globalisation, Poverty and Inequality.* Cambridge: Polity Press.

Koenig-Archibugi, M (2004). Transnational corporations and public accountability, *Government and Opposition*, 39(2), 234–259.

Macdonald, K (2007). Public Accountability within Transnational Supply Chains: A Global Agenda for Empowering Southern Workers? In *Forging Global Acountabilities: Participation, Pluralism and Public Ethics*, A Ebrahim and E Weisband (eds.). Cambridge: Cambridge University Press.

Ravenhill, J (2006). Is China an economic threat to South East Asia? *Asian Survey*, 46(5), 653–674.

Ravenhill, J (ed.) (2009). *Global Political Economy* (Second Edition). Oxford: Oxford University Press.

Walter, A and G Sen (2009). *Analyzing the Global Political Economy.* Princeton: Princeton University Press.

CHAPTER 6

The Rise of China and India

Pradeep Taneja

University of Melbourne

Over the past decade or more, a great deal of attention has been focused on the rise of China and India, especially the economic and security dimensions of their emergence as significant players on the world stage. One of the motivations behind this growing interest in the two Asian countries is a desire to understand the impact that their dynamic economic growth is having on the international political economy. Some in the developed world worry that the rapid economic growth in the world's two most populous nations, and their voracious appetite for natural resources, will push the global prices of essential commodities higher and add to the cost of living pressures for consumers in other parts of the world. Others worry about losing their jobs as domestic manufacturers move production offshore to China and companies outsource their back-office operations to India. Such concerns reflect a view of the international economy as a zero-sum game. The reality is much more complex. The emergence of China and India as economic giants in Asia presents the rest of the world with both challenges and opportunities. The balance in this regard for individual countries depends on a number of factors, including their competitive position in the global economy, the strengths and weaknesses of their economic structures, the openness of their economies, and the quality of their infrastructure and institutions. Given the critical importance of access to natural resources for China and India, the resource-rich countries such as Australia and Brazil are in a particularly strong position to benefit from their economic rise. However, like every other country, they also face challenges from these rising powers.

China and India may be relatively new in the league of major economies in modern times but they have historically enjoyed a dominant position in the world economy. In 1700, according to the late economic historian, Angus Maddison, India and China together contributed more than forty-five percent of the world's gross domestic product (GDP). With the advent of modern mass production technologies in the era of industrial revolution, however, and the European colonial expansion and exploitation of colonised societies, the relative positions of China and India in the world economy declined sharply. The effect of colonialism on these economies was so powerful that by the time they gained their freedom in the late 1940s, their collective share of the world economy had dropped to less than nine percent in 1950 (The Maddison Project, 2008).

While historians have been trying to explain the reasons why — over the past three centuries — the West came to dominate not only China and India but the rest of the world (see for example Niall Ferguson, 2011), a new sense of optimism has come to pervade Asia. The twenty-first century, it is felt, will be the Asian century. This optimism has been fuelled by the recent high economic growth rates registered by both China and India. China's high growth trajectory began fifteen years ahead of India's but the latter has managed to confound experts by growing at an average annual rate of more than eight percent in the first decade of this century, breaking free of the so-called Hindu rate of growth, which was the historical average of three and a half percent per year experienced during the 1960s and 1970s. It was not long ago when the two Asian behemoths were "pejoratively dismissed as either chronic basket cases doomed forever to depend on the generosity of others or as the 'sick men of Asia', trapped in an extravagantly wasteful and coercive Oriental despotism of their own making" (Sharma, 2009, p. 4). With their embrace of open markets, however, China and India are now hailed as economic powerhouses that are already having far-reaching impact on the global balance of economic power. In 2001, an economist with the investment bank Goldman Sachs coined the acronym BRICs — Brazil, Russia, India and China — to highlight the shift in economic power from developed to developing countries. A subsequent study by the same bank predicted that by 2040 the combined GDP of BRIC economies could be larger than that of the United States, Britain, France, Germany, Italy and Japan. It also forecast that in 2050 China's GDP would be US$44.5 trillion and India's US$28 trillion, making India the world's third largest economy behind the United States, which is projected to have a GDP of US$35.4 trillion.

China and India are both in the middle stages of market-oriented development, have a billion-plus population, and share a legacy of strong state involvement in economic management. But there are also significant differences between these two countries. This chapter looks at the development experiences of both these countries to understand the similarities and differences between their approaches to global integration. It begins by first discussing the background to China's open-door policy before examining the factors that have made China one of the fastest growing economies in the world. It includes an examination of the process of China's integration into the world economy and its emergence as the 'factory of the world', supplying labour-intensive manufactured goods to every domain. China's strengths in what is technically known as vertical specialisation will also be considered because of its important role in the country's export success. This will be followed by a look at India's open economy policy, which began in 1991, not as part of a systematic development strategy but as a way to deal with a short-term balance of payments crisis. Regardless of its origins, however, India's policy of deregulating its domestic economy and opening up its doors to foreign trade and investment has transformed the country from an economic laggard into a dynamic high-growth economy. No account of the modern Indian economy would be complete without a look at the country's information technology industry and its role in India's economic rise; this chapter is no exception in this regard. The chapter concludes by outlining the social and political challenges that both China and India face and the hurdles they need to overcome to achieve their economic goal of becoming economic superpowers.

CHINA'S RISE

In China, the private sector was almost completely eliminated and market economy institutions were abolished following the revolution which brought the Chinese Communist Party to power under the leadership of Mao Zedong in 1949. Agricultural land and production were collectivised and large-scale industry was placed firmly in the hands of the state, while small-scale enterprises were organised as local collectives. In the 1950s, lacking an alternative model of socialist development, China borrowed heavily from the Soviet Union and the Soviet-style centrally planned command economy system was introduced with a view to achieving rapid economic development. While the actual degree of central control over the economy varied during the Mao Zedong era (1949–1976), there were no privately owned companies, and foreign trade was highly restricted and controlled by a handful of state-owned trading companies. Following the split with the Soviet Union in 1960, China became even more isolated from the outside world and only a negligible amount of trade existed with some European and developing countries. Although China began to expand trading relations with Western countries and Japan in the early 1970s, it was not until the launch of the open-door policy by Deng Xiaoping in 1978 that foreign trade and investment began to grow rapidly.

The beginning of this new era in Chinese politics and economy marked a significant change in China's attitude to the rest of the world. China was now keen to play an active part in the world economy and benefit from it. Unlike in the past, foreign trade was no longer seen as a means of earning some foreign currency to import essential machinery and raw materials to keep the state-owned mills running. It was now seen as playing an important role in China's future economic growth. Merchandise trade began to occupy a growing share of China's GDP, reaching thirty-nine percent in 2000 and then rising to sixty-six percent in 2006 (Jha, 2010 p. 24). China's share of world trade also began to climb rapidly. At the onset of its open-door policy, China was ranked thirty-second among the world's trading nations. By 1996 it had risen to the eleventh place. In 2010, China was the largest exporter of goods and the second biggest importer in the world. It was the number one trading partner of many countries, including six of the Group of 20 (G20) major economies (Australia, Japan, India, South Korea, Russia and South Africa). It was also the number two trading partner of the United States, Canada, Mexico and Brazil. At present, Chinese companies are scouring the world for investment opportunities and foreign companies are increasing their investments in China, which are in turn boosting China's share of world trade.

Special Economic Zones

One of the first initiatives launched by the Chinese government as part of its open-door policy was the establishment of Special Economic Zones (SEZs) to attract foreign capital and technology and to promote exports. Encouraged by the success of export processing zones in Taiwan and several other Asian countries, China decided, in August 1980, to establish a number of SEZs in its southern coastal provinces. Of the original four SEZs, the first three — Shenzhen, Zhuhai and Shantou — were located in Guangdong province and the fourth — Xiamen — in Fujian province. These sites were chosen for their close proximity to Hong Kong, Macau (at the time colonies of Britain and Portugal respectively) and Taiwan. The location of the SEZs was also significant because many of the overseas Chinese hailed from these areas, where they still had strong family ties and cultural links. A key element of the open-door policy was to attract wealthy members of the Chinese diaspora to invest in China. Hong Kong had already demonstrated the great entrepreneurial spirit of the Chinese people by becoming one of the most prosperous cities in the world under the free market policies of the British colonial administration. Macau was also more prosperous under Portuguese rule than its neighbouring region in China. Just as China had begun to open its doors to overseas Chinese capital, the rising labour and land costs in Hong Kong were forcing local companies to move production offshore.

The creation of the original four SEZs, the establishment of a fifth in Hainan in 1988 and the subsequent opening of other parts of China to foreign investment provided Hong Kong and Macau companies with a great opportunity to lower their production costs by moving to China. The spectacular success of Shenzhen SEZ, for example, can be attributed as much to the efforts of the Chinese government as to the huge inflow of investment capital from the overseas Chinese. With thousands of Hong Kong companies and overseas Chinese firms from Southeast Asia investing in the SEZs, the local governments from various parts of China and state-owned Chinese companies also flocked there to take advantage of the preferential policies and more modern infrastructure. Another important motivation behind the mainland Chinese firms entering the SEZs was to develop international links and gain valuable business experience.

As the SEZs developed into mega cities, however, the cost of production rose, forcing the footloose and highly price-sensitive export-oriented industries to move again. The towns and villages located outside the official boundaries of the SEZs, but still within the booming Pearl River Delta in the southern Guangdong province, became a magnet for all manner of export industries. As Martin Jacques (2009, p. 158) writes, "during the eighties, the Guangdong economy became a microcosm of the future shape and comparative advantage of the fast-changing Chinese economy, with Hong Kong entrepreneurs moving their manufacturing operations out of the city-state to neighbouring Guangdong province". Once sleepy little towns like Foshan, Dongguan and Zhongshan (in the Delta region) turned into major manufacturing centres in less than two decades. In addition to Guangdong and Fujian provinces, home to the SEZs, other coastal provinces, such as Zhejiang and Jiangsu near Shanghai, quickly industrialised on the back of the export success of mostly privately owned small and medium enterprises and Sino-foreign joint venture firms. The wave of export-oriented industrialisation that began in the south during the eighties spread north and eastwards during the nineties.

Although the power to approve new SEZs rested with the central government in Beijing, provincial and local governments all over China began to create 'economic and technological development zones' to attract overseas Chinese and foreign firms. Many of these new zones turned out to be a waste of already scarce agricultural land because their location and the quality of their infrastructure were not suitable for export-oriented foreign firms. A large number of high technology zones were also established in major cities to attract high technology foreign companies and to provide a favourable environment for local technology firms to develop. For instance, Beijing's Zhongguancun Science and Technology Park, surrounded by some of China's best universities, was already home to numerous regional headquarters and research and development centres. It became a manufacturing base for many large and well-known international firms.

Vertical Specialisation

China's economic success has been defined in large measure by the ability of the country to forge strong investment and technological links with foreign countries.

Many of the Hong Kong, Taiwanese and other overseas Chinese companies that began to invest in mainland China in the wake of the country's open-door policy already had well-developed commercial linkages with overseas customers and suppliers. They were already part of the vertical trading chain in which intermediate and semi-finished goods were shipped from one country to another to complete the manufacturing process. By opening its economy to foreign trade and investment, China was now becoming part of the global vertical trading chain, which was spread across many countries and in which each country specialised in particular stages of a finished product's production sequence. As was to be expected, the more labour-intensive parts of the production process were carried out in low-wage developing countries. This type of trade drove the growth of the East Asian economy for several decades and was the result of the increasing interconnectedness of its production processes.

Because of its large, literate and disciplined labour force, China has been successful in integrating its manufacturing sector with global production and trading networks through vertical specialisation in labour-intensive processes and product lines. This has given a huge boost to China's economy and created tens of millions of manufacturing jobs, providing employment to a steady stream of rural workers who are no longer content with subsistence farming. Many of the much sought after high-technology and high-value consumer products such as smart phones and tablet computers are assembled in China, by Chinese and Taiwanese-owned companies that employ tens of thousands of workers on low wages. These workers often work long hours for a fraction of the income earned by their counterparts in countries where the bulk of the products they make are sold.

The Role of Foreign Direct Investment

Foreign direct investment (FDI) has played a more important role in China's industrialisation than it did in Japan, South Korea or Taiwan during their rapid growth phases. Since the beginning of its open-door policy in 1978 China has absorbed more than five hundred billion US dollars in FDI, which is ten times the amount received by Japan between 1945 and 2000 (Jacques, 2009, p. 158). In 2010 alone, China received one hundred and six billion dollars in foreign direct investment (Ding, 2011). While initially the main motivation behind foreign companies investing in China was to take advantage of its cheaper labour costs to produce goods for exports, the new FDI projects frequently had the already quite large and fast growing domestic Chinese market in their sights. After joining the World Trade Organisation in 2001, China had to change hundreds of domestic laws that had hitherto protected domestic companies from foreign competition. The changes in these laws and the resultant access to the Chinese domestic market for foreign companies not only boosted exports to China, it also encouraged foreign firms to increase their investments in China as new areas of investment opened up. For example, under the terms of China's accession to the WTO, China committed itself to liberalising the environment in which its banks and other financial institutions operated. Earlier on, foreign banks were not allowed to undertake local currency business in China and strict geographical restrictions were in place concerning the establishment of foreign banks. China agreed to remove these restrictions by 2005 under its WTO commitments.

In reality, however, there remains many problems with the implementation of China's WTO commitments. While historically the majority of FDI inflows to China had gone into the manufacturing sector, the services sector has now begun to outperform the manufacturing sector in attracting FDI, receiving 46.8 percent of the total US$10.03 billion in January 2011 (Ding, 2011). A growing number of foreign banks and insurance companies have taken advantage of the more liberal investment environment in China to start operations there. The path to China's domestic market for foreign firms, however, especially in the services sector, is still lined with numerous administrative barriers that foreign companies find hard to overcome, leading to a large number of disputes involving Chinese and foreign companies. Chinese companies have also been the biggest target for anti-dumping complaints filed with the WTO.

Massive Infrastructure Spending

China's emergence as a manufacturing power would not have been possible without rapid improvement in both the quality and quantity of its basic infrastructure. Starting from a very low base in the early 1980s, China invested hundreds of billions of dollars in building new roads, subways, highways, ports, airports and high-speed railways. The quality of China's infrastructure even drew praise from Barack Obama during the 2008 American presidential election campaign when he told an audience, in Chester, VA, "Think about the money that China has spent on infrastructure; their ports, their train systems, their airports are vastly superior to us now". While this may not be true across the board, it is a fact that China has invested heavily in infrastructure development. According to the World Bank, China spends fifteen percent of its GDP each year on infrastructure, builds 200,000 kilometres of roads per year, and adds one gigawatt of power generation every other week (World Bank, 2011). The country plans to spend over US$430 billion to build an extra thirty thousand kilometres of rail lines by 2015 (People's Daily, 2011).

The speed with which China has been able to build infrastructure is evident from the fact that while until 2004 China did not have a single kilometre of high-speed railway, by 2011 it had built the world's longest high-speed railway network.

As the foregoing discussion illustrates, China has come a long way from Mao Zedong's egalitarian and isolationist economic policies and disastrous political campaigns of the fifties and sixties in order to emerge as the world's second largest economy after the United States. This has been made possible by more than three decades of reforms involving the de-collectivisation of agriculture, the decentralisation of economic decision-making powers, the de-controlling of prices, the encouragement of private enterprise, and the integration of China with the world economy.

Despite these very significant changes, the role of the state in China's economic development remains very strong. Many strategically important sectors of China's economy remain under the control of the state through state-owned enterprises. Important industries such as mining, iron and steel, telecommunications, banking, insurance and civil aviation remain dominated by state-owned companies.

These companies are now actively engaged in expanding their operations beyond China's shores, leveraging China's huge foreign currency reserves to guarantee future supplies of much-needed energy resources and other essential commodities by investing in far-flung parts of the earth. It is not surprising, therefore, that the one part of the world where China's economic rise has been felt very strongly, and where Chinese companies have been investing heavily, is Africa. As Jacques (2009, p. 321–332) points out, the drawing power of Africa for China is understandable. China needs vast quantities of raw materials of all kinds to fuel its economic growth. While China does have significant natural resource endowments, its demand for these resources has continued to outgrow domestic supply, thus necessitating a search for alternative sources. Instead of relying on the market to supply these commodities, China has been eager to lock in long-term supplies by buying up oil and gas fields and mines not only in Africa but also in other parts of the world. China is not the only rising power hungry for energy and other natural resources, however.

Indian companies, too, are scouring the world for opportunities to invest in energy and mineral resources. China's state-owned companies often go head-to-head with Indian companies in different parts of the world in bidding for exploration or mining rights. With their deep pockets and the strong backing of the Chinese government, plus generous foreign aid packages thrown in as inducements, Chinese companies frequently emerge triumphant in their competition with Indian firms. It is, therefore, fitting that we now turn our attention to the rise of India as an emerging power.

THE RISE OF INDIA

India is the world's largest democracy with more than seven hundred and thirty million registered voters who jealously guard their right to vote and frequently use it to punish governments that fail to meet their expectations. China, on the other hand, has been ruled by the authoritarian Chinese Communist Party (CCP) for more than sixty years. The CCP exercises a monopoly on political and military power and exerts a strong influence on the economy. A parallel party structure at every level of the government and corporate organisations ensures that the Party's interests are protected at all times. In India, by contrast, political parties have no direct influence over corporate entities, including those owned by the government. The country's defence forces are also barred from getting involved in political matters. Regardless of the above differences, China and India have much in common, however, especially a history of the 'eerily similar' central planning (Sharma, 2009, p. 7).

When India gained independence from British colonial rule in August 1947, the nationalist leaders of the country also opted for an independent path of economic development, which in practice meant a healthy suspicion of multinational corporations and a strong preference for public sector (state-owned) enterprises over private business interests. Far from outlawing private and foreign businesses as China had done, however, the Indian government's economic policies under the country's first prime minister, Jawaharlal Nehru, remained relatively open and investor-friendly in the first decade after independence. India did implement a centrally planned model of economic development in 1951 but it did not adopt a closed economy model. Unlike in China, where the five-year plans were designed to allocate resources and set production targets for state-owned enterprises (SOEs), in India the same goals were to be achieved through an elaborate system of regulatory and licensing requirements imposed on the private sector. India also had, and continues to have, five-year plans, but they were never as detailed as the Chinese plans, even after they grew in complexity after 1957. Another feature of India's central planning was the practice of reserving certain sectors of the industry for exclusive development by the public sector. Perhaps the most damaging for the competitiveness of Indian industry, however, was the policy of reserving more than eight hundred products for manufacture exclusively by small-scale factories. These included items such as toys, ready-made garments, cutlery and home electrical appliances, for which production was increasingly outsourced to Southeast Asia and later China by American and European companies. Although the motivation behind this policy was to create jobs for the unemployed, it was a missed opportunity for India to take part in global production. Faced with a series of foreign exchange crises starting in 1957, the Indian government abandoned its earlier more liberal trade policies and began to heavily restrict imports, promoting instead a policy of import substitution. Domestic manufacturers were protected from foreign competition behind heavy tariff and non-tariff barriers.

Although India's state-owned industrial enterprises played an important role in the country's industrialisation after independence, even at the height of economic autarchy, their share in the country's GDP was less than twenty percent (Jha, 2010, p. 45). This left enough room for the private sector to develop and grow, albeit under a strict regulatory and licensing regime. India's public and private enterprises of all shapes and sizes were thus able to operate without facing the pressure of foreign competition. As is often the case with trade protection, the main loser was the Indian consumer who had to deal with regular shortages of consumer goods (e.g. scooters and motorcycles) and pay high prices for poor quality locally made products — when these were available. In short, India's economic policies stifled growth and were responsible for India remaining among the slowest-growing economies in the world for four decades until 1991.

India's Embrace of Globalisation

As indicated above, India's decision to open its economy to foreign trade and investment was the result of a balance of payments crisis that came to a head in 1991. In June 1991, a new government led by Prime Minister Narasimha Rao was sworn in following general elections in which his Congress Party had won. This was as a result of a sympathy wave generated by the assassination of the former prime minister, Rajiv Gandhi, in May that year. The Party had not won enough seats to form a government in its own right, however, and had to rely on minor parties for support. The dismal state of the country's finances was already known to everyone in the country even before the elections. Due to the paralysis of the political system between 1989 and 1991, however, when a succession of minority governments came and went, nothing could be done to avert the crisis. Iraq's invasion of Kuwait in 1990 and the subsequent drying up of the remittances from Indian workers in the Middle East pushed India to the edge of financial abyss.

Prem Shankar Jha, a noted Indian journalist, summed up the extent of the crisis in the following words, "The fiscal deficit climbed to 8.4 percent of GDP, the external current account deficit climbed to 3.5 percent of GDP, inflation nudged 13 percent (which was double India's historical inflation rate), and foreign exchange reserves were down to US$1.1 billion" (Jha, 2010, p. 175). Left with very few options and on the verge of defaulting on its foreign debt, the government had to ship part of the country's gold reserves overseas to access the international overnight market in order to avoid a loan default (Sharma, 2009, p. 76). In return for emergency assistance from the International Monetary Fund (IMF), the newly elected Rao government agreed to implement a wide-ranging economic reform programme. As part of the reform agenda, the government agreed to devalue the rupee, free the exchange rate, dismantle the system of industrial licensing, drastically cut tariffs, and remove the remaining bans and quantitative restrictions on imports. It also agreed to cut government expenditure in order to bring down the fiscal deficit. This was indeed a very bold set of policies that inevitably attracted a great deal of criticism and protest from many segments of Indian society. It did signal the end of an era, however. The control-bound and inward-looking economy was over and the new market-friendly and outward-looking one had begun.

The net effect of these policies was that "the organisation of the economy — how income is earned and spent, how capital is raised, how business is run, how labour is employed and work done, how goods and services are traded across borders, how profits are shared, re-invested, and taxed, and how the state treats private enterprise — became by the mid-2000s fundamentally different from how it was in 1990" (Alamgir, 2009, p. 1). There was also a clear change of mood and a heightened sense of optimism about the country's future among India's middle classes as unprecedented opportunities opened up for career enhancement, entrepreneurial pursuits, asset acquisition and wealth generation. As foreign financial institutions were allowed to invest in India's stock markets, stock indices began to soar higher and higher and many Indians who had never shown any interest in shares, or could not afford to, began buying and selling shares for the first time. While some multinational companies such as Unilever had been in India for a protracted period, the entry through foreign direct investment of numerous well-known international firms not only created new, high paying jobs, it also offered international brand goods to Indian consumers at affordable prices. The availability and quality of consumer goods changed dramatically, winning the support of middle class Indians for the government's new market-oriented economic policies.

Some scholars have argued that Indian leaders have always had a 'globalist' orientation but that it was not until China's rapid economic growth and rising international stature that they began to prioritise material objectives as part of their globalist agenda (Alamgir, 2009). Prior to that, India's globalist orientation was based on ideational concepts such as non-alignment, pacifism, democracy and self-determination. The rise of China also engendered a strong sense of rivalry and competition in India. Alamgir (2009) argues that it is this feeling of rivalry with China that has sustained the support for India's new open-economy policy despite the unpopularity of some elements of the policy and attendant protests and demonstrations by disaffected sections of the population.

While India has adopted many of the same economic policies as China, it has lagged behind its north-eastern neighbour in terms of integration into the regional and global production and trading networks. A large proportion of inward FDI in China is 'vertical'. It is characterised by the fragmentation of the production process by international corporations who undertake each stage in countries where it can be done at the lowest cost. As a result, industry accounts for about forty-seven percent of China's GDP, facilitated by China's successful participation in global production networks through vertical specialisation. By contrast, industry contributes only about twenty-seven percent of India's GDP. As much of the inward FDI into India is horizontal (market-seeking) rather than vertical (export-promoting), the share of FDI-driven exports in India's manufacturing exports is less than ten percent. If India is to increase living standards and domestic consumption, it will need to create more jobs in the manufacturing sector for its large unskilled workforce. In order to attract more foreign investment in manufacturing, India must undertake further microeconomic reforms, including changing labour and bankruptcy laws, investing in education and technical training and improving its physical infrastructure, such as roads, highways and ports.

Infrastructure Deficit

The need for developing better and more efficient infrastructure has already been recognised by the Indian government. Infrastructure spending has also increased over the past decade and, according to the World Bank, the country will spend nine percent of its GDP on infrastructure in 2011 (World Bank, 2011). One area of weakness in infrastructure that is easily visible to any visitor to India is the poor quality of its roads. To remedy this situation, the government embarked on an ambitious programme of highway construction in the late 1990s under the National Highway Development Project (NHDP). Given the high fiscal deficits run by both the central and state governments in India, the financial capacity of the government to invest in much-needed infrastructure has been severely constrained. A novel feature of NHDP is that nearly two thirds of the funding for this project comes from a levy on fuel rather than the usual practice of relying on general tax revenues (Bardhan, 2010, p. 58). Similarly, the power sector in India has also suffered from inadequate investment and inefficient management. Most Indian businesses and households have to endure daily power cuts, and power costs for manufacturing in India are thirty-five percent higher than in China (Bardhan, 2010, p. 56). This fact alone seriously undermines the competitiveness of Indian industry. But here, too, there are signs of improvement as changes in legislation have begun to inject a degree of competition and efficiency in the power sector. The competitiveness of Indian industry is also dented by higher transportation costs; average freight tariff per tonne-kilometre on Indian railways is sixty percent higher than in China (Bardhan, 2010, p. 59). In the telecommunications sector, however, the gap between India and China is not as big as in other areas. While China's average teledensity (the number of telephone lines per one hundred inhabitants in a given area) is higher than India's, the consumers in India enjoy lower call charges. India's telecommunications industry is more competitive and private companies play a much bigger role in the sector than in China.

Overall, there are a number of reasons why India lags behind China in infrastructure. First, despite the authoritarian nature of Chinese politics, the fiscal system in China is more decentralised and local authorities enjoy much more executive power and operational autonomy than in India. Second, India's democratic system has meant that politicians often indulge in electoral populism and do not allow state-owned utilities to recover costs by forcing them to keep user charges low. If they cannot recover costs, they have no means of reinvesting in added capacity and improving service delivery. Moreover, faced with regular elections, Indian politicians engage in short-term behaviour by bestowing immediate benefits (or private goods) on selected constituents rather than investing in long-term public goods. Finally, India's infrastructure deficit is also a result of what Shalendra Sharma (1999, p. 20) has called "weak and fragmented administrative and institutional capacities of the country's democratic regime". The Indian bureaucracy, with a few exceptions, does not seem to be as good at implementing projects as its counterpart in China and other parts of East Asia.

India's Software Success

India's success in developing a highly competitive information technology (IT) industry is something that even the Chinese view with envy. It is sometimes said that the IT industry in India developed not because of the government but in spite of the government. This implies that the government had no positive role to play in the development of this industry. This is not entirely true. The central government and the various state governments in India have been actively establishing software technology parks since the early 1990s and these have generally been very successful. In 1998, for example, the government of Andhra Pradesh, in the country's south, created an $850 million state-of-the-art software park in the state capital, Hyderabad, in which the government holds eleven percent equity (Yahya, 2009,

p. 379). The then Chief Minister of the state, Chandrababu Naidu, personally wooed the chief executive officers of major multinational IT companies to invest in Hyderabad. It was because of his efforts that Microsoft decided to set up its Indian head office in Hyderabad rather than Bangalore, which was already well known as India's Silicon Valley. The Indian government has also created a very favourable business environment for both Indian and foreign IT companies to invest in the sector. More importantly, however, it was the establishment of the elite Indian Institutes of Technology (IITs) and the Indian Institutes of Management (IIMs) by the government of India in the fifties and sixties that provided the initial manpower for the IT industry. Many of the founders of India's own globally successful software companies are themselves graduates of IITs and IIMs.

Starting with almost nothing in the 1980s, the IT and IT-enabled services (ITES) industry has become India's largest export income earner with exports of forty billion US dollars in the 2007–2008 financial year. Export earnings are projected to rise to fifty-nine billion US dollars in 2011 (Reuters, 2011/2/11). The industry employs two million people directly and another eight million indirectly (Illiyan, 2008, p. 1088). Even more impressive is India's share in the global (IT services) outsourcing market, which rose to fifty-five percent in 2010 from fifty-one percent a year earlier (Reuters, 2011/2/11).

On the whole, India's services sector is large in comparison with other countries at a similar level of income. It contributes to fifty-five percent of India's GDP, a significantly higher figure than China's forty-two percent (Lommen, 2011). This has led some economists to ask whether India can 'leapfrog manufacturing' and become a middle income country on the back of knowledge-based service industries. This is unlikely unless India can dramatically increase its literacy and higher education participation rates, which are currently lower than in China. India will also need to significantly improve the quality and quantity of its physical infrastructure. Even with such improvement, India will still need an acceleration of manufacturing to provide employment to its large and growing population and work hard to maintain the competitive advantage it has gained in the IT sector.

CONCLUSION

China and India are the emerging giants of the twenty-first century, each with populations of more than one billion people and a rapidly developing economy. Both are becoming significant international players, through direct and indirect action, in international finance, investment and corporate entrepreneurship, as well as becoming large and expanding consumers of natural resources. The high-speed economic growth in both countries has lifted hundreds of millions of people out of poverty. It has also created opportunities and challenges for people in other parts of the world. In a recent study of Western responses to globalisation in the face of the rise of China and India, Mark Thirlwell (2007) questions whether the developed world can cope with the emergence of these new powers. Perhaps a better question to ask is whether these two countries can cope with the large-scale transformations that have shaped not only their economies but also their societies and polities.

In both countries, inequities in the distribution of wealth are increasing. While both boast a rising number of billionaires each year, not everyone has benefited equally from the economic growth of the past several decades. This is leading to rising social tensions. In China each year the number of 'mass incidents', as popular protests and riots are officially called, is increasing and the state is resorting to more repressive measures to contain the spread of such incidents. With the spread of new telecommunications technologies, like the internet and social media, the Chinese authorities are increasingly finding it difficult to control the free flow of information. Every rumour of a perceived abuse of power by a government official or communist party cadre spreads very quickly despite the best efforts of the country's cyber police to contain it. Maintaining at least eight percent growth each year has become an absolute necessity for the Chinese leadership, failing which the prospects of social discontent and highly destabilising popular protests could rise significantly. It was at least partly because of these concerns that the Chinese government responded to the 2008 Global Financial Crisis with a massive four trillion yuan ($586 billion) stimulus package.

Both the countries also face the grave environmental consequences of rapid economic growth. Both are confronting serious water shortages. It was, therefore, not surprising that despite their otherwise difficult bilateral relationship, China and India coordinated very closely their positions at the Copenhagen climate change conference in 2009.

In addition, political leaders in democratic India have to always keep one eye on the electoral cycle in making economic decisions. As a result, economic policies that may be in the long-term interest of the country, but might cause short-term pain, are often avoided because of the fear of their impact on the next election. Open market policies and the relatively easy access to credit have created unexpected problems in rural India (see Vakulabharanam and Motiram, 2011). Poor harvests, lower than expected prices, and exploitation by middlemen is driving a large number of farmers to commit suicide each year since the early 1990s (see Sainath, 1999). Although the government has introduced a number of initiatives to alleviate poverty in rural India, including a multibillion dollar employment guarantee scheme, corruption and inefficiency are often blamed for the relative lack of their effectiveness.

REFERENCES

Alamgir, J (2009). *India's Open-Economy Policy: Globalism, Rivalry and Continuity*. New York: Routledge.

Bardhan, P (2010). *Awakening Giants: Feet of Clay: Assessing the Economic Rise of China and India*. Princeton, New Jersey: Princeton University Press.

Ding, Q (2011). FDI Growth to Remain Robust over Coming Year, *China Daily*, 18 February. http://www.chinadaily.com.cn/bizchina/2011–02/18/content_12037480.htm [14 December 2011].

Ferguson, N (2011). *Civilisation, the West and the Rest*. London: Allen Lane.

Illiyan, A (2008). Performance, challenges and opportunities of Indian software export, *Journal of Theoretical and Applied Information Technology*, 4(11), 1088–1106.

Jacques, M (2009). *When China Rules the World: The Rise of the Middle Kingdom and the End of the Western World*. London: Allen Lane.

Jha, P (2010). *India and China: The Battle between Soft and Hard Power*. New York: Viking/Penguin.

Lommen, Y (2011). Unlock the potential of services sector. *China Daily*, 22 February, p. 9.

Reuters (2011). India's Software Exports Seen Up 16–18 pct in FY12. Reuters News Agency, 2 February 2011. http://in.reuters.com/article/2011/02/02/idINIndia-54597320110202 [14 December 2011].

Sainath, P (1999). *Everybody Loves a Good Drought: Stories from India's Poorest Districts*. London: Headline Book Publishing.

Sharma, S (2009). *China and India in the Age of Globalisation*. New York: Cambridge University Press.

Sharma, S (1999). *Development and Democracy in India*. Boulder and London: Lynne Rienner Publishers.

The Maddison Project (2008). http://www.ggdc.net/maddison/oriindex.htm [14 December 2011].

Thirlwell, M (2007). *Second Thoughts on Globalisation: Can the Developed World Cope with the Rise of China and India?* Double Bay, N.S.W: Longueville Books for Lowy Institute for International Policy.

Vakulabharanam, V and S Motiram (2011). Political Economy of Agrarian Distress in India since the 1990s. In *Understanding India's New Political Economy: A Great Transformation*, S Ruparelia, S Reddy, J Harris and S Corbridge (eds.). Abingdon: Routledge.

World Bank (2011). Infrastructure. http://web.worldbank.org/WBSITE/EXTERNAL/NEWS/0,,contentMDK:20127296~pagePK:64257043~piPK:437376~theSitePK:4607,00.html [14 December 2011].

Yahya, F (2009). The rise of India as an information technology (IT) hub and challenges to governance, *South Asia: Journal of South Asian Studies*, 32(3), 374–389.

CHAPTER 7

Europe's Political Economy: The Search For Stability

Philomena Murray

University of Melbourne

Even with only 7% of the world's population we still generate almost 22% of the world's GDP.

Herman Van Rompuy, 2011

This chapter examines the political economy of the European Union (EU). It seeks to illustrate that the EU is not simply an economic project but rather that it is a political and social experiment in supranational and transnational cooperation. The economic imperatives of the EU are perhaps its most obvious characteristics, yet the political motivations behind it were clearly in evidence from its origins as a new international organisation that pooled national sovereignty in the aftermath of the devastation of the Second World War. The EU is both an economic and a political project, therefore, and as such has been distinguished by distinct phases of development. Economic policy was pursued at times for political ends, but both imperatives were evident from the beginning. In addition, a civic component was increasingly developed in terms of workers' rights and social policies.

The radical and innovative approach adopted in the 1950s by the EU's founders to organise its modes of production — and establish its unique institutional structure — remain key signifiers of the EU. This has been evident in the pooling of both policy management and governance structures with regard to coal and steel production in the early 1950s, in the European Coal and Steel Community, and in the EU as it developed a market based on twenty-seven constituent states and a currency union based on seventeen of these states. This chapter traces the development of the EU as an economic entity and a political entity. There were times when economic achievements were dominant and times when political integration was pre-eminent. The basis of the EU's origins was the need for political stability. This was deemed achievable in terms of economic integration and political institutions. It is argued here that political stability within the EU is no longer a key concern, however. Rather, economic stability has become the overarching priority of the EU's leaders and policy makers. The interstate reconciliation that formed the foundation stone of the initial Franco-German bargain was a political compromise that had beneficial economic outcomes. Now the Franco-German bargain — sponsored by Germany's dominance as Europe's paymaster — has become the cornerstone of the search for economic stability at a time of grave economic and financial crisis. The political bargain has changed from the pooling of national sovereignty in order to achieve peace, stability and trade production to a search for ways to secure economic stability. The desire for the EU to be the world's most influential trader remains a core EU interest, but internal economic stability is now paramount as internal solutions to EU problems dominate the minds of the EU's leaders and its citizens.

The EU's political economy is a combination of its economy, polity and society. Its grand strategies are encapsulated in the Single Internal Market. This has made possible effective trade and competition policies that have had a considerable external impact. At the same time, the EU has developed a distinctive historical narrative based on the achievement of peace, stability and prosperity among the nations of Western Europe and later among an enlarged EU of twenty-seven member states. This narrative has been highly significant in terms of its policy implications and the rhetoric involved. It has won widespread admiration as an example of successful interstate cooperation (Rifkin, 2004 and Leonard, 2005) and as a paradigm for the achievement of reconciliation among member states (Gardner Feldman, 1999).

In early 2011, for example, in an article in the *New York Times*, Paul Krugman argued that the euro is essentially a political as well as an economic project and that this has been the European strategy "ever since the Schuman declaration". The point is to deliver a series of economic integration plans that do double duty, "they're economically productive", but they also create "de facto solidarity", moving Europe closer to "political union" (Krugman, 2011). This chapter argues that politics and economics have always determined European integration, in other words, that political objectives and economic imperatives have always been intertwined.

Integration refers to the initiative to unite states in a single grouping for the benefit of constituent members. A challenge to understanding the EU is that European integration is also a long-term objective and process. It has been defined as close cooperation among member states in order to achieve a state of political union. In addition to achieving economic integration, that is, monetary integration is also evident. Indeed, in these terms the EU is the most advanced example of regional integration in the world.

Integration is examined in the scholarly literature, and to an extent presented by the EU itself, in a number of often confusing ways. These can be grouped as integration as a process, integration as policy making, integration as an end-goal, and integration as international influence (Murray, 2009, p. 228).

Early attempts at economic cooperation were evident well before the visionary ideals emerged of an EU or of a European Community (EC) in the 1950s. The European continent was home to the first trade and occupational guilds and to the trading cooperative known as the Hanseatic League. Europe was the birthplace of the industrial revolution. It was the birthplace of the nation state. The EU was to rewrite the rulebook for sovereignty with the pooling of national power in a new political, legal, economic and diplomatic form. The EU also set many of the regulatory norms that are currently in place regarding international trade. Yet Europe's integration was created out of war and out of a desire for reconciliation and stability. Many of its most important decisions were made when it was undergoing a period of crisis. It is currently yet again in crisis, however, there are many politicians and scholars who consider the EU not only to be a successful economic, political and social entity, but to be a model for governance, both economic and political, in other parts of the world.

This chapter now traces the EU's trajectory from a war-ravaged continent to one enjoying prosperity and economic success and subsequently to its current crises. It seeks to illustrate that the EU is characterised by a distinctive combination of several factors — relatively sound economic management and leadership, a commitment to social values, and a commitment to a political system that is characterised by embedded and entrenched institutionalism and rule-based behaviour. Europe, the cradle of the nation state, often seems — through its supranational tendencies — to be trying to bury it. Europe, the cradle of industrial development — a revolution that seemed to be the defining characteristic of economic prosperity — now finds itself in economic crisis. It is in recession and that has challenged its ability to meet its commitment to implement effective economic policies, financial regulations, social cohesion, educational advances and poverty reduction. In essence, it has sought to create an economy, polity and society that are based on shared objectives and values that are harmonised throughout its twenty-seven member states. The EU is also characterised by expansion — in terms of its membership, its policy scope and reach, its institutional and treaty embeddedness, and its polity. All of these have been the subject of dispute, admiration and opposition.

ORIGINS AND DEVELOPMENT OF ECONOMIC INTEGRATION

In July 1951, the European Coal and Steel Community (ECSC) Treaty was signed in Paris by Germany, France, Italy, the Netherlands, Belgium and Luxembourg. It came into force in 1952. Two important treaties were signed by the same six countries in Rome on 25 March 1957. (The ECSC had a fixed life of fifty years and ceased to exist in 2002, when the policy areas of coal and steel were subsumed within the EC Treaty.) The first, the Treaty Establishing the European Economic Community (EEC), created the European Economic Community (EEC). The second established the European Atomic Energy Community (Euratom).

Economic integration became the hallmark of the EU with the establishment of a customs union, the abolition of tariffs and quotas, the development of a Common Commercial Policy, and a Common Agricultural Policy. Indeed, economic integration was perceived as "the most concrete and visible achievement of the European Union since the signature of the Rome Treaty" (Andreosso-O'Callaghan, 2005, p. 49). The 1957 Rome Treaty provided for the establishment of a common organisation for agricultural markets and single prices, backed up by financial solidarity and European Community preferences. The most controversial — and for a considerable number of Europeans, the most successful — policy was the Common Agricultural Policy (CAP). The CAP's objectives were, firstly, to increase agricultural productivity; secondly, to ensure a fair standard of living for farmers; thirdly, to stabilise agricultural markets; fourthly, to guarantee regular supplies of food; and finally, to ensure reasonable prices for consumers. It was criticised, however, for being protectionist and discriminatory by businesses, civil society groups, trade unions, development aid groups, and international interlocutors.

At the centre of the EU's integration was the creation of the Single Market, a neo-functionalist development from the Common Market established in the 1950s. The treaty framework for its creation was set out during negotiations in 1985 for a Single European Act that would establish the means to adopt the requisite legal instruments in order to eliminate the technical, regulatory, legal, bureaucratic, cultural and other protectionist barriers to the free movement of goods, services, labour and capital within the EC. Tariffs and quotas were abolished at the end of the 1960s but many technical and administrative obstacles to free trade persisted. The Single Market has been credited with creating some two and a half million new jobs since 1993 and generating more than €800 billion in extra wealth. The four freedoms of movement — of goods, services, people and capital — are underpinned by a range of supporting policies. The EU pursues a very strong antitrust policy, for example, that is backed up by its recourse to the European Court of Justice. Companies may not fix prices or carve up markets. Workers, for the most part, may move around freely to seek employment. This is supported by the fact that there is mutual recognition by the EU member states of many academic and professional qualifications. Certainly economic stability and prosperity have been achieved, over several decades now, for the EU and its citizens.

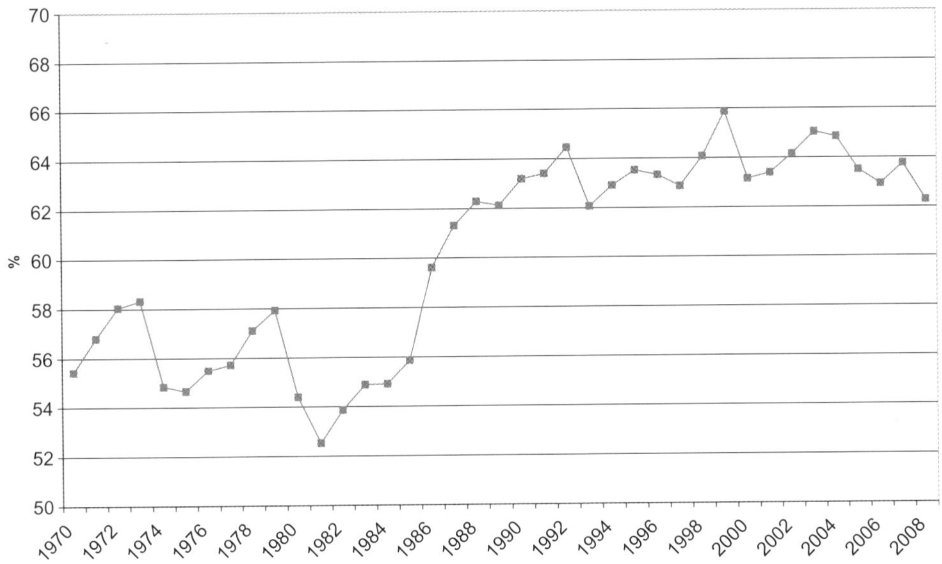

Figure 1: Intra-regional trade share in the EU.

Source: Regional Integration Knowledge System, http://www.cris.unu.edu/riks/web/. Eurostat provides the following figures for the following years, for intra-EU trade in goods: percentage of total external trade in goods: 2001:66%; 2002:67%; 2003:67%; 2004:67%; 2005:66%; 2006:66%; 2007:66%; 2008:65%; 2009:65%, at http://epp.eurostat.ec.europa.eu/portal/page/portal/globalisation/indicators [2 November 2010].

The EU's political economy and political system have developed in an incremental fashion. Since the 1950s, they have expanded in terms of their roles, their membership, their impact and their policy portfolios. National economies have been deregulated and a new regulatory order has been introduced that is trans-EU. It now consists of some five hundred million people. It has attempted to influence international trade agendas with this regulatory order and to reshape the rulebook of international trade diplomacy as a norms entrepreneur. At the same time as it has advocated trade liberalisation though the WTO and other fora, however, it has been characterised as agriculturally protectionist. The EU is a major producer of goods and services internationally while at the same time most of its trade is among its own member states. It has the highest level of intra-regional trade of any regional body in the world. As Figures 1 and 2 illustrate, there is extensive intra-regional trade within the EU. This is in marked contrast to the Association of Southeast Asian Nations (ASEAN), for example, which has the next most extensive intra-regional trade.

SEEKING POLITICAL STABILITY

The EU's narrative of belonging, of peace and of values is a distinctive one. It has been characterised on the one hand by a grand design at the supranational level

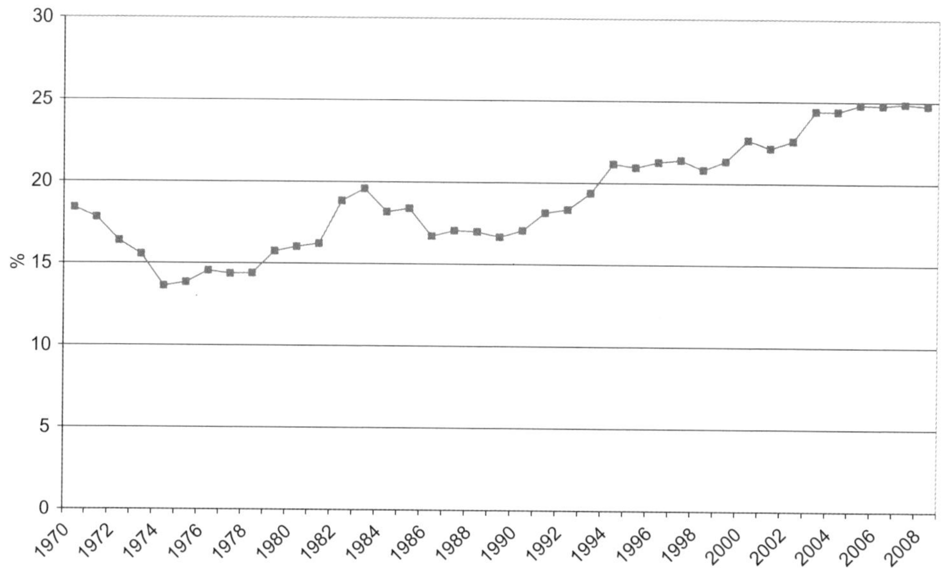

Figure 2: Intra-regional trade share in ASEAN.

Source: Regional Integration Knowledge System, http://www.cris.unu.edu/riks/web/ (accessed 2 Nov 2010).

and by often intransigent national opposition on the other. It has been characterised by visionary ideals and plans throughout the twentieth century ranging from the Spinelli-inspired European federalist movement to reports by 'Wise Men', such as the Tindemans report on European Union in 1975 and the Delors report on Economic and Monetary Union (Murray and Rich, 1996).

The EU has always attracted substantial criticism for being both too intrusive in the lives of European citizens and not being activist enough. It combines differing ideologies and ideals about political economy and polity though it is essentially capitalist in market design. This said, it is social democratic in many of its policy initiatives, such as the policies designed to promote cohesion, which provide, for example, support and funding for the development of disadvantaged regions and for youth and the long-term unemployed. In addition it has a solidarity fund that makes provision for emergency financial aid. It is inclusive of citizens of other member states, allowing for the free movement of citizens and allowing them to live, work, invest and establish businesses under its Single Market programme. It provides the opportunity to undertake university study in other member states under its Erasmus programme. And yet it continues to constitute a Fortress Europe for many immigrants and refugees. Its social policy has been created on a market foundation despite those policies having achieved a momentum of their own in the form of workers' rights, equality in the workplace, and maternity leave.

A distinctive feature of the EU is that it possesses its own budget. This involves a unique distributive mechanism where some member states are net contributors (Germany, France, the UK and the Netherlands) and some are net recipients (many Eastern and Central European countries, Portugal, Greece and Ireland). The aim of cohesion in determining the redistribution of funds among states and regions is a distinctive characteristic of the EU. The cohesion funds were established to satisfy a desire for social justice, to strengthen the weak economic areas of the EU, to promote solidarity and harmonious development, to create a European 'social space', and to create an EU-wide socio-economic and political entity by establishing a more even pattern of development across member states. It established a number of structural funds: the European Agricultural Guidance and Guarantee Fund (EAGGF); the European Social Fund (ESF); the European Regional Development Fund (ERDF); and a Fisheries Guidance financial instrument. These allocate one third of the EU budget to regional economic regeneration and to countering unemployment. More recently they have been supplemented by a number of rescue packages for Greece, Ireland and Portugal, which are funded by the eurozone and the International Monetary Fund.

DEVELOPING A KNOWLEDGE-BASED ECONOMY AND SOCIETY

In addition to constituting the world's largest trader for some decades now, the EU has also developed its own services industries, often in direct competition with the US, Japan and now China. It has developed a new objective, which is to become the largest knowledge-based economy in the world.

This was first called the Lisbon Strategy, the key objective of which was to transform the EU into the most dynamic knowledge-based economy in the world by 2010, based on education and training systems that were referenced globally and were of global quality. The objective of the Strategy was for the EU to become the most "dynamic and competitive knowledge-based economy in the world by 2010, capable of sustainable economic growth with more and better jobs and greater social cohesion and respect for the environment" (European Council, 2000, Section 1). It set out goals to be achieved in this regard by 2010: firstly, investment in research and development to increase to three percent of GDP; secondly, the reduction of red tape to promote entrepreneurship; and thirdly, the achievement of an employment rate of seventy percent (sixty percent for women).

The first five years saw few concrete results. There was confusion and a lack of action due to complex structures that had multiple goals, as well as unclear division of responsibilities and tasks. The Lisbon Strategy was relaunched in March 2005, therefore, with an emphasis on growth, employment creation, and the transferral of more ownership to member states via national action plans. It set out four priority areas: research and innovation; investment in people and the modernisation of labour markets; the liberation of business potential, particularly for small- to medium-sized enterprises; and energy and climate change.

The 2020 Strategy, the successor to the above, also seeks growth in terms of knowledge. To this it adds the creation of an inclusive society and the construction of a larger economy that is internationally competitive (Murray, 2011). Meanwhile the Bologna Process, itself not originally an EU initiative but one increasingly subsumed into an EU-style framework, has developed into a new university-level way of monitoring university standards. This complements the Lisbon Strategy's response to the challenges that arise from a globalising world and an aging population.

Why was the Strategy not widely adopted by national politicians, economists, or members of the civil society, even though it encompassed most of the economic and social policies advocated by European governments (Robert Schuman Foundation, 2007)? One reason was the financial crisis that commenced in late 2008. This undermined the Strategy's progress since member states were obliged to focus on their national priorities. When a European Commission staff document (2010a) reported that the EU had failed to meet its two targets of re-employment and research and development (R&D) spending, it was deemed that the financial crisis was to blame. In terms of spending on R&D, for example, there was only a marginal improvement from 2000. As a proportion of GDP, R&D rose from 1.2% to only 1.9% in 2008.

The successor to the Lisbon Strategy, the EU 2020 Strategy, has three priority areas: growth from knowledge; the creation of an inclusive society; and the building of a greater economy that is competitive at the international level. It also encompasses targets with regard to employment, research and innovation, environmental protection, and poverty alleviation. It seeks to raise the employment rate of the population aged 20–64 from the current sixty-nine percent to at least seventy-five percent; to invest three percent of GDP in R&D by improving the conditions for R&D investment by the private sector; and to develop a new indicator to track innovation. This carries over a target from the Lisbon Strategy. It further seeks to reduce greenhouse gas emissions by at least twenty percent compared to 1990 levels, or by thirty percent if the conditions are right, to increase the share of renewable energy in Europe's energy consumption to twenty percent, and to achieve a twenty percent increase in energy efficiency. Its educational objectives are to reduce the share of early school leavers to ten percent from the current fifteen percent and to increase the share of the population aged 30–34 having completed tertiary education by thirty-one percent to at least forty percent. In terms of societal objectives, it seeks to reduce the number of Europeans living below national poverty lines by twenty-five percent, thus lifting twenty million people out of poverty. Drawing on the lessons of the problems with national and EU-level coordination experienced by the Lisbon Strategy, the 2020 Strategy also seeks to complement both common and national targets and to adapt them to individual circumstances.

The preliminary national targets for the implementation of the 2020 Strategy are set at relatively minimal levels. This is in contrast to the optimistic, promissory levels that have tended to characterise many EU objectives in the past. This is because there are concerns at the EU level that there is a trend towards renationalising many EU policy areas and because of the challenges faced by member national governments with regard to their economic crises. It is not to be expected that the 2020 targets will realise the EU's long-term ambitions at this stage. A mid-term review on their progress will be held in 2014.

Despite the expectation that many of the objectives may be delayed, the institutions of the EU have reassessed other economic policies that are part of the 2020 Strategy. In November 2010, the European Commission's Directorate General for Trade (2010d) released a communication (and a series of support documents) detailing how the EU's trade and investment policy are contributing to the Strategy. With the overarching aim of bringing about faster growth, the communication stated that the EU's economic future lies in keeping a "competitive edge in innovative, high-value products" that generate "long-term and well paid jobs" (p. 6). As part of its 2011 action plan, it identifies as a key focus the development of better coordination between its internal and external markets, with a specific focus on goods and services regulation.

The EU's new trade policy, as linked to the 2020 Strategy, regards the following as key challenges:

> Cutting tariffs on industrial and agricultural goods is still important, but the brunt of the challenge lies elsewhere. What will make a bigger difference is market access for services and investment, opening public procurement, better agreements on and enforcement of protection of IPR [intellectual property rules], unrestricted supply of raw materials and energy, and, not in the least, overcoming regulatory barriers including via the promotion of international standards. Through trade, we should also promote the greening of the world economy and decent work (European Commission, Trade, 2010d, p. 4).

RECENT DEVELOPMENTS IN THE SINGLE MARKET

In April 2011 the EU Commission proposed the implementation of the Single Market Act, consisting of twelve 'levers' to boost growth and strengthen confidence. Entitled *Working Together to Create New Growth*, this recent report states (European Commission, 2011, p. 4):

> At the heart of the European project since its inception, the common market — which has now become the internal market — has for over 50 years woven strands of solidarity between the men and women of Europe, whilst opening up new opportunities for growth for more than 21 million European businesses. An area of free movement for goods, people, services and capital, the internal market has been further developed since 1993 by the consolidation of economic integration, the euro and solidarity and cohesion policies. Today more than ever it has become a part of people's everyday life in their professional and private activities and as consumers. It is the real growth engine within the European economy.

This document is the key EU strategy for economic recovery within the Single Market. It regards the Single Market as the core economic driving force of the EU — the one which remains the "most effective means of responding to the current economic crisis". It recognises that the Single Market's growth potential has not been fully exploited and that it must "open the doors to new, greener and more inclusive growth". The new strategy sets out twelve projects to relaunch the Single Market for 2012. These are based on growth, competitiveness and social progress. They range from "worker mobility to SME finance and consumer protection, via digital content, taxation and trans-European networks" (European Commission, 2011). The twelve instruments (in Table 1) summarise the EU's current politico-economic position — less production-based and more internal market and services-based. In particular, the Commission emphasises the positive outlook for services in contrast to goods. Services are regarded as the "driving force behind job creation" because EU growth averaged 2.1% per year from 1998 to 2008 whereas the services sector grew by an average of 2.8% per annum. The Commission (2010c, 2011) wishes to build on the fact that employment in the services sector grew by 2% per year, compared with just 1% for the economy as a whole.

The EU's political economy is primarily based on its own internal policies, such as the Single Market, although increasingly these have considerable international impact. It guarantees the free movement of goods and services and many professions as well as capital among its twenty-seven member states. It provides for the EU-level coordination and harmonisation of government regulations, corporation laws and trademark registrations. Its system of indirect taxation, a

Table 1: The 12 instruments of the single market act, 2011.

Instrument	Objective
1. Access to finance for small and medium enterprises	Common rules for venture-capital funds, across member states.
2. Worker mobility in the Single Market	Enhanced mobility for qualified workers. Removal of legal obstacles. Recognition of professional qualifications.
3. Intellectual property rights	Provision of unitary patent protection for inventions.
4. Consumers: Single Market players	Guarantee of consumer rights, including dispute settlement and redress.
5. Services: strengthening of standardisation	Revision of the European standardisation system to extend it to services, making it more effective, efficient and inclusive.
6. Stronger European networks	Strategic projects to do with transport, energy and electronic communications networks.
7. Digital Single Market	Legislation to guarantee mutual recognition of electronic identification and authentication
8. Social entrepreneurship	Development of a European asset management industry, with mutual investment funds
9. Taxation	Encouragement of the most energy-saving or environmentally friendly practices with revision of the Energy Tax Directive.
10. A more socially cohesive Single Market	Strengthening the Workers' Directive and fundamental social rights as part of the exercise of economic freedoms.
11. A revised regulatory environment for business	Reduce regulatory and administrative constraints. Simplification of accounting directives as these relate to financial reporting obligations, especially for small and medium enterprises.
12. Public procurement	Modernisation of the legislative framework, with environmentally friendly, socially responsible and innovative goods and services, simpler and more flexible procedures, and easier access for small and medium enterprises.

goods and services tax known at the Value Added Tax, is comprehensive across the member states, although states can choose how to apply it.

The external policies are to do with the EU relating to market access. They encompass the common external customs policy and tariffs. The EU also has a track record of providing financial support for programmes for candidate countries who wish to accede to the EU and developmental aid and humanitarian assistance to developing countries. Indeed, the EU is the world's largest donor of developmental aid, accounting for almost sixty percent of world development aid. It plays a leading role in humanitarian assistance. It is involved in peace promotion and civilian crisis management in many parts of the globe and has been involved in both brokering peace deals and in monitoring those deals, as in the case of the Aceh Monitoring Mission.

It also projects itself as an international actor into trade and international relations more generally. In the Laeken Declaration of December 2001 it stated that its objective was to be a manager of globalisation. In the *European Security Strategy*, two years later, it stated that the EU was "inevitably a global player". In short, the EU presents itself as an intermediary between globalisation and the nation state, between globalisation and crisis (Rumford and Murray, 2003).

ENLARGEMENT OF MEMBERSHIP

The original European community has grown over time in policy scope and remit. Most obviously, it has expanded its membership. In 1973, the first enlargement took place when the United Kingdom, Ireland and Denmark joined. This was followed in 1981 with Greece's accession and in 1986 when Spain and Portugal joined. With the reunification of Germany, the former German Democratic Republic joined the European community in 1990. After the Single Market was launched, enlargement negotiations commenced once again and in 1995 Austria, Finland and Sweden joined. The end of the Cold War heralded a new and closer relationship between the former East and West on the European continent and a 'big bang' enlargement took place in 2000. Eight Eastern and Central European states joined the EU at this time (the Czech Republic, Estonia, Hungary, Latvia, Lithuania, Poland, the Slovak Republic and Slovenia) along with Malta and Cyprus. This was followed in 2007 by the accession of Bulgaria and Romania. Enlargement has been regarded at the official level as the EU's most effective foreign policy tool. It has also been seen as a means of enhancing the EU's influence in international negotiations.

By the time of the last two enlargements, it had become clear that enlargement fatigue had set in. There was considerable opposition to the sharing of the benefits of the EU political economy, such as employment and the freedom of movement of workers. In societal terms, racism and exclusionism were evident in the form of opposition to the nationals of newer member states coming into more established Western ones. Exclusionist policies were increasingly rearing their ugly heads regarding both East and Central Europeans on the one hand and non-EU immigrants on the other.

TREATY AND INSTITUTIONAL EXPANSION

Alongside the expansion of the EU's membership, the EU has developed an embedded institutional arrangement that is unique in terms of its actors, processes and the merging of state sovereignty. It is often characterised by tensions between national interests and EU interests. In 1966, the Luxembourg Accord resulted in an uneasy compromise between nationalism and Europeanism. In 1970 and 1975, new EC budget provisions established the independence of the EU Budget. In 1978, a

European Monetary System (EMS) and an exchange rate mechanism (ERM) were set up by the Council, although not all member states joined — the UK and Denmark decided not to participate at that time. Institutionally, 1979 saw the first direct elections of the European Parliament. These were held in June, increasing the democratic legitimacy of the EU as an institution. In 1986, the Single European Act established mechanisms for the completion of an internal market, which happened in 1993. Following the fall of the Berlin Wall and the Delors Initiative for Economic and Monetary Union, two intergovernmental conferences led to the 1992 Treaty on European Union. This was signed in Maastricht and also came into force in 1993.

The Treaty on European Union (TEU) introduced new forms of interstate cooperation in areas including defence, justice and home affairs. These forms were not supranational. Rather, they were intergovernmental. They added to the existing community system thereby creating a new structure with three pillars, Community, a Common Foreign and Security Policy (CFSP), and Justice and Home Affairs. This is what became known as the European Union.

Further treaty reform followed with the signature of the Treaty of Amsterdam in 1997 and the Treaty of Nice in 2001. These came into effect in 2003. Just as enlargement fatigue was to become increasingly evident in the aftermath of the fall of the Soviet Union, so too did institutional reform and the creation of new or revised treaties lead to increased reform fatigue. The permissive consensus in favour of increased economic and political integration was gradually eroded after the early 1990s and was to come to an end by 2005 when the French and Dutch publics opposed, in a referendum, the proposed EU Constitutional treaty, despite the latter having been signed in 2004. As a result this treaty was never ratified. Its intention to provide for more streamlined decision making and a more effective and coherent foreign policy was never realised. A two-year 'period of reflection' was subsequently undertaken during which the core elements of the Treaty were incorporated into a new treaty, the Treaty of Lisbon. Another nail in this coffin was the Irish public's rejection in 2008 of the subsequent attempt to ratify this Treaty. However, the rejection was reversed the following year when a second referendum was held and the Treaty was finally ratified.

SEEKING ECONOMIC STABILITY: CRISIS, CURRENCY TRIALS AND TRIBULATIONS

EU treaties have effected considerable change and have led to innovative new arrangements, the most remarkable and controversial being a single currency. This was provided for in the 1992 Maastricht Treaty on a European Union, which set out the conditions that member states must fulfil in order to adopt the euro (Art. 140 and Protocol No. 13, Lisbon Treaty). These 'convergence criteria' addressed, firstly, price stability, with an average inflation rate not to exceed more than 1.5% in relation to the three best-performing member states; secondly, budgetary discipline, with a budget deficit to be less than 3% of GDP and a government debt ratio not to exceed 60% of GDP; thirdly, currency stability, with the observance of normal fluctuation margins with regard to the exchange rate mechanism of the European monetary system for at least two years without devaluations; and finally, interest rate convergence, with an average nominal long-term interest rate not to exceed by more than 2% that of the three best-performing member states in terms of price stability.

With the introduction of the euro, monetary policy became the responsibility of the European Central Bank and the national central banks of the member states that had adopted it. Together they now make up the European System of Central Banks (ESCB). The ESCB's primary objective is to maintain price stability so that the European economy will not be damaged by inflation. Its tasks are to conduct foreign exchange operations, to hold and manage the official foreign reserves of the member states, to define and implement the monetary policy of the EU, and to promote the smooth operation of its payment systems.

For many years the political economy of currency collaboration continued apace. In 1999, the exchange rates for the currencies of countries participating in the European Monetary Union (the EMU) were irrevocably fixed. On 1 January 2002, euro notes and coins were issued and after a phase of adjustment, the euro became the only legal tender currency in those countries which had chosen to participate (Austria, Belgium, France, Finland, Germany, Greece, Ireland, Italy, Luxembourg, the Netherlands, Portugal and Spain), a group which became known as the eurozone. This group was joined by Slovenia in 2007, by Malta and Cyprus in 2008, by Slovakia in 2009, and by Estonia in 2011.

The EU is currently facing a severe crisis. Figures present a grim picture of large government deficits both within and outside the eurozone. Eurostat (2011) reported in 2011 that in 2010 the largest government deficits, as a percentage of GDP, were those of Ireland (–32.4%), Greece (–10.5%), the United Kingdom (–10.4%), Spain (–9.2%), Portugal (–9.1%), Poland (–7.9%), Slovakia (–7.9%), Latvia (–7.7%), Lithuania (–7.1%) and France (–7.0%). The lowest deficits were those of Luxembourg (–1.7%), Finland (–2.5%) and Denmark (–2.7%).

A number of regulatory mechanisms and task forces were subsequently formed to deal with this debt crisis. These included the European Financial Stabilisation Mechanism (EFSM), which agreed on 9 May 2010 to allocate €500 billion, with a further €220 billion from the International Monetary Fund, to member states in difficulty. These allocations were to be replaced by a permanent European Stability Mechanism in 2013. The Task Force on Economic Governance, established in March 2010, developed proposals for better budgetary discipline and an improved crisis resolution framework. It recommended that a permanent crisis mechanism be established to safeguard the financial stability of the euro area and that sanctions be imposed on euro area member states who failed to comply with eurozone requirements. A 'European Semester' came into effect in September 2010 to coordinate the EU and eurozone budgetary and economic policies with the EU's Stability and Growth Pact and its 2020 Strategy. This meant that there was no possibility for a nation to 'go it alone' in budgetary and economic terms. It ensured that all national economic and fiscal policies were assessed in Brussels before they were adopted by member states. The EU's institutions, the Commission and Council, while not tasked to block a national government's budget, could, in cases of a government's failure to comply with EU recommendations, take strict action such as issue alerts, impose sanctions, and in the case of eurozone countries, apply annual fines of 0.2% of a country's GDP. The European Stability Mechanism (ESM), adopted in late 2010, allowed for a permanent crisis mechanism to be established in mid-2013 to replace the European Financial Stability Facility. This was to provide assistance to euro area member states in financial distress, with conditions relating to the implementation of strict economic and adjustment programmes.

A further innovation was the introduction of Bank Stress Tests. Since July 2009, the Commission said that banks which required state aid should undergo stress tests in order to assess the viability of their restructuring plans. The stress test's objective was to provide "policy information for assessing the resilience of the EU banking system to possible adverse economic developments and to assess the ability of banks in the exercise to absorb possible shocks on credit and market risks, including sovereign risks" (Committee of European Banking Supervisors, 2010; European Banking Authority, 2011). Increasingly, in other words, national policy was being subsumed under the umbrella of the EU.

Yet more decisive action was required as the situation of debt and lack of growth became increasingly serious. Summits of EU leaders took place in the second half of 2011, to attempt to restore confidence and deal with the risk of further risk contagion. Tensions marked these meetings and none more obviously than at the December 2011 European Council Summit, where the UK took the remarkable step of exercising the veto against an agreement signed by the other twenty-six member states of the EU. The EU's search for both economic and political stability remains increasingly elusive even as its leaders seek to agree on governance structures and fiscal rectitude. The problems are not only regarding the types of measure to be adopted for the deepening crisis, however. The EU is experiencing a leadership crisis, with deep divisions among its member states. Its current crisis of governance is characterised by a lack of agreement on the achievement of EU solidarity. This is in part a crisis of competence and a legitimacy crisis within the EU (Longo and Murray, 2011).

The eurozone remains under serious threat and world leaders are stepping up their criticisms of the EU's inability to rein in its members and its debts. European economic growth will be sluggish for some time; unemployment is on the increase, especially among young people, and there is little sense of confidence in the ability of the EU to solve its problems. Indeed, the EU is now being seen as the problem rather than a potential solution. The EU is experiencing a crisis of expectations regarding its promises and its actual capabilities, which is compounded by the fact that many national leaders are reluctant to admit this. European leaders will continue to work on a solution, albeit in a very European way that may seem to outsiders to be technocratic, lacking in solidarity and over-political in tone.

CONCLUSION

The EU cannot simply be examined as an economic entity since it has always been a political project. It has always impacted upon European society as well.

Indeed, it entails a distinctive narrative based on peace, stability and prosperity, one punctuated by several important constitutionalising moments. It is a narrative that highlights reconciliation and one that is couched in terms of an economic way to deal with historical rivalries and bitter wars. In the process particular memories have been privileged. There has also been a significant expansion of its role from its origins as an economic and political entity in Western Europe to one that encompasses twenty-seven European states and a series of neighbourhood strategies.

The EU has active policies of engagement with its region, its neighbourhood, other regions and the world at large. It engages with the rest of the world in multilateralist, regionalist and inter-regionalist ways.

The EU's development has been marked by courage and innovation. The diverse political bargains it has involved have largely stood the test of time which is why there is reason to be satisfied with the increase in prosperity and harmony that has been the result. There is reason to be concerned about the EU's economic crises, however, and with competition from the US, Asia and the BRICs (Brazil, Russia, India and China — recently joined by South Africa). The EU's development has at times been characterised by a sense of superiority and hubris. This has been evident in its policies towards parts of Asia and Africa. It has been evident in the suggestions that it is a model for other parts of the world, in the concept of conditionality and in its promotion of human rights. Certainly, its power base has been shifting. It is not based on hard power now. It has come to draw more on its powers of persuasion and influence, particularly within its own region.

In short, the EU's political economy combines economic, political and social elements. It also encompasses cultural and educational cooperation, the Bologna

Process, the 2020 and Lisbon Strategies, as well as concerns about the world economy in 2020 and beyond. The EU is a capitalist, a social democratic and a liberalist project. It is often teleological and even messianic in its zeal. It is incrementalist in its policy implementation procedures. Its social policy has met largely market ends yet also achieved a momentum of its own. The role and impact of the EU's policies for social and economic cohesion, with redistribution being key determinants, grow increasingly strong. It is famous for its agricultural protectionism. It is less famous, perhaps, for its development aid and humanitarian assistance.

Many EU strategy documents and policy statements assert that the EU is a global player and a manager of globalisation. The EU projects itself as an intermediary between globalisation and the nation state. The role of the Westphalian state has been revised and recast as the EU seeks to reconceptualise what states do, what regional entities are, and what international relations is. In some of these areas it has competitors. Regional bodies such as the Association of Southeast Asian Nations, for example, do not wish to reconceptualise the sovereign state in the same way.

To the extent that the EU has recast the state, the role of the economy, and regional governance, it has done so in a distinctively European way. It constitutes, for many observers, a model of its own. It seeks trade liberalisation yet its primary focus is on its European economic protection, while there is a trend towards national economic protectionism as well. It seeks to be a knowledge economy and yet defining what this means is not clear. Its wealth is collective but it has a German backbone in the sense that Germany constitutes the EU's economic powerhouse. It remains unique, however, and as such is likely to do so for many years to come.

REFERENCES

Andreosso-O'Callaghan, B (2005). History and Process of European economic Integration. In *Regional Integration — Europe and Asia Compared*, W Moon and B Andreosso-O'Callaghan (eds.). Aldershot: Ashgate.

Committee of European Banking Supervisors (2010). EU Wide Stress Test, 23 July. http://www.eba.europa.eu/EuWideStressTesting.aspx [2 November 2010].

European Banking Authority (2011). The EBA Announced A New Round of Stress Tests, http://www.eba.europa.eu/News—Communications/Latest-news/The-European-Banking-Authority-up-and-running-and-.aspx [14 January 2011].

European Commission Staff (2010a). Working Document: Lisbon Strategy Evaluation Document 114 final. Brussels, 2 March, http://ec.europa.eu/archives/growthandjobs_2009/pdf/lisbon_strategy_evaluation_en.pdf [2 November 2010].

European Commission (2010b). Communication from the Commission to the European Parliament, the Council, the European Economic and Social Committee and the Committee of Regions, Trade, Growth and World Affairs. *Trade Policy as a Core Component of the EU's 2020 Strategy*, COM, 612 final, Brussels.

European Commission (2010c). Communication from the Commission to the European Parliament, the Council, the Economic and Social Committee and the Committee of Regions: Towards a Single Market Act For a highly competitive social market economy, COM (2010) 608 final/2, Brussels 11 November 2010.

European Commission, Trade (2010d). Trade, Growth and World Affairs. Trade Policy as a Core Component of the EU's 2020 Strategy, Brussels.

European Commission (2011). Communication from the Commission to the European Parliament, The Council, The European Economic and Social Committee and the Committee of the Regions, *Single Market Act.* Twelve levers to boost growth and strengthen confidence. "Working together to create new growth", SEC(2011) 467, Brussels, April. http://register.consilium.europa.eu/pdf/en/11/st09/st09283.en11.pdf [29 October 2011].

European Council (2000). Presidency Conclusions, Lisbon, 23–24 March.

Eurostat, Eurostat News release, 60/2011 (26 April 2011). Provision of deficit and debt data for 2010 — first notification. Euro area and EU27 government deficit at 6.0% and 6.4% of GDP respectively. European Commission, http://epp.eurostat.ec.europa.eu/cache/ITY_PUBLIC/2-26042011-AP/EN/2-26042011-AP-EN.PDF (accessed 28 April 2011).

Gardner, Feldman, L (1999). Reconciliation and Legitimacy: Foreign Relations and Enlargement of the European Union. In *Legitimacy and the European Union*, T Banchoff and M Smith (eds.). London: Routledge.

Krugman, P (2011). The Euro and the European Project, 3 January. http://krugman.blogs.nytimes.com/2011/01/03/the-euro-and-the-european-project/ [accessed 4 January 2011].

Leonard, M (2005). *Why Europe will Run the 21st Century.* London and New York: Fourth Estate.

Longo, M and P Murray (2011). No ode to joy? Reflections on the European Union's legitimacy, *International Politics*, 48(6), 667–690.

Murray, P (2011). Ideas of regionalism: The European case, *Japanese Journal of Political Science*, 12(2), 305–322.

Murray, P (2009). Uses and Abuses of the Concept of Integration. In *Sage Handbook of European Studies*, C Rumford (ed.). London: Sage.

Murray, P and P Rich (eds.) (1996). *Visions of European Unity.* Boulder: Westview.

Rifkin, J (2004). *The European Dream: How Europe's Vision of the Future is Quietly Eclipsing the American dream.* New York: Tarcher/ Penguin.

Robert Schuman Foundation (2007). *The Lisbon Strategy: the European Route to Globalisation.* Strasbourg.

Rumford, C and P Murray (2003). Globalisation and the limitations of European integration studies: Interdisciplinary considerations, *Journal of Contemporary European Studies*, 11(1), 85–93.

Van Rompuy, H (2011). Europe in the New Global Game. *The Economist*, http://www.economist.com/node/17493309 [accessed 7 February 2011].

Part Two

Global Trade

CHAPTER 8

Global Trade: An Overview

Ralph Pettman

University of Melbourne

Who trades with whom in the international political economy and why? For many analysts and policy maker a question like this is little more than a distraction from the main business of world affairs, which they see as being the practice of 'high politics'. Analysts like these call international political economy 'low politics'. They would not talk about it at all except that ministries like the Australian Department of Foreign Affairs, for example, now calls itself the Department of Foreign Affairs *and Trade* and defines its fundamental purpose not only in terms of enhancing Australia's security but also in terms of the contribution it makes to Australia's economic growth and market performance. Only relatively recently, in other words, have questions about trade been deemed legitimate ones to ask if one wants to be considered a serious student of world affairs. Even now, international political economy in general and trade issues in particular are seen as the second string to the international relations bow.

The most significant feature of the international political economy, as Blainey highlights in this *Handbook*, is that humankind lives in the middle of what has been called an industrial revolution, however difficult this is to define. The significance of this revolution is impossible to overestimate.

It was a revolution originally based on the trade in luxury goods. It became in turn a key feature of a massive, global upsurge in production and consumption. To quote Masefield's famous poem on historical *Cargoes* (Masefield, 1924):

> Quinquireme of Nineveh from distant Ophir,
> Rowing home to haven in sunny Palestine,
> With a cargo of ivory,
> And apes and peacocks,
> Sandalwood, cedarwood, and sweet white wine.
>
> Stately Spanish galleon coming from the Isthmus,
> Dipping through the Tropics by the palm-green shores,

With a cargo of diamonds,
Emeralds, amythysts,
Topazes, and cinnamon, and gold moidores.

Dirty British coaster with a salt-caked smoke stack,
Butting through the Channel in the mad March days,
With a cargo of Tyne coal,
Road-rails, pig-lead,
Firewood, iron-ware, and cheap tin trays.

The industrial revolution proper was preceded by a surge in the extent and substance of Europe's maritime reach. This surge is said to have been contingent not so much upon a breakthrough in shipping design as upon the ability of Europeans to read the world's winds, as well as its latitude and eventually its longitude.

This surge was initially most evident in the exploratory advantage it gave the Portuguese and the Spanish. With weapons made of iron that were able to use gunpowder, the Spanish, for example, took advantage of their capacity to cross the Atlantic to impose dominion over much of the central and south Americas. Genocide ensued, as did the appropriation of vast quantities of silver and gold. It was subsequently clearly evident in the advantage it gave the Dutch, the French and the English.

The technological breakthrough that made for steam locomotion changed the picture again. Applied to machine manufacture, steam technology magnified worker output far beyond that envisaged by Adam Smith. It made possible the creation of industrial factories and farms. These, together with a revolution in transportation technology, led to radical changes in long-distance trade.

Why this breakthrough occurred and why it occurred first in Europe is a story, like all such stories, told in a number of different ways, each contingent upon the particular analytical language in which the narrative is couched. Marx, for example, talked not only of changes in the means of production but of the effect these changes had upon whole modes of production, like feudalism with its tribute and capitalism with its commodities. He highlighted class and class struggle. Weber, by contrast, talked of the imperatives of a particular form of Protestant predestination and the role this played in the rationalisation of capital and labour. He highlighted a more sacral cause. Sombart talked of the newly wealthy in the Europe of the late Middle Ages, who with riches derived from usury and the plunder of the Orient and Africa were keen to win social status commensurate with their commercial one. With the secularisation of love in the growing cities, he said, large numbers of courtesans set new standards in fashion and splendour. This in turn — the desire of elites for luxurious goods, that is — brought about large-scale industrialism and full-scale capitalism.

The material consequences of the industrial revolution were apparent in an extraordinary increase in the production of commodities. This made it necessary for many more people to consume what was produced. Mass consumption ensued. Old luxuries, like sugar, became commonplace. The long-distance trade in luxuries gave way to long-distance trade in what became necessities while all the world's markets succumbed to what was called the 'wide, compelling leer' of merchandise.

The need to disburse such material abundance required a new kind of system. In this system production and consumption no longer served a larger cultural and social purpose. They became that purpose itself.

'Doing business' became the rationale for whole cultures. Manufacturers were encouraged to build production chains abroad to take advantage of cheaper wages. Advances in transport technology, like the containerised shipping detailed in Chapter 11, allowed finished goods to be assembled from semi-finished ingredients made in many different countries. The volume of world trade occurring inside transnational firms began to rival the volume of trade occurring between nation states. Meanwhile, advances in communication technologies like the computer made it possible to source both primary and finished goods in many different countries and allowed them to be finished and consumed in many different others. This was facilitated by currency exchange services, investment services, and insurance and accounting services, that began to be offered globally from a few key centres, like Wall Street in New York.

The expense of these technologies made it necessary to expand distribution. Recovering the investment required made it necessary to sell products globally with the result being yet more world trade.

Modernist explanations of this system highlight the historic significance of mercantilism, or economic nationalism. European state-makers learned early to meet the increasing cost of politico-strategic rivalry and the growing expense of their armies and navies by increasing taxes and fostering domestic loyalties. This meant fostering greater politico-economic activity, albeit politically protected activity.

In its current form, mercantilism involves protecting local industries and encouraging exports, mainly by controlling imports using tariff and non-tariff barriers. It is about consumer self-sufficiency and the maximisation of a country's productive advantage. It is more likely now to be achieved by means of vertical integration, that is, by ownership of all of the steps in a particular production process, from the foreign factory or field to the retail shop shelves at home. It is also likely to be more about industrial subsidies than about trying to monopolise, say, the supply of a particular raw material.

The main exception is oil, although another is precious metals. The latter were used to underpin the value of money. It was only when the leaders of the world's richest country, the United States, finally stopped backing the value of the US dollar with that of gold and started relying solely on the country's productivity and prestige to maintain the worth of its currency in the eyes of the world that this system broke down.

Neomercantilism remains an option for all state-makers. However, unless they are merely kleptocrats, state leaders have to balance the desire to foster their country's trade against a desire to ensure that their workers do not end up adding value to other people's production chains.

Meanwhile, there is economic liberalism. Economic liberalists think that the appropriation of the world's goods and services is part of what it means to be an individual. People are not only rationalistic, they say. They are also opportunistic and calculating. As such, they prize the freedom to make of their calculative capacity whatever they want. Economic liberalists see individuals as individuated, that is. They see them as the sole 'proprietors' of their own selves and skills, inside a society of 'relations of exchange' between such proprietors, inside a polity that maintains the underlying order that these relations require and little more. Economic liberalists talk about reducing the extent to which state-makers regulate markets and the tax burden that producers and consumers bear. They talk about the need for personal incentives and about long-distance trading regimes predicated upon a commitment to unimpeded exchange. They talk about economic development and free trade as being fair trade (see below). They talk about the number of states in the world proliferating and becoming increasingly dependent upon each other for traded necessities. And they see the 'trading state' as preferring commercial cooperation and reciprocity.

The economic/liberalist story of global trade is basically about demand. The wants of those in industrial societies remain unsatisfied, economic liberalists say, because even when people get more they want more. Rather than be satisfied with what they have when compared with those who are less well-off, people ostensibly envy the rich if they are not rich and think of themselves as less than rich if they are rich. This means that despite the productivity of the world's industrial factories and farms, there is never enough and never will be enough. Resources, economic liberalists say, are always limited. Regardless of the overall increase in wealth that industry makes possible, goods and services will always be 'in demand'.

Economic liberalists see the most efficient way to meet demand, not in terms of economic planning, but in terms of free markets, where the price mechanism determines supply. In practice, since it is possible to increase demand by advertising and to fix prices by making monopolies or oligopolies, economic liberalists also recognise the need for someone to hold the market's ring. They recognise the need for state-makers who have the power to intervene to ensure that the pursuit of short-term gain does not preclude long-term supply. They also recognise the need for international ring-holding so that long-distance trade does not suffer from the sort of beggar-thy-neighbour competition that might destroy the whole system. Hence the advent of institutions like the World Trade Organisation discussed in detail by two of the contributors in the subsequent chapters, the advent of regional trading blocs like the EU discussed above, where countries use local affinities to keep borders relatively open, and the advent of hegemonic countries like the US that police the stability of the system as a whole.

Economic socialists see the global appropriation of goods and services differently again. They see markets as better managed, not by the price mechanism, that is, Adam Smith's 'hidden hand', but by non-market means. They prefer state-planned production and distribution. They see people as being basically altrusitic enough to realise that the failure to feed, clothe, house, educate and medically treat everyone on earth, despite there being the industrial means to do so, as due to the failure to construct the appropriate systems of production and supply. They also see people as altruistic enough to act accordingly, that is, good enough to countenance fewer life choices and opportunities if it means everyone having life's basic necessities.

Marxists, meanwhile, see the appropriation of the world's goods and services in the context of global capitalism. They highlight how trade is bourgeois trade and serves the interests of the owners and managers of the means of production.

Constructivists, by contrast, highlight what people learn to value and subsequently seek to acquire. They see trading regimes as determined accordingly.

Meta-marxists combine both materialist and mentalist views. They highlight the control by members of the bourgeoisie of the means of cultural production and the use of advertising and the like to create trading regimes convenient to the bourgeois cause.

Those pushed to the margins by the modernist project consider the question of who trades with whom in the world — and why — in other ways. Feminists, for example, highlight gender disparities and how more men than women are able to appropriate the world's traded wealth.

Environmentalists tend to highlight those who do today's trading exchanges at the expense of the viability of tomorrow's planetary ecology. To them trade is a manifestation of a production system that pollutes, exhausts non-renewable resources, and promotes overpopulation.

Indigenous peoples highlight the costs of contemporary trading practices to their cultures and to the values these cultures espouse. These values are often very different from the ones that global appropriation currently promotes and protects, for example, they are often much more respectful of environmental viability.

Those who critique the whole modernist project, of which current global trading practices are a part, do so in even more radical ways. Global trading looks very different, for example, when discussed in terms of Buddhist economics, where the idea of 'right work' prevails and the ultimate aim is not to satiate the material needs of the discrete self but to realise nirvana, that is, the spiritual potential of the non-discrete self.

If the primary feature of IPE is the industrial revolution its secondary feature is the transnational firm. As is discussed in the upcoming chapter on corporations, it is estimated that only a few hundred firms now do most of the world's production, while only a handful control the international trade in all basic commodities, from food to minerals. In pursuit of company profit these firms use advances in transport and communications to take their production processes to where those who actually do the work cost less. They may employ only a small percentage of the global work force but it is the leading edge of that force that they exploit.

There have been considerable changes in this regard since the industrial revolution began. Those who lived where the industrial revolution took place first began by exchanging their factory-made goods for primary commodities. This division of global labour changed, however, as the manufacturing process was broken up to allow the more labour-intensive parts of it to be put where workers were cheap. The factory, as pioneered by Henry Ford, with its designers, its dedicated machines producing large production runs, its assembly lines kept in constant motion, and its distribution and sales personnel all in one place, was replaced by more flexible and fragmented enterprises. These dispersed the different stages of the production process across countries and even across continents.

The globalisation of production process that the industrial revolution made possible is most obvious to marxists and socialists. They see very clearly the way global firms create integrated production chains to maximise profits, though even economic liberalists and nationalists talk today about entrepreneurs connecting up national economies.

What does this talk actually mean? Analysts and policy makers refer blithely to world production and global firms and trade within and between them and their host countries but what does this mean? To really answer questions like these it is necessary to get close and listen to what is going on, however, and as the Conclusion to this *Handbook* argues, to take part. Most of this *Handbook*'s readers will not have worked for a large global corporation so talk about them will not be very meaningful. There are second-hand accounts, though, which provide some idea of what they involve. They provide at least a vicarious sense of what global trade entails today. Meanwhile there are particular debates that provide something of this sense, too.

FREE TRADE VERSUS FAIR TRADE

For example, why call free trade unfair? If this question is framed using the approach taken in the Introduction then why free trade might be called unfair prompts a similarly diverse range of possible responses. These are, in the order in which the Introduction discusses them:

- because free trade practices make it difficult, if not impossible, to protect a state and its people from those with economic power, particularly where the state and its people are like David and those who have economic power are like Goliath (this is economic protectionism);
- because analysts fail to understand how beneficial free trade is and how a world free trade order is the best conceivable alternative we have (this is economic liberalism);
- because free trade is not equitable, that is, it does not provide fair prices regardless of the supply and demand conditions; nor does it promote purchasing practices that actively prohibit child and slave labour, unsafe workplace conditions, and environmental degradation; nor does it plan to provide explicitly for social development, stable relationships between sellers and buyers, and contractual transparency (this is economic socialism);
- because free trade is one dimension of a capitalist world political economy that is *bourgeois* and as such represents the exploitative interests of those who own and manage the means of production rather than the interests of those who sell their labour for a wage and do the work, that is, the *proletariat* (this is classical marxism)
- because if we do call free trade unfair then the unfair aspects of present-day world trade practices will become readily apparent and it will be possible to do something to redress these aspects (this is constructivism);
- because trade is only called free by those who own and manage the means of production as a way of persuading the *proletariat* that it is good for them, thereby making it harder for them to see the exploitative character of capitalist trade relations — which are for short-term profit and only incidentally for the social good (this is meta-marxism);
- because in a world political economy like the one we currently have — that systematically discriminates against women — more freedom of any kind, including the trading kind, means more of such discrimination and this will result is more unfairness, particularly for women of colour and women of the lower classes and castes who are the most marginalised of all (this is feminism);
- because in a world political economy like the one we currently have — that exploits the natural environment to detrimental effect — more freedom of any kind, including the trading kind, means more of such discrimination and this will result in growing unfairness to the generations that will (hopefully) come after us (this is environmentalism);

- because in a world political economy like the one we currently have — that exploits indigenous peoples and places their cultural viability in jeopardy — more freedom of any kind, including the trading kind, means more of such discrimination and this is unfair, particularly to those indigenous peoples most marginalised by this kind of political economy (this is Fourth Worldism);
- because free trade is a doctrine that has yet to be cast in falsifiable terms and subjected to public and repeated tests that provide us with scientific conclusions, and this is unfair to everyone since it means we must continue to argue its fairness by assertion and not in the light of reliable findings (this is hyper-rationalism);
- because free trade is a rationalist practice that fails to turn reason back upon itself so as to unsettle the certainties of free trade as a doctrine and this is unfair to those who want to create thinking spaces for people marginalised by the rationalist project in general and the free trade doctrine in particular — people like women, environmentalists and the poor (this is postmodernism);
- because free trade cannot be discussed except in a language and language not only defines identity in specific and contingent ways, it carries within it assumptions that craft the conclusions analysts come to about free trade, and this is unfair to those who want to create speaking spaces for those marginalised by the rationalist project (this is poststructuralism);
- because free trade is a rationalist practice that represents a conscious intention to have less inhibited trading relations and this is unfair to everyone since those inhibitions are not as readily removed as might at first appear, being the result of sexual proclivities or desires for power or meaning or species-specific proclivities only accessible via research into myths (this is psycho-analysis);
- because free trade is a rationalist practice and as such is unfair because it obscures the reductionist quality of such a statement — reductionist in that it fails to convey the emotional significance of what, as a doctrine, free trade costs in experiential terms (this is romanticism);
- because free trade is a rationalist practice and as such is unfair because it obscures the extent to which people intend what they think in this regard they are attending to (this is phenomenology);
- because free trade is a rationalist practice and as such promotes and protects the objectifying and the individuation that rationalism is predicated upon and this is unfair to those who want to trade in such a way as to promote and protect a sense of human community (this is pre-modernism or post-pre-modernism);
- because free trade is a rationalist practice and as such promotes and protects the secularism that puts the sacral at mind's length as anti-rational, and this is unfair to those who want to trade in such a way as to promote and protect the belief that usury is wrong, for example, as in Islam (this is sacralism).

Most of these approaches are not found in the literature on free trade and discussions of its fairness or unfairness. Most of this literature is relatively superficial, not because those who provide it are shallow or ignorant but because they mostly do not realise how radically their consciousness has been crafted in very particular ways and how getting to the root of this question might require going outside how they think.

The literature mostly provides the first three reasons, that is, the economically nationalist, liberalist and socialist ones. Occasionally there is a foray into the fourth, that is, the marxist reason. This leaves many more reasons, however, with regard to whether free trade is fair, being unaccounted for. These reasons are irrelevant, most analysts and policy makers tend to say, and that is why they are not to be found in the literature. But are they irrelevant?

The hegemonic analytic language of today is undoubtedly economic liberalism. Being hegemonic does not mean that the part truth that economic liberalism articulates is the whole truth. It means that economic liberalism is the dominant analytic language and therefore the one most likely to be found promoted and protected by international political economy analysts.

For an example of the advocacy of this analytic language, consider the popular and influential weekly magazine the *Economist* and an article it published on May 13, 2004 called "How much damage does protectionism do to the world economy?" The article began by saying, "Mercantilism has been defunct as an economic theory for at least 200 years, but many practical men in authority remain slaves to the notion that exports must be promoted and imports deterred. Over 40% of the European Union's budget is dedicated to defying Ricardo's theory of comparative advantage", that is, to "subsidizing picturesque farms in Burgundy at the expense of efficient farms elsewhere". Meanwhile, "[t]ariffs of 500% on rice imports indulge Japan's nostalgia for its lost agricultural past". Subsidies like these, it says, represent the "naked transfer from taxpayers to corporate mendicants". They are also an "indirect transfer to overseas consumers, who enjoy artificially depressed prices as a result of the handouts". On the other hand, trading tariffs raise money for treasuries "at the expense of foreign exporters" while at the same time creating higher prices for the "home consumer". Do the gains to the one offset the losses to the other? "Emphatically not", the *Economist* says. As far as it is concerned it is unfree trade that is unfair trade and it is free trade that is fair trade. "Tariffs and subsidies drive a wedge between demand and supply ...", it says. Tariffs and subsidies impose "'deadweight costs' on any economy". They also encourage "worthless overproduction (of goods that could cost more to make, sans the subsidy, than consumers are prepared to pay)". Making the situation more fair, the *Economist* says, simply means eliminating tariffs and subsidies. This means doing away in turn with the economic distortions they cause. It means stopping prices from doing their 'proper job' of equating 'supply and demand'. The general argument is straightforward, then, it is free trade, as Ricardo first argued, that ensures that an economy makes the best use of its resources and it is free trade that deploys labour to its best advantage.

A great deal hangs here off the writings of one ostensible authority. "Under a system of perfectly free commerce", says Ricardo, "each country naturally devotes its capital and labour to such employments as are most beneficial to each. This pursuit of individual advantage is admirably connected with the universal good of the whole. By stimulating industry, by rewarding ingenuity, and by using most efficaciously the peculiar powers bestowed by nature, it distributes labour most effectively and most economically: while, by increasing the general mass of productions, it diffuses general benefit, and binds together by one common tie of interest and intercourse, the universal society of nations throughout the civilised world" (Ricardo, 1951[1817]). This sounds excellent but is it? Nations exchange goods in a market, as Adam Smith says in the *Wealth of Nations*, because of the absolute advantages they thereby enjoy (Smith, 1993[1776]). The Scots could grow grapes in glass houses and produce wine that way, but why bother to do so when by growing oats, which presents them with no particular horticultural problem, they can harvest a crop they can exchange for wine from somewhere else more sunny; somewhere that uses its absolute advantage — which is sunshine — to grow grapes and make wine? Barter like this is easy to understand. It involves the direct exchange of goods or services for other goods or services. But what about a country that is better at growing both oats and grapes? Why would it bother to trade? As Ricardo argues in his book *On the Principles of Political Economy and Taxation* (in a chapter "On Foreign Trade"), it is still better for such a country to specialise in what it is comparatively better at making or doing and to trade with that, rather than making or doing both things and consuming the output at home. He makes a comparison in this regard between England and Portugal. Consider England, he says, where cloth is produced using one hundred men's labour for a year and where wine is made using one hundred and twenty men's labour for a year. England should really import wine because it takes more men to make that. It should put its men to work making cloth because it is cheaper to do so and England can be more competitive internationally with this product. Now consider Portugal, he says, where cloth is made using ninety men for a year and wine is made using eighty men a year. Portugal can make both wine and cloth cheaper than England, however, Ricardo says that because it is still better for Portugal to make wine, which is the product it is comparatively good at, it should do so and it should import cloth. If England and Portugal trade, he says, England can get wine which took eighty men a year in Portugal to make, and have cloth which took one hundred men in England to make. Portugal can get cloth which took one hundred men a year in England to make and have wine which took eighty to make at home. Both will ostensibly be better off.

The whole contemporary case for free world trade depends on the argument made above. Ricardo says that if both countries make their own wine and cloth, Portuguese consumers can get both products cheaper. He then says that this is only a "seeming advantage", however, since the "quantity of cloth and wine together produced in ... [Portugal] would be diminished ...", indeed, "[e]stimated in money, the whole revenue of Portugal would be diminished". So what? For the poorer country, the absolute disadvantage involved in being more poor is always going to be greater than any relative advantage there might be in being poorer more 'efficiently'. Might the solution to being poorer lie in not looking for some relative advantage with regard to the goods and services to be sold or traded abroad, but to getting an absolute advantage? This is exactly what a number of Asian countries, like Japan, Korea, Taiwan and China — unimpressed by nineteenth-century liberalist logic — chose to do to become more 'developed'. It was no accident that the Japanese first translated the works of the German economic protectionist Friedrich List and followed his advice. They translated Adam Smith and David Ricardo only second.

All of this is obvious to economic protectionists and economic socialists as well as to marxists since they all make very different assumptions about the motives of those who want to open state economic borders. Economic protectionists say that free trade favours the most developed. It throws countries open to exploitation by those with politico-economic power. It increases specialisation and it decreases flexibility and national security. People need to be self-sufficient. Economic socialists say that free trade results in disparities in wealth. It allows markets to determine the distribution of goods and services. It increases wage differentials and decreases access by the poor to what they need. Marxists say that free trade is exploitative. It allows owners and managers to extract surplus value from the world's workers for their own ends, not that of the workers. The latter need to become aware of their collective plight and revolt, not to accept protection from the predatory profiteering practices of global capitalists.

CONCLUSION

In conclusion, consider coffee, which is a global industry worth in excess of seventy billion US dollars annually. Coffee workers have a hard life. Labour conditions are appalling. Luckily, commodities do not convey this to the consumer who would otherwise be acutely aware, with every cup, of the blood, sweat and tears it took to produce and deliver. Commodities do not stink or complain or get sick from exhaustion or the chemicals used to make them. They smell and taste like coffee. They do not manifest the human aspects of their manufacture and supply.

The fair trade movement was initiated to do something about the human dimension to this industry. The movement's market share is still small, though half a million of the developing world's four million coffee farmers are signed on with TransFair USA, which covers about one eighth of the relevant labour pool. This has improved the working conditions of those in this pool since democratically-run cooperatives are different from exploitative entrepreneurs.

For Starbucks, a fairer coffee-trade regime worldwide is about allaying protestors and getting it out of the press. It can offer a new product that has a cause-related feature, thereby expanding its business and making more money. Fair trade coffee is just another product on its shop shelves. It is one tenth of one percent of all that it buys, and all that it buys is only one percent of the world's coffee. It is about business and consumer preference.

Despite the use of the fair trade movement to a capitalist purpose it still presents an alternative to the liberalist approach. Economic liberalism has no interest in how profits are distributed. It sees free trade as making for greater productivity and the wealth subsequently generated as 'trickling down' to the producers themselves, thereby 'floating the boats' of the working poor. It has no interest in the way wealth floods up to the owners and managers of the means of production leaving the working poor 'high and dry'.

Hence the importance of considering free trade in general in terms of fair trade in particular. Hence the significance of seeing the free trade doctrine from more than one perspective.

REFERENCES

Masefield, J (1924). *Cargoes.* http//www.poemhunter.com/poem/cargoes/ [14 December 2011].

Ricardo, D (1951 [1817]). On the Principles of Political Economy and Taxation. In *The Works and Correspondence of David Ricardo,* Vol. 1, P Sraffa (ed.). Cambridge: Cambridge University Press.

Smith, A (1993 [1776]). *An Inquiry into the Nature and Causes of the Wealth of Nations.* Oxford: Oxford University Press.

CHAPTER 9

A Multilateral System

Stephen Woolcock

London School of Economics

The multilateral trading system is currently seen as failing due to the lack of any agreement in the current Doha Development Agenda (DDA) negotiations of the World Trade Organisation (WTO). Is this really the case and if so what are the current difficulties besetting the system? Are they endemic or are they due more to a lack of 'political will'?

This chapter argues for a differentiated approach to the health of this system. It bases its assessment on an analysis of the longer term development of global trade. It then discusses the challenges facing the multilateral trading system, such as whether it can be effective as well as inclusive, and concludes by arguing that it can, but not in all aspects of trade policy and not with regard to all of their members.

IS THE MULTILATERAL SYSTEM FAILING?

The case that the multilateral system is failing is essentially based on the view it has not been possible to conclude the current DDA negotiations. These were intended to be a fairly short multilateral round of negotiations but have been less than vigorous and have been on 'life support' for much of the last ten years.

The reasons for this are often given as systemic in nature. First, it is argued that the WTO has become too big or too inclusive to be effective. In other words a larger number of active members makes decision making in the WTO impossible. In this context it is worth noting that the original organisation was far smaller and signed by just thirty-two Contracting Parties (CPs) in 1948. Even when more countries — especially developing countries — became CPs during the 1960s and 1970s, there was in effect a two-tier membership due to the use of Part IV of the General Agreement on Tariffs and Trade (GATT). This broadly exempted developing countries from major commitments but also denied them any real influence. The key decisions, including the negotiation of multilateral trade rounds in the

1960s and 1970s (if not in the 1980s and 1990s) were taken by a fairly small group of relatively like-minded developed countries.

The WTO now faces difficulties because it includes more members. More importantly the use of a Single Undertaking to conclude the Uruguay Round (discussed below) to replace Part IV, means that developing countries now expect to have a say in the rules of the game. In other words the interests of the members have become too heterogeneous for agreement to be reached, with the result that countries are resorting more and more to preferential (in fact bilateral) trade agreements that further weaken the WTO by removing the incentive to conclude multilateral negotiations (Heydon and Woolcock, 2009; Baldwin and Thornton, 2008).

Related to this is a second systemic reason for the difficulties facing the WTO. This is a structural shift in the relative importance of major trading countries with the emergence during the 2000s of China, India, Brazil, and other major developing countries. While India and Brazil sought for decades to influence GATT negotiations, they had little market power. Their economies were fairly small compared to the major OECD economies. They had poor or at best uncertain growth prospects and they were not ready to offer market access in any case. Thanks to the increased leverage (due to their recent growth rates), as well as the alliances they have built with other developing countries, these major emerging markets now have the ability to shape outcomes. The rapid emergence of China as a major player has been a decisive factor, since its accession to the WTO in 2001, in shifting the balance of market power within the WTO. The picture is further complicated by the fact that the subject matter of negotiations has become more and more complex and intrusive with regard to national policy autonomy. With the reduction of tariff and other border measures, the focus of WTO negotiations — like the GATT before it — has moved to behind-the-border issues that encroach more and more on national policy autonomy and as a result are much harder to negotiate.

The difficulties facing the WTO can also be seen as a result of its success. Successive rounds of tariff liberalisation have brought tariffs on manufactured goods among developed countries down to around four percent. While average tariffs on agricultural products and 'bound' tariffs in developing countries are higher, the fact that the WTO faces the challenge of dealing with behind-the-border issues is because many 'at the border' barriers have been removed. (A tariff is 'bound' when a WTO member agrees to a set maximum tariff. The country concerned may have a lower applied tariff, as is the case in many developing economies. The difference between the applied and the bound tariff is then called the 'water' in the tariff. Developing countries would like to retain this because it gives them 'policy space' to increase protection for sectors that are seen to be important for development. Developed economies that have bound tariffs at low levels wish all WTO members to move towards that goal.) The fact that the WTO has now become a global trade organisation can also be seen as a problem of success. The challenge of remaining effective with more members is, after all, due to the increased number of WTO members. The former centrally planned economies have all moved to join the WTO with the only major economy outside the WTO now being Russia, which is itself negotiating accession. Developing countries and emerging markets seek a greater say in the WTO because of its relevance. This could well have something to do with the fact that in the WTO it is one member-one vote, so it is more 'democratic' than other international organisations such as the International Monetary Fund, where there is weighting according to the importance of countries.

Another problem of success could be that agreement is difficult to reach in the WTO because the rules mean something. WTO rules are binding and members that do not comply can be dragged into a rigorous dispute settlement process. When negotiating such binding agreements governments are more cautious than when negotiating less binding agreements. International agreements that are less binding or take the form of softer laws are likely to be easier to conclude.

THE MAIN TENSION THAT CHARACTERISES THE WTO

The following section looks more closely at the main tension that characterises the challenges, facing the WTO, namely, that between effectiveness and inclusiveness. Before doing so, it is worth clarifying what these terms mean. Effectiveness can have a number of meanings. First, there is the issue of the WTO's effectiveness as a forum for negotiating further liberalisation or more generally enhancing market access. As noted above, the GATT was effective in bringing tariffs and other border measures, such as quotas, down to low levels in developed countries. The difficulty finalising the DDA, which is largely a conventional market-access negotiation since the Cancun WTO Ministerial meeting in 2003, does raise some doubts about the effectiveness of the WTO as a forum for negotiating enhanced market access.

Often linked to this is the effectiveness of the WTO in negotiating new rules governing international trade. In analytical terms, if not in practice, rules can be distinguished from market access in the sense that they set out common standards for national policies, such as in the case of Trade Related Intellectual Property Rights (TRIPs), Sanitary and Phytosanitary (SPS) standards, or rules on national subsidy programmes. The negotiation of such rules has often gone hand-in-hand with negotiations on market access. As will be discussed below in the context of the DDA, the prospect of the WTO being effective in negotiating such rules looks even less promising than that for market access. Important issues for rules, such as the so-called Singapore issues (investment, competition and government procurement) have been dropped from the DDA agenda altogether. The only one remaining is trade facilitation (Lee and Wilkinson, 2007).

The effectiveness of the WTO can also be measured with respect to enforcement, that is, with respect to maintaining discipline in the trading system. In this regard the WTO has done quite well so far. With only a few exceptions WTO members have complied with the decisions of the stronger dispute settlement mechanism introduced as a result of the Uruguay Round (see below). Even during the recent downturn in trade and economic activity following the 2007/8 financial crisis there was no general flouting of the rules or recourse to protectionism. This contrasts, for example, with the period in the early 1970s when the post oil-shock recessions led to various measures aimed at circumventing GATT rules in the form of voluntary export restraints or dubious applications of contingent protection measures that went under the name of new protectionism.

Finally, in relation to effectiveness, there is the question of how good the WTO is in implementing agreements. For many areas of policy, especially technical barriers to trade or other regulatory measures, the conclusion of an agreement is only the beginning. If such measures are not to pose barriers to market access and international competition, there is a need for continuous efforts to address the new standards and regulations that governments introduce all the time. This is the ongoing work of many specialist committees of the WTO that provide forums for consultation and discussion between WTO members. The work in these largely unnoticed committees removes many potential barriers to market access, while ensuring that national governments can introduce regulations in the pursuit of legitimate policy aims such as health and safety, environmental protection, or prudential control. It is only a minority of cases that end up as disputes and go through the formal, legalistic, dispute-settlement procedure. Most are resolved through dialogue and discussion. In assessing the effectiveness of the WTO it is important, therefore, to consider all these dimensions to the work of the WTO and not to focus exclusively on whether the DDA has been completed.

It is also helpful to deconstruct what is meant by inclusiveness. If inclusiveness means having all of the WTO members involved in every decision then the numbers really do constitute a difficulty. In practice, negotiations within the WTO context — as in most other multilateral settings — are conducted among a smaller group of key countries. In the GATT this took the form of the infamous 'Green Room' (see below) where the outline of agreements would be concluded among a small group of CPs invited by the Director General of the GATT. These agreements would then be put to the full GATT membership for approval. This was not an inclusive process. Quite often the non-invited CPs had no idea what was being discussed and could not, therefore, even make representations to the GATT Secretariat, or to potential allies or coalition partners that were invited.

Inclusiveness can also relate to how the trading system accommodates more active members. During the 1980s the Newly Industrialising Countries (NICs) were effectively integrated into the system, largely as the result of pressure from the OECD countries. The NICs constituted a competitive challenge to the OECD, particularly with regard to manufactures, and the OECD countries were keen that they 'graduate' and assume more commitments and responsibilities under the GATT. In 2000 the WTO saw similar efforts to integrate the new major emerging economies of China, India and Brazil more fully into the system. An important distinction however, was that while the NICs were happy to accept the norms laid down by the developed OECD economies, the emerging markets wanted to shape the rules.

Inclusiveness in the GATT/WTO has not meant that all members have the same status and obligations. As noted above, for many years the GATT functioned as a two-tier system with developing countries largely exempt from significant obligations in terms of liberalisation but also sidelined with regard to key decisions. Today the least developed country (LDC) members of the WTO still benefit from special and differential treatment (S&DT) and are granted tariff-free and quota-free access for most if not all of their exports to the major developed country markets. (Quota-free, duty-free access for LDCs — as opposed to developing countries — is subject to negotiation. Some developed economies, such as the EU with its Everything but Arms policy, already provide it. The issue is whether this should be one hundred percent or whether certain sensitive sectors — in which the LDCs are usually competitive — should be excluded.) In terms of their short- to medium-term interests, therefore, there is little need for LDCs or even smaller DCs to be included in all negotiations. The treatment of LDCs must, however, be distinguished from that of the major emerging markets, which are a prime target of developed country exporters — and thus developed country governments — in seeking to secure market access. LDC governments also find it difficult to be included in all the negotiations or meetings of the WTO. Given the limited capacity of many LDC governments and the large number of meetings that take place, it is impossible for them to be involved in all meetings or even all negotiations. This is clearly a factor in terms of inclusion.

Finally, with regard to inclusiveness, there is the issue of whether stakeholders other than the governments of WTO member are or should be included in decision making. After pressure for such access during the 1990s from a range of non-governmental organisations (NGOs), the WTO embraced transparency. This, together with the inclusion of stakeholders in national delegations (although seldom at the negotiating table) appears to be the current *modus vivendi*.

THE EVOLUTION OF THE GATT/WTO SYSTEM

The nature of the current multilateral trading system has been shaped by its origins and by its evolution over the more than sixty years since the establishment of the General Agreement on Tariffs and Trade in 1947. A formal trade organisation was supposed to have formed part of the post-1945 Bretton Woods system. Indeed trade was supposed to have been negotiated before the monetary regime and the IMF. But there were difficulties due to British reluctance to end imperial preferences. In 1947 the GATT was negotiated in Geneva. This was, as the name states, a general agreement on a set of rules and a set of tariff reductions. It did not involve a formal treaty or an international organisation, although a Secretariat was subsequently established in Geneva. The Havana Charter that was negotiated in 1948 included the GATT and a formal International Trade Organisation (ITO), as well as much more besides, but the Havana Charter was never ratified by the US Congress (Diebold, 1952). The GATT, which had been adopted by executive order in the US rather than by Congressional treaty ratification, was therefore a practical alternative or fallback that provided US exporters with reduced tariffs and the enhanced market access that they sought. The US government took at least the first steps towards removing the preferential trading arrangements that had damaged trade and the international economy during the interwar years. With no formal treaty basis, however, the GATT emerged as a member-driven forum for negotiation.

The trading regime has over the years become deeper and wider — deeper in the sense that the regime has grown to cover more issues, often ones that are more intrusive with regard to national policy autonomy; wider in the sense that starting from just thirty-two CPs in 1947 it has grown to include, first, most developing countries as they have achieved independence and, second, the former centrally planned economies as these made the transition to market economies in the 1990s. How the GATT/WTO has balanced this deepening and widening has shaped the nature and the effectiveness of the regime.

At the outset the GATT was concerned with market access only in the form of tariff reduction. The 1947 negotiations resulted in tariff reductions in the order of twenty-five percent. In addition the GATT embodied a number of core principles, some codified in the GATT agreement and some of a more implicit political nature. The codified principles guaranteed non-discrimination in the form of the most-favoured-nation principle (MFN), as expressed in Article I, and national treatment as expressed in Article III. MFN meant and means that any concession or tariff reduction extended to one trading partner has to be extended to all the others. National treatment meant and means that imported 'like products' must be treated the same as nationally produced products: hence national treatment.

(The reference to 'like-products' is important for current trade discussions on issues such as climate change. The GATT interpretation of like products means that products that have the same physical characteristics must be treated the same. In other words, there can be no differentiation between products on the basis of how they are made. This means no discrimination between products according to whether they are produced using a lot of carbon or very little, or using workers that do not benefit from union membership or are fully paid up union members.) The GATT contained a number of important exceptions to these rules. These exceptions have been important over the years and remain so today. The exceptions regarding customs unions and free trade arrangements in Article XXIV are still very ill-defined despite being the legal basis for proliferating preferential trade agreements. There were other important exceptions in the form of anti-dumping (Article VI) and safeguard measures (Article XIX) that have also over the years been the basis for contingent protection.

In addition to the principles set out in the agreement, the underlying basis for liberalisation under the GATT has been reciprocal market access. This stems from the political economy of trade liberalisation in the US as set out originally in the 1933 Reciprocal Trade Agreements Act, which reversed the disastrous protection of the Smoot-Hawley Tariff of 1930. In other words, the US sought to liberalise on the condition that other countries did. This differed from the British policy of unilateral trade liberalisation, which shaped the latter half of the nineteenth century. It was the political basis for getting support in the US Congress to begin the liberalisation process. As the US provided the leadership in the post-1945 period it shaped the agenda, and thus the GATT process, in its own image. Within the GATT reciprocity was defined broadly to mean a broad balance of benefits from the trading system, or 'global reciprocity.' Thus, in the multilateral rounds that followed, success depended on trade-offs between market-access concessions designed to ensure that such reciprocity existed.

After the initial GATT negotiations, there was little further liberalisation during the 1950s and the beginning of the 1960s. Indeed, the cause of multilateralism was undermined by the 1953 waiver for US agricultural support that provided the precedent for the exclusion of agriculture from the GATT rules for the next forty years. The lack of forward movement in the GATT during the 1950s was probably due to the focus on reconstruction in Europe and Japan and partly to the fact that the Europeans had little to offer in terms of market access until their economies recovered. There was some widening of membership, with the Federal Republic of Germany (1950) and Japan (1955) becoming Contracting Parties to the GATT, but the next round of major liberalisation did not come until the Kennedy Round (1963–1967). This was initiated by the US, which proposed a new comprehensive round in 1961. The principle US motivation was to limit the effects of the common external tariff (CET) of the European Economic Community (EEC) and to establish GATT discipline over the EEC's Common Agricultural Policy (CAP) (Preeg, 1970). (The existing bindings of EEC member states were changed with the creation of the CET, so the issue was whether the CET would constitute a net decrease or increase in tariffs for US exporters to the EEC. Article XXIV of the GATT required the CET to be, on balance, no higher than the previous tariffs, but the US concerns were to do with what 'on balance' meant.) Strategic in the form of consolidating the Western capitalist system in the depths of the Cold War, was another important factor (Evans, 1971). European integration therefore had a two-fold impact on the trading system. It provided an incentive for a further round of liberalisation and gave the EEC sufficient leverage to bring about a reduction in US tariffs. On the other hand, the EEC provided a precedent in terms of the application of Article XXIV, allowing customs unions as an exception to the MFN principle. During the Kennedy Round the GATT Contracting Parties also established Part IV of the GATT in response to the increased number of newly independent countries becoming Contracting Parties. In so doing a two-tier system was created, one for the OECD and one for developing countries.

The 1970s saw a consolidation of this two-tier system. Part IV of the GATT was incorporated into the Tokyo Round of GATT negotiations (1973–1979). The effort to introduce stronger rules on non-tariff measures (NTM), which was driven by a US desire to clamp down on the provision of what it saw as unfair support given to its European and Japanese competitors, resulted in qualified MFN codes (Winham, 1986). These were codes on subsidies and countervailing duties, government procurement and technical barriers to trade, that were signed only by OECD Contracting Parties and therefore did not apply to the developing countries. The US again sought and failed to bring agriculture (in other words the European Common Agricultural Policy) under GATT discipline. Based on a price support system, the CAP resulted in European Community (EC) exports of agricultural products being subsidised when EC prices were above world prices. Such subsidised exports then competed in third markets with the US and other more competitive agricultural producers. The Tokyo Round also saw a consolidation of the 'club-model' of international trade policy in which the US-led, core OECD countries shaped the rules. For example, the codes on NTM were based on work done in the OECD. Relations with developing countries were shaped by the ideology-driven debate on a New International Economic Order (NIEO), which included among other things the demand of the 'G77' group of developing countries for a greater say in governing the international economy. Towards the end of the Tokyo Round the Newly Industrialising Countries (NICs) began to emerge as a distinct group of developing countries. This posed a competitive challenge to the OECD countries which responded by negotiating 'voluntary export restraint agreements'

(VERs) outside of the GATT system. (Efforts to reform the Article XIX safeguards agreement of the GATT to accommodate pressure from OECD countries for selective safeguards against the NICs failed in the face of opposition to such a clear breach of the core GATT principle of MFN.) Anti-dumping duties were also used as contingent protection measures since these could equally be targeted at specific sectors, which was at odds with the principle of MFN. Faced with the protectionist measures taken by the major importers against their manufactured goods the NICs began to move towards a position favouring stronger GATT discipline.

During the Uruguay Round (1986–1994) the ideological North-South divide of the 1970s was no longer such a central issue. The NICs favoured stronger rules as a defence against contingent protection. The paradigm shift towards more liberal trade and investment policies had by the mid-to-late 1980s also spread to many developing countries. These were more and more shifting from import-substitution protection towards outward-looking development strategies. The US was again the main driver in the run up to the Uruguay Round (Bergsten and Cline, 1982). This time the aim was to extend the multilateral rules to cover areas in which the US still retained a competitive position. This was meant to help the US balance-of-trade but also to compensate for the growing opposition to liberal trade in traditional sectors such as manufacturing. Hence the inclusion of services, driven by the US financial sector in particular, and hence the drive to protect intellectual property rights (IPRs), which came most notably from the US pharmaceuticals sector. The European Community, Japan and other OECD countries eventually came to accept the case for this extension of multilateralism as well as an agenda that included a serious effort to bring agriculture under GATT discipline. The agenda was shaped by what came to be called the 'quad' (the US, the European Community, Japan and Canada). This was often a US — EU dialogue given Japan's reluctance to adopt a prominent position and Canada's relatively small market. The G77 group of developing countries, that owed its existence to the Non-Aligned Movement, became less important as developing countries began to shift towards an acceptance of the GATT as the forum for trade. In its place there were more functional coalitions such as the Cairns Group, which included developed and developing countries interested in more liberal agricultural policies. A 'hard core' group of ten developing countries, led by India and Brazil, still resisted comprehensive negotiations within the GATT, but even Brazil switched, leaving India unable to block the launch of the Uruguay Round.

There were three outcomes to the Uruguay Round (Croome, 1995; Schott, 1994; and Stewart, 1993). First, the scope of the regime was extended to include the so-called new areas of services, trade-related intellectual property rights (TRIPs), and investment. The inclusion of agriculture for the first time, as well as a range of other more technical issues, meant the round was indeed comprehensive and included measures that reached deeper into national policy autonomy and in some areas — such as intellectual property rights protection and sanitary and phytosanitary measures — required a degree of policy harmonisation. Second, the trade regime became more rules-based in the sense that the dispute settlement procedures were strengthened and made more legalistic. The power-based 1947 GATT regime, where outcomes were determined by negotiation but invariably favoured the more powerful parties, was replaced by a system in which all parties were (at least in a formal sense) equal under the 'law'. Third, the two-tier structure of membership was replaced by a Single Undertaking (covering a revised GATT from 1994, a General Agreement on Trade in Services [GATS] and the TRIPs agreement) that all members of the WTO had to accept. The ending of the two-tier system widened the effective membership of the WTO by bringing all countries into a single system regardless of their level of development. (Developing countries and especially the least developed countries still received special and differential treatment in the form of longer transition periods, technical assistance, or other exceptions.) A final change was the creation of the World Trade Organisation (the WTO) itself, although in many respects this was less significant because the WTO largely codified existing GATT practices (Jackson, 2000).

To sum up, then, by the end of the Uruguay Round the multilateral trading system deepened the system in the sense that WTO provisions began to intrude more into national policy autonomy than had been the case with the original GATT. Under GATT, national treatment ensured non-discrimination but said nothing about the substance of any national policy provided it was not disproportionate and did not constitute a hidden barrier to trade (Cottier and Mavroidis, 2000). The Uruguay Round also led to a widening of effective membership that coincided with the end of the Cold War and the beginnings of accession for countries in transition from centrally planned economies. The WTO became a global trade organisation. As discussed below, the WTO is a one-member one-vote organisation, but *de facto* influence is clearly different. From a US-led regime in 1947, the GATT changed into a US-led club in the 1970s and a virtual US–EU duopoly in the 1980s. By the middle of the 1990s the EU began to assume the role of the main driver of new multilateral negotiations, as the US shifted to a policy of competitive liberalisation.

DECISION MAKING WITHIN THE WTO

The WTO assumed most of the GATT practices in terms of decision making. Although formal decision making is based on one-member one-vote, so that the smallest member can theoretically veto any agreement, the practice is consensus. As in the GATT this normally means that the agreement tabled is adopted, provided there is no member present who is decisively against. If members are not present, as is the case for some LDCs, they have no influence. There are, however, formal provisions for voting. For example, unanimity is required to change the basic principles of the WTO, such as any changes to Articles I (MFN) or III (national treatment). On certain issues, such as a waiver from GATT rules like the one that provides for EU preferences for developing countries under the Cotonou Agreement, there is scope for a two-third majority vote (see WTO Doc WT/L/93). In the case of the interpretation of WTO agreements there is also provision under Article IX for weighted votes of three quarters of the members and for accession by two thirds. The creation of a formal institutional structure in the WTO has not changed the nature of the beast, however, in that it is still predominantly a member-driven organisation. Initiatives on new negotiations are taken by the members and not the WTO Secretariat.

In practice, work on key decisions is undertaken in smaller groups. These can be informal or more formal, as with the Chair's Consultative Group. This is a more transparent version of the old 'Green Room process'. It is more transparent in the sense that all members are now informed that meetings are taking place, which was not the case with the old Green Room. Every effort is also made to ensure that key interested parties are involved or informed. Final decisions are always taken in the General Council, however, or ultimately in the Ministerial Meeting of the WTO that is supposed to take place every two years. In the initial years of the WTO, that is, after 1995, a number of WTO Ministerial meetings became a focus of intense public interest and of campaigns by non-governmental organisations. In recent years the WTO Ministerial Meetings have not attracted such interest. In the wake of the Seattle and Cancun WTO Ministerial meetings there was a debate on whether there was a need for institutional reform in the WTO (Schott, 2000; Sutherland Report, 2007; Warwick Commission, 2007). The response has been pragmatic. Efforts have been made to open up the previously opaque Green Room process and to further enhance the transparency of decision making by publishing more or less all of the formal position papers discussed within the WTO.

Below the level of the Ministerial Conference the key decision making body in the WTO is the General Council. This includes all member countries. It also sits as the Dispute Settlement Body, which adopts the reports of dispute settlement panels (see below) and is the Trade Policy Review Body. The latter considers the Trade Policy Reviews that are produced for all WTO members and that constitutes an important element in the promotion of transparency in trade policy. (The trade policies of all WTO member countries are subject to regular review. This consists of reports by the government of the country concerned and the WTO Secretariat. The reports are then discussed in the Trade Policy Review Body. Large economies face a review every two years, least developed countries far less often.) Below the

General Council are the Councils for Trade in Goods, Services and TRIPs. Below each of these councils are a fairly sizable number of specialist committees that monitor the application of WTO rules and commitments on an ongoing basis. (For details of the workings of the WTO and other information on specific issues see the WTO website *www.wto.org.*)

For negotiation, a Trade Negotiations Committee (also consisting of representatives from all member countries) is established to provide horizontal control of the 'vertical' negotiations within specific negotiating committees. These negotiating committees can be seen as operating on the more technical level and are generally chaired by a senior trade official from a member country, with the WTO providing the secretariat functions and working behind the scenes to promote agreement. The chairs of each negotiating committee may propose compromise texts but will generally work to reduce the areas of disagreement within each negotiating topic. In addition to these vertical negotiations there is a need to agree on trade-offs across issues, however, since the General Council is too big these horizontal negotiations take place in the Chair's Consultative Group, or in more ad hoc groups such as the Group of 11 that met during the spring of 2011 to try and find a final agreement in the DDA. The final political level negotiations take place at a ministerial level. The role of the Director General of the WTO has become more important over time as more high profile candidates have assumed this position. If agreement is close the Director General may table a compromise proposal, as Arthur Dunkel did in December 1990 during the Uruguay Round. But this tends to happen only when there is broad political support for agreement.

In terms of inclusiveness, LDCs are very hard pressed to maintain much of a presence in Geneva. Whilst the major economies will have experts based in Geneva or will fly them in from national capitals to cover technical meetings, some LDCs have no trade people in Geneva and often cannot afford to fly in experts. As many decisions in trade hinge on details to do with tariff schedules, exclusions, or the coverage of rules, this can mean LDCs are not adequately represented, though this disadvantage can be partially compensated for by cooperation between smaller WTO members through the work of coalitions like the G20 or the Africa Group, or through technical support from developed members.

Before leaving the topic of decision making it is important to stress the strengthened dispute settlement procedure agreed to as part of the Uruguay Round. The GATT developed a reasonably effective system of dispute settlement based on conciliation, and if that failed, on decisions by a panel of independent experts. Under the pre-Uruguay Round arrangements, GATT Contracting Parties were able to block the establishment of a panel and veto the adoption of a panel report. Despite this the system worked reasonably because the major countries wished it to work and most sought to comply with panel decisions.

The Understanding on Dispute Settlement adopted as part of the Uruguay Round strengthened the rules and made dispute settlement more legalistic. WTO members now have an effective right to a panel, even though conciliation is still encouraged and extensively used. It is no longer possible to veto a panel decision, which can only be blocked if there is a consensus among all WTO members to do so (including the country destined to 'win' the case). The fail-safe in cases where a panel might misinterpret GATT rules is recourse to the Appellate Body of the WTO which is made up of a panel of senior trade officials and lawyers. (The GATT still exists in the form of the GATT 1994 that replaced GATT 1947. The WTO also incorporates the GATS and the TRIPs into its body of trade law.)

The decision of the Appellate Body is final. This shift has made the WTO a more rules-based and legalistic system and has arguably strengthened enforcement. It has been criticised for lacking legitimacy, though, with quasi-judicial decisions taken in Geneva that affect national policy preferences. There has also been concern expressed about 'legal activism' in which Appellate Body interpretations reach beyond what has been agreed at the political level in the General Council or Trade Negotiating Committee. In practice, the dispute settlement procedure is now used more sparingly than in the initial years, and the Appellate Body has been constrained in its interpretation of these agreements.

THE DOHA DEVELOPMENT AGENDA (DDA)

The first Ministerial Meeting of the WTO was held in Singapore in 1996. This was still shaped by the prevailing views of the 1990s according to which there was a need to complete the process of strengthening the international system by including investment and other issues in international negotiations. With globalised production moving ahead, it was seen as an anomaly that there were comprehensive rules on trade but no multilateral rules for investment. At Singapore investment was therefore included on the WTO's work programme, along with competition policy, government procurement and trade facilitation (Schott, 1996). These became the 'Singapore issues' that have been most consistently supported by the EU and constituted a key part of the efforts to launch a new and more comprehensive round of negotiations able to include them. The EU received only lukewarm support from the US in advocating this. Meanwhile it faced active opposition from many developing countries. (The US favoured the OECD as a forum for 'multilateral' negotiations on investment and negotiations were initiated on a Multilateral Investment Agreement in 1966. These paralleled work at the WTO but the MAI famously failed in 1998.) In 1998, at the second WTO Ministerial meeting that marked fifty years of the GATT, the US agreed to support efforts to launch a new trade round but these failed in Seattle in late 1999 due to differences between the OECD economies, opposition from developing countries (which believed the agenda was again being imposed upon them), and a lack of resolve on the part of national governments in the face of growing civil society opposition to what was seen as another step towards globalisation.

The DDA was finally launched in Doha in December 2001, thanks in part to the use of 'constructive ambiguity' in the wording of the communiqué. This was a technique that had often been used in GATT negotiations where compromise wording was used to paper over differences. The failure in Seattle was also due in part to failed efforts to agree on an explicit, clear agenda. The EU remained the main 'demandeur' for a new comprehensive round, in which it sought progress on the Singapore issues and market access for its services and manufactures in the larger emerging markets in return for concessions on agriculture. The EU strategy favored multilateral negotiations over preferential agreements and it adopted a *de facto* moratorium on new preferential trade negotiations from 1999. In contrast to previous rounds, the US provided only qualified support for a comprehensive round and from 2001, when it finally obtained new Trade Promotion Authority from Congress, the US administration began pursuing a strategy of 'competitive liberalisation'. This was a pragmatic approach in which bilateral, regional or multilateral approaches to liberalisation were to be pursued depending on which offered the best prospect of results. Developing countries flagged their intention to have a greater say by first making the launch of the DDA conditional upon a statement interpreting the TRIPs agreement in a way that favoured developing country interests. This was the Doha Declaration on TRIPs and essential medicines. Secondly, India, assuming a leadership role for developing countries, insisted on an 'explicit consensus' on the final agenda. As some smaller developing countries were sometimes not present in negotiations and often remained silent when they were, specifying the need for an explicit consensus clearly gave the DCs a more powerful veto right.

Between 2001 and 2003 a limited commitment to negotiate and a general economic slowdown meant progress towards reaching an agreement on the 'modalities' for the DDA was slow. In an effort to move things along, the EU and the US produced a joint text on agriculture in 2003. Given that transatlantic differences on agriculture had determined the pace of the Uruguay Round there was a belief that an EU–US agreement would help. In practice, the reverse was the case. The joint text was seen by the major developing countries as a bid to sustain transatlantic duopoly over the trade agenda and an effort to ensure continued scope for protection for their special agricultural interests while pushing for developed country concessions on services, non-agricultural market access (NAMA) and the Singapore issues. Brazil and India, plus China and other developing countries, formed the G20 and came forward with alternative proposals that made the overall ambitions of the round dependent on the willingness of the EU and the US to make concessions on agriculture. The 2003 WTO Ministerial Meeting in Cancun, which was supposed to map out a course for the DDA, failed, even though the EU had effectively taken the three most controversial Singapore issues off the table.

A more modest agenda was put together in the shape of the August 2004 Framework Agreement. This excluded the Singapore issues, except for trade facilitation, and focused on the traditional topics of agriculture and NAMA. Even services slipped down to a less than central position in the negotiations and although other topics were included, such as rules on regional trade agreements, anti-dumping, and some aspects of intellectual property rights, it became clear that the main substance of the negotiations concerned agriculture and NAMA. In these negotiations the G20 sought progress on agriculture from both the US (reductions in domestic support) and the EU (elimination of export subsidies and better market access). In return the EU and the US sought reductions in tariffs on manufactures in the major emerging markets of the G20 as well as progress on services. As always this simple depiction of the G20 against the EU and the US, or perhaps the OECD countries, is inaccurate. In reality the picture was much more complex, with tensions within both 'blocs'. For example, there was certainly some concern among China's G20 partners as well as within the US and the EU about lowering tariffs on products in which China was already very competitive.

The DDA stumbled on through times when there appeared to be some progress, such as at the Hong Kong WTO Ministerial meeting, and other times when it was barely alive (Lee and Wilkinson, 2007; Jones, 2010). In 2007, and especially in 2008, major efforts were made by the various negotiating groups in Geneva and in high-level meetings out of the glare of the news media that accompanied big summits to make progress. In December 2008 an agreement was nearly reached on the modalities for tariff and subsidy reductions in agriculture, however, the negotiations failed on the issue of special safeguard measures (SSM) under which India — with support from China — wanted scope to reimpose tariffs in the event of any import surge of agricultural products that might threaten its numerous and politically important subsistence farmers. The US, in particular, saw the Indian proposal as a way of maintaining or even increasing protection rather than safeguarding food security. In reality, however, the main hindrance to agreement was a lack of political support among a limited number of important WTO members.

The DDA remained for a protracted period in considerable doubt. Efforts to find agreement failed again in the spring of 2011. This time the differences were more in NAMA, with the US pressing for more commitments from the emerging markets to liberalise selected sectors, something Brazil, China and India argued was supposed to be voluntary. While continued failure to conclude the negotiations raised doubts about them ever being concluded, especially as all WTO members began resorting to more and more preferential agreements, the need to maintain the credibility of the WTO was enough to sustain it.

CONCLUSION

What can be concluded in terms of the balance between effectiveness and inclusiveness outlined in this chapter? In terms of negotiating reciprocal market opening it can be argued that the GATT was effective and tariffs were significantly reduced. With no market access agreement under the WTO as yet, it is not possible to conclude this for the WTO as an organisation. In a sense the WTO is suffering from the success of the GATT in that developed WTO members now have little to offer in terms of market access concessions.

In terms of rule making, or establishing expectations regarding behind-the-border measures, and in terms of keeping pace with globalisation, the system looks rather less effective. There are as yet no comprehensive provisions on investment even though this represents probably the most important vehicle for globalisation. (The GATS agreement covers investment in services in the shape of the so-called mode three commitments on establishment. But these are limited in the case of many countries by restrictive scheduling. The Trade Related Investment Measures agreement of the Uruguay Round also covers aspects of investment policy in that it prohibits host countries from imposing six core performance requirements on inward investors, including local content requirements.)

The TRIPs agreement, when it was adopted in 1994, included positive integration in the form of a commitment to apply specific standards for the protection of intellectual property rights. It is arguably less than effective, however, due to a lack of ownership or commitment to it on the part of developing countries. The history of the Uruguay Round suggests that agreements based on bargaining that involves trading market access (in textiles and clothing) for rules (in the shape of the TRIPs) are unlikely to be sustainable. Multilateral rules will only be sustainable (that is, effective in the longer term) when supported by the countries that apply them. This suggests that multilateral rule making requires more persuasion than bargaining.

In the GATT and the WTO all debate has been seen as a prelude to negotiations on commitments. This means that WTO member governments, and in particular developing countries, which are unsure of the likely benefits of including something on the trade agenda will err in favor of caution and avoid engaging in any debate for fear that this will be the first step down a slippery slope to further undesired commitments. The WTO is therefore not the best forum for seeking consensus on rule making.

The fact that the DDA has been reduced to the negotiation of modest reciprocal market-access commitments appears to confirm this view. (The question of where such rules should be developed goes beyond the scope of this chapter, but a forum is needed that can replicate what the OECD did for the old 'club'. A wider club is required that contains countries which do not appear to automatically share the liberal democratic norms of the OECD.)

In terms of its ability to hold the ring by keeping markets open despite protectionist pressures the WTO appears to have been reasonably effective, as evidenced by the limited recourse to protection or contingent protection during the economic recession following the 2007/8 financial crisis. This statement needs qualification, however. One important reason for the lack of protectionist measures was the existence of global supply chains. The now numerous companies involved in these have no interest in seeing barriers imposed on trade within the chains. Another way of looking at this is that globalisation during the 1990s and 2000s has led to companies freeing themselves of their national identities and shifting to global production systems. These companies no longer wish protection as the previous 'national champions' did. The rules-based system of the WTO can therefore be seen as a force for the stability and predictability that international companies seek when engaging in trade and investment. The WTO dispute settlement procedures could also be classified as effective. These have strengthened enforcement and made all WTO members more equal before the law of the WTO. Small WTO members have succeeded in getting redress when major members have failed to comply with their commitments. At the same time some of the fears about the WTO being swamped with cases, or the Appellate Body engaging in legal activism, do not seem to have been justified. The credibility of the WTO as a system of rules will be weakened, however, if the 'legislative' branch that agrees on new provisions or negotiates new rounds fails.

What about inclusiveness? Does the larger, more active membership of the WTO mean it will inevitably become less effective? The GATT system adjusted to a wider and more effective membership over the years. Initially this took the form of the OECD club replacing US hegemony in the 1970s. In the 1980s and subsequently, more countries joined the OCED club, which then shaped the GATT agenda. The Uruguay Round succeeded in establishing a single framework for all WTO members in the shape of a Single Undertaking, so in a formal sense the WTO became more inclusive. The challenge facing the WTO now is to adjust to China, India, Brazil and other emerging markets that cannot be easily integrated into the OECD club, but have to be included if any WTO agreement is to be reached. In other words the old 'club' will have to put up with some new disruptive members that are not willing to accept all the existing norms. If it can do this then the numbers issue should not present a problem as the smaller developed and least developed economies may be dealt with by simply offering them tariff free access.

REFERENCES

Baldwin, R and P Thornton (2008). *Multilateralising Regionalism: Ideas for a WTO Action Plan on Regionalism.* London: Centre for Economic Policy Research.

Bergsten, C and R Cline (1982). *Trade Policy in the 1980s.* Washington D.C.: Institute for International Economics.

Cottier, T and P Mavroidis (eds.) (2000). Regulatory Barriers and the Principle of Non-discrimination in World Trade Law. *The World Trade Forum Series, Vol. 2. Studies in International Economics.* Ann Arbor: University of Michigan Press

Croome, J (1995). *Reshaping the World Trading System: A History of the Uruguay Round.* Geneva: World Trade Organisation.

Diebold, W (1952). The End of the ITO. *Princeton Essays in International Finance, No. 16.* Princeton NJ: Princeton University Press.

Evans, J (1971). *The Kennedy Round in American Trade Policy: The Twilight of the GATT?* Cambridge, Mass.: Harvard University Press.

Heydon, K and S Woolcock (2009). *The Rise of Bilateralism: Comparing American, European and Asian Approaches to Preferential Trade Agreements.* Tokyo, Japan: United Nations University Press.

Jackson, J (2000). *The World Trading System: Law and Policy of International Economic Relations.* 2nd Edition. Cambridge, Mass.: MIT Press.

Jones, K (2010). *The Doha Blues: Institutional Crisis and Reform in the WTO.* Oxford: Oxford University Press.

Lee, D and R Wilkinson (2007). *The WTO after Hong Kong: Progress in, and Prospects for, the Doha Development Agenda.* London: Routledge.

Preeg, E (1970). *Traders and Diplomats: An Analysis of the Kennedy Round of Negotiations under the General Agreement on Tariffs and Trade.* Washington D.C.: Brookings Institution.

Schott, J (2000). *The WTO after Seattle.* Washington D.C.: Institute for International Economics.

Schott, J (1996). WTO 2000: Setting the Course for World Trade. *Policy Analysis in International Economics,* No. 45 (September). Washington D.C.: Institute for International Economics.

Schott, J (1994). *The Uruguay Round: An Assessment.* Washington, DC: Institute for International Economics.

Stewart, T (1993). *The GATT Uruguay Round: A Negotiating History (1986–1992).* Deventer: Kluwer Law & Taxation.

Sutherland Report (2007). *The Future of the WTO.* Geneva: World Trade Organisation.

Winham, G (1986). *International Trade and the Tokyo Round Negotiations.* Princeton NJ: Princeton University Press.

Warwick Commission (2007). *The Multilateral Trade Regime: Which Way Forward?* The Report of the First Warwick Commission. Coventry: University of Warwick.

CHAPTER 10

GATT and the WTO

Susan K. Sell

The George Washington University

The hallmarks of the global trading system are robust institutional evolution and increasing complexity. Built from the misery of the Great Depression and the ashes of World War Two, post-war planners designed the multilateral trading system to re-engage the world's economies and yet still allow nations to preserve a significant measure of economic autonomy. The global trading system was enshrined in a compromise of 'embedded liberalism' (Ruggie, 2007). The 'embedded' aspect refers to the social bargain that reflected a Depression-era penchant for Keynesian-inspired government stimulus spending and a commitment to full employment and social safety nets. The idea was to permit some measure of autonomy to cushion national economies from global market fluctuations. The 'liberalism' component reflects the rejection of the economic nationalism and imperialism that led to global war in favour of multilateralism, economic liberalism and integration. The foundational underpinnings of the post-war global trade regime were transparency, multilateral diplomacy, and re-integration of the global economy. The Soviet Union and its satellite nations were invited to join the Bretton Woods institutions (which also included the International Monetary Fund and the International Bank for Reconstruction and Development), but declined. They established Eastern counterparts under COMECON instead. In that sense, the Bretton Woods institutions were less global than intended.

This chapter provides a brief historical overview and analysis of the role of the private sector in getting new issues into the trade regime in the Uruguay Round. Focusing on some North-South issues of contention, it goes on to discuss post-Uruguay controversies, forum-shifting, and some concluding concerns. Overall, the trade regime has grown increasingly complex and inequality persists in ways that make negotiations difficult.

HISTORICAL OVERVIEW

Participating nations adopted The General Agreement on Tariffs and Trade (GATT) treaty in 1949. At that time nations failed to establish an international trade organisation, however, the treaty aimed to get the world economy moving again after the economic nationalism and economic contraction of the interwar period that had cut world trade by nearly seventy percent.

GATT included important founding principles such as national treatment, the most-favoured-nation clause, and non-discrimination. National treatment committed treaty members to deal with imported goods no less favourably than domestically produced goods. For example, if domestic widgets were taxed at four percent, imported widgets had to be taxed at the same rate. National treatment was designed to prevent discrimination against foreign goods once they entered the domestic market. 'Most-favoured-nation' meant nations were obliged to treat all signatories as they did their 'most-favoured' ones. For instance, if treaty member Nation A gave treaty member Nation B a special deal, Nation A had to extend that deal to *all* treaty members. 'Non-discrimination' referred to 'at-the-border' measures. It meant signatories had to refrain from discriminating against others' goods when they entered their borders so that said goods could be accepted at the same tariff rates.

While the foundational principles that enshrined the multilateral approach helped reopen the world economy after World War Two, nations were also permitted sufficient flexibility to address their domestic concerns. The GATT included safeguards and escape clauses according to which members could be exempt from GATT strictures under specific conditions. Significantly, a number of tradable goods were completely off the table. The most glaring instance of this was agriculture. This omission was deliberate; GATT did not require states to liberalise their agricultural markets. Many argue that today agriculture remains the Achilles' heel of the multilateral trading system and is in large part responsible for the stalled Doha Round of multilateral trade negotiations discussed in the previous chapter.

Over time, through successive negotiating rounds, GATT has led to the increasing liberalisation of trade in goods and now services. In the beginning GATT negotiations focused on the simple issues — external tariffs. These are comparatively easy to address because they are highly visible and transparent. A twelve percent duty is a twelve percent duty, period. Early on, negotiators haggled item-by-item, but in the Kennedy Round between 1964 and 1967 negotiators adopted the more efficient method of reducing tariffs by *product category* rather than by item. This led to an unprecedented post-war reduction in tariffs.

As the international trading system continued to develop, more difficult problems began to arise. Beginning in the early 1970s, during the Tokyo Round of negotiations, GATT signatories started to address the problem of non-tariff barriers (NTBs). The Tokyo Round was the first that extensively addressed NTBs. It concluded with agreements covering technical barriers to trade, import licensing, government procurement, subsidies, countervailing duties, and customs valuations. NTBs are more opaque and difficult to detect. They often reflect domestic political commitments that are more resistant to multilateral pressure. Many countries, for example, have numerous health and environmental standards. Europeans do not wish to eat the hormone-fed beef that the United States produces. Europeans fear that the hormones will have negative health consequences. The United States (the US) argues that Europeans are discriminating against US beef and are therefore violating multilateral trade agreements. NTBs are problematic because it is not often easy to tell whether the NTB is, for example, a genuine health and safety issue or whether it is merely protectionism in disguise. In the 1980s the US and Japan engaged in heated trade conflicts over NTBs with each side accusing the other of cheating on everything from cars to apples to film to baseball bats.

Trade negotiations have gotten more difficult as negotiators have made great progress on 'at-the-border' issues like tariffs. Tariff negotiations are still thorny, especially given the remarkable economic diversity represented by the one hundred and forty-nine nations now participating. However, NTBs and other forms of possible trade discrimination, such as subsidies and export controls, often reach deep into domestic regulatory environments. Overturning them can threaten to destabilise delicate political bargains. Agricultural subsidies have become a particularly thorny issue in trade negotiations. As a result of the deeper reach of multilateral trade policy-making into domestic regulatory domains, multilateral trade rounds have gotten progressively longer. The Kennedy Round of 1964 to 1967 lasted only three years whereas the Uruguay Round lasted from 1986 to 1994. The Doha Round went to ten years and counting. Over time the mix of countries increased as well. It came to include a huge range of least developed countries, 'emerging markets', and new up-and-coming powerhouses like China, India and Brazil. During the Kennedy Round, sixty-two countries participated. In the Uruguay Round one hundred and twenty-three countries participated. The Doha Round, which began in 1999, included one hundred and forty-nine negotiating countries. All of these factors complicated multilateral trade policy-making.

Mainstream contemporary analysis of the politics of international trade tends to be light on the politics and long on the assumptions of rationalistic choice that Ralph Pettman outlined in his Introduction. Stemming from so-called neo-liberal institutionalism, and addressing the problem of 'cooperation under anarchy' (Oye, 1985), this branch of scholarship assumes that rationalist/liberalist actors freely enter into cooperative arrangements that make each other better off (so-called 'Pareto-optimisation'). What these analysts tend to neglect, however, is that over eighty percent of the world's population is poor. Their overwhelming focus on OECD countries blinds them to what the vast majority of the world's population face with regard to trade policy. When it is West African cotton farmers or governments seeking to provide low-cost effective generic medicines for their citizens, multilateral trade policy can look a lot less like a 'win-win' proposition and a lot more like a destructive imposition by the strong and rich. When former US Trade Representative Robert Portman famously announced in the wake of the disastrous Cancun negotiations in 2003 that the key distinction was between the 'Can Do' and the 'Won't Do' countries (or more accurately, 'wouldn't do what the US wanted them to do'), he betrayed both ignorance of and insensitivity to the plight of the poor. Perhaps more accurately the latter were (and are) 'Can't Do' nations — or maybe even 'Shouldn't Do' nations.

The problem is that the multilateral trading system was erected long before the majority of the world's countries could participate in it. At the time of GATT's founding many countries were still colonies and had yet to achieve independence. Those who stood to gain the most from an open trading system made the rules. The asymmetrical and self-serving circumstance of GATT's birth still lingers today in the World Trade Organisation (WTO) (Wilkinson, 2006). That is one of the major reasons for the volatility of the Doha Round that began in 1999. Inequality is baked into the cake.

Cognizant of this built-in bias in favour of wealthier nations, developing countries established in 1964 the United Nations Conference on Trade and Development as a counterpart to the 'rich man's club' that was GATT. UNCTAD produced studies and negotiating supports that reflected developing countries' concerns and GATT signatories eventually assented to some developing countries' requests for accommodation. In 1971, for example, GATT established a *Generalised System of Preferences* (GSP) that offered non-reciprocal market access for developing countries' goods. Richer signatories offered market access for particular goods and developing countries did not have to reciprocate. In practice, however, the GSP still exempted many goods where the developing countries were most competitive (including textiles — under the Multi-Fibre Arrangement — and various agricultural products).

Over time, and particularly after the oil price shocks and subsequent debt crises of the 1970s and 1980s, UNCTAD's role receded. As more countries adopted neo-liberal economic policies, UNCTAD was overshadowed by GATT and the International Monetary Fund (IMF).

WATERSHED: THE WORLD TRADE ORGANISATION

The Uruguay Round of GATT negotiations began in 1986 and ended in 1994. This round was distinctive in many ways. First of all, negotiators decided that it would be a 'single undertaking'. This meant that participants had to vote the entire package up or down; no longer could states opt for an *a la carte* approach to multilateral trade policy. Secondly, the negotiations featured an expanded agenda that included investment, services, and intellectual property. Private sector actors played unprecedented roles in pushing these new agenda items in the trade context. Thirdly, developing countries played far more prominent roles in the negotiating process than they had in past rounds (Watal, 2003; Singh, 2008). Fourthly, the negotiations resulted in the establishment of an international institution, the World Trade Organisation, that was given real enforcement powers. Fifthly, it was the most liberalising round in GATT history. Each of these features will be discussed in turn.

The institutional innovation of the single undertaking approach was a significant change. In the past GATT did not 'pinch very hard'. States were free to pick and choose which elements of trade agreements they would bind themselves to and which they would reject. State autonomy was not compromised in major ways. GATT agreements were voluntary. With the single undertaking approach, this more selective option was eradicated and with it the scope for state autonomy shrunk. In the Uruguay Round, if states wanted to be part of the multilateral trading regime they had to assent to all parts of the agreement.

Given the reduced autonomy produced by the single-undertaking approach, the introduction of new issues into GATT became very important. Private sector actors from OECD countries pushed very hard (with mixed success) to include their pet issues into the trade regime. In the Uruguay Round these issues: intellectual property, services, financial services, and investment, were now incorporated into the trade negotiations. Of these four issues, the private sector actors were most successful in developing extensive and binding multilateral intellectual property rules for member states.

The Agreement on Trade-Related Intellectual Property Rights (TRIPS) established extensive obligations for national legislators. Under TRIPS all member states were required to enact implementing legislation, adopt enforcement measures, offer patent owners a twenty-year monopoly right, and face the threat of trade sanctions if they failed to comply with the relevant provisions. This approach privileged the rights of property owners and raised the costs of information and technology. The short-term consequences were a significant transfer of resources from developing country consumers and firms to developed countries' firms. TRIPS represented a decisive victory for private sector interests and was not exactly a 'win' for developing countries.

Early in the negotiations, incorporating intellectual property into the trade regime was a hard sell. While the OECD pushed hard on behalf of its private sector software, its agricultural chemical, as well as entertainment and pharmaceutical firms, countries like Brazil and India argued that intellectual property policymaking belonged to the World Intellectual Property Organisation (WIPO) and not GATT. These countries knew that a trade-based intellectual property agreement would lead to unwelcome changes in their national legislation and cause them to compromise important domestic bargains such as keeping pharmaceutical products off-patent so that medicines remained affordable. By 1989, however, through a combination of US coercive economic pressure (the threat of trade sanctions) and the promise of better market access for agriculture and textiles, these countries ultimately assented to the incorporation of intellectual property into the trade regime. Indeed, they came to discover that the actual choice was no longer between WIPO and GATT, but rather between GATT and continued bilateral coercive economic pressure and the threat of trade sanctions. TRIPS established a one-size-fits-all regime for member states, although it did incorporate some flexibility to reserve some domestic policy space.

The efforts to incorporate trade in services fared less well. Beginning in the early 1970s the financial services sector, led by American Express and the insurance giant American International Group, invented the term 'trade in services' to bring investment squarely into the international trade regime (Dunoff, 2001, p. 103). The global growth in the trade in services and the intensification of competition in the larger markets sharpened service providers' concerns over differences in the domestic regulatory environments. OECD-based private sector actors sought expanded market access and the elimination of regulatory obstacles to a free trade in services. Many services depended on the proximity of the provider and the consumer and therefore required international direct investment to establish offices in host countries. OECD-based service providers were able to insert services into the trade regime, but the resulting General Agreement on Trade in Services (GATS) established a more tentative *a la carte* approach to services trade.

Developing countries, led by India and Brazil, protested over the inclusion of services in the Uruguay Round but agreed to negotiate a separate services agreement. GATS is a private sector victory insofar as the services trade is now embedded in the multilateral trade regime. The private sector lobbyists were ultimately disappointed with the results, however. They failed to achieve an ambitiously liberalising agreement, in part due to opposition from both developing countries and the Europeans. GATS is rather weak and dilutes the twin GATT pillars of non-discrimination: most-favoured-nation (MFN) status and national treatment. GATS signatories are free to include a list of sectors in an Annex to which GATS will not apply. Since GATS failed to open foreign markets to their satisfaction, US private sector actors did not get their wish. They sought, therefore, to maintain their negotiating leverage by invoking sectoral (or mirror-image) reciprocity — withholding MFN privileges from those competitors in restricted markets. National treatment was watered down through a 'positive list' approach in which national treatment applied only to those sectors listed in a member state's schedule of commitments. At the end of the day there was no significant rolling back of barriers to the services trade.

While negotiating the GATS, the financial services sector proved to be particularly challenging. Asian countries' reluctance to open their financial services sectors became a major sticking point. In the interests of keeping the GATS negotiations moving forward, participants agreed to negotiate basic principles and a separate financial services agreement after the conclusion of the Uruguay Round. Frustrated US negotiators walked out at the end of 1995 citing little progress towards opening Asian markets. Between 1995 and 1997, with the US absent, the Europeans took the lead in the negotiations and worked to narrow differences among the parties. They kept the negotiations alive and moving forward. By 1997 the Europeans succeeded in getting the US to rejoin the deliberations. The Asian currency crisis of July 1997 spurred an unexpected and successful conclusion to the negotiations. OECD governments and the International Monetary Fund urged Asian countries to adopt market-opening measures to inspire investor confidence. In the throes of the economic crisis and desperate for foreign capital, Asian countries finally assented to opening their financial services markets. US financial services firms Citicorp, Goldman Sachs, Merrill Lynch, and the insurance industries, set up command posts near the WTO and conferred with US negotiators throughout the talks. Negotiators reached a broadly liberalising Financial Services Agreement on 13 December 1997.

As in all the new issue areas, the US private sector spearheaded the effort to achieve a multilateral trade agreement on investment during the Uruguay Round. This was the least successful of its efforts to bring a new discipline to the trade regime. A number of factors stymied the effort and kept the agreement extremely weak. Developing countries opposed the inclusion of investment issues, so negotiators addressed Trade-Related Investment Measures (TRIMS) on a separate track. Countries with large markets, such as India and Brazil, had considerable negotiating leverage vis-à-vis potential foreign investors and were not eager to bind their own hands, that is, to give up their policy space and leverage. Fundamental disagreements between OECD members hampered progress on a meaningful accord as well. Splits between private sector actors and foreign policy makers in the US also meant that the US government was not on board with full-bore investment liberalisation. The US foreign policy-making community at times opted to ban investment from certain markets for security reasons (e.g., the Helms-Burton Act prohibited investment in Cuba and there was also the Iran-Libya Sanctions Act). The US also sought to reserve the right to discriminate with regard to its investments for national security purposes. TRIMS neither guaranteed the rights of establishment nor full national treatment for foreign investors. TRIMS was, in effect, a lowest-common-denominator approach to investment and failed to liberalise significantly.

As noted in the previous chapter, the most innovative change to the multilateral trading regime was the establishment of the WTO. The WTO was charged with administering all of the multilateral trade treaties, including GATT, GATS, TRIPS, TRIMS and the Financial Services Agreement. Most significantly, the WTO included a Dispute Settlement Mechanism (DSM) and a Dispute Settlement Body (DSB). Now trade disputes would be adjudicated through a formal, legalistic, and enforceable process. This meant that the multilateral trade regime 'pinched' much harder than before. Members were not free to ignore negative rulings and rules under the WTO constituted hard law. They were both legally binding and enforceable.

Many have argued that this rule-based system replaced the old power-based one and therefore that the new system was more equitable. Weaker parties could take stronger trade partners to the WTO if the latter violated the rules. The Dispute Settlement Body could review the case and make a judgment. If the stronger party was found to have violated the rules, the WTO could authorise the weaker party to apply trade sanctions against the stronger party. This institutional innovation did not eliminate fundamental power asymmetries, however. In principle it was supposed to reduce the bilateral economic coercion that the US exercised extensively throughout the Uruguay Round. The US continued to persist in exerting threats and pressure, however, and the EU began to apply such pressure as well. Some analysts have also pointed out that the dispute settlement mechanism was very expensive to use (an average case costing around three hundred thousand US dollars). This prevented poor countries from availing themselves of such an option (Shaffer, 2003, p. 148). While wealthier developing countries found it useful, less wealthy countries found it inaccessible.

With the WTO now administering 'hard' law that was truly enforceable and with the addition of numerous new disciplines within the trade regime, the Uruguay Round was the most liberalising round in the history of the multilateral trading regime. Committing more states than ever before to opening up their economies to trade in services, financial services, textile trade (through the agreed-upon phasing out of the protectionist Multi-Fibre Arrangement), it was this round that went a long way towards opening up the world economy. China became a member of the WTO and was bound by its rules. The fact that the Soviet Union collapsed at this time also meant that a number of former Eastern bloc nations were able to gain full membership and those that did not join may yet seek entry.

POST-URUGUAY CONTROVERSIES

The years since the conclusion of the Uruguay Round have been rocky for the world trade regime. The unexpectedly costly and controversial provisions, especially TRIPS, disillusioned developing countries. The unwanted bilateral economic pressure that the US exerted on them did not go away, despite the widespread expectation that a strong multilateral agreement would end such bilateral bullying. Europe followed suit and began exerting economic pressure in Economic Partnership Agreements (EPAs) to achieve Uruguay-plus trade concessions from weaker and more vulnerable partners. At the same time developing countries waited in vain for the promised agricultural liberalisation of OECD markets. New post-Uruguay pressure to add even more disciplines to the trading regime — the so-called 'Singapore issues' like competition policy and transparency in government procurement — came as an unwelcome shock to countries still reeling under the weight of their new Uruguay Round commitments.

In the wake of the Uruguay Round the fiercest controversy erupted over TRIPS. In the late 1990s sub-Saharan Africa was in the throes of a devastating HIV/AIDS pandemic. Brazil and Thailand also had significant HIV/AIDS-infected populations. TRIPS required all member states to offer patent protection for pharmaceutical products and restricted the conditions under which states could issue compulsory licenses (seizing a patent and compensating the owner). In response to their health crises, both South Africa and Thailand opted to invoke TRIPS Articles 30 and 31 that permitted compulsory licensing. Under these Articles, states were able to grant compulsory licenses for a patented product. In effect, the state could license another party to produce the patented product without the patent-holder's permission. Compulsory licensing permitted countries with a pharmaceutical manufacturing capacity to produce generic versions of drugs and thus to provide them more affordably.

In 1997 and 1998, Thailand planned to produce a generic version of a particular AIDS drug. The US, acting at the behest of the US-based Pharmaceutical Research and Manufacturing Association (PhRMA), threatened to impose sanctions on core Thai exports. In response Thailand dropped its compulsory licensing plans. Even though TRIPS permitted the planned Thai action, US threats deterred Thais from exercising their rights.

In December 1997, South African President Nelson Mandela signed into law the South African Medicines and Medical Devices Regulatory Authority Act. This law was broadly designed to relinquish apartheid legacies with regard to medical care. It authorised the Minister of Health to issue compulsory licenses for manufacturing generic HIV/AIDS drugs; again, a practice that was permissible under TRIPS. Article 15c of the Act permitted parallel-importing so that South Africa could take advantage of discriminatory pricing-policies and import the cheapest available patented medicines. Notably, parallel-importing is perfectly TRIPS-compliant. The PhRMA, however, feared South Africa's potential as a competitive generic drug supplier and angrily denounced the new law. Forty-two local licensees of the PhRMA filed a suit challenging the legislation in Pretoria's High Court. By 1998 the US Trade Representative was backing the PhRMA, had placed

South Africa on its 301 Watch list, and had urged South Africa to repeal its Medicines Act. In June of 1998 the US suspended South Africa's duty-free treatment under the US Generalised System of Preferences.

The South Africa case inflamed HIV/AIDS activists in South Africa and a grassroots Treatment Access Campaign (TAC) engaged in social mobilisation to oppose the PhRMA's heavy-handed approach. Soon TAC was joined by an international coalition of public health activists and NGOs including Medecins san Frontieres, Consumer Project on Technology, and Health Action International. In the US the AIDS Coalition to Unleash Power (ACT UP) mobilised a protest against the Clinton administration's PhRMA-friendly policy towards South Africa. Compelling arguments about the way preventing access to affordable medicines led to unnecessary deaths presented the stakes in the starkest of terms. The US support of the PhRMA looked to many like a preference for pharmaceutical profits over saving lives. ACT UP ultimately targeted then-Vice President Albert Gore's presidential campaign, protesting using noisemakers and banners that said "Gore's Greed Kills!" Within one week of ACT UP's activities on the campaign trail, the Clinton Administration withdrew two years' worth of harassment towards South Africa over its Medicines Act. After a barrage of negative publicity, the PhRMA ultimately dropped its lawsuit against South Africa in March 2001.

Brazil also exercised its rights under TRIPS. It repeatedly threatened compulsory licensing in its negotiations with drug companies to encourage them to drop their prices. Brazil provided anti-retroviral drugs free to HIV/AIDS patients as a matter of public policy. The US threatened Brazil with a WTO challenge at the behest of its non-generic pharmaceutical firms. Brazil refused to back down and the US finally withdrew its case in June 2001.

The African Group, India, and Brazil worked together to address the HIV/AIDS issues in the context of TRIPS. They sought clarification of the conditions under which they were permitted to issue compulsory licenses. The US aggressively challenged virtually every instance of states trying to avail themselves of the flexibilities afforded by TRIPS, while developing countries sought a declaration that said that nothing in TRIPS should prevent member states from taking steps to protect public health.

Meanwhile, the post-Uruguay road to a new trade round was rocky indeed. At the 1996 Singapore Ministerial meeting, Europe and the US raised four new issues that they sought to add to the next round of trade negotiations: trade facilitation (customs issues); transparency in government procurement; trade and investment (since TRIMS was so weak); and trade and competition. Developing countries protested the inclusion of these new issues as they were just starting to absorb the impact of the WTO agreements. Since the OECD had yet to make good on the Uruguay promises, the developing countries were in no mood to embrace yet another costly agenda. A certain amount of distrust permeated all the discussions.

In 1999 the Seattle Ministerial meeting that was to launch the next trade round collapsed in the so-called 'Battle in Seattle'. Violent protests and sharp disputes between the Europeans and the US abruptly shut the meeting down.

Member states successfully launched a new trade round at the Doha Ministerial meeting in November 2001. Referred to as the 'Doha Development Agenda' the round was sold as an effort to respond to those concerns of developing countries that had arisen as a result of the Uruguay one. To them the post-Uruguay gains felt one-sided with the US continuing to aggressively push its preferred intellectual property policies through bilateral and regional trade negotiations. Clearly the US was promoting something that went above and beyond TRIPS.

At the outset of the November 2001 Doha meeting the developing country public health coalition announced that it would refuse to negotiate any of the industrialised countries' agenda items unless they first agreed to a declaration on TRIPS and public health. The timing was propitious. In the wake of the terrorist attacks on the US on 11 September 2001, mysterious packets of anthrax were sent around the US. Both Canada and the US were eager to have ample stockpiles of Bayer's drug Cipro, the only effective treatment for anthrax. Canada and the US both threatened Bayer with the compulsory licensing of Cipro. Bayer subsequently dropped its prices and assured governments that it would provide the drug. The irony of the US and Canada threating to issue compulsory licenses in response to the prospect of a handful of deaths and the US's harassment of developing countries seeking to do the very same in response to tens of thousands of deaths was lost on no one. Finally, on the third day of the Doha ministerial meeting, negotiators agreed to the Doha Declaration on TRIPS and Public Health. The Declaration affirmed members' rights to issue compulsory licenses and the freedom to determine grounds for such licenses. This episode illustrated developing countries pushing back after the Uruguay Round.

In the new round, developing countries remained mobilised and on guard for Uruguay-style inclusion of new issues that seemed devoid of benefit for them. They also remained focused on ensuring that developed countries finally make good on their Uruguay promises of agricultural market access. At the 2003 Cancun ministerial, developing countries firmly opposed the incorporation of the so-called 'Singapore issues'. A number of think tanks and NGOs provided them with extensive analyses that highlighted the negative impact that the investment agreements would have on their economies (Kellow and Murphy, 2010, p. 239). The stalemate over investment contributed to the acrimonious collapse of the Cancun negotiations.

Agricultural market access was another flashpoint in Cancun. Negotiating as the G21, developing countries opposed agricultural subsidies and singled out developed country cotton subsidies as particularly damaging to West African cotton growers. The Europeans and the Japanese continued to insist on including the 'Singapore issues'. Meanwhile, the less-developed countries refused to agree to lower their tariffs on non-agricultural goods, much to the chagrin of US trade representatives.

After the collapse of Cancun, the head of WTO, Pascal Lamy, wrote a letter to WTO members pledging to drop the 'Singapore issues'. The letter reflected a widespread consensus that progress on agricultural issues would be essential to keep negotiations going forward. The developing countries sought progress on agriculture, special and differential treatment, technical assistance, and capacity building. Concerns for special and differential treatment arose in the light of the difficulty many countries faced in implementing their Uruguay Round obligations. Developing countries wanted more technical assistance and capacity building to help them fulfil their Uruguay obligations before agreeing to new issues. Led by Brazil, China and India, they demanded an end to agricultural subsidies.

Tensions over these issues continue. In 2008, at negotiations over the Doha Development Agenda in Geneva, developing countries called for an end to agricultural subsidies and India and China sought the right to raise tariffs to protect their farmers in cases of import surges or price declines (Special Safeguard Mechanism). OECD countries balked at reducing subsidies further and pressed for reduced barriers to non-agricultural imports and services.

With the ongoing global financial crisis stoking a renewed interest in protectionism, the Doha Round remained contentious. The rising economic powerhouses of China, India, and Brazil were shifting the tectonic plates that underpinned post-World War Two trade policy. And economic tensions bedevilled the cohesion of the G20 (the industrialised countries), that is, there were differences in approach to economic recovery in the wake of the 2007 financial meltdown.

In November 2010, at the G20 and the Asia-Pacific Economic Cooperation (APEC) summits, world leaders called for a more forward moving Doha Round. They pressed negotiators to conclude the Round in 2011. After nearly a decade the negotiators still had not been able to resolve major outstanding issues. The US was pressing for much greater access to Brazilian, Chinese and Indian markets. These emerging economic powerhouses resisted these demands, however. Dissatisfied with the failure of the US and Europe to reduce agricultural subsidies and various agricultural supports, a pervasive sense of inequity coloured the talks. Developing countries argued that they were being asked to make much deeper commitments than the US and Europe and that the relative sacrifices were inequitable. Clearly the post-Uruguay experience heightened sensitivity to unequal deals. If industrialised countries wanted to insist on deep reductions in tariffs on non-agricultural goods, they were called on to reciprocate with deeper cuts in agricultural subsidies. While some of the agricultural controversies cut across North-South lines (and reflected exporters' versus importers' interests), the G20 agricultural developing countries pressed back hard on sectors such as US cotton. Brazil's success at the WTO over US cotton subsidies gave this challenge momentum. No matter what, however, the negotiators had a tough road ahead to arrive at an acceptable deal for all parties.

FORUM-SHIFTING

Simultaneous bilateral and regional trade deals added further complexity to these multilateral trade negotiations. Frustrated by the slow pace of the multilateral trade negotiation process, many countries entered into less cumbersome bilateral and regional agreements. These agreements ran parallel to the multilateral processes and frequently involved deals between highly unequal partners. These agreements also tended to feature provisions and disciplines that went well beyond the WTO agreements. For example, US bilateral and regional trade and investment agreements with weaker parties invariably required intellectual property provisions that were far more restrictive and encompassing than those TRIPS required. These deals tended to reduce developing countries' flexibility (for example, by prohibiting parallel importing or sharply restricting the conditions under which states might issue compulsory licenses). At the same time they increased developing countries' commitments to protect things that were not covered in TRIPS or they extended coverage for longer periods of time than TRIPS required.

In order to seek a better deal, parties sometimes shifted forums to press their agendas in more hospitable negotiating venues. Parties shifted horizontally, from one multilateral venue to another, as the US did, in order to bring intellectual property from WIPO into GATT. Or they shifted vertically, from multilateral to regional and to bilateral forums. Stronger parties with larger markets pressed for more concessions in these vertical forum shifts (Benevisti and Downs, 2007). For instance, during the Uruguay Round industrialised countries were unhappy with the weakness of TRIMS. In a vertical forum shift, therefore, they entered into plurilateral negotiations among like-minded parties. They moved away from the transparency and glare of the WTO. Although the Multilateral Agreement on Investment (MAI) negotiations ultimately broke down, they were an attempt to achieve a much more liberalising agreement on investment. Similarly, after all the focus on access to HIV/AIDS medicines in the WTO, industrialised countries, led by the US, shifted back over to WIPO in an effort to get stronger intellectual property rights than TRIPS allowed. Industrialised countries pressed to negotiate a Substantive Patent Law Treaty (SPLT) in WIPO that offered higher levels of and more extensive protection than TRIPS. Developing countries countered by insisting on negotiating a Development Agenda within WIPO. Having mobilised around the medicines issue in the WTO, developing countries sought more consideration of their development concerns and a recalibrated balance between private property rights in knowledge-goods and access to innovation and affordable medicines. Playing hardball as they had at Doha, they refused to discuss the SPLT unless the industrialised countries first addressed their development and access concerns in WIPO.

Rebuffed in WIPO, industrialised countries shifted forums again in their quest to raise international property protection. Just as in the case of the MAI, industrialised countries vertically shifted from the multilateral WIPO to the pluri-lateral Anti-Counterfeiting Trade Agreement (ACTA) negotiations. These non-transparent negotiations sought to codify intellectual property protections of a kind far beyond TRIPS. The ACTA included plans for an enforcement body like the Dispute Settlement Body in WTO. If parties agreed to ACTA this raised questions about the latter's relationship to the WTO and WIPO and the role these two organisations might play in intellectual property going forward. Undoubtedly, ACTA provisions will continue to appear in US and EU bilateral and regional trade agreements. Thus ACTA provisions are likely to be imposed upon the majority of developing countries. Europe and the US are also pursuing a Trans-Pacific Partnership Agreement (TPP) that seeks to go even further than ACTA in guaranteeing higher levels of intellectual property protection. Just as in the TRIPS case, however, it is private sector intellectual property holders, seeking more protection of their movies, music, software, drugs and profits, who are driving this particular process.

CONCLUSION

The trade regime is increasingly complex. A persistent sense of inequality means that the relatively simple and straightforward early days of the GATT are long past.

Recent developments also highlight the way mainstream analysts who depict multilateral, regional, and bilateral trade agreements as contract stories of rational actors arriving at mutually beneficial 'win-win' solutions obscure important aspects of contemporary trade relations. It is these stories that inspire perspectives like Robert Portman's. It was his account of 'Can Do' versus 'Won't Do' countries, that is, that arguably resulted in the Cancun collapse of 2003. It was his account that obscured the fact that 'Can't Do' and 'Shouldn't Do' countries make up the majority of WTO members. 'Can't Do' countries lack the capacity to implement agreements or may be politically constrained from doing so. Thinking of 'Shouldn't Do' countries alerts us to the very real distributive consequences of trade deals and the fact that, while there are winners, there are many losers as well. Even if aggregate welfare increases with the successful completion of a trade round, the highly skewed distribution of that welfare is a fundamentally political issue that goes a long way towards accounting for increasing multilateral stalemates and protracted and contentious negotiations. The next chapter of the trade regime will feature a much larger role for Brazil, India and China and much greater pressure on the US and Europe to accommodate the formers' interests. It will not be dull.

REFERENCES

Benevisti, E and G Downes (2007). The empire's new clothes: Political economy and the fragmentation of international law, *Stanford Law Review*, 60(2), 595.

Dunoff, J (2001). The WTO in transition: Of constituents, competence and coherence, *George Washington University International Law Review*, 33(3), 983.

Kellow, A and H Murphy (2010). Democratic Accountability in Global Governance: Business and Civil Society in Multiple Arenas. In *The Challenges of Global Business Authority*, T Porter and K Ronit (eds.). Albany: State University of New York Press.

Odell, J (ed.) (2006). *Negotiating Trade: Developing Countries in the WTO and NAFTA*. Cambridge: Cambridge University Press.

Oye, K (ed.) (1986). *Cooperation under Anarchy*. Princeton: Princeton University Press.

Ruggie, J (2007). Global Markets and Global Governance: The Prospects for Convergence. In *Global Liberalism and Political Order: Toward a New Grand Compromise?* S. Bernstein and L Pauly (eds.). Albany: State University of New York Press.

Sell, S and A Prakash (2004). Using ideas strategically: The contest between business and NGO networks in intellectual property rights, *International Studies Quarterly*, 48, 143–175.

Shaffer, G (2003). *Defending Interests: Public-Private Partnerships in WTO Litigation*. Washington D.C.: Brookings Institution.

Singh, J (2008). *Negotiation and the Global Information Economy*. Cambridge: Cambridge University Press.

Wilkinson, R (2006). *The WTO: Crisis and the Governance of Global Trade*. London: Routledge.

CHAPTER 11

Containerisation

Lance Hoovestal

University of Melbourne

The post-World War Two liberalist framework achieved at Bretton Woods offered both freedom and openness. This was essential for the development of a new era of global trade.

From this approach, however, emerged one innovation that is arguably the most uncelebrated of the twentieth century. This innovation altered global trade more than any other and is none other than the freight container.

This technological advance transformed the global economy by becoming the core component in a complex system that spectacularly lowered the cost and time of transporting goods globally. Indeed, the container was such a dynamic force that it left nothing about the world market untouched.

In itself the freight container is an unimpressive piece of equipment. It is simply a steel box bound by welds and rivets, with two doors at one end. The container is not mysterious; nonetheless, no technological innovation in sea transport is more significant. This is why many call this twenty-foot long (6.1 metres), eight-foot wide (2.4 metres), and eight and a half-foot tall (2.6 metres) instrument the 'heart of the global economy'.

In the late 1930s a young US trucking entrepreneur named Malcom McLean grew increasingly frustrated with the laborious, costly and slow process of cargo loading and unloading. This led McLean to search for a more effective and efficient way to handle cargo. His idea was to carry loaded trailer trucks aboard ships in a coastal service.

THE INVENTION OF THE CONTAINER

What distinguished McLean's thinking from that of previous entrepreneurs was his desire to radically simplify the whole process. He sought to improve bulk shipping by reducing the whole process to a single system in which every part was interrelated and had an explicit function (Kendall and Buckley 1994; Levinson, 2006). As with many such innovations this one was met with strong industry resistance.

Despite such resistance, however, on April 26, 1956, a partially converted World War Two vintage tanker, the *Ideal X*, departed from Port Newark, New Jersey, for Houston, Texas. McLean and one hundred dignitaries watched as two revolving cranes with booms seventy-two feet (21.9 metres) above the dock moved on tracks parallel to the *Ideal X*, placing a container on board every seven minutes. The ship was loaded in less than eight hours and McLean and his executives flew to Houston to watch its arrival. There they all watched as the tanker arrived with the boxes on its deck loaded with cargo.

For McLean, however, the real triumph came when the costs were tallied. Loading loose cargo in 1956 onto a medium-size cargo ship cost US$5.83 per ton. McLean's experts pegged the cost of loading the *Ideal X* at US$0.15 per ton.

Suddenly, it was economically viable to ship machine parts from Japan, for example and sell them at a price North Americans could pay. The time it took to unload a freighter also dropped — from weeks to days — thus enabling ships to carry more cargo and not sit idly in port.

McLean's crucial insight led to a concept quite different from anything that had been done before. He understood the ramifications that containerisation would have for world transport and the global economy as a whole. He appreciated that reducing the cost of shipping goods required not just a metal box but an entirely new way of handling freight. Every part of the system, including ports, ships, cranes, storage facilities, trucks, trains, and the operation of all these systems together, had to change. This brought the container to the forefront of contemporary technology. McLean's insights ushered in a change so dramatic that even the experts at the International Container Bureau, (originally the Bureau International des Conteneurs (BIC), who had been pushing containers for decades, were astonished at what he achieved (Cudahy, 2006; Levinson, 2006).

Levinson (2006, pp. 1–2) writes that the "value of this utilitarian object lies not in what it is, but in how it is used. The container is at the core of a highly automated system for moving goods from anywhere, to anywhere, with a minimum of cost and complication along the way". It greatly simplified the trans-shipment of goods from one form of transport to another, increasing the security of shipments and reducing the time and cost involved in moving freight over long distances. Moreover, it dramatically improved the efficiency with which manufactured and processed goods could be shipped to anywhere in the world, thus transforming the entire shape and content of global trade.

With the arrival of the shipping container the cost of shipping fell sharply since ships could be loaded by a several dozen longshoremen instead of hundreds. Pilferage and breakage also greatly decreased since it was no longer necessary to construct wooden crates to shelter individual items. It became practical, that is, to ship consumer goods of all sorts around the globe. International shipping increased accordingly, given the growth in the potential volume of the goods it became possible to ship (*The Economist*, 1997). Factories were also able to move to cheaper locations and away from crowded city ports such as New York City and the London Docks. Container terminals did not have to be located near large population centres. All they needed was space, railway access, good roads, and workers prepared to handle the containers. Many stevedores in the older ports did not have these things, nor did these ports have the infrastructure to handle the carriers of containers (*The Economist*, 1997). Many did, however, and these were the ones which brought about the container revolution.

As already indicated, the consequences of the container for global trade were immediately apparent. In the mid-1970s, for example, it took twenty-four hours to ship ten billion US dollars worth of international trade. In the contemporary world, by contrast, that amount gets shipped in one second. The world's largest trading nation, the US, received more than ten million containers at its seaports in 2007 or approximately twenty-eight thousand containers every day. Containers now account for approximately ninety percent of the world's traded cargo by value.

Consequences like these affirm the container as the primary reason for the growth of new industries, products, production processes, delivery systems, and wealth creation regimes. These new industries and systems constitute in turn the key single consequence of the container: economic globalisation.

THE CONTAINER AND INTERCONNECTEDNESS

The container underpins the contemporary world economy's interconnectedness. This interconnectedness brings together ideas, labour, capital, services, and goods without regard to national borders. Its victims have resisted these technologies, or are simply unable to adopt them because they are omitted from the key demand and supply chains. Its beneficiaries, however, have utilised computers to guide container networks to create an integrated global economy. The web of transport they now have traversing the world via oceans, rail, or highways has engendered an explosion of global trade and a change in the market of a kind not seen since the early days of the industrial revolution. In the contemporary world the principal dynamics of globalisation — open markets, free trade, transnational corporations (TNCs) scanning the globe in search of more cost efficient production sites — are all predicated upon a world container shipping system with sufficient capacity to move products to global markets (Dicken, 2003; Levinson, 2006).

Globalisation can be depicted in various ways since it is not a single system. Basically, however, globalisation denotes global interdependence. Along with economic interdependence, which consists of trade, finance, and interdependence in terms of direct investment, there are forms of interdependence with regard to education, technology, ideology, culture, the environment, judiciaries, military strategies and diplomatic relations. Our current age is unlike any other since earlier ages imposed formidable constraints on the velocity and volume of global interdependence.

Though globalisation is described in diverse ways, as Dicken (2003) argues it has one fundamental aspect: the development of transportation and communications technologies that have overcome the friction represented by time and space. Neither of these areas of technology can be regarded as the cause of globalisation. Without them, however, today's complex global market system simply could not exist. Transportation and communication technologies perform two distinct though closely related and complementary roles. Communications systems are the means by which information is transmitted from place to place in the form of ideas, instructions and images. Transportation systems are the means by which materials, products and other tangible entities, including people, are transferred from place to place.

No matter how globalisation is depicted, one issue remains constant, namely, the way leaps in technological innovation, such as the advent of the computer and the freight container, have been major catalysts in creating the contemporary globalisation phenomenon. Today, globalisation is an undeniable reality. Moreover, it is the main contemporary characteristic of world trade.

TRANSNATIONAL CORPORATIONS

At this point it is worth noting how out of the post-World War Two strategic and economic environment there arose a momentous global actor, the transnational corporation (TNC). Through their decisions either to invest or not to invest in particular geographical locations, TNCs have become key shapers of the contemporary political economy and of the globalisation process. They are also the main users of the freight container. The container allows TNCs to maintain an efficient flow of materials, components and finished products between dispersed operation centres. It is their material lifeblood.

TNCs and the state are fundamentally linked since TNCs are corporations, that is, legal entities formerly subordinate to the state. In principle the state controls corporations, subjects them to taxes, and entangles them in regulations and restrictions. In practice, however, TNCs break these shackles by becoming part of the integrated world economy and by moving their operations accordingly. This allows them to escape burdensome sovereign state controls, to search for workers who cost less, to search for favourable tax environments and raw material supplies, and to look for new markets for their goods and services. In this sense, TNCs are rootless and shapeless and cannot be corralled by state institutions. Most of the world's largest TNCs hail from developed nations. However, the 'nationality' of TNCs is typically obscured by the extent to which they have foreign affiliates in the developing world. In a sense TNC currency deals and market manipulations take place in a vacuum, where no international body prevails. TNCs can truly be said to be 'masterless'. They are arguably the true masters of those who make states.

The proliferation of TNCs and of international production following World War Two reflected a world in which capital and technology had become increasingly mobile while labour remained relatively immobile. The advantages TNCs sought included low-cost skilled labour, greater proximity to key markets, and investment incentives such as corporate tax advantages. The result of the resulting internationalisation of industrial production created a novel web of interlocking relationships among states and TNCs.

TNC's have the capacity to seek low-cost inputs to production by exploiting geographical differences in prevailing wages. Critics claim that when TNCs take advantage of geographical differences in wages they stimulate competitive bidding for their mobile investments. They argue that this results in the exploitation of labour worldwide as wages are driven down. The link between globalisation and cheap labour, critics say, has contributed to the "globalisation of poverty" (Wilkins, 1998; Dicken, 2003).

This has been accompanied by the reshaping of the economies in developing nations and the redefinition of their role in the new world economic order. National level economic reforms are implemented concurrently in a large number of individual countries. The global economy is nourished accordingly by the 'race-to-the-bottom' (RTB) and the relocation of significant portions of advanced nations' industries to parts of the world where work is made cheap.

The 'reform and opening' of China's economy in 1978 allowed China to utilise its huge supply of cheap labour in order to attract the foreign direct investment (FDI) which TNCs offer and to become an integral part of the world economy. The production structure in East Asia has been fundamentally altered due to China's ability to attract increasing amounts of FDI from other East Asian economies. This is due to China's almost unlimited pool of cheap labour and pro-business FDI policies. FDI's most immediate contribution lies in the movement of monies from mature industries in source economies to countries like China. The majority of these industries fall into labour-intensive and export-oriented categories, for example, Amway, Apple, AT&T, Audi, Canon, Estee Lauder, General Electric, General Motors, Gillete, Heinz, Honda, IBM, Ikea, Kraft, Nike, Panasonic, Sony, Toshiba, Toyota, Walmart, just name a few. 'Made in China' demonstrates a strong competitive advantage in international markets because the commodities concerned embody the best blend of Asian resources, including, for example, intellectual innovation from the research and development (R&D) departments of

Tokyo, Shanghai and Singapore, cheap rubber from Indonesia, and cheap labour from China. All these resources are allocated and manipulated by TNCs to cater for their interests, the most important of which are cost minimisation and profit maximisation.

Alliances between local strategic and economic elites and TNCs have inevitably mixed cooperation with conflict, as each set of actors leverage their power to gain the most from the alliance. In many cases, local elites form alliances with TNCs that are characterised by outright bribery and illicit campaign contributions. The common citizens who stay outside these alliances can suffer greatly from the distorted policies they create. Other critics focus on the process of 'denationalisation', where foreign capital absorbs local assets. This process is characterised by TNCs exploiting profit-making opportunities in developing countries, expatriating the profits to their home countries and developing indigenous industries and firms. Perhaps most significant is the effect of competition for international capital on national governments. Local, state, and national governments engage in bidding wars to attract TNCs and their unique resources. TNCs scour the globe for investment opportunities, pitting governments against each another, forcing political leaders to decide between fiscal policy autonomy and attracting FDI. TNCs must be considered in the light of their exceptional mobility. They are able to petition national governments to gain political favours in the form of tax breaks and an agreeable regulatory environment. The flexibility of contemporary TNCs allows them to effectively create competitions between states for their investment.

THE 'RACE-TO-THE-BOTTOM'

The 'race-to-the-bottom' epitomises such a world, namely, one in which state responsibilities have shrunk and the reach and influence of the private sector has expanded. A major concern of policy makers and researchers is that private sector FDI may relocate inferior, low-wage jobs from high-income countries to labour-abundant economies, forcing a competitive and comprehensive downward decline in wages all around. Essentially, TNCs play off one state against another while states themselves strive to outbid their rivals to capture or retain particular TNC activities. The concerns regarding the RTB are part of a more general apprehension that when negotiations for investment occur between large companies and small countries, the weak, poor countries will yield to unreasonable demands from the stronger corporations.

The RTB issue places labour market dynamics at the forefront of the globalisation debate. This global competition generates pressure to lower wages and labour standards across the world. Pressure arises, for example, when TNCs seek to escape from compromise and transfer operations to lower-cost foreign sites in which there are no collective and other labour rights of the kind that are recognised in prosperous, industrialised states. National and TNC competition generates cost minimisation strategies which have potentially unfavourable effects on wages and on the conditions of employment. The risk of plant relocation or investing abroad rather than at home offers leverage which owners of FDI can utilise against workers and governments alike. In the process, the regulatory capacity of governments is weakened, providing more opportunities to compete for more FDI and export markets.

The RTB is a brutal and well-known global reality in which critics say poor countries end up the net losers. The RTB can nonetheless be seen as a positive dynamic for developing nations for several reasons. These include the behaviour of TNCs in poor countries and the behaviour of the unions and their allies in rich countries. Though lower labour standards exist in poor countries, this does not necessarily mean TNCs take advantage of them. The gains to be made by doing so can be outweighed by several other factors, particularly those to do with reputation. TNCs, which account for an overwhelming percentage of FDI in poor countries, cannot necessarily afford to be seen unloading hazardous substances into the environment or treating their workers badly. With developing, and in some cases functioning democracies in many poor countries, plus the growth of non-governmental organisations (NGOs) and instantaneous global communication networks, the probability that TNCs will engage in practices that might diminish their reputation and ultimately their profits is relatively small. The consequences for their reputation of profiting from host-country negligence are sufficient enough to outweigh, for many TNCs, the extra profits that might be made by the 'taking advantage' strategy.

The RTB dynamic is manifest at a time when human affairs are undergoing a process of globalisation. The world is experiencing greater cultural and economic integration, that is taking place along with a progressive decentralisation of authority and fragmentation of society. These global shifts are underpinned by the penetration of economic market relations into many aspects of global life. The proliferating global economy reduces institutions to instruments in the global dispersal of the market economy. The synergy of the market and the state is furthered by a global system of governance which is largely manifest in the form of rules that embody the rationale of market-oriented growth. While government and TNC collaboration is clearly apparent, and may even be necessary, the global RTB dynamic demonstrates the market's ability to both unify and fragment by placing more intense demands on the state. The state now finds itself confronted with more elaborate layers of organisation which traverse its territorial boundaries while TNCs become less dependent on the state for a wider range of economic functions.

States undoubtedly face a major dilemma in this regard. If they do not join the economic bidding battle they face the very real probability of being left out of TNCs' investment plans and thus left out of a greater role in the global economy. Many of the small low-income and lower-middle income nations must increasingly ask themselves whether they should surrender control to TNCs. Within the RTB paradigm governments are increasingly compelled to offer greater incentives and forfeit elements of their sovereignty due to the relentless competition to attract and retain TNCs (Dicken, 2003; Mehmet, 2006).

Dicken (2003, p. 304) writes that ultimately "the relationship between TNCs and host countries revolves around their relative bargaining power: the extent to which each can implement their own preferred strategies". Underpinning the bargaining power process, however, sits the fundamental fact that states and TNCs need one another. States need TNCs to help in the process of material wealth creation while TNCs need states to provide the infrastructures, both physical and institutional, that can support their profit-making pursuits.

RE-ENTER THE CONTAINER AND SUPPLY-AND-SALE NETWORKS

Re-enter the container. This did not bring TNCs and the issues they give rise to onto the world scene. It did, however, dramatically amplify the extraordinary degree to which they affect the contemporary world.

Following World War Two global trade quickly began to outstrip its pre-war equivalent. A particularly revealing aspect of the worldwide reorganisation of capitalist production was the shift of manufacturing capacity from the established high-income countries to the lower-income newly industrialised countries (NICs). The advanced economies of Europe, Japan, and the US began to be linked significantly through trade flows after the 1960s. The falling communication and transport costs allowed for a 'dividing up' of the 'value chain' of production. Different stages of the production process came to be carried out in different parts of the world, depending on the comparative advantages offered by various production sites. Advances in communications and transportation, such as developments in computer technology and, most notably, transport technology (the container) meant that the organisational and cost issues that had previously impeded the relocation of industries were largely resolved.

In the contemporary world globalisation presents in the form of novel production and distribution processes. It is manifest in the form of myriad world industries that now source supplies from all the corners of the globe and sell them likewise. In this picture the humble container is the central and essential feature. As producers have sought to reduce the cost of their products, for example, they have created global supply-and-sale chains where semi-assembled and semi-finished components are routinely shipped in containers across oceans and borders to be finished elsewhere and sold on — potentially to anywhere.

The majority of containers moving around the world today hold not finished products but industrial components such as synthetic resins, engine parts, waste-paper, screws, and other intermediate goods. The supply lines needed to deliver these components cheaply to the right factory at the right time are not highlighted by the TNCs that use them. Nor are they evident to consumers. Nonetheless, they are the hidden backbone to the global political economy.

Supply-and-sale networks have evolved largely to exploit the availability of the raw materials which particular countries offer, to benefit from labour cost differences, and to realise global product-differentiation opportunities. The container is the key technological item that facilitates these networks. It continues to transform global production and distribution. It allows producers to outsource ever greater amounts of their manufacturing processes and to augment their profits in the process. It also allows them to reach ever more remote points of sale. The container, in short, has made possible many new possibilities with regard to inputs and outputs. For example, when relative labour costs in Japan increased, Singaporean labour rates became more attractive. This, combined with an acute decrease in the costs of transportation due to containerisation, allowed Japanese TNCs to develop new ways of organising and managing their businesses. These innovations led to competitive advantages which were manifest in a reliance on specialist outside suppliers and the ability to operate a truly global production system. These characteristics are readily seen in contemporary global supply chains and in the world's manufacturing and sale systems.

Supply-and-sale networks are inherently complex, both from a structural and an operational perspective. They display the characteristics of complex systems since a large number of firms may be operating simultaneously with many supply-and-sale partners, interacting using a variety of information and material flows. The layout of supply-and-sale chains largely determines the level of process complexity. Complex production processes require a greater volume of information monitoring. This is evident in systems such as 'just-in-time' (JIT) manufacturing. The JIT concept, which began with the Toyota Motor Company in Japan after the 1973 oil shock, seeks to increase quality and efficiency through the elimination of large inventories. Rather than store costly inventory itself Toyota chose to rely on freight containers that would arrive 'just-in-time', essentially using the container as a mobile warehouse. This cut costs. In economic terms, inventories represent waste. Whether sitting on warehouse shelves or on the deck of a ship, their owners must pay for them but they have not yet sold them. They incur costs while they wait. The primary objective of the Toyota production system was to reduce this cost and to eliminate the consequent waste. Waste in production takes different forms: excessive production of resources, overproduction, unnecessary capital investment, and excessive inventory. Waste in production for Toyota was regarded as the main type of waste due to its excessive inventories. Extra inventory creates unnecessary capital investment such as extra labour, equipment, and the facilities needed to transport and stock it. With JIT, Toyota was being innovative in a number of ways. For example, rather than make most of its own components, as its competitors did, Toyota signed long-term contracts with outside suppliers. The suppliers became radically involved with Toyota. They aided in production design and became well-versed with the details of Toyota's production plans. Toyota also sought to eliminate the testing time of supplier components before use as well as requiring suppliers to adopt strict quality standards with very low rates of error. The suppliers agreed to make their goods in small quantities, as required by Toyota's assembly lines, and to deliver them within very specific time frames for immediate use, hence the name, just-in-time. Keeping inventory to a minimum brought discipline to the entire manufacturing process. With little inventory, however, there was little margin for error, forcing every firm in the supply chain to perform at optimum capacity. Moreover, the savings in freight costs, in inventory costs, and in the time-to-market, resulted in ever-longer supply-and-sale chains.

In the pre-container era a multi-dimensional process like this would have been impossible to sustain. High transportation costs would have prohibited it. They would have acted as trade barriers in the same way high tariffs impede imports.

Today, however, it is common for a single supply chain to have up to two thousand third-tier (raw material) suppliers. Where transportation costs remain high they may shelter the jobs of production workers from foreign competition. This can however impose higher prices on consumers.

The global supply chain is a system whose components include material suppliers, production facilities, distribution services, and customers linked together through the feed-forward flow of materials and the feed-back flow of information. As a consequence numerous analysts have stated that contemporary competition now takes place, not between individual companies but between supply-and-sale chains (New and Westbrook, 2004; Donovan, 2004).

National wealth creation is a synergy of intricate social and economic processes that interface within the global environment. There are many arguments as to the factors determining why some cities, regions and nations are rich and some poor.

Myer (1996) has reviewed eighteen nations and their attempts to create wealth. He found several patterns of economic change regarding wealth creation.

He describes these in terms of the integration of four activities, the first three of which are an equitable distribution of income, a rising market demand for goods and services, and an increasing share of the savings made possible by the gross domestic product (GDP). The final activity, which he finds greatly aids national wealth creation, is the amount of investment in physical capital or infrastructure which promotes international trade. This includes container ports. Investment in infrastructure results, he says, in a progressive conversion from a reliance on domestic markets to increasing integration into the international economy. Ports which accommodate containerisation act as vital trade facilitators and in the process become examples of infrastructure engendering global economic integration and aiding in wealth creation.

Infrastructure serves two major purposes. It provides public-sector services and private-sector inputs. Infrastructure includes mass-transit transportation, education buildings, electricity grids, gas and water-supply facilities and distribution systems, waste treatment facilities, correctional institutions, police, fire and judiciary services, highways, roads, and airport and port facilities. Considerable investment in infrastructure is vital if a nation is to increase its wealth and become a part of the global economy.

CONTAINERISATION AND INFRASTRUCTURE

It is little wonder, then, that a key consequence of containerisation has been the rapid upgrading of infrastructural capacity by developing countries. This particularly pertains to ports. The fundamental rationale behind having a world-class port infrastructure is the capacity it provides to reduce the order-to-delivery time to hours or days. This depends largely on the ability to move raw materials, components, and final products from suppliers and distributors to manufacturers and consumers. The timely transport of cargo relies in turn on the capacity of a country's highways, railways, airports, coastal and inland waterways and ports.

Container infrastructure requires capital-intensive investments which many industry leaders and government officials reject for a variety of reasons, including lack of resources or simply a refusal to implement new technologies and processes. Many of the largest ports of the contemporary era were either secondary ports initially or did not even exist before containerisation. For example, in the 1960s Felixstowe was a port ninety miles (144.8 kilometres) from London. It was so insignificant that the main union did not even enlist its workers, so that when a strike closed other major ports Felixstowe became Britain's largest container port. On the west coast of the US, ports have historically lagged behind those on the east coast in trade volume. West coast ports have invested heavily in container capacity, however, and today they far outpace the east coast in trade volume. In 2009 Singapore was the world's busiest port in terms of total tonnage, trans-shipping a fifth of the world's containers. Despite its lack of land and natural resources its national income per person is higher than that of Spain and New Zealand and five times that of its nearest neighbour, Malaysia. Furthermore, the destination of the first container ship, Houston, Texas, long ago passed its neighbour (the container-resistant port of New Orleans) as the Gulf of Mexico's largest port. Each of these examples demonstrates that contemporary comparative advantage is shaped by those actors that invest most in innovative technologies such as the container (Bogart, 2006; *The Economist*, 2007d; World Shipping Council, 2009). Meanwhile, cities that were traditionally centres of maritime commerce, such as New York and Liverpool, have seen their waterfronts decline with startling speed due to their slow or inadequate response to containerisation. Previously quiet harbours such as Busan, South Korea and Seattle have moved instead into the front ranks of the world's container ports along with the large new container ports built in places where none were before, like Tanjung Pelepas in Malaysia. Small towns, distant from great population centres, use their comparative advantages, like cheap land and low wages, to become crucial elements in global economic networks by developing world-class container ports (Levinson, 2006).

The difference in port facilities is evident in the fact that of the twenty ports handling the greatest number of containers in 2003, seven had little or no container traffic in 1990 and three of the seven had not existed before. Their creation was a deliberate response to the economics of container shipping, in which keeping the ship moving is what matters most. The large ports constructed in China, Malaysia, and Thailand during the 1990s were investments in the changing configuration of global trade. Factories whose goods used these ports found in them the lowest rates and costs that saved money as well as time. A nation with an outdated infrastructure or with inefficient ports was a country that faced obstacles in finding a larger role in the global economy. The World Bank, for example, estimated that if Peru had been as effective at port management as Australia then this alone would have increased its foreign trade by one-quarter (Levinson, 2006c).

Containerisation represents a dilemma for national economies, nonetheless, and particularly for the port industry. Many of the investments required to make containerisation successful are made by the port industry. It must supply physical and soft infrastructure to manage an effective and efficient facility. Physical infrastructure refers to operational technology such as the berths, gantry cranes, yards, tugs and storage areas. Physical infrastructure also includes intermodal transport such as roads and railways. Soft infrastructure refers to the manpower employed. The efficient distribution of both types of infrastructure aids in diminishing a sea craft's turnaround time. This in turn augments a port's ability to accommodate more vessels and a larger container flow.

While the port industry bears much of the investment burden regarding containerisation they also face the possibility of being under-utilised or comprehensively neglected by shipping lines. Which ports shipping lines choose to visit is often based upon their consideration of the conditions of the entire chain, as opposed to the specific assets of a specific port. The conditions of the entire chain include the effectiveness and efficiency of the intermodal infrastructure, such as mini-bridge rail services and established highway carriers. Despite the capital intensive nature of containerisation and the risk of being bypassed by shipping lines, however, port investment in container infrastructure is the only way to ensure that a particular port will have the opportunity to reap the benefits offered by containerisation and by the unprecedented proliferation in world trade (Slack, 2001).

When the *MSC Pamela* sailed into Felixstowe, Britain's biggest container terminal, on her maiden voyage in 2005, Hutchison Whampoa, the port's Hong Kong owners, realised they were looking at the future. They quickly renewed their efforts to build more deep-water berths. At one thousand and fifty-three feet (three hundred and twenty-one metres) in length and with an ability to carry the equivalent of more than nine thousand containers, *Pamela* was then the world's largest container ship. This did not remain true for long, however. Ships with twice that capacity are in production and leading global ports such as Felixstowe will have to react quickly if they are not to become an economic afterthought, like many ports before them (Donovan, 2004; Levinson, 2006).

As the container continues to grow in significance the successful movement of freight beyond ports and along and between the nation's highways, inland waterways, railroads, warehouses, distribution centres, container yards and terminal facilities becomes more and more vital for nations seeking to increase their role in the global economy. This requires the comprehensive integration of modes of transportation.

Containerisation promotes the spread of intermodal infrastructure by placing cargoes in standard-sized boxes that can be moved by all three modes of surface transportation without being opened and repacked. In the mid-1970s, US and international intermodal loading increased dramatically, reflecting the greater use of containers and trailer loads that used some combination of rail, trucking and shipping. Intermodalism became an emblem for all transportation improvements, not just in the freight area but also as planners began to see the problems of growth and congestion as being more manageable due to more efficient planning and interconnectivity.

A competent intermodal infrastructure enables goods to be moved in and out of ports, thus preventing overcrowding and minimising the amount of storage capacity required, whether for dry-bulk, containers, or any other form of freight. The intermodal infrastructure is vital to a country's economic future as it gives inland populations access to ports and thus to global markets. This reality is particularly evident in China. Its rapid economic growth and integration into the global economy has placed a significant burden on its intermodal infrastructure and has made necessary considerable upgrade spending. For example, the amount spent between 2001 and 2005 on China's roads, railways and other fixed assets surpassed the total amount spent in the previous fifty years. Intermodal infrastructure is a vital element in the trade system, both domestically and internationally. The global network of ocean, road, and rail routes connects almost any two points on the earth's surface. It also gives cargo access to a country's hinterland. The comprehensive performance of the container system and of particular ports is part of the development of this system. Fundamentally, a nation's economy is only as competitive as its inland and outbound connections.

The use of containers has transformed all the different modes of transport. A seamless network has arisen that moves freight from its place of origin to its destination with unprecedented speed and efficiency. As noted above, the container has greatly simplified the loading and unloading of cargo and permitted the dynamic utilisation of containers on ships, trains, and trucks, thus breaking down the barrier between land and sea. Shippers now think of transportation as a service that, like all other components of a company's supply-and-sale chains, needs to be integrated into its overall operations. Carriers no longer view themselves as operating in a singular transportation mode but within one dynamic and inclusive process (Donovan, 2004; Greenburg *et al.*, 2006).

The Economist (1997, p. 86) contends that with the arrival of the container, a manufacturer in South Korea, for example, is for the first time able to ask a shipping line to deliver its exports to the US mid-west. The shipping line may negotiate with a railway to haul the container from Los Angeles to Chicago; hire a road hauler to transport the container from Chicago to South Bend; and take responsibility for meeting delivery schedules at every stage of the journey while sending a single invoice for the entire shipment.

The significance of an effective container infrastructure was outlined in a study by the World Bank in 2005. This study describes how differences in port efficiency and an adequate infrastructure can have a cost-effect that is equivalent to differences in five thousand miles (8046.7 kilometres) of shipping distance (Hill *et al.*, 2008).

The attempt by a state to create wealth is dependent upon its ability to integrate many actions, including its ability to adopt technologies like the container and its willingness to invest in the associated infrastructure. In addition, a society must maintain the kind of national trade policies and procedures that allow it to reap the full benefits of containerisation.

The container compels states to alter national policies and procedures such as those pertaining to excessive red tape, the enforcement of contracts, and standards regarding the movement of cargo. These issues largely determine a state's ability to increase its global trade competitiveness and claim a greater role in the international economy (Myers, 1996).

In the 2005 World Bank study (Hill *et al.*, 2008, p. 19) it was found that customs clearance times for a twenty-foot container ranged from about one day for Hong Kong and the Netherlands, two days for Ireland and Mauritius, twenty-one days for the Syrian Arab Republic and twenty-five days for Uzbekistan. In Kazakhstan it takes ninety-three days to export a twenty-foot container of cotton apparel, and in Mali sixty-seven days. In Sweden it takes only six days. In Namibia, the cost of all trade-related container transactions, including inland transport from the ocean vessel to the factory gate, amount to slightly more than three thousand US dollars. In Germany these costs amount to only eight hundred and thirteen US dollars and in Sweden little more than five hundred US dollars. A typical export transaction requires forty-two approval signatures in the Democratic Republic of the Congo (DRC), forty in Azerbaijan, thirty-nine in Nigeria, and thirty-three in Mali. It requires only two in Australia, Austria and Canada, and only one in Germany. The swiftness of the latter transactions has ramifications for vessel turnaround time. For example, vessels in Algerian, Nigerian and Russian ports average approximately seven days turnaround time compared with Germany where it is two days, and the US, where it is one.

Although ninety percent of international trade is transported by water some states have disregarded its importance in realising economic growth. For example, African nations have the most inefficient ports in the world. In African ports, the amount of time a ship must wait in port to load and unload its cargo surpasses the global average by several days. It is, for example, four times that experienced in Asian ports. In 2010 no African port was listed in the top seventy most productive in the world.

Djankov, Freund and Pham (2008) have researched how time delays affect global trade. They have used World Bank data to examine the days it takes to move standard cargo from the factory gate to the ship in ninety-eight countries. They have found that each additional day that a product is delayed prior to being shipped reduces trade by more than one percent. In other words, each day is equivalent to a country distancing itself from its trade partners by an average of seventy kilometres. Efficient document processing, the reduction of procedural red tape, the enforcement of contracts, adequate harbour maintenance, sufficient infrastructure, tight security, and the use of standard protocols to move cargo, all have far-reaching consequences for states' trade competitiveness. States with inadequate trade policies and procedures find it more difficult to create enduring wealth, to implement new ways of managing global production systems, and to divide up the production process into global supply-and-sale chains. Not unexpectedly, these nations face greater difficulties in finding a larger role in the global economy.

CONCLUSION

Since the pioneering voyage of the *Ideal X* on April 26, 1956, the container has affirmed its role as the main catalyst in helping to create novel industries, products, production processes and delivery systems. It has provided global actors with the freedom to break out of the constraints of their state canopies and to become integral components in globalised economic networks. These networks connect individuals, firms and countries in relational structures on different organisational and geographical levels.

The container has proven to be a significant part of the transformation of global politics, culture, and particularly the global economy. It has done this by shaping globalisation and by becoming the core element in a system which allows for goods to traverse the world in a timely manner and at a price much below what was possible before.

The web of containers traversing the world via its oceans, rail networks, or highways has engendered an explosion of international trade and a profound change in the world political economy of a kind not experienced since the early days of the industrial revolution. As noted above, in the contemporary world the principal dynamics of economic globalisation — open markets, free trade, and TNCs scanning the globe in search of more cost efficient production and sale sites — are predicated upon a container shipping system with sufficient capacity to move components to assembly points and products to world markets (Dicken, 2003; Hill *et al.*, 2008).

In short, the traffic in goods that is at the heart of the contemporary global political economy would be impossible without the freight container. It has fashioned a world of interconnectedness by becoming the nucleus of a network in which goods traverse the globe at prices which were formerly prohibitively high. This interconnectedness is founded upon the freedom to trade with the rest of the world. This freedom has enabled states to exploit their comparative advantages. This has had innumerable effects in turn on the international political economy (Levinson, 2006).

REFERENCES

Camilleri, J and J Falk (1992). *The End of Sovereignty?* Aldershot: Edward Elgar Publishing.

Cudahy, B (2006). *Box Boats. How Containers Ships Changed the World*. New York: Fordham University Press.

Dicken, P (2003). *Global Shift. Reshaping the Global Economic Map in the 21st Century*. New York: The Guilford Press.

Djankov, S, C Freund and C Pham (2008). *Trading on Time*. The World Bank, 22 May, http://www.doingbusiness.org/Documents/TradingOnTime_APR08.pdf [17 August 2010].

Donovan, A (2004). The impact of containerisation: From Adam Smith to the 21st century, *Review of Business,* 25(3), 10–15. [Business Source Premier database, accessed 22 January 2008].

Greenburg, M, P Chalk and H Wills (2006). *Marine Terrorism. Risk and Liability.* RAND Centre for Terrorism Risk Management Policy, http://www.rand.org/pubs/monographs/2006/RAND_MG520.pdf [12 July 2009].

Hill, C, T Cronk and R Wickramasekera (2008). *Global Business Today: An Asia-Pacific Perspective.* Sydney: McGraw-Hill.

Levinson, M (2006). *The Box. How the Shipping Container Made the World Smaller and the World Economy Bigger.* Princeton: Princeton University Press

Mehmet, O (2006). Race to the Bottom: The Impact of Globalisation on Labour Markets — A Review of Empirical and Theoretical Evidence. In *Globalisation and the Third World. A Study of Negative Consequences,* B Ghosh and H Guven (eds.). New York: Palgrave Macmillan.

Myers, R (1996). Introduction. In *The Wealth of Nations in the Twentieth Century. The Policies and Instituional Determinants of Economic Development,* R Meyers (ed.). Stanford: Hoover Institution Press.

New, S and R Westbrook (2004). *Understanding Supply Chains. Concepts, Critiques, and Futures.* New York: Oxford University Press.

The Economist (1997). Delivering the Goods, 15 November, 345 (8043), 85–86. [Business Source Premier database, accessed 25 August 2007]

Wilkins, M (1998). Multinational Corporations: A Historical Account. In *Transnational Corporations and the Global Economy,* R Kozul-Wright and R Rowthorn (eds.). Basingstoke: Macmillan Press Ltd.

Part Three

Global Finance

CHAPTER 12

Global Finance: An Overview

Mark Triffitt

University of Melbourne

Money makes the world go round, or so the saying goes. It has a neat ring about it, suggesting that the laws of global finance, like gravity and momentum, have a Newtonian certainty about them. Certainly, the collapse of communism and central state planning in the early 1990s left only one set of economic rules with which to organise global financial flows. And so for the last twenty years or so, the world, without the limits that rival ideologies have historically imposed on capitalism, has embarked on a radical exploration of globalised finance.

The 'physics' of free market finance states that capital markets should be left largely unregulated by governments and politicians. The world of global finance is self-regulating; it is too 'natural' and rationalistic to warrant the interference of states and their messy, unpredictable politics. Markets are constantly striving and achieving equilibrium as they seek to allocate resources and capital in the most efficient manner. So when governments try to intervene in this highly complex order of financial flows, disequilibrium and disorder is sure to follow. In other words, finance rules over politics.

What is now referred to as the Global Financial Crisis (GFC) of 2008 — the biggest financial meltdown since the Great Depression — upended these cosy certainties. No longer is global finance, like gravity and momentum, unquestionable or unquestioned. Indeed, the folly that created the GFC was played out on such a cosmic scale, costing trillions of dollars of shareholders' and taxpayers' money and resulting in the virtual shutdown of financial and banking systems the world over, that the legitimacy of global finance and capital markets seemed to evaporate overnight. In its place came forth the polemics of long-time doubters and newly minted opponents of free markets. What the GFC demonstrated, they claimed, is the un-sustainability of the global financial system. Governments should not be subordinate to global finance: what is required is constant regulation to keep what is a virulent genie in its bottle or box. In short, politics must rule over finance.

Political economic theory and advocacy has long been divided into these two camps; the GFC simply re-energised and repolarised the debate. As this chapter highlights, however, the fractious relationship between global finance and politics, at both a state and international level, is nothing new. Sometimes politics is in the ascendency. At other times finance prevails over politics. The debate that calls for one to subordinate the other, or that politics and global money are functionally and morally separable, misses the point. The bottom line is that each has always needed the other. What is different in the twenty-first century is the way in which this relationship has become counterintuitive, however. Such are the contradictions and unpredictabilities of twenty-first century globalisation. Global finances are not explained or explainable in conventional terms. The weaker states appear, as global financial flows become increasingly omnipotent, the stronger and more crucial they are. Similarly, the weakened state of global markets in the aftermath of the GFC disguises the fact that financial systems can never be truly subordinate to states, no matter how hard politics tries to keep the genie contained.

A BRIEF HISTORY OF FINANCIAL FLOWS

Global finance is, in some ways, as old as civilisation. The precursor of the contemporary world trade system, as noted above, started in the third millennium BC (Bernstein, 2008). This early trade needed to be lubricated by various forms of exchange. Thus we can think of the flow of silk, gold and other commodities between the traders of ancient Mesopotamia, India and China as providing with them the first trickles of global finance.

It is fair to say that the organisation of finance into the system that we know today began to consolidate in sixteenth century Europe. Even in these early stages, finance and politics were combined. Europe had long been a warring continent, but by the 1500s the escalating costs of massed armies and weaponry had brought many states and their monarchs to the edge of fiscal ruin. New sources of revenue, over and above the annual tithes and taxes levied upon their subjects, were urgently required. The solution came in the form of government bonds. In return for receiving a lump sum to pay for that year's campaign, the cash-strapped monarch sold the rights to future years' tax revenues at a discount: in effect, the present costs of warfare were offset against the future. Those who constructed these financial instruments — in effect the first merchant bankers — profited handsomely from buying the rights to this revenue stream at the discounted cost, then on-selling this income stream to investors (typically the upper classes), who were paid back their investment in annual instalments plus an amount in interest.

These initial arrangements, while rudimentary, carried with them the features that characterise modern finance. Firstly, it involved a mindset that created or ascribed value to something that was not yet real or present. Secondly, it created relationships based on a future projection of one's self. The notion of selling future revenue earned by a future self is a basic function of modern commercial life (this is done every day with credit cards which permit the purchase of goods today with income that will be earned in the future). At the time, however, it was seen as an ingenious concept because of its fundamental distance from traditional ways of thinking that situated the world and its wealth largely in the here-and-now.

This future projection of the self involved another fundamental aspect of modern finance, namely, risk. Ascribing value to a future time or relationship which, by definition, could not ultimately be known or controlled, carried with it uncertainty. Finance was bound, therefore, to construct various methods that sought to manage, through prediction and quantification, this uncertainty. In other words, modern finance became self-perpetuating because — through the mere act of conjuring wealth out of the future — it created a demand for the ongoing financial management of the future, which by definition is never-ending. Thus, money not only made the world go around, but made itself go around.

The third important element of modern finance was its ability to challenge and break down hierarchies of wealth. By creating mechanisms whereby the creation of financial wealth became tied both to the future and to tradition, pre-capitalist barriers to the entry to wealth and finance (linked as they were to birth and history) began to be less dominant in determining economic class. Certainly, the first purchasers of government bonds were not commoners, but neither were they kings or queens. They were the first non-sovereigns to gain direct access to a share of the sovereign's wealth — a significant landmark in the distribution of that wealth. Wealth became not only more plentiful through the expansion of the monetary supply but also more accessible and *dangerous* — important factors when considering the growing democratisation and complexity of modern finance.

The success of government bonds — an early demonstration of the fundamental link between states and finance — involved the practice of inventing a financial future to pay for the present extend to private ventures in need of large amounts of capital. The other beneficiary of this arrangement was the joint-stock company, the forerunner to the listed stock firms that dominate today's global markets. The principle behind joint-stocks was much the same as bonds. Investors bought a share of a company in return for the right to access a share of its future earnings. By projecting themselves into the future, they gained access to potential reward, as well as exposed themselves and their investment to potential risks.

Whereas bonds helped governments to finance intra-European wars, stocks paid for Europe's colonisation of the rest of the world. Many of these early joint-stock companies were established to pay for the exploration of faraway lands and the appropriation of their natural resources, notably land, precious metals and furs. The names of the most prominent and successful of these — Hudson, Mississippi, East India, Africa, the South Sea Company — indicate the extent to which joint-stock companies underpinned the geographic spread of Western colonialism over the course of the seventeenth and eighteenth centuries. These companies were not only the prisms through which the patterns of financial flows, directed from Europe to other continents, grew to dominate global finance, but as 'states-within-states' they also often acted as agents of foreign policy as directed by their home governments.

Many profited handsomely from their joint-stock investments: returns from an overseas trading venture could often run into a multiple of hundreds. Others lost their proverbial shirts, however, in what were typically high-risk ventures. The process of the democratisation of wealth mentioned above gathered pace because of the proliferation of joint-stock companies and their comparatively modest entry price in terms of the purchase price of individual shares. Yet the gradual seeping down of wealth created a mass of capital flows which could, from time to time, turn dangerously irrational. The momentum of the many rushing to invest in a stock of no lasting value (like the 'tulip mania' of the seventeenth century that elevated the stock price of tulip companies only to see it fall just as quickly when the mania wore off) could be seemingly unstoppable. Momentum represented an overly inflated representation of the future earnings of a joint-stock company, combined with an inflated perception among investors of how wealthy their future selves would become if the price of the stock kept being bid up. Under these circumstances, financial markets, which were supposed to manage future risk, demonstrated how — through a combination of scale and mania — could become a monumental risk to themselves in the present. More often than not these financial bubbles burst and the money flows that between the eighteenth and nineteenth centuries were gradually connecting Europe with North and South America as well as East Asia, receded until confidence and the reservoir of global capital was replenished.

The role of states in the development of globalised finance remained central, even if not always obvious. Joint-stock companies, for example, required states to develop special legislation to legitimate what were at the time highly innovative commercial arrangements. More generally, the legal infrastructure to support and protect capital flows across national borders was progressively developed. European powers also spent heavily on navies in order to protect new sources of revenue and pacify the trade routes on which their economies — and their global financial flows — were now heavily dependent.

THEMES AND VARIATIONS

At the risk of oversimplifying complex changes over two centuries, developments until the middle of the twentieth century were variations on the themes outlined above. Global finance became not an end in itself but was invariably directed at realising, or rather financing, some tangible commercial outcome or project, like rail lines and canals, that propelled capitalism to even faster rates of production and consumption. All the while, states continued to prop up finance markets through the continual tapping of bond markets for money, not just to underwrite wars and conquest but to pay for the increasing social welfare and economic responsibilities that accompanied the development of the nation state. Wealth expanded and became more accessible, not always at a consistent rate but in a way that fed off itself. More and more people down the economic and social chain were able, as a consequence, to call themselves investors.

The development of communication technologies in the nineteenth century was critical. Both the telegraph (known retrospectively as the Victorian internet) and early telephony helped to speed the movement of capital and information about capital, allowing for it to be more rationally and quickly invested. Compared to the near-instant speeds of contemporary financial dealings, the advances of earlier times seem paltry. But they were crucial in the evolution of global monetary flows, not just because they carried money and information quicker than previously thought possible. They also created and solidified reliable linkages between established and emerging financial centres around the world, spreading good and bad news alike. This whetted the appetite of the masses at large for investment and investing.

The growing nexus of capital markets and investment exchange spurred two further developments, the first of which was the way — as the scale of these flows increased and quickened due to technological developments — governments began to feel an increasing need to have a direct influence over capital flows. Central banks, which were the banking arms of states — became increasingly important as hands-on conduits and regulators of stable money supplies for governments and the economies they administered. Their mandate was to ensure that the amount of currency circulating within, as well as to and from, their economies was in synch with the nation's stocks of gold. The Great Depression and World War Two began to stretch this money-gold relationship toward breaking point as nations and their central banks opted for Keynesian demand-side management and a massive expansion of government-backed money to deal with both crises. The fact that this odd and enduring relationship between national and international flows of capital, and a nation's fixed stock of precious metal (otherwise known as the gold standard), effectively regulated the flow and value of global finances up until the 1970s, demonstrated the extent of state influence over the movement of capital. This held for most of the twentieth century.

The other development was the increasing consolidation of global financial power among two or three major Western cities. Initially, these hubs were Western

European — London and Paris in particular. The centrifugal power of mass communications played a crucial role in facilitating the role of the United States, however, which was a hemisphere removed from the Old World and the traditional sources of wealth. It became the new centre for global finance. Fuelled by a massive immigrant influx, a seemingly unlimited supply of land, and a comparatively egalitarian, can-do society, the US economy took the European model of capitalism and supercharged it. Creative destruction, hailed as the hallmark of modernist economics, became the hallmark of US development. Nowhere was this more apparent than in the finance market, that is, in the frenetic trading pits of New York and Chicago, where financial flows began to unshackle themselves from the tangible investments of so-called 'real economy'. Futures markets, in which the future became a discrete and tradeable commodity in its own right, were one of many US financial innovations that helped oust London and Paris as the epicentres of global financial flows.

As the new financial centre of the world, the US took over the privilege of shaping the rules of the global financial game. Initially, it assumed custodianship of the gold standard, which had been a European invention. As the twentieth century evolved, however, new global regulatory arrangements were required, particularly following the fiscal and physical carnage of the 1930s and 40s. In the mid-1940s, the US instituted the Bretton Woods agreements, a curious mix of looser and tighter financial controls on international capital. These eventually led to currency flows replacing gold stocks as the arbiter of global monetary management.

For all these changes and shifts in the focus, direction and speed of financial flows, it is fair to say that — compared to today's more intensely horizontal and networked patterns of global financing — capital markets remained for most of the twentieth century essentially hierarchical and bounded. Economies remained industrially oriented, organised around command-and-control structures that aligned the interests of big business, big financiers and increasingly bigger government bureaucracies. This corporatist approach to capital flows, evidenced by the gold standard and various state-based and international monetary and pricing controls, combined to ensure that the flows of global finance were relatively predictable and sluggish. By the 1970s, electronic trading was starting to quicken the pace of these flows and spur the scaling-up of asset volumes, which further broadened and deepened public participation in stocks and bonds. Yet, even during the 1920s and the 1980s, the decades of the twentieth century most associated with manic investment by the masses, the numbers of those who directly held shares or bonds were modest compared to the worldwide legions of so-called 'mum-and-dad' investors who were directly involved in all manner of financial exotica offered by today's local and global markets.

The biggest stopper on the unbridled flow and development of global finance was geopolitical. For most of the twentieth century, free markets were not the dominant mode of capital formation and distribution that free marketeers liked to think they were in retrospect. Communism, then fascism, deprived capitalism and its money flows of access to between one-third and half the world in terms of territory and population. Powerful and lowly states alike, if they were seriously of a mind to practice autarky, could do so by retreating into alternative economic systems that placed ideological or racial factors ahead of market forces in determining the allocation of scare resources. (For an account of the way Nazi Germany undermined its war economy through highly irrational, racially based financial practices, see Tooze, 2006.) Fascism's reign was relatively brief, but communism carried on as an effective barrier to truly global flows of free market finance until the 1980s, when the contradictions of ideologically and militarily driven technocrats seeking to micromanage complex, large scale economies led to the collapse of the Soviet empire.

THEORISING FINANCIAL FLOWS

At this point, it is worth reviewing traditional theories of the structure and development of global capital markets, since for most of the twentieth century they played a significant role in simplifying and explaining what had become an increasingly complex and aggrandising system — one that reached into most corners of the globe, subjecting and subsuming traditional forms of commercial exchange within its exacting, rationalised boundaries. As outlined at the start of this chapter, these theories can be divided into two camps. One sees markets as positive and empowering. The other sees them as perverse and alienating. Despite their dissimilar assumptions about the inputs and outcomes of free financial flows, they have a common view in that they both see capital markets reflecting the fact that financial order is achieved, not though stasis, but through the logic of relentless expansion.

Those in the Newtonian corner of global finance explain the global triumph of capital markets as proof of the inherent superiority of the 'physics' of free market forces in assigning rational value to scarce resources and speeding their allocation to where they are needed most. Thus, the 'perfect information' which markets provide in terms of matching the supply and demand of resources accounts for why capital and its flows work exceptionally well. Its mechanisms and logic, like gravity, are fundamentally 'right'.

The concept of dysfunctionality lies at the heart of the opposing marxist and other anti-marketeer views of capital. These perspectives are profoundly less optimistic about financial flows and their consequences. In their terms the world has always been divided into two classes — those who own the means of production and those who are condemned to spend their days in economic and political subordination. Capitalism is the latest and the last phase of man's exploitative relationships in this regard. There is nothing innately legitimate about the capitalist system, that is. Indeed, rationalist/liberalist market theory is no more than an ideological construct designed to mask capital's profound imperfections and inequalities. Capitalists and their corporate manifestations have the inside track on wealth creation and they conspire with the state to perpetuate a system geared toward unending, alienating growth.

Marx conceived his theories at a time when the nation state was relatively dominant and the globalisation of capital was still being developed. In order to align anti-market theory with the nexus of economic and financial arrangements that transcended national economies in the twentieth century, world-system theorists effectively globalised Marx's framework. Rich, core countries became the nation state equivalent of capitalists: the world's developing and underdeveloped countries beccame its proletariat. The core sent capital to the periphery to fund the extraction of raw resources and cheap labour, while getting most of this productive value back as investment returns. Capital flows became, in short, a tightly controlled conveyor belt, sending and returning wealth to the core while exporting dependence and deprivation to the margins.

While the differences in their perceptions and views were profound, both market and marxist theories agreed on a diminished role for the state as global capital flows expanded and intensified. As noted above, rationalist/liberalist market theories viewed the state as anathema to 'perfect' markets: global finance runs so fast and is so nimble, propelled across datelines and national borders by elite money managers and state-of-the-art information technologies, that any action or intervention by states and their cumbersome, rule-bound bureaucracies can only spark a myriad of unintended and unfortunate consequences. For anti-market theorists, the state seemed to assert itself over economics and finance and in this way ensured a more equitable distribution of resources, but in reality it was capitalism's handmaiden, its role being restricted to providing the necessary legal and ideological props for global capital markets to perpetuate themselves. World-system theorists saw the state as obliging international finance regulators, such as the World Bank and the International Monetary Fund, to enforce global financial rules and coordinate bailouts when they failed.

The marxists were correct in highlighting rationalist/liberalist market theory as an ideology. The idea of movements in financial markets being subject to immutable laws and being therefore eminently predictable was, until the 1950s, an extremely oversimplified view advocated by a minority of economists and financiers. Over the past half-century, the relative lack of empirical justification and theoretical justification behind the theory's core tenets was neatly sidestepped by a plethora of pure and applied finance theories and formulae. Having been given an unchallenged status in business schools and corporate boardrooms worldwide, rationalist/liberalist market theory embedded itself in every facet of capital markets and their management. (For a telling account of how rationalist/liberalist market theory graduated from the margins to the mainstream in terms of understanding and ordering the world of modern finances, see Fox, 2009.)

Yet the marxist approach, with its reliance on the view that the social, economic and political arrangements that order the world in the twenty-first century were essentially the same as those that characterised the nineteenth century when Marx was writing, was also a gross oversimplification. For marxists, the economic and political world — for all the profound complexities and un-predictabilities introduced into political and financial systems this century — remained relatively monolithic. Value, as it related to capital and capital formation, remained uniform and unvariegated. Access and barriers to wealth were largely decided by class and its hierarchies. These in turn were determined by a static view of what constitutes the means of production. Given what is essentially a command view of the world — a world where the sources of authority and control flow from top to bottom, North to South, core to periphery — it seemed but a small step to viewing international political economy and capital flows as being controlled by shadowy figures in multinational corporate boardrooms. These figures were so omnipotent and yet so stealthy in the execution of their hegemonic plans that they could only be described as 'masters of the universe' (this being the name given to New York's elite financiers in a classic satire of 1980's Wall Street, Wolfe, 1988).

RADICAL GLOBALISATION

Both rationalist/liberalist market theory and marxism perpetuate the conventional view that global finance in the twenty-first century is simply an extrapolation, or a stepwise change, in the dynamics that have underpinned capital markets in previous eras. On the one hand, market theorists see the same highly ordered system of market forces, even though these forces have undergone significant broadening and deepening over the past two decades. Anti-marketeers view today's global finance — while acknowledging that modes of production in terms of capital formation and distribution are no longer as static and hierarchical as before — as simply a more cunning and subtle variation on old-style, hegemonic capitalism.

To see the world as it is, and particularly the role of global finance in driving change (as well as the capacity and function of states to manage it), it is necessary first to acknowledge what it has become. The past two decades have ushered in fundamental alterations to both economies and polities, and their relationship, in ways that are more profound, more complex, and moving more quickly than at any period since the industrial revolution.

The early chroniclers of the current age saw this transformation as important and unique. The New Economy was the (unsurprising) moniker for it, based as it was on the transformative power of information and communications technologies and the rapid globalisation of markets. When the dot com boom and bust in the early 2000s discredited this transformative potential, 'globalisation' became the signature tune of the time, used either as a catch-all, pejorative term by anti-free marketers or as a rallying cry for those trumpeting the explosive expansion of free markets. Either way, 'globalisation' lent itself to superficial comparisons between today and previous periods, such as the first decade of the twentieth century, when free markets and global capital appeared similarly unconstrained by states and their regulations. (The title of Frieden's history of global integration highlights how today's globalisation is largely seen as a repeat of past eras of global integration, particularly the decade before World War One. See Frieden, 2006.)

This chapter argues for a different approach. Certainly, globalisation — in the form of the integration of capital, information and labour across national boundaries — existed before, but compared to today's form, this was globalisation for beginners. Many of the characteristics of previous modes of globalisation are evident today but they have been supercharged to such an extent that they have resulted not simply in quantitative changes but in a qualitative transformation of the way global systems are organised. These changes have effectively unshackled the temporal, spatial and ideological constraints that previously kept free markets relatively restrained, making them truly global and giving them an intensity not remotely seen before. Today we live in a period of *radical* globalisation.

This new era was triggered by the collapse of the Soviet Union in 1991, however, it was not just a geopolitical event. It facilitated a massive enlargement of the global free market. What could not be conquered by the West during four decades of Cold War was achieved conclusively by economics and finance in less than one. It left communist China, the world's potentially most populous marketplace, no choice but to shift its tentative programme of market reforms into high gear. India, meanwhile, which throughout the 1970s and 80s continued to organise its economy around state regulation and intervention, also began to transform its economy along free market lines. In the blink of an eye (in historical terms), the global free market doubled the number of producers and consum ers to three billion or so — the largest and quickest expansion of a single, economic system that the world is ever likely to see. The Soviet Empire's collapse also meant the end of competing ideologies. Communism was not only discredited *in toto* but its profound and instant de-legitimisation meant any ideological view tied to leftist politics or central planning was tarred by association. This left a single, effectively unchallengeable ideology with which to understand and manage the world.

Concurrently, rapid advances in information and communication technologies (ICT) in the early 1990s — particularly the internet and ongoing developments in digital technology — overlaid the prior levels of unprecedented complexity, thus unleashing further geographical and ideological expansion. Again, this tends to be seen as an evolution, that is, as a trend, rather than as the revolution it actually was and will continue to be for the foreseeable future. Computers and other digital technology were stock business and household items for some years prior to the 1990s. Once linked by expensive but limited mainframe networks which could only be afforded by governments and big business, however, they were able to process and store information in isolation from each other. The scale and speed of the development and rollout of 'linking' technologies in the second half of the 1990s — notably the internet as well as satellite technologies and mobile telephony — fundamentally transformed and up-scaled the processing power of individual ICT devices by joining them together in a low-cost way, even as these devices became increasingly more powerful and reliable as a way of processing and reconfiguring larger and larger amounts of information. (The worldwide web, the backbone of radical globalisation and the new global finance system, took just three years to reach fifty million users, compared to radio and television which took forty years and fifteen years respectively to reach forty million users. The internet now has two billion users, with the number doubling between 2005 and 2010. See Thussu, 2006, pp. 208–209.)

FLOWS INTO TORRENTS

What does this mean for global finance and the power embedded within its systems? The short answer is *everything*. Radical globalisation, by incorporating all economies into a single, totalising free market system, has meshed financial systems into an infinitely more integrated and complex whole. In the past, looser forms of global integration, which kept capital formation and distribution on a less tight leash, meant developing economies typically played the subordinate role to major developed economies as a destination for the latter's surplus capital. The biggest impact has been the creation of an unprecedented volume of money upon which the global financial system now feeds. Such has been the scale of finance creation over the last two decades, lowering the entry barriers to capital markets for, at a macro-level, developing nations, and at a micro-level, tens of millions of new, small investors, that the traditional hierarchies of capital and capital ordering have been upended. In the process, the balance of financial clout has been tipped towards a constellation of emerging economies.

It is easy to forget that China, the emerging leviathan of the global financial system, is still a developing economy after nearly thirty years of marketisation. The financial and economic systems of the developed world, and particularly the US, have become dependent not only on the continuing capacity of China to absorb their investment but to inject it with its stupendous trade surpluses. In this way, the developing world now underpins the living standards of rich nations in a pattern of counter-flows and counter-dependence that is not likely to end anytime soon. As China moves up the economic value chain, India — the world's second most populous nation — will take its place, followed by a band of smaller, strategically positioned developing economies which are also directing greater volumes of their savings into sustaining the increasingly debt-laden Western economies.

Rapidly evolving ICT technologies have also been critical in developing new forms of financial flow. Their generative power not only joins financial markets because of their lightning speed but it massively increases the production and distribution of new financial products. This money bears little relation to real economic production. As the future, and future selves, become endlessly created and recreated through computer pulses that trigger and shape most of the financial world's daily activity, money begets money in ways which are almost entirely virtual.

In terms of the Newtonian metaphor, this combination of volume and speed equals momentum. To be sure, global finance is no stranger to momentum, particularly the type in which capital accumulates in large volumes and is directed disproportionately, creating in the process asset bubbles in stocks or property that are followed by a crash. Capital feast gives way invariably to famine. (The Great Crash of 1929, the first truly global financial meltdown, was created by irrational surges of funds being poured into stock exchanges around the globe followed by a sudden collapse in investor confidence. This saw these amounts — and more — extracted in such a rush that it paralysed the world economy for more than a decade. Yet the volume of money traded in the year preceding the Great Crash was a fraction of the amount traded on any given day in today's global markets.) With vast amounts of virtual money being generated and sped from one international money market to another in a fraction of second, mega-momentum has become a defining characteristic of twenty-first century global finances. Flows have become torrents, which can be and often is a good thing. Massive supplies of capital directed quickly, with pinpoint precision, to where they can be most efficiently deployed, has been a major factor in the achievement of higher levels of global economic growth for much of the past two decades and in particular, in achieving better standards of living for hundreds of millions of people in emerging economies as well as increased prosperity for many in developed economies. At times, however, this rush of virtual finance — or so-called 'hot money' — has become a stampeding herd of future selves unlike any other. In 1998, for example, a so-called Asian financial crisis occurred because currency speculators withdrew their capital from the region in such large amounts that it crippled most of the economies concerned and threatened to bring the whole global economy to its knees.

Unprecedented volume and speed has been one part of the transformation. As the blunt face of global finance, it is easy to define and measure in terms of both its positive and negative features. What makes momentum both highly beneficial and highly unstable at the same time, however, is its combination with the new geometries of global finance. Specifically, this refers to the cross-cutting linkages that now micro-marble the world of finance due to the same factors that contribute so significantly to the volume of global finance. The complexity and opacity of these linkages makes them extremely difficult, if not impossible, to quantify, understand, or to predict.

WHAT'S UNDER THE ROCK?

The internet and other digital technologies have created a financial world in which an infinite number of financial and fiscal gardens are enmeshed. Moreover, all of them are full of lovingly tended investments planted by hundreds of millions of small and large investors around the globe, fed and watered by the rationalist/liberalist market theory that underpins them, and the 'perfect information' practices that pertain to that theory. The ubiquitous linkages afforded by digital technology, however, also connect these gardens with serpents, which come in many shapes and sizes. Some of these can be obvious, like the emerging or sub-developed countries that are now deeply embedded in the global financial world and whose financial and governance structures and standards can fall well short of what radical globalisation requires in terms of a functional financial system. (The Russian and Mexican bond crises in the second half of the 1990s, and more recently, the Greek and Irish fiscal crises of 2010, were both testament to how global markets can go seriously awry when investors are linked up to the financial systems of emerging economies. These are far less rigorous, and even outright corrupt, in their use of other people's money.) The serpents are more likely to be stealthy and hidden, however, even within the most lovingly tended gardens. The GFC, it should be remembered, was homegrown. It emanated from the core of the US financial system in the form of subprime loans, that is, home finance provided by some of the world's largest and reputable banks to low or no-income Americans who, by definition, had no chance of servicing these loans, let alone paying them back. (In a real sense, this was the apotheosis of the long process of democratising access to wealth, referred to above.) When the extent of these high-risk loans became known, particularly the way in which they had been on-sold as part of so-called low-risk investments purchased by investors around the world, not only did it shatter the balance sheets of many of the world's largest financial companies but, more critically, it shattered the confidence of investors in the integrity of the global financial system. The blame for what now seems to be, on hindsight, an obvious case of financial stupidity, has been sheeted home to greedy bankers, obtuse mortgage providers and lax regulators. All this is true at a superficial level but the real problem lay ultimately with the levels of unknowable and, ultimately, uncontrollable levels of complexity that have been dug into the global financial system due to radical globalisation.

Despite all the talk of the infallibility of rationalistic liberalism in terms of identifying and quantifying risk, as well as the unprecedented levels of financial information on tap to anyone with access to a computer, the reality is that complexity has risen to such levels that for most of the time no one really knows or understands the chain of financial production and distribution, that is, who is investing in what, who really owes what, how much, and to whom. For rationalist/liberalist market theory to remain predictive and legitimate in such an inchoate environment — in other words, to adhere to the principle of 'perfect information' — it must apply itself to increasingly smaller and smaller parts of the financial world. Thus, we find financial markets full of experts speaking authoritatively about the size and growth of a particular tree, the pattern of its trunk rings, and the depth of its roots. None, in truth, can claim a sustained or deep understanding of the relationship of their special tree and the next tree, however, let alone the forest in which both reside. In short, no one can know what is going on in the financial world with either the certainty required by rationalist/liberalist market theory or, for that matter, by marxist hegemony theory. This means that no one is in control.

DERIVATIVES

One of the biggest changes to the global financial world and one that speaks directly to the geometries of new finance and the diminution of overarching order has been the increasingly deep dependence of financial systems on what are called derivatives. The exponential growth of this twenty-first century financial instrument of choice (the value of traded derivatives rose from $870 billion to $450 *trillion* between 1987 and 2007) has been a key reason for both the massive increase in the global money supply and the whole system's complexity (Fox, 2009, p. xii). The explosive growth in derivatives has been blamed largely on the deregulation of the global financial system. To some extent this is correct, although it is important to note that the complexity and the speed with which new forms of derivatives are created mean they are effectively impossible to understand even by those in the financial sector, let alone by those governments that seek to regulate them.

Derivatives are effectively contracts for which value is *derived* from underlying assets such as shares, bonds and currencies. They seek to manage the risks associated with investing in these more mundane assets. The biggest culprit is therefore systematic: the explosion of all sorts of political, market and governance risks associated with the unprecedented unleashing of free markets, and the technological tools (read ICT and linking technologies) that have facilitated the production of vast new pools of finance that have created their own risks and sophisticated, risk management requirements.

Derivatives have become the intermediaries between investors and investments. This means in effect that the investors may end up being many times removed from the actual investment that determines whether they make or lose money.

Compared to traditional investment practices, in which the investor takes on the role of a future self investing directly in the future performance of an asset like a stock, bond, or currency, derivatives allow an investor to create another future self — or indeed, any number of selves — to minimise the risk of investing in that asset. What is more, these derivatives can be bought and sold in their own right, which means the 'derivative' future self can split into other derivative future selves in order to manage the risk created by managing the risk.

SECURITISATION

This complexity has been amplified by a financial technique known as 'securitisation', which is the other significant global financial innovation in recent years. This is where different kinds of debts owed by many unrelated future selves are bundled into a single asset and sold to other unrelated future selves such as pension funds, which are conduits for the investments of other future selves like retirees. It sounds mind-numbing though this is, in fact, a simplified representation of how everyday global finances work in the age of radical globalisation.

This complexity also helps explain how something so self-evidently short-sighted as providing subprime home loans to the unemployed could be disguised as something benign and 'rational'. In order to manage a world so infinitely varied and dynamic that even the future (that fundamental mindset that propels investors and investment) is beyond any real understanding, financial markets need to keep coming up with new and more exotic financial products. This is one of the paradoxes of modern finance: by managing itself so 'effectively', it stores up subterranean chains of venomous serpents.

CONCLUSION

Is global finance an accident waiting to happen? Yes it is, but not in the way marxists and other anti-marketeers would have it. The global financial system is not inevitably doomed as it tracks towards a mega-implosion and a legitimacy crisis too big to be addressed by bail-outs. Despite its systemic flaws, when the global financial system works — which it does most of the time due to its rigorous, ICT-driven attention to micro-detail — it works extremely well: in fact better than the global financial system has ever worked. The vast range of markets and the new participants now at its disposal, combined with constantly improving ICT technologies that speed the financing of innovations, lead to diverse and new products and services. These carry both the seeds of recurrent meltdown and are the system's trump cards in terms of perpetuating its legitimacy.

At one level, therefore, the ascendency of financial markets is greater than ever. (As noted above, even if financial markets were approaching a legitimacy crisis, states have no practical way of successfully regulating them on a day-to-day basis.)

At another level, the stronger that free capital markets appear to be, the more fragile they are. By introducing infinitely more links into the supply and consumption of global finance, and by becoming increasingly dependent on often unpredictable torrents of financial production and distribution, the system becomes significantly more volatile and vulnerable to disruption. Thanks to the new 'physics' of global momentum, strengths can become weaknesses in an instant. Thanks to the system's new 'geometries', gardens nourish serpents that, when they awaken, rapidly spread themselves unpredictably.

So, at a time when the influence of states over financial markets looks to be historically at its weakest, their ascendency, as well as that of monetary authorities like the IMF, has never been greater. The massive scale of the fiscal and regulatory resources that need to be brought to bear to address financial meltdowns, both in terms of lenders of last resort and as agents external to increasingly micromanaged markets, means only states have the capacity to comprehend and act on the bigger picture.

To be sure, this power is reactive rather than strategic. It rests on constructing fiscal floodwalls to halt negative momentum and to assume emergency oversight of financial torrents. The height and strength of these floodwalls also depends on how much money governments can afford. This demonstrates in turn how the old rules and certainties of finance — in which boundaries like the gold standard served to place reasonable limits on the supply of money — have changed for good. The large amounts spent by states and international authorities to right the global financial ship in the wake of the GFC are the best indication that in an age of radical globalisation, the invention of new finance, and the ability of states to draw upon it, is virtually limitless, however. Meanwhile the capacity for modern finance to have its venom used by governments as an antidote for its recurrent crises is perhaps its greatest paradox.

REFERENCES

Bernstein, W (2008). *A Splendid Exchange: How Trade Shaped the World.* New York: Atlantic Monthly Press.

Fox, J (2009). *The Myth of the Rational Market: A History of Risk, Reward, and Delusion on Wall Street.* New York: HarperCollins.

Frieden, J (2006). *Global Capitalism: Its Fall and Rise in the Twentieth Century.* New York: W.W. Norton and Company.

Thussu, D (2006). *International Communication: Continuity and Change.* London: Hodder Arnold.

Tooze, A (2006). *The Wages of Destruction: The Making and the Breaking of the Nazi Economy.* London: Allen Lane.

Wolfe, T (1988). *The Bonfire of the Vanities.* London: Cape.

CHAPTER 13

The International Monetary Fund

Nidhi Dutt

University of Melbourne

For more than sixty years the International Monetary Fund (IMF) and the World Bank have been the bastions of the global economy. They are best described as parents of an often unruly, unpredictable, and at times irrational modern-day financial system. For decades they have guided governments, leaders, other financial institutions and organisations through the good times and the bad; through times of economic expansion and contraction; and through periods of crisis and growth. To a greater or lesser extent, both have tried to evolve as the needs of the world's increasingly interdependent economy have changed. And since the Bretton Woods conference in 1944 both have fulfilled numerous roles. Depending on the requirements of the situation and the economic and political sensitivities of the country or region in which they have worked, they have been observers, managers and/or rescuers. Like their roles, their histories have been chequered. They have borne the brunt of the blame for financial crises but they have also, more often than not, been the first port of call for governments facing severe financial trouble.

As pillars of the modern-day financial system they have also meant different things to different governments. Take the IMF, for example. For some it has been the guiding hand of economic integration and the bearer of enticing free market principles. For others it represents the heavy-handedness of competitive capitalist economics as dictated by Western countries like the US.

Over time the internal mechanics and the balances of power within these institutions has also changed. Today, despite its still highly politicised and weighted voting system, the World Bank has more developing world voices taking part in decision making than ever before. Indeed, emerging economies like Brazil, China and India are finding themselves in greater positions of power and influence now within global forums such as this and not just because of their bigger financial contributions to or their investments in such institutions, but simply because of their growing importance in the global economy. The changing balance of power in what were once known as institutions of the first world is a testament to, and a measure of, the significant changes taking place in the global political economy today and of the transitions in the 'developing world'.

As the global economic crisis of recent years has shown, it is no longer just developing or transitional countries that rely on international financial institutions for assistance and guidance. During the tough times of recent years, Western countries have also sought the help of the IMF, since the Fund is also known as the lender of last resort for them too. Decades ago it would have been unimaginable that countries such as Iceland, Greece or Ireland would experience the kind of financial vulnerability they faced in 2010, let alone be in need of IMF assistance.

The financial crisis that ensued following the 2008 subprime mortgage crisis in the US also showed that the modern-day financial system had runaway capabilities that few previously suspected. As a result, the major questions of those analysing the role of the IMF and the World Bank in the twenty-first century has become: can these institutions prevent crises from taking place in a global politico-economic environment as unpredictable and volatile as the current one? Or is today's market far too big and erratic for these two ageing parents to handle?

What follows highlights the work of the IMF. This is not to demean the significance of the World Bank. It is to allow for a more detailed discussion of the role the IMF plays in the IPE.

THE IMF

For more than six decades the IMF has made its presence felt all over the world. By and large it has been most active in developing countries, managing economic liberalisation or helping to prevent or deal with financial crises. It has, more often than not, walked what is a fine line between assistance and dictation. Many of its reform programmes, and in particular those it fostered during the 1990s, have been described as aggressive and restrictive.

The IMF (and the World Bank's) handling of big economic issues, as well as its participation in events of financial significance, has been a source of constant and heated debate the world over. There is little denying that these two global institutions are important, however, if not integral parts of the modern-day financial system. Irrespective of whether leaders, governments, economists or citizens like them, there is little doubt that most would prefer them to exist. The challenges that institutions like the IMF (and the World Bank) face today, and are likely to face in the years and decades to come, include the need for them to break away from their 'first world' heritage and to internationalise their policies to better reflect the changing scope and nature of the global marketplace. To fully assess and appreciate the role of institutions like the IMF, however, it is important first to frame them in their contemporary economic and political context.

THE IMF'S HISTORY

When institutions like the IMF were founded there were very few stable unilateral or multilateral channels of communication and dialogue between nation states. At that time the need for large, overarching forums such as the IMF was great. As the world regrouped, however, and regions arose, state-to-state, government-to-government dialogue, negotiations and agreements increased. While the tendency of leaders to want to cut deals, especially when it came to political economics, on a one-on-one level did not render institutions like the IMF totally useless, it did, however, begin to limit their role in economic policy provision, development and integration.

The desire of international bodies to stay current and relevant cannot be overstated. At some point, during one period of their history or another, all international financial agencies, organisations and institutions find they have to fight for their survival. Often more important than just survival is the need to prove their own worth and relevance, not only to individual governments and countries but also to the financial system as a whole. Those organisations formed after, or as a result of World War Two have had to fight the hardest to play a prominent, front-line role in the modern-day financial system. Note that this has had little to do with their age. Rather, it has had most to do with the fundamental reasons for their original establishment, the way in which they have been controlled and operated, and the balances of power within them.

When it comes to the role and work of international institutions, one of the most delicate topics is the extent to which they further and foster economic and political policy prescriptions with regard to respective countries and governments. Historically the IMF has been accused of championing the development ideologies of the US and attempting to bring countries into Washington's sphere of influence. Here the critical discussion is not how or why the IMF has championed relatively pro-Western policies in the developing world but how countries like the US have been able to leverage themselves within such institutions to the point of being able to make them do such ground work for them.

As observers looked back on the IMF's work in the developing world, particularly in the latter years of the twentieth century, the questions many asked were: did the Fund actually benefit from peddling pro-Western policy? Did its decisions to leverage and openly support some policies and not others hinder its success in particular parts of the world?

The work of the IMF in Latin America during the 1990s is a useful place to start in answering questions like these. It is here that they start to become clear.

WHO IS THE MESSENGER?

International financial institutions have long been assigned the challenge of taking globalisation to the developing world. Their ability to marry Western notions of politico-economic liberalism with an existing domestic financial and political infrastructure has by and large determined the effectiveness of their reform prescriptions. It can be argued that liberal institutionalism was critical to the implementation of free market economics in Latin America during the 1990s. But as a 'crisis manager', the IMF failed to adequately protect the economies of Mexico, Brazil and Argentina from financial collapse — caused in part by its own neoliberal economic and monetary reform policies. Effectively, the Fund's inconsistent response to these crises undermined the region's faith in economic liberalism and, ultimately, the success of the US Treasury's 'Washington Consensus' agenda.

To illustrate how the IMF administered key economic policy prescriptions in Latin America throughout the twentieth century, this chapter will explore and assess three regional financial crises that were triggered in the 1990s. These crises culminated in the currency collapses of Mexico in 1994, Brazil in 1999, and Argentina in 2001 respectively. Each section will highlight the cause of each crisis, the IMF's response, and the administration of the 'Washington Consensus' in each case. Throughout the 1990s, Latin American countries actively worked with international financial institutions like the IMF to reform their economic and political infrastructures in a bid to legitimise their desire to play a more prominent role in the contemporary, globally integrated free market. Each section will consider these specific bids.

THE NEED TO BE RELEVANT

Since the 1970s the IMF's role in the global financial system has been determined by the evolution of free market economics. Established in July 1944 at the Bretton Woods Conference in the US, the IMF's main purpose was to oversee the adjustable-peg exchange rate system through surveillance, standard-setting and crisis prevention. With the collapse of the adjustable-peg for international currencies in the 1970s, the IMF was reinvented and given a new purpose, namely, the prevention, management and containment of financial crises in developing countries. Its reinvention coincided with the need for a global economic watchman during the international debt crisis of the 1980s. According to Helleiner (2008), it was at this critical time in the world's financial history that the IMF was given a new lease of life.

With the policy and capital backing of the US, the IMF was put in charge of "stabilising the financial underpinnings necessary for real national economies to become more deeply interdependent and more reliably prosperous through expanded trade" (Pauly, 2008, p. 265). Today, the IMF acknowledges that over the course of modern economic history it has had to be amenable to change to stay current and relevant in an evolving world political economy (International Monetary Fund, 2008, p. 245). The timing of the IMF's redirection during the 1980s cannot be undervalued, however. As Pauly (2008) points out, the main crises capable of derailing the international system late in the twentieth century occurred in emerging markets. As the integration of developing countries into a global marketplace became more important, so too did the need for an institution that could look after the transition. In effect, the IMF's crisis management role became more obvious as "capital account liberalisation became a clearer collective policy objective at the international level" (Pauly, 2008, p. 266).

During the 1990s the IMF built close working relationships with developing countries throughout the South and Central Americas. In the short term these mostly bilateral connections were mutually beneficial. For instance, the IMF was able to administer neoliberal economic reforms in countries like Mexico, Brazil and Argentina that led to their deeper integration into the global financial system. By accepting and implementing the prescribed reforms, these countries enjoyed an increase in foreign investment and domestic growth. For variable lengths of time, they all basked in the novelty of being the star pupils of a formidable international financial institution.

Throughout this time the regional influence of the Fund's key contributor, the US, also grew. The IMF's multilateral network provided the perfect means by which the international superpower could simultaneously connect with and influence a number of countries — economically and politically. This was no accident. It was rather a strategic (and well-calculated) tenet of US foreign policy at the time. Fundamentally, the US's leverage within the IMF and its relative control of the institution's economic reform policies was inextricably linked to the dollar value of its capital investment. This is why Momani claims that "it would be naïve to argue that the United States contributes significant amounts to the Fund's liquidity without the expectation of having its voice heard on key strategic allies at all levels of the Fund's decision-making process" (Momani, 2004, p. 898).

As the case studies of Mexico, Brazil and Argentina illustrate, there is a fundamental loss of economic sovereignty and monetary autonomy associated with the neoliberal reforms prescribed by institutions like the IMF. Despite the Fund's well-documented policy-prescription failures in Latin America, Asia and Africa throughout the 1990s, however, defenders of international financial institutions still argue that forced economic conversion is the price developing countries still have to pay for deeper integration and wider access to the contemporary, interdependent marketplace. Additionally, they continue to support the notion that the benefits of being brought into the fold far outweigh the initial political damage and financial costs (or losses) that domestic markets incur. Thirkell-White goes so far as to contend that "the maintenance of a functioning international economy has always relied on international political coordination, whether institutionalised or not" (Thirkell-White, 2005, p. 30).

Fundamentally, since the 1970s, international financial institutions like the IMF have — often through little choice of their own — become organisers of the modern marketplace. Their prominence in the global economic system has made them convenient channels or conduits through which Western states like the US have been able to entice developing countries into democratising their political systems and liberalising their domestic economies.

THE 'WASHINGTON CONSENSUS' — A ONE-WORLD STRATEGY

The 'Washington Consensus' was one of the US Treasury's strongest post-war economic manifestos: a clear and focused blueprint for the creation of a self-regulated international market, free of government control. Coined by the US economist John Williamson in 1989, the term 'Washington Consensus' refers to a set of ten policy prescriptions that formed the basis of the US's foreign economic reform package during the 1990s. Broad argues that the ten prescriptions can be broken down into five key categories: trade liberalisation, deregulation, privatisation, financial liberalisation and debt-crisis management (Broad, 2004, p. 129). The main purpose of the 'Consensus' was to integrate developing countries, particularly those in the Americas with which the US had bilateral economic and political ties, into a free market financial system (Gallagher, 2007). It aimed to do this by breaking down protectionist trade barriers and political systems through overt and covert neoliberal economic reform.

Economic reform provided the US with a chance to pursue political change within the region. Up until the late 1980s, Latin America's political landscape was dominated by authoritarian regimes. And while the US did not share or agree with the political visions of its regional partners, up until the late twentieth century it was amenable to establishing economic links with them. As globalisation dawned, however, authoritarianism was no longer acceptable to the US or compatible with its definition of democracy. By the end of the twentieth century, the US had become less amenable to integrating 'closed' authoritarian regimes into an 'open' global market. As a result democracy became part and parcel of the 'Washington Consensus'. From there on and throughout the 1990s, the developing countries of the Americas were required to install civilian, democratic regimes for two reasons: to reap the rewards of a free market economy and to be entitled to the financial, political and military protection of the world's most powerful nation. Through the 'Washington Consensus' the US was able to revolutionise the political economy of the region. Whereas in the past US policy supported the relationships between authoritarian regime and capitalism, Gamarra claims that in the 1980s Latin America "conveniently highlighted a relationship between open, competitive political systems and market economies" (Gamarra, 1994, p. 3).

Throughout the 1990s the 'Washington Consensus' served as an important cornerstone of US foreign economic policy. Despite its prominence in the government's international policy portfolio, however, its success was greatly contingent upon its institutionalisation. The policy prescriptions it entailed proved too rigid, demanding, and invasive to be sold by the US Treasury in unilateral terms. The 'Washington Consensus' (and the neoliberal ideology to which it was attached) needed to be funnelled through a global, multilateral network. At the time the IMF appeared to be the perfect institution for the purpose. For the US the benefit of disseminating neoliberal economic reforms through such an organisation was two-fold: it was able to reach more countries in the region simultaneously and protect itself against accusations of being overly aggressive and invasive in its pursuit of a self-regulated, integrated global economy, free of government control. The IMF is best described in this period of global financial history as an 'agent' of the US — one of many bodies the Treasury used during the early years of globalisation to promote economic and political neoliberal reform in developing countries.

The IMF sold the 'Washington Consensus' to policy makers in poor countries as the only way to secure a place in the new 'global' economy. Additionally the institution convinced developing countries it was the best way to guard against economic isolation and volatility in an age of deepening interdependence. As the case studies of Mexico, Brazil and Argentina demonstrate, this sales pitch did two things contrary to the IMF's expectations, however: it lulled political leaders into a false sense of financial security, and it encouraged irresponsible economic and political decision making under the security blanket of financial institutions like the IMF — a risk best described by analysts as moral hazard. Essentially the 'Washington Consensus' was the US Treasury's economic blueprint for the 1990s: a set of policy prescriptions that sold economic liberalism as the only way to achieve peace and prosperity. As an agent of economic reform the IMF attempted to implement the 'Washington Consensus' in countries like Mexico to build economic stability, promote deeper integration, and remedy financial crises.

1994 — THE MEXICAN *PESO* CRISIS

The 1994 Mexican *peso* crisis is best known as the first emerging market crash of the 1990s. The crisis had a long gestation period (Edwards and Naim, 1997) but it was the eventual collapse of the *peso* that actually marked the end of the Mexican miracle: a period of politico-economic restructuring and repositioning that was described by the IMF as a time of "remarkable economic transformation" (International Monetary Fund, 2008). The Mexican miracle was based on drastic economic reforms prescribed by the IMF and administered by the Mexican government from the late 1980s through to 1994. The reforms included the liberalisation of the country's banking and trade sectors. This made Mexico's banking sector more amenable to foreign capital investment while the trade reforms broke down protectionist barriers, making the country more open to foreign goods and services, particularly those from the US. Here it is important to note the domestic social and political contexts within which the eventual currency collapse took place. The crisis occurred at a time when Mexico's economy was one of the strongest in the region, yet its political system was one of the weakest. In 1994, then-President Carlos Salinas was fighting numerous domestic battles, including a guerrilla insurgency in the poverty-stricken state of Chiapas. His battle for political survival was partially responsible for the prolonged mismanagement of Mexico's burgeoning economy and the government's failure to recognise the signs of an impending crisis.

By the mid-1990s Mexico's economy was buckling under the weight of unfettered and unregulated capital inflow along with a growing current account deficit. In a bid to ease the pressure in December 1994, the newly elected government of President Ernesto Zedillo devalued the *peso* by 15.3%. The move broke the *peso's* peg to the US dollar and sent the domestic banking system into a tailspin. Investor panic resulted in a huge speculative attack on the nation's banks and a massive flight of capital. The currency collapse reversed all the financial gains Mexico had made as a result of implementing the IMF-prescribed capital account liberalisation policies throughout the 'miracle years' of the 1990s. Despite having successfully administered economic reform as outlined in the 'Washington Consensus', the IMF had failed to ensure that Mexico's financial system was equipped with the checks and balances to prevent such an enormous and debilitating financial crisis from building and culminating in an all-out currency collapse.

Fundamentally the *peso* crisis was the result of unregulated capital inflow, an unsustainable current account deficit, and political uncertainty. These problems did not manifest overnight. Analysts argue that the signs of a looming crisis were visible as early as 1990 (Edwards and Naim, 1997). The *peso* crisis did send alarm bells ringing across the region, however. Contagion spread to other Latin American economies, like Brazil, but no country feared a financial crisis in Mexico more than the US. Having signed the North American Free Trade Agreement (NAFTA) with its neighbour in January 1994, the US was susceptible to every shock in the Latin American market. Highlighting the significance of the US-Mexico economic bond, Hakim wrote, "The United States' most important relationship in Latin America is with Mexico. No other country in the world affects the lives of Americans as much, and no other country is more intensely affected by US policies" (Hakim, 2001, p. 57).

With the financial backing of the Clinton administration, early in 1995 the IMF threw Mexico a fifty-two billion US dollar lifeline. The bailout was contingent upon the Mexican government's acceptance and implementation of more sweeping economic reforms. Based on the policies outlined in the 'Washington Consensus', these reforms included fiscal and monetary policy adjustments, the establishment of a floating exchange rate, market liberalisation, and the provision of financial emergency measures. Through the implementation of these reforms, the Fund tried to do two things: protect the US and (to a lesser extent) the global marketplace from contagion, and facilitate an environment of continued economic reform within Mexico itself.

The IMF's reaction to the Mexican currency crisis is best described as delayed. The financial storm that lashed the US's neighbour had been brewing long before the *peso* collapsed in December 1994. Unfettered foreign capital investment and a large current account deficit throughout the 'miracle years' placed pressure on an already weak domestic banking sector that was still reeling from a national debt crisis in 1982. It was evident that the Fund saw the crisis building. Despite surveillance being a key plank of its mandate, it failed to provide the Mexican government and foreign investors with clear and adequate warning signs of the financial catastrophe that was likely to ensue if unfettered growth and investment were not curtailed. As late as March 1994, the IMF's Managing Director, Michael Camdessus, claimed that Mexican authorities were pursuing "fundamentally sound economic policies" (Edwards and Naim, 1997, p. 101). In this instance the IMF's response is best viewed as self-preservation rather than institutional negligence. During the 1990s Mexico was one of the crisis manager's star pupils — a shining example of neoliberalism, democracy, and free market principles in action. It was the best example the IMF had of the successful implementation of the 'Washington Consensus'. The Fund intervened in Mexico to protect its investment in the country's economic reforms and to defend its administration of American neoliberal politico-economic policies. Without such an intervention, it is unlikely that similar free market reforms would have spread throughout Latin America, and from a regional perspective, the IMF would have been marginalised to the point of redundancy.

1999 — THE BRAZILIAN *REAL* CRISIS

When the Brazilian economy fell upon tough times in 1999 the IMF was attempting to re-establish its credibility as a global 'crisis manager' and keep the ideals of free market economics afloat. This followed its lacklustre response to the 1997 East Asian financial crisis. Throughout the 1990s, under the direction of the IMF, Brazil implemented the 'Washington Consensus'. It did this through a series of economic reform programmes that aimed to rein in the country's wayward economy and regulate its banking sector. Despite these apparent corrections, however, Brazil faced ongoing macroeconomic difficulties: an overvalued *real* and a huge current account deficit. Similar to Mexico's *peso* crisis, Brazil's financial meltdown had a long gestation period. As early as August 1997, foreign capital began flowing out of the country. This was largely due to the contagion caused by the East Asian financial collapse.

With its reputation as a global 'crisis manager' in tatters the IMF moved to rebuild international confidence by acting pre-emptively in Brazil. Late in 1998 the Fund acted to cushion the blow of capital flight and provide the government with a forty-two billion US dollar financial aid package. Additionally, the international financial institution began consulting President Cardoso's government on the '*Real* Plan' — devised to once again stabilise the national currency and reform Brazil's domestic banking sector. The huge IMF aid package and the new fiscal plan failed to stem the outflow of foreign capital, however. The *real* was subsequently floated in January 1999 and Brazil entered a period of economic recession. As Cason said at the time, "the Brazilian stabilisation solution was resting on a house of cards. If fiscal, monetary and exchange rate policies were not reconciled, then the house would collapse" (Cason, 2001, p. 203). This was because the Brazilian currency crisis was a combination of three factors: political and economic policy failures; a weak banking system operating with an overabundance of liquidity; and an over-dependence on increasingly volatile capital flows (Santiso, 2003, p. 26).

As a 'crisis manager' the IMF's response to the Brazilian meltdown was two-dimensional. Prior to the collapse it provided the Brazilian economy with financial cushioning and actively supported the government in its implementation of a fiscal restructuring programme. For all intents and purposes the *real* rescue package was meant to be 'preventative' as opposed to 'curative' (Chossudovsky, 1999). The IMF echoed this sentiment in a statement on 4 February 1999, in which it claimed "The firm implementation of these policies should promote a lasting recovery of confidence, both domestically and abroad, an indispensable condition for the resumption of sustainable growth of output and employment towards the end of 1999" (IMF, 1999). When the *real* eventually collapsed, the IMFs role in the crisis changed, however. Its focus shifted from prevention to protection and rebuilding. Late in 1999, as Brazil slipped deeper into recession, the Fund began to oversee the implementation of more liberal economic reforms, such as those embodied in the 1998 '*Real* Plan'. These reforms were deemed necessary not only to restore domestic and global confidence in the Brazilian currency but also to manage the spread of contagion throughout the region and beyond.

The IMF's actions in Brazil highlight an institutional urge, and a push from within, to get back to a particular kind of basics. The Fund's response to the second major currency crisis faced by Latin America in the 1990s was in keeping with its historical mandate of surveillance. In fact, for the first time in a series of crises, the IMF began to fulfil its role as an early-warning system for the globally integrated, modern-day marketplace (Wroughton, 2008). It is also important to note that the institution's return to traditional (neoliberalist) values was by and large to prove it could still play a valuable role in the international financial system, following its lacklustre management of the 1997 East Asian financial crisis.

In the case of Brazil, the IMF responded pre-emptively for three reasons: to restore international confidence in its ability to identify and contain financial crises; to prevent contagion from reaching the world's largest economy — the US; and to keep Brazil on the path of neoliberal economic reform — a process it began in the 1980s. The main difference between the IMF's response to Mexico's *peso* crisis in 1995 and Brazil's *real* crisis in 1999 was timing. In Mexico, the institution's response was hesitant and delayed. In Brazil, it acted pre-emptively to cushion the blow of an eventual currency collapse. The IMFs response to the *real* crisis highlighted the time-centric and reactionary nature of the organisation, though. It was clear that the international crisis of confidence in the role and capabilities of the IMF following the East Asian financial crisis was critical to the Fund's pre-emptive action in Brazil.

By institutionalising the management of the '*Real* Plan', the IMF successfully ensured the ongoing administration of the 'Washington Consensus' in Brazil. Furthermore, it reaffirmed, in fact even guaranteed, the US's political and economic clout in the region. As the crisis unfolded, it created an environment within which the stronghold of Wall Street creditors over monetary policy was bolstered under the stewardship of the IMF (Chossudovsky, 1999). As a 'crisis manager', the IMFs response to the collapse of the *real* was remarkably different to its intervention in Mexico in 1994. And while it was able to regain some of the credibility it had lost five years earlier, it failed to capitalise on any such gains during the Argentine *peso* crisis of 2001.

2001 — THE ARGENTINE *PESO* CRISIS

The Argentine *peso* crisis completely stretched Latin America's faith in free market economics and signalled the end of rosy relations between the IMF's star pupils and Wall Street. From the early 1990s the IMF guided Argentina through a series of intense fiscal reforms based on the principles of economic liberalisation as embodied in the 'Washington Consensus'. Collectively known as the convertibility plan, academics describe the reforms as "one of the most drastic and far-reaching experiments in neoliberalism" (Onis, 2004, p. 377). Central to the reform process was the establishment of a currency board system. This aimed to stabilise the Argentine economy and democratise the country's banking system by making it more accountable and transparent. While the currency board allowed Argentina to regulate its domestic market by altering its price stability point, it stifled monetary autonomy by stripping the government of its ability to finance budget deficits and create new money (Onis, 2004).

By the second half of the 1990s capital was flowing freely into Argentina. Its openness to foreign capital made it the darling of investment banks and bond managers around the world. Despite the inflow of capital during that time, however, Argentina's current account deficit and external debt burden mushroomed. By 2001 the country had been in recession for three years and its economy was crumbling. International market volatility sparked by the terrorist attacks in the US on September 11 that year, together with domestic political instability, prompted the interim government to take action. It announced a moratorium on debt payments, sending shockwaves through the domestic banking sector. Panicked investors began withdrawing large sums of money from Argentine banks, triggering a run on the national currency. The Argentine *peso* eventually collapsed at the beginning of 2002. This had a devastating effect on the domestic economy, causing serious poverty and curbing investor confidence. The result was an unstable political situation, waning social support for IMF-administered reforms and a decaying political and economic infrastructure. This created in turn a national system not of prosperity but of profound financial crisis.

The IMF detected the makings of an Argentine financial crisis as early as 2000. In that year, with the political backing of the Clinton administration, it had attempted to prop up the Argentine economy with a forty billion dollar conditional aid package. The conditions (based on the economic reform policies outlined by the 'Washington Consensus') included a drastic and immediate reduction in the country's budget deficit. The bailout provided only momentary relief, however. It failed to stop the Argentine economy from slipping further. On the brink of default in November 2001, Argentina turned to the IMF for more support. After much deliberation and a divisive internal debate, the Fund offered Argentina nine billion dollars in the first months of 2002 (Setser and Gelpern, 2006).

As a 'crisis manager' the IMF's response to the Argentine *peso* crisis is best described as disjointed. The Fund clearly detected the problem early enough but it bailed out of Argentina's financial system when its pre-emptive rescue plan failed. At the time, it claimed the Argentine government had failed to adequately implement the fiscal reforms it had prescribed to remedy the crisis. When the *peso* eventually collapsed, however, the Fund was unwilling to provide further financial and consultative assistance, or at least, to do so fast enough to avert a complete domestic banking disaster and prevent the spread of contagion.

The IMF's response in the case of Argentina can be attributed to two factors: frustration with the government's economic and political malfunctioning and a change of leadership in the US. For two decades the democratic administration led by US President Bill Clinton used large monetary handouts or financial aid packages to guard against contagion and to protect the integrity of the 'Washington Consensus'. The Republican Party, led by George W. Bush, swept into office in 2001 with a new politico-economic foreign policy: one that still prioritised Latin American relations and the US's regional influence but did not support the Clinton administration's bailout policy. The case of Argentina highlighted a distinctive move away from jumbo packages and economic policies driven by the fear of contagion (Setser and Gelpern, 2006, p. 477). This said, it was clear that throughout the 1990s the US Treasury had actively supported the implementation of neoliberal economic reforms by institutions like the IMF in Latin America and for two reasons: a desire to standardise national and regional economies and to exert further economic and political influence in its own backyard. While the IMF was largely unsuccessful in keeping Argentina on the track to economic liberalisation, the Fund's oversight of the country's convertibility plan in the 1990s and the provision of a huge Treasury-backed financial aid package in 2000 did demonstrate the US's desire to dominate the region by reforming domestic economic and political systems one country at a time.

THE MOST CONDUCIVE MEDIUMS

The crises described above highlight the critical role that liberal institutionalism has played in the spread of democracy and the spread of free market economics as embodied in John Williamson's 'Washington Consensus' of 1989. The three case studies of the currency crises that struck Latin American states during the 1990s highlight how the reform prescriptions embedded in this manifesto were too rigid and invasive to be implemented by the US on a unilateral basis.

The success of the 'Washington Consensus' was contingent upon its institutionalisation and the IMF — given its post-1970s mandate and multilateral, global reach — was the most convenient and effective institution for the challenge. Through it the US Treasury department was able to dictate neoliberal fiscal reforms to developing countries, particularly those in the Americas that were of economic and strategic importance. The case studies of the financial crises that struck Mexico, Brazil and Argentina in the 1990s indicate that despite the loss of economic sovereignty and monetary autonomy, the governments of these countries initially welcomed the 'Washington Consensus' and the IMF's involvement in their financial, business and domestic reform processes. They signed up to the reforms in a bid to become bigger players in the contemporary, integrated marketplace. It was the IMF's response to these countries in their times of financial need, however, that greatly jeopardised the success of the 'Washington Consensus' and America's postmodern politico-economic policies. The IMF's mismanagement of its reform programmes and its mishandling of these crises also curbed the region's faith in neoliberalist reform at large. The financial crises experienced by Mexico, Brazil and Argentina unequivocally highlighted the fact that the IMF was not a 'crisis manager'. Rather it was a reactionary institution whose behaviour was dictated not by the needs and requirements of the modern marketplace but by its own necessity to remain a viable, credible and integral part of the global financial system.

THE FIGHT FOR SURVIVAL

There is one question above all others that international agencies and organisations have not only had to entertain but attempt to find an answer to in recent decades. This is: how to stay relevant in the modern-day financial system?

While they continue to attempt to find answers to this question they are obliged to consider a number of other factors. By structure and design, agencies like the IMF and the World Bank are not fast-changing or fast-moving bodies. Their complex bureaucracies and systems of governance render them unable to take action quickly, especially when it comes to their own management and administrative practices. Their relative immobility in comparison to the speed with which the market and its parameters change continue to be a challenge for these agencies and is likely to remains so for the foreseeable future.

It must also be noted that the economic and political landscapes they attempt to do business in are very different from those that both agencies were established to deal with. It can feasibly be argued, for example, that the concentration of the world's wealth and power is shifting and is now being transferred beyond the Western world. For the greater part of the last sixty years these organisations have never looked to Asia and the Pacific, Africa, Latin America or the Middle East for leadership and momentum, let alone capital and financial investment. They have interacted with the aforementioned regions of the world by way of assistance or guidance in times of crisis or during periods of development. Put simply, they have always helped the countries and governments of these regions but they have never faced a situation, like they do today, where they have had to acknowledge and take note of what their economic and political clout and decision-making capabilities really mean.

While trying to establish how to stay relevant, the IMF and the World Bank have also had to acknowledge that governments and their constituents — be they Ireland or Pakistan — are highly protective today of their political as well as their economic sovereignty. Take the IMF for example: historically, its policy prescriptions were underwritten by an almost guaranteed loss of control of key decision-making powers on the part of the governments or leaders who required their assistance. While it may have been accepted as part and parcel of their work in the past, in today's fast-paced, competitive, global financial system, terms and conditions like these are far more difficult for governments to accept. Control is far less easy to concede. Leaving aside the economic ramifications, states and their leaders have come to realise that the political fallout from making such concessions to an international financial institution can be detrimental and possibly counterproductive.

The performance of both institutions, during times of crisis and development, has been well-documented. Citizens in every corner of the world know of these agencies and what they do. When considering their future it is important to keep in mind that they were first and foremost products of their time, however. Their respective roles and duties changed and evolved as the world's economic and political landscapes required but it is not clear how much flexibility they continue to have. How much can they be moulded in the years to come? At one extreme, analysts ponder the idea of getting rid of them altogether. At the other are those who say there is no viable alternative and that they must be maintained.

CONCLUSION

The mistakes and shortcomings of the IMF and the World Bank are familiar components of the story of the contemporary international political economy, so are their respective triumphs and achievements.

The difficulty and the challenge now lies in balancing the ledger. It lies in ascertaining what these international financial institutions are currently doing well and what they are not.

It lies in reforming them so that they can continue to do well in the future or in abolishing them if their usefulness is at an end. In this regard it is important to note that relevance, in today's high-speed politico-economic environment, is only ever — at best — a relative business.

REFERENCES

Broad, R (2004). The Washington consensus meets the global backlash: Shifting debates and policies, *Globalisations*, 1(2), 129–154.

Cason, J (2001). Brazil: Political Institutions and Delayed Reaction to Financial Crisis. In *The Political Economy of International Financial Crisis*, S Horowitz and U Heo (eds.). Singapore: Institute of Southeast Asian Studies.

Chossudovsky, M (1999). Brazil's IMF-Sponsored economic disaster. *The Third World Network*. http://www.turnside.org/title/latin-cn.htm [27 September 2008].

Edwards, S and M Naim (1997). Introduction: Anatomy and Lessons of Mexico in 1994. In *Mexico: 1994 Anatomy of an Emerging-Market Crash*, S Edwards and M Naim (eds.). Washington, DC: Carnegie Endowment for International Peace.

Gallagher, K (2007). Economic reform and foreign direct investment in Latin America: A critical assessment. *Progress in Development Studies*, 7(3), 217–233.

Gamarra, E (1994). Market-Orientated Reforms and Democratisation in Latin America: Challenges of the 1990s. In *Latin American Political Economy in the Age of Neoliberal Reform*, W Smith, C Acuna and E Gamarra (eds.). New Brunswick: Transaction Publishers.

Hakim, P (2001). The Uneasy Americas. *Foreign Affairs*, 80(2), 46–61.

Helleiner, E (2008). The Evaluation of the International Monetary and Financial System. In *Global Political Economy*, J Ravenhill (ed.). New York: Oxford University Press.

International Monetary Fund (2008). *World Economic Outlook*. The International Monetary Fund, http://www.imf.org/external/pubs/ft/weo/2008/02/pdf/annex.pdf [14 December 2011].

International Monetary Fund (1999). *Joint Statement of the Ministry of Finance of Brazil and the IMF Team*. The International Monetary Fund, http://www.imf.org/external/nb/1999/nb9905.htm [27 September 2008].

Momani, B (2004). American politicization of the International Monetary Fund, *Review of International Political Economy*, 11(5), 880–904.

Onis, Z (2004). Argentina, the IMF, and the limits of neo-liberal globalisation: A comparative perspective, *The Review of International Affairs*, 3(3), 375–392.

Pauly, L (2008). The Political Economy of Global Financial Crisis. In *Global Political Economy*, J Ravenhill (ed.). New York: Oxford University Press.

Pauly, L (1999). Good governance and bad policy: The perils of international organisational overextension, *Review of International Political Economy*, 6(4), 401–424.

Santiso, J (2003). *The Political Economy of Emerging Markets: Actors, Institutions and Financial Crises in Latin America*. New York: Palgrave Macmillan.

Setser, B and A Gelpern (2006). Pathways through financial crisis: Argentina, *Global Governance*, 12, 465–487.

Thirkell-White, B (2005). IMF Legitimacy: Principles and Institutions. In *The IMF and the Politics of Financial Globalisation — From the Asian Crisis to a New International Financial Architecture?* B Thirkell-White (ed.). United Kingdom: Palgrave Macmillan.

Wroughton, L (2008). Sidelined in U.S. crisis, IMF's day may still come. Thomson Reuters, http://www.reuters.com/article/reutersEdge/idUSN2140108620080921?sp=true [27 September 2008].

CHAPTER 14

Corruption and Financial Crises

Leslie Holmes

University of Melbourne

Since the early 1990s corruption has been a prominent topic in the social sciences. This is largely because of what Naím (1995) calls a 'corruption eruption', namely, a substantial increase in the scale of corruption worldwide.

Given the considerable problems involved in trying to measure this increase, it is unclear whether or not there really has been a radical increase in corruption rates. There can be no question, however, that there is a considerable amount of corruption in the contemporary world and that the general *awareness* of it has grown substantially over the past two decades.

Numerous suggestions have been put forward to explain this growth, several of them relating to the end of the Cold War. Until the end of the 1980s, the fact that most of the world's states were in one of two camps — one oriented towards the US, the other towards the USSR (a third group of states consciously opted not to align with either camp and so formed the Non-Aligned Movement) — meant that Washington was generally unwilling to criticise actual or potential allies for their corruption for fear that this might encourage such states to align with the Soviet bloc. Once the latter had collapsed, this constraint on the US government disappeared.

Another reason connected to the end of the Cold War is that Western states became more introspective during the 1990s. They were more willing then, than during a period of ideological competition, to examine and acknowledge their own flaws.

Thirdly, the transition to democracy that began in many post-communist states around 1990 was accompanied by much freer press reporting of negative developments. This included much greater coverage of corruption.

Moving away from the Cold War, and a fourth factor, is the way a number of individuals from the World Bank became increasingly aware during the 1990s of the negative effects of corruption on aid to developing states. One of them, who had been in charge of World Bank operations in East Africa (Peter Eigen), was so convinced that corruption was hindering the development of poorer states that he left the Bank in 1993 and founded what was to become the world's leading anti-corruption INGO, Transparency International (TI). Two years later, in 1995, James Wolfensohn became President of the World Bank and soon declared corruption to be the leading cause of poverty in the world. In line with this, the World Bank adopted a number of measures in the second half of the 1990s designed to both measure and reduce corruption.

A heightened interest in corruption resulted in a dramatic increase in the number of anti-corruption NGOs around the world. One downside to this expansion was the growth of what has been called the 'anti-corruption industry' (Sampson, 2010). Many of these NGOs — especially in developing and transition states — were dependent on foreign funding. Since it was usually in the NGOs' interests to make the corruption situation in their country look as serious as possible, so as to ensure continued external funding, the scale and nature of corruption was in some cases exaggerated. This, too, helps to explain the perception of a 'corruption eruption'.

The growing awareness was also reflected in the fact that many of the world's leading IOs, both global and regional, adopted explicit anti-corruption measures aftere the mid-1990s. These included the OECD (Anti-Bribery Recommendations 1994; the Anti-Bribery Convention adopted 1997, effective 1999); the Organisation of American States (Inter-American Convention against Corruption, 1996); the Council of Europe (the Criminal Law Convention on Corruption, 1999; the Civil Law Convention on Corruption, 1999); the Asian Development Bank (ADB) and the OECD jointly (the Anti-Corruption Action Plan for Asia and the Pacific, 2001); the African Union (the Convention on Preventing and Combating Corruption, 2003); and the UN, whose Convention against Corruption (adopted 2003, effective December 2005) is described by the UN itself as the world's first and only legally binding universal anti-corruption instrument.

International awareness of the corruption issue was raised further in the 2000s in the aftermath of the events of 9/11, as states and IOs became increasingly conscious of the role of money laundering in terrorist activities, and of the connections between terrorism, organised crime and corruption (Masciandaro, 2004; van Duyne *et al.*, 2004; Holmes, 2007; Chaikin and Sharman, 2009). While the OECD had shown serious concern about money laundering in the 1980s, and had in this context established the Financial Action Task Force (FATF) in 1989, the focus for many years was primarily on laundering by organised crime. The events of 9/11 significantly broadened the FATF's focus, which came to include money laundering by both terrorist organisations and corrupt officials.

In sum, corruption has become a major global concern. The rest of this chapter will be devoted to considering the role corruption has played in three financial crises — the Asian and the Russian in the 1990s and the GFC that finally erupted in 2008. After briefly describing these three financial crises, the chapter will consider some possible meanings of the concept of corruption, since the answer to the question 'how significant a role did corruption play in the three financial crises?' depends in part on the definition of corruption adopted. This will be followed by a brief overview of the problems that arise in trying to measure corruption and its impact. It will consider some of the empirical evidence with regard to corruption's role in the financial crises mentioned above; some of the explanations for corruption; and some conclusions. The underlying argument is that corruption, however defined, has been a contributory factor in all the financial crises considered but that its significance lies primarily in the fact that it symbolises the problems of the neoliberal approach to capitalism.

THREE FINANCIAL CRISES

There have been numerous financial crises in the past two centuries; the focus here is on just three recent ones. The first is the major crisis that affected many Asian states in 1997–1998. This crisis emerged in July 1997 when the Thai currency was suddenly and substantially devalued. Major devaluations of the Indonesian, Malaysian and Philippine currencies soon followed. These devaluations had numerous negative ramifications for the countries concerned.

The second crisis erupted less than a year after the Asian crisis had emerged and was similar to it. Thus the Russian crisis, which erupted in August 1998, was marked by a sudden, dramatic decline in the exchange rate of the ruble. Clear signs of serious economic problems had already emerged by May 1998, however, when the government's repayment of its debts began to exceed its gross budgetary revenues. Another sign was a major loan package to Russia from the IMF in July 1998 (for details see Tikhomirov, 1998). As with the Asian one, the Russian financial crisis had significant negative knock-on effects on the economy concerned.

In terms of its impact — on the number of countries affected, the duration, and likely after effects — the GFC has been by far the most significant financial crisis since the October 1929 Wall Street Crash. This time the tipping point was not exchange rates — though the value of the US dollar did decline — but the collapse of a 'blue chip' financial services firm, Lehman Brothers, which filed for bankruptcy in September 2008. The significance of this lay not only in the prestige of the company until shortly before its collapse — it had weathered numerous crises since its establishment in 1850 — but in the fact that this was by far the largest bankruptcy in US history, and that it symbolised the fact that a liquidity crisis had hit US banking. Once again, there had been numerous signs earlier of the emerging crisis: these included the sudden downturn in US house prices in 2007; Lehman Brothers withdrawal from the subprime mortgage sector in August 2007; the abnormally large (0.75%) lowering of interest rates in one hit in January 2008;

a major stimulus package in February designed to avoid a US recession; the announcement in March that almost eight percent of US mortgages had been foreclosed or were seriously in arrears; and the US government takeover of the major mortgage lenders and guarantors (Fannie Mae and Freddie Mac) in September. This time, the financial crisis was not essentially confined to one country or region. Within months most of the world's leading economies had fallen into recession, and many continued to experience severe economic problems.

Each of these three crises was complex and none can be explained in terms of just one factor. It is worth noting, however, what have been identified as the primary factors.

The Asian crisis was explained by the IMF in terms of weak banking practices that were linked in turn to corruption of various types (including 'crony capitalism' — an example of Types B and D in the taxonomy elaborated below). Others explained it primarily in psychological terms, that is, a mass panic resulting in abnormally high withdrawal rates from leading banks. Others again blamed IMF policies.

Contagion from the Asian crisis was seen as a major factor leading to the Russian crisis. So was poor management of the transition to a marketised and privatised economy with the collapse of the Soviet Union.

In the case of the GFC, many observers pointed to the subprime mortgage crisis in the US as the root of a much bigger general crisis in liquidity, which was caused in turn by excessive risk-taking. All of these explanations were valid, but all of them were incomplete, which is why many analyses also identified misconduct — corruption — by state officials, corporations and banks as contributory factors.

CORRUPTION'S ROLE IN THE FINANCIAL CRISES

Determining the role corruption played in the three crises nominated above is a complex and controversial task. One of the problems applies to most research projects related to corruption, namely, obtaining adequate and reliable information. This is not the only difficulty, however. Another relates to the meaning and nature of corruption. Thus, to no small extent, the answer to the question: 'how significant was the corruption factor in the three financial crises?' depends on at least two subjective decisions — how corruption is defined and how it is measured.

DEFINITIONAL ISSUES

Corruption is a concept whose meaning can vary, not only across time but also across countries and cultures and even within them. Since one person's bribe is another person's gift, many pages could be devoted to consideration of the definitional issues involved in discussing corruption. Given space limitations, the focus here is on just two key parts of the debate. Both relate to the scope of corruption — who and what it covers. In order to minimise confusion, corruption is conceptualised here along two axes. The first relates to who or what is potentially corrupt and so is called the 'identity' axis; the second refers to what is included under the term 'corruption' and is therefore called the 'range' (of corruption) axis.

Consider first the 'identity' axis. The most common definition of corruption is 'the private abuse of public office' or something very similar. While the meaning of 'private' can be debated, the key point for the purposes of the present analysis is the emphasis on 'public office'. This is usually interpreted to refer to positions within the state machinery, whether elected or appointed, and whether these positions are in the administrative, repressive or ideological apparatuses (the latter two terms are from Althusser, 1971, pp. 142–148). Using this first definition of corruption does not mean that private agents are excluded; indeed, they are frequently involved in corruption by paying bribes to state officials. This first definition does require the improper involvement of an officer of the state, however.

Until the end of the 1990s, TI employed a definition almost identical to that quoted in the previous paragraph — 'the abuse of public office for private gain'. But at the start of the 2000s, TI broadened its definition to 'the abuse of entrusted power for private gain'. By replacing the term 'public office' with 'entrusted power', TI intended to demonstrate that misconduct purely in the private sector was as much in its sights as misconduct in the state had long been. According to the new TI definition, a private corporation offering bribes to another, or deliberately operating — either alone or in collusion with other firms — against the interests of the public and the market, could be said to be engaging in corruption. Much of what TI includes in its broader definition already had a label — corporate crime — and in many ways it is preferable and less confusing, to continue to use the latter term. But so many commentators and organisations have now adopted TI's broad definition that it will be accepted for the purposes of the analysis here.

The other key aspect of the debate — the basis of our second axis — focuses on the 'range' of actions and non-actions (e.g. 'turning a blind eye') to be included under the term corruption. Many commentators limit their analyses to acts involving pecuniary advantage and focus on bribery. In most cases the acts will be illegal. Other commentators advocate a broader approach, however, that includes what is called 'penumbra' (that is, 'gray area') corruption. This conceptualisation includes favouritism of various kinds, notably nepotism and cronyism. Many acts included under this broader conceptualisation are subject to social criticism but are not illegal. Again, any assessment of the role of corruption in financial crises needs to specify whether a narrow or broad range of activities is being included.

Using these two axes, a four-cell matrix can be constructed, and the labels for each cell — A to D — can be used to address the primary research question (see Figure 1). Thus type A corruption must involve at least one state official and relate to pecuniary advantage. Type B must involve at least one state official and include penumbra corruption. Type C must include all activities included under A, but can also involve purely private sector misconduct — it is limited to improper (often illegal) acts that involve pecuniary benefit. Type D corruption is the broadest and includes penumbra activity, whether in the state or private sector.

The focus in the rest of this chapter is primarily on types A and C and of the interaction between them. Given the Naím quotation cited at the start of this chapter, it is clear that corruption in its narrower senses had become a major problem well before any of the three crises cited. While it was a contributory factor to all of them, it was ultimately a background factor. Corruption in the broader sense — particularly within the banking and corporate sectors — was a factor in all three, however, it pertained particularly to the GFC. This is not to claim that corruption in either sense was the *only* or even the primary factor in any of these crises. As noted above, each manifested a unique combination of explanatory variables. It is argued here, however, that the ramifications of the general context in which both state and corporate corruption thrived — neoliberalism and globalisation — *were* a major cause of all three crises and that the corruption involved symbolises this. Before advancing this proposition, it is necessary to consider some of the measurement problems involved in attempting to assess the scale and nature of corruption.

MEASUREMENT ISSUES AND SURVEY RESULTS

Official statistics on corruption — such as legal ones on the number of convictions each year, or economic ones on the losses caused by it — are only ever the tip of the iceberg (in the case of legal data) or guesstimates (in the case of economic ones). They may even be misleading. Unlike most crimes, corruption typically has

A Narrow identity; narrow range	B Narrow identity; broad range
C Broad identity; narrow range	D Broad identity; broad range

Figure 1: Corruption conceptualisation matrix.

no obvious and identifiable victim. The 'victim' is often 'the state' or the 'society', so there is no one to report it and hence far less investigation by law enforcement agencies. Moreover, many penumbra forms of corruption are not illegal anyway in many of the world's jurisdictions. This compounds the problem of invisibility. At the same time a higher number of convictions in country X than in country Y might not signify a higher level of corruption in the former but rather a more determined anti-corruption effort than in the latter. In fact, country X may actually have a *lower* rate of corruption than country Y, though there is ultimately no way of being certain about this.

Given these issues, analysts have in the past fifteen to twenty years devised a number of other techniques for assessing the level of corruption in particular places at particular times. The most common methods are perceptual and attitudinal surveys (what respondents believe the situation to be and their opinions on this situation); experiential surveys (respondents' actual experiences of corruption, primarily bribery); tracking surveys (in which, for example, an agency such as the World Bank tracks aid monies across each administrative level involved in dispersing them to determine how much eventually reaches the intended beneficiaries); and proxy measures (for example, making inferences about the scale and the main areas of corruption on the basis of anti-corruption measures adopted by governments).

Space limitations preclude consideration here of the advantages and disadvantages of these various techniques (for recent and comprehensive analyses of each, and of their respective drawbacks, see Sampford *et al.*, 2006; June *et al.*, 2008). Suffice to note is that there are problems with all of the existing measurement methods, but that the seriousness of the issue means that most analysts now agree that combining as many methods as possible ('multi-angulation') to form a picture of the corruption situation is a worthwhile exercise — methodological shortcomings notwithstanding.

Still the most commonly cited measure is TI's Corruption Perceptions Index (CPI), published annually since 1995. This aggregates and averages perception surveys conducted by other agencies and produces a score for a given country on a 0–10 scale; the higher the figure, the lower the perceived level of corruption. For the purposes of the present exercise, another of TI's indices, the Bribe Payers' Index (BPI), is also worth mentioning. Following the publication of the early CPIs, a number of developing countries complained that they had fared badly in these because the focus was on state officials accepting or demanding bribes, rather than on who was paying or offering bribes. TI responded by inviting countries to rate the likelihood of firms from other countries offering bribes to their officials. The BPIs are not conducted as frequently as the CPIs (the first was in 1999), but are a useful counterweight to the latter, given that the focus shifts from bribe recipients to bribe donors. In terms of the distinction drawn in this chapter between narrower and broader conceptions of corruption, the fact that the BPI in essence considers corporate behaviour more than the conduct of state officials is useful. On the other hand, it still does not focus explicitly on either B2B (business to business) corruption or on B2P (businesses misleading or explicitly cheating the public for their own benefit) corruption. In addition, the BPI scores countries rather than corporations, so that its value is limited for identifying all possible culprits. For these reasons, case studies of particular corporations is another valuable method for analysing the role and nature of corruption in the three crises being considered here.

But before citing specific cases, and despite their real limitations, the absence of alternatives renders it worthwhile to note the *overall* findings of the CPIs and BPIs. Considering the CPI first, corruption has clearly been a significant problem since the first indices appeared in the 1990s, and the situation shows no sign of improvement. Thus the press release that accompanied the publication of the 2010 (the most recent) CPI included the following:

> The 2010 CPI shows that nearly three quarters of the 178 countries in the index score below five, on a scale from 0 (perceived to be highly corrupt) to 10 (perceived to have low levels of corruption), indicating a serious corruption problem.

Similarly, the press release on the 2008 (most recent) BPI included the following statement:

> While most of the world's wealthiest countries already subscribe to a ban on foreign bribery, under the OECD Anti-Bribery Convention, there is little awareness of the convention among the senior business executives interviewed in the Bribe Payers Survey.

Some of the evidence of various types of corruption can now be considered.

EVIDENCE OF CORRUPTION

Types A and C to A

There is so much evidence on Type A corruption in all types of systems over recent decades that it would be both impossible and superfluous even to provide an overview here (useful starting points are Williams *et al.*, 2000; Williams and Theobald, 2000). Note that the problem is by no means confined to developing and transition states, however. Several Western leaders have been implicated in major corruption scandals since the 1990s, including Germany's Helmut Kohl, France's Jacques Chirac and Italy's Silvio Berlusconi. If corruption levels relate in part to the example being set at the top, then it is not surprising that they appear to have risen in recent years.

Examples of corporations paying bribes to (that is, actively corrupting) state officials to secure contracts overseas, and hence being involved in C to A corruption, are numerous, especially in the years preceding the GFC. Among the most serious cases are those of the UK aerospace firm BAE (the allegations were made public in 2003) in a case that involved the highest levels of political interference and raised a number of questions relating to British security. Formal investigations commenced in 2004 and BAE agreed in 2010, with the UK's Serious Fraud Office and the US Department of Justice, to pay almost four hundred and fifty million US dollars in fines. Then there is Statoil in Norway (allegations were made public in 2003); Daimler-Chrysler in Germany and the US (allegations were made public in 2004); Siemens in Germany (there were numerous allegations, as a result of which the company was blacklisted by the Singaporean authorities for five years in 1996 and by Italy for one year in 2004 — major publicity about bribery in 2006 led to the CEO resigning in 2007); and the former Australian Wheat Board or AWB (allegations were made public in 2005), a scandal that was investigated by the Cole Commission in 2005–2006 and which — controversially — identified most of the corporation's improper acts vis-à-vis Iraq as 'kickbacks' rather than bribes. Finally, there was Alcatel-Lucent in France (allegations were first made public in 2009 and intensified in 2010). (For details on most of these cases, see Holmes, 2009).

It is clear from even this small selection of cases that transnational C to A corruption has been widespread in recent years — but also that it was common well before the GFC. This type of transnational corruption appears to have applied less to the other two crises, which were based more on domestic factors.

If narrow identity-related definitions of corruption are used (cells A and B), there is at first glance only limited evidence of any *direct* relationship between them and the financial crises nominated. Indeed, the point has been made explicitly — if not totally convincingly — with regard to the Asian Crisis that there was no connection at all (Furman and Stiglitz, 1998, p. 5 and pp. 56–62; Radelet and Sachs, 1998, pp. 1–2 and pp. 48–49; Weder, 1999); this contradicts the IMF's analysis cited above, although it must be borne in mind that the IMF's reference is largely to types B and D corruption. Although some well-regarded analyses (e.g. Buchs, 1999; Desai, 2000) make no reference to corruption playing any role in the Russian crisis, there is a clearer relationship there than in the Asian case. The very nature of the Russian privatisation and marketisation project often involved an unhealthy and murky relationship between state bureaucrats and entrepreneurs, so that the pejorative term '*nomenklatura* privatisation' was commonly used to describe it (on the role of corruption in the Russian crisis see Cox, 2000). In 2009, TI explicitly identified the lack of transparency and accountability as lying "at the root of the financial crisis" (Zinnbauer *et al.*, 2009, pp. xxiv) — a point explored below. Moreover, it is worth noting that the eurozone country most seriously impacted by the European sovereign debt crisis that was a spin-off from the GFC — Greece — was the one ranked throughout the 2000s in CPIs (which focus on type A corruption) as the most corrupt EU15 state (that is, the EU as it was until its May 2004 expansion).

Although awareness of serious corporate misconduct — corruption — has intensified over the past decade, it is not a new phenomenon. Thus Clinard and Yeager (1980, p. 155) wrote the following — which basically relates to C to A corruption — some three decades ago:

> Probably nothing has tarnished the image of corporations within recent years more than the public revelation of the widespread illegal payments made to attain certain corporate objectives.

The situation has significantly worsened since Clinard and Yeager made this observation.

Types C and D

Opting for the broader definitions, there is once again a great deal of evidence of misconduct in and from the private sector — though less so with regard to the Asian and Russian cases than both during and prior to the GFC. The nature of the misconduct varies.

Some of the best-known examples of private sector corruption in the 2000s include cases where corporations were deliberately misleading their shareholders and the general public about their performance. As already noted, much of this could be described as corporate crime or misconduct, depending on the precise details. Given that so many analysts now use the term corruption loosely, however, it can also be labelled B2P corruption.

Among the numerous examples are One.Tel (Australia, 2001); Enron (US, 2001, see O'Brien, 2003, pp. 71–114); Freddie Mac (US, 2002 — for understated earnings, although there were also allegations of having contributed to the legislative committees that regulate it, that is, of C to A corruption); Halliburton (US, 2002 and again in 2005 — it was required to repay the US government almost thirty million dollars for overcharging for food provided, via a subsidiary, to troops in Iraq); WorldCom (US, 2002); Parmalat (Italy, 2003); Fannie Mae (the Federal National Mortgage Association) (US, 2004 — for 'erroneous' accounts reporting, though there were also allegations in 2008 of contributing to the legislative committees that regulated it, that is, of C to A corruption); AIG (US, 2004); the Anglo Irish Bank (Ireland, 2008); and Lehman Brothers (again in 2010 — though it had acknowledged improper behaviour in 2003). Once again, it is clear that this type of corruption was common enough well before the advent of the GFC.

These and many other cases have undermined the Western publics' trust in the corporate sector and the legitimacy of neoliberal capitalism more generally. This point inheres in the following quotation from a Nobel Prize winner for economics, Joseph Stiglitz (2006, p. 187):

> For many people, multinational corporations have come to symbolise what is wrong with globalisation; many would say they are a primary cause of the problems.

CORRUPTION AND THE GLOBAL FINANCIAL CRISES (THE GFC)

Clearly, corruption in both its narrower and broader senses has been widespread in recent years. Since all the forms identified above were widespread before, during and after any of the crises — especially the GFC — examined here, it might be inferred that corruption's contribution to them was at most marginal. To make this assumption would be quite wrong, however. It must be borne in mind that while crises can appear suddenly, they usually build up over time and are more or less predictable (that is, they will occur though the precise timing can be difficult to determine in advance). They also present their own risks.

Before elaborating on this argument, an important point needs to be made about the directionality of any causal relationship between corruption and financial crises. How does this work?

REVERSE EFFECTS

In examining the connection between corruption and financial crises, it has so far been implied that any causal relationship that exists is in the direction of corruption contributing to crisis. But financial crises can stimulate corruption. Thus the press release for the 2009 CPI implicitly identified an aspect of the GFC that was seen by the current Chair of TI, Huguette Labelle, as likely to *increase* corruption:

> At a time when massive stimulus packages, fast-track disbursements of public funds and attempts to secure peace are being implemented around the world, it is essential to identify where corruption blocks good governance and accountability, in order to break its corrosive cycle.

More recently, a 2010 report produced by international auditing and professional services firm Ernst and Young concluded that the GFC had made firms in the mining and metals sector more likely to engage in corporate impropriety (Fontanot *et al.*, 2010). While more empirical evidence is required before this sector-specific finding can be generalised, the drivers identified in the case of mining and metals can be found in most branches and sectors, and are likely to have led to an increase in fraud and corruption across a wide range of industries.

SOME EXPLANATIONS

The point has been reached at which it is appropriate to probe below the surface and consider a more abstract way in which corruption and the various financial crises are related. The focus here is on economic globalisation and in particular its ideology — known variously as neoliberalism, economic rationalism, or the 'Washington Consensus' — and its practical ramifications. For the purposes of the present discussion, the key feature of neoliberalism is that the state seeks to offload or distance itself from responsibilities it once assumed, and to justify this through propaganda that often presents such a move in terms of 'common sense', 'necessity' or 'the public (especially taxpayers') interest'. Salient aspects of the approach include outsourcing, privatisation, downsizing/right-sizing, and deregulation. Outsourcing to the corporate sector sometimes even extends to what has traditionally been seen as one of the state's primary and most sacred responsibilities, defence. (For a feisty analysis of the blurring of the public and private sectors see Galbraith, 2005, pp. 30–34.) States subscribing to this ideology advocate greater economic competition; the free transnational movement of capital; and open markets, both domestically and internationally. As part of the process of offloading, neoliberal states also advocate 'governance', rather than government. While this could and in theory should represent a higher stage of democracy in that it increases the number of agencies involved in decision making and decision implementation, in practice it all too often means that the state has simply become more irresponsible. Indeed, in practice it often involves *less* democracy. Firstly, many of the additional agencies are not subject to public control to any meaningful extent. At least the senior decision makers of liberal democratic *states* are generally subject to regular, free and genuinely competitive elections. Secondly, and related to the first point, transparency often *declines* as the state offloads or shares tasks with the private sector. In many countries, for instance, some information that was once available via freedom of information acts is now protected from public scrutiny by commercial-in-confidence laws. This clearly relates to TI's 2009 earlier-cited identification of the roots of the GFC.

It is sometimes claimed that fewer state responsibilities mean less corruption. Thus analysts such as Daniel Mitchell of the CATO Institute (2010) maintains that the bigger the state — in the sense of the more tasks it performs and the larger the bureaucracy relative to the population — the greater the capacity for, and hence the greater the scale of, corruption. This is based on the assumption that more state tasks mean more opportunities for corruption. This argument is unconvincing, however, for three reasons.

Firstly, increased state responsibilities often mean that the state does not outsource tasks to the private sector. Its officers are ostensibly less prone to being corrupted by competing private interests as a consequence.

Secondly, if the state does offload tasks to the private sector, this usually involves either privatisation (increasing short- and medium-term opportunities for corruption) or contract-based outsourcing (which results in new, ongoing opportunities for corruption). It also often implies more state supervision, since the public in democracies usually demand this, and such supervision typically involves greater scope for discretionary decision making by state officials. Since, according to Klitgaard (1988), the discretionary powers of state officials are one of the prime explicators of corruption — the more such powers, the more corruption (unless there is also much greater accountability) — it becomes obvious why this process can increase corruption. In sum, all of these changes — privatisation, outsourcing and enhanced supervision — create new opportunities for type A and C to A corruption.

Finally, both of the first two points above are based on the assumption that the narrowest definition of corruption (Type A) is being used. If Type C is incorporated into the analysis as well, it can be argued that corruption's primary location will simply be shifted from the public to the private sector. The more there is deregulation and the more the focus is placed on having a 'small state', the greater the likelihood of this occurring. One of the more naïve and self-deceptive assumptions of many neoliberals is that companies will self-regulate and 'police' themselves. There is by now abundant evidence that this is usually wishful thinking. Private enterprises exist to maximise profit and, in the case of most licit firms, also to endure. These objectives typically override other ethical commitments.

Another way of challenging the 'bigger government means more corruption' argument is to make a simple calculation based on the points just made. If a state deregulates, there is a greater likelihood of corruption in both the broader and narrower senses (especially types A and C), whereas increasing the size and responsibilities of the state *may* increase corruption in its narrower senses (especially type A), but will probably reduce type C to A — *inter alia* because of greater state regulation — and types C to A.

In sum, while there will always be some corruption, however defined, it is likely to increase or decrease according to the ideological context and the policy decisions made within that context. It will be recalled that it is a particular type of capitalism — neoliberalism — and a particular approach to economic globalisation that is being 'blamed' here for much of the GFC and earlier crises. There are alternative models of capitalism, for example, the social democratic model worked very well for Sweden and Germany for decades. And Keynesianism is back on the agenda now since 2008, because even die-hard economic rationalists have been forced to admit that state intervention in economies saved many of the latter from complete meltdown.

The process of re-evaluating neoliberal economics was already underway long before the GFC. Harvard economist Jeffrey Sachs, for example, who was described by the *New York Times* in June 1993 as "probably the most important economist in the world" and by *Time Magazine* the following year as the world's best-known economist, strongly criticised the IMF for having both exacerbated and fundamentally misunderstood the nature of the Asian financial crisis of 1997–1998 because of its ideological blinkers (Sachs, 1997). The IMF did acknowledge in 1999 that it had made mistakes in Asia, especially in Indonesia (Borsuk *et al.*, 1999). It did so reluctantly, however, and it did not subsequently introduce *fundamental* changes to its neoliberal approach. Stiglitz (2003) also criticised the World Bank, of which he had at one time been Chief Economist and Vice-President, as well as the IMF, for their lack of transparency and ideological dogma. He argued that their approach had exacerbated both the Asian and Russian financial crises. Even the guru of monetarist 'Chicago School' economics, which is a key component of neoliberalism, admitted in 2002 that he had been wrong to urge post-communist transition states — during the 1990s — to "privatise, privatise, privatise". Milton Friedman (2002, pp. xvii–xviii) acknowledged that the establishment of the rule of law needed to precede privatisation (for one of the most trenchant critiques of Friedman's approach see Klein, 2007, pp. 49–57). Notwithstanding these early and notable examples, the GFC intensified the trend among thinking economists to question many of the underlying principles of neoliberalism.

CONCLUSION

It is not being argued here that corruption was the principal or even a major cause of any of the crises examined. Rather, it is contended that corruption, whether in its narrower or its broader forms, was a significant contributory factor. More generally, the argument is that neoliberalism and the whole ethos that accompanies it (ends are more important than means; profit comes before due process, before people and before non-calculative forms of morality; the role of the state in the economy should be made minimal) was a major factor, and that increased corruption, particularly of types A, C, and C to A, is a function of its ideological tenets. It is *exacerbated* by and *symbolises* neoliberalism.

So: what are the prospects? Neoliberalism is now being questioned in many forums and the role of the state looks set to increase again, while the approach of the leading economic IOs is likely to be modified as a result. Many of the calculative ethical practices advocated by radical neoliberals, which have fuelled corruption in both its narrow and broad senses, are being challenged. More and more states and IOs are practising debarment (blacklisting). Thus the World Bank's first debarment of a *large* corporation (that is, as distinct from a small- to medium-sized enterprise) was announced as recently as July 2004, at about the same time the EU began to advocate this as a means to fight corruption and corporate crime. This might be seen as an encouraging sign that the cosy relationship that existed until then between many states and major corporations was coming to an end. This relationship, as it was known until the early 2000s, is seen in the different treatment meted out to misbehaving small- and medium-sized corporations compared to that meted out to giant corporations. Thus, of the top ten recidivist US corporations in the period 1990–2002, only one (General Electric) was actually debarred (Drew, 2005, p. 274) and then only for a few days (for up-to-date details on US corporate misconduct see the Federal Contractor Misconduct database on the "Project on Government Oversight" website). Governments have been highly dependent on large corporations, notably for party financing, employment, and as major suppliers to governments (of the top ten recidivists seven, including the top five, were in the defence industry).

Unfortunately this dependency continues and is likely to limit the extent to which states and IOs debar firms. This bodes ill for the much stricter government control of corrupt corporations. Moreover, the global anti-corruption situation post-2004 (especially for C and C to A) are at best mixed. According to a 2010 TI assessment (Heimann and Dell, 2010, p. 11), only seven out of thirty-six signatory states to the OECD anti-bribery convention were actively enforcing it and three of these (Denmark, Italy and the UK) had been deemed *not* to have been actively enforcing it just one year before. While one of the exemplary states in both 2009 and 2010 was the US (the others being Germany, Norway and Switzerland), there was as of 2010 only moderate enforcement in nine countries and 'little or no enforcement' in twenty-one others. Although the UK was by 2010 finally addressing the major BAE scandal, countries such as Australia, Canada, and New Zealand fared badly. Considering that the Australian government had been implicated in a major scandal that involved a large corporation (the AWB scandal), this scorecard must raise doubts about the global anti-corruption struggle given that the twenty-one states deemed to be doing little or nothing had signed up to the convention more than a decade earlier.

In addition, in bailing out the private and especially the financial sector, many states have created significant problems for themselves. Thus the sovereign debt problem exemplified by Greece has seriously affected many other European states including Hungary, Iceland, Ireland, Portugal and Spain. It is rapidly becoming a major problem for the global political economy.

Is it all too late, then, so that even state-makers cannot now correct the mess that corruption, excessive risk-taking, and inadequate regulation of the private sector have created? Is the global political economy really in 'freefall', to quote the title of Stiglitz's 2010 book on the GFC and its aftermath?

While most indicators give little cause for optimism about the near future, the longer term outlook is not *necessarily* hopeless. Globalisation has begun to shift wealth and even the international political economy's whole centre of gravity.

There are massive new consumer markets, for example, most notably in China and India. These countries might be able to take over the baton as the most developed parts of the world gradually decline.

The new powerhouses are at present relatively corrupt (both internally and when doing business overseas) according, that is, to our (rather imperfect) ways of measuring this. Does this mean that we might simply have to become accustomed to corruption, in both its narrow and broad senses, as 'normal'? Conversely, if the apparently strong negative correlation between Gross Domestic Product (GDP) and type A corruption levels — the higher the former, the lower the latter — is valid and holds, then rising standards of living and the GDP in these countries might be accompanied by a decline in their corruption levels. This is especially true for China, where the government is still far more interventionist in the economy than are most Western governments. In addition, if the development of the so-called BRIC states (Brazil, Russia, India, China) reduces the gap between the poorer and wealthier nations, one of the principal drivers of contemporary corruption should be reduced in salience.

Perhaps the partial move away from neoliberalism, and the putative renewed focus on good governance at both state and corporate level, will turn the recent rotten trends around. Conflict of interest laws are constantly being tightened. Shareholders are currently fighting back.

Occasionally, as in the case of IKEA in Russia, corporations publicly resist bribery demands. More corporate executives and corrupt officials are receiving heavier sentences. (It will be worth tracking the development of 'quadruple bottom-lining' by corporations in terms of the above. During the 1990s, many firms introduced triple bottom-lining, that is, a summary not only of their economic performance for the year but also of their social and environmental contributions. There is now pressure on them from some quarters to introduce a fourth bottom line, that is, one on improvements in governance that could include details of the anti-corruption measures involved.)

Then again, all of this might be a drop in the ocean. While there are some signs that corruption in its various meanings is being seriously addressed, there remain many counterweights.

Corruption is certainly likely to remain a serious problem for the foreseeable future. As such it is likely to remain a contributory factor to, and be affected by, any new financial crises.

REFERENCES

Althusser, L (1971). *Lenin and Philosophy and Other Essays.* New York: Monthly Review Press.

Borsuk, R, G Goad and M Phillips (1999). IMF Admits Errors in Asian Crisis, But Defends its Tight-Money Policy. *Wall Street Journal*, 20 January.

Buchs, T (1999). Financial crisis in the Russian federation, *Economics of Transition*, 7(3), 687–715.

Chaikin, D and J Sharman (2009). *Corruption and Money Laundering: A Symbiotic Relationship.* New York: Palgrave Macmillan.

Clinard, M and C Yeager (1980). *Corporate Crime.* New York: Free Press.

Cox, C (2000). *Russia's Road to Corruption.* Washington DC: US House of Representatives.

Desai, P (2000). Why did the ruble collapse in August 1998? *American Economic Review*, 90(2), 48–52.

Drew, K (2005). *Fighting Corruption and Promoting Integrity in Public Procurement.* Paris: OECD.

Fontanot, P, R Cockerell and T Koekemoer (2010). *Fraud and Corruption in Mining and Metals.* Sydney: EYGM.

Friedman, M (2002). Preface: Economic Freedom behind the Scenes. In *Economic Freedom of the World: 2002 Annual Report*, J Gwartney and R Lawson. Vancouver: Fraser Institute.

Furman, J and J Stiglitz (1998). Economic Crises: Evidence and Insights from East Asia, *Brookings Papers on Economic Activity*, (2), 1–114.

Galbraith, J (2005). *The Economics of Innocent Fraud.* London: Penguin.

Heimann, F and G Dell (2010). *Progress Report 2010: Enforcement of the OECD Convention on Combating Bribery of Foreign Public Officials in International Business Transactions.* Berlin: Transparency International.

Holmes, L (ed.) (2007). *Terrorism, Organised Crime and Corruption: Networks and Linkages.* Cheltenham: Edward Elgar.

Holmes, L (2009). Good guys, bad guys: Transnational corporations, rational choice theory and power crime, *Crime, Law and Social Change*, 51(3–4), 383–397.

June, R, A Chowdhury, N Heller and J Werve (2008). *A User's Guide to Measuring Corruption.* Oslo: UNDP.

Klein, N (2007). *The Shock Doctrine: The Rise of Disaster Capitalism.* London: Penguin.

Klitgaard, R (1988). *Controlling Corruption.* Berkeley and Los Angeles: University of California Press.

Masciandaro, D (ed.) (2004). *Global Financial Crime: Terrorism, Money Laundering and Offshore Centres.* Aldershot: Ashgate.

Mitchell, D (2010). Big Government Means Big Corruption. International Liberty, http://danieljmitchell.wordpress.com/2010/01/10/big-government-means-big-corruption/ [20 December 2011].

Naím, M (1995). The Corruption Eruption, *Brown Journal of World Affairs,* 2(2), 245–261.

O'Brien, J (2003). *Wall Street on Trial: A Corrupted State?* Chichester: Wiley.

Radelet, S and J Sachs (1998). The East Asian financial crisis: Diagnosis, remedies, prospects, *Brookings Papers on Economic Activity,* (1), 1–74.

Sachs, J (1997). The IMF is a Power unto Itself. *The Financial Times,* 11 December, p. 11.

Sampford, C, A Shacklock, C Connors and F Galtung (eds.) (2006). *Measuring Corruption.* Aldershot: Ashgate.

Sampson, S (2010). The anti-corruption industry: From movement to institution, *Global Crime,* 11(2), 261–278.

Stiglitz, J (2003). *Globalisation and its Discontents.* New York: Norton.

Stiglitz, J (2006). *Making Globalisation Work.* Camberwell, Vic: Penguin.

Stiglitz, J (2010). *Freefall.* New York: Norton.

Tikhomirov, V (1998). The Russian Economic Situation and the Failure of Market Reforms. In *The Russian Crisis and its Impact on Australia,* L Holmes (ed.). Melbourne: Contemporary Europe Research Centre.

van Duyne, P, M Jager, K von Lampe and J Newell (eds.) (2004). *Threats and Phantoms of Organised Crime, Corruption and Terrorism.* Nijmegen: Wolf.

Weder, B (1999). *Model, Myth or Miracle?: Reassessing the Role of Governments in the East Asian Experience.* Tokyo: United Nations University Press.

Williams, R, J Moran and R Flanary (eds.) (2000). *Corruption in the Developed World.* Cheltenham: Elgar.

Williams, R and R Theobold (eds.) (2000). *Corruption in the Developing World.* Cheltenham: Elgar.

Zinnbauer, D, R Dobson and K Despota (eds.) (2009). *Global Corruption Report 2009: Corruption and the Private Sector.* New York: Cambridge University Press.

Part Four

Globalisation and the North/South Divide

CHAPTER 15

Globalisation and the North/South Divide: An Overview

Thomas W. D. Davis

University of Melbourne

'North' and 'South' have been established terms of use in debates about international political economy since the 1960s. In their most basic form the terms are regarded as a shorthand for distinguishing 'rich countries' from 'poor countries'. 'The North' is taken to include the industrialised, high-per-capita income, national political economies of which the majority are located in the Northern Hemisphere. 'The South' describes those countries with high levels of poverty and comparatively low levels of industrialisation, large numbers of which exist in the Southern Hemisphere.

There are significant exceptions to this simplistic geographic demarcation. Australia and New Zealand, which are both high-income, developed political economies, are located in the 'deep south' of the Southern Hemisphere; meanwhile, a plethora of low-income, developing countries are found north of the equator.

A purely geographic interpretation of 'North' and 'South' belies a richer conceptual history, therefore, where the 'North-South divide', from the late 1960s to the early 1980s, challenged the 'East-West' bipolarity of the Cold War as an organising principle of international relations and international political economy. While the North-South distinction continues to be employed, long after the East-West divide has fallen from use, there is some question, addressed in this chapter, as to its contemporary relevance to the current global situation.

In its first iteration, the 'North-South divide' attempted to describe a deep international political and economic division rather than an accurate map of global poverty. Its proponents argued that one set of countries, the former colonial powers based in the North, had established, and then unequally benefited from, the structures and institutions of international politics and global capitalism, and had little interest in remedying that inequality in order to reduce poverty in the South.

The standard historical narrative of the 'North-South' debate takes as its starting point the emergence in the 1960s of a political notion of 'the South' as being a comparatively homogenous group of low-income countries bound together by their shared experiences of poverty, colonial subjugation, and structural exclusion from the benefits of the global political economy. This politicisation of the developmental divide reached its peak with the New International Economic Order (NIEO) movement of the 1970s before gradually fading over the course of the 1980s and the early 1990s. Its arrival accompanied the advent of the Non-Aligned Movement and the entry of large numbers of de-colonised states to the UN General Assembly. Its end was hastened by the Northern-supported rise of neoliberal politico-economic theory and its attendant globalisation.

With the contemporary economic axis of the world inexorably tilting toward East Asia, it has become a live question as to whether this narrative deserves a coda. Does the 'North-South divide' continue to have economic and political relevance? Is a newly minted form of Southern political consciousness now forming in response to the economic inequalities associated with globalisation?

While 'North' and 'South' still have currency as a linguistic shortcut in academic and practitioner debates and dialogues, it is less obvious whether, in the twenty-first century, users of these terms are as concerned as their predecessors were with the political dimensions of international structural and institutional inequality. With the broadening and deepening of globalisation, the value of the global 'North-South' divide as a description, as an explanation or as a normative ideal in relation to international development and the international political economy has become rather muddied.

Part of the problem lies in the vagueness of the definition of 'North' and 'South'. By demarcating countries based on their levels of economic development, the 'North-South divide' is subject to all the technical and philosophical difficulties inherent in determining the nature and causes of global poverty and inequality. There is also considerable debate over how to interpret the relationship between economic globalisation and global income inequality. Large numbers of the most poor (those who exist under the US$1.25 per day absolute poverty line set by the World Bank) now live in middle-income, fast-growing economies, which is indicative of how economic globalisation has created wealth and poverty in places and in ways not envisioned by earlier champions of the 'South'.

The desire on the part of lower income countries to describe themselves collectively as 'the South' is also no longer obvious. Acceptance of the benefits of neoliberal economic policy is far from universal. At the same time there have been few recent coordinated attempts by developing states to alter core international economic and political institutions. Southern political coalitions were always fragile, and there are serious queries as to whether the interests of low-income countries have become any better aligned since the 1980s.

Finally, there are the increased numbers of actors who claim a stake in the North-South debate. For example, local and international NGOs, human rights institutions, and community-based organisations (CBOs), linked through transnational advocacy networks, have a level of engagement in development discourses that was not in evidence in earlier decades when the North-South conflict was the focus primarily of states and international organisations.

While it would be easy to dismiss the 'North-South divide' as having little ongoing relevance in a world that is increasingly economically, politically and culturally connected, as well as transnational, then, the continuing existence of entrenched poverty, the growth of global income inequality, the aggressive anti-Western sentiments of some communities within the 'developing world', the increased economic and political relevance of the middle-income BRIC (Brazil, Russia, India, China) countries, and, most importantly perhaps, the rise in claims for human rights, suggests there remains an important need to understand the multiple economic and political connections between the rich and the poor. In investigating the link between the North-South debate and globalisation, this chapter charts several phases in the evolution of the 'North-South divide' as an analytical and political tool in international political economy. It examines the conditions in which the notion of 'the South' rose to prominence, before turning to the manner in which it then began to fade from view (and the possible impact of economic globalisation on that process). It finishes with an analysis of how it might be reconceived in the light of dominant, twenty-first century interpretations of international politico-economic processes. By way of conclusion it suggests that, while the 'North-South divide' may be too clumsy an appellation to capture fully the interactions between the global rich and the global poor, it still provides a useful conceptual stepping stone towards a more appropriate explanation of those connections and how they might drive future developmental change.

THE RISE OF THE NORTH-SOUTH DIVIDE

To understand why the 'North-South divide' became such a significant feature of global politics and economics, and to begin to isolate potential explanations for what is currently occurring in North-South relations, it is important to first provide the historical context within which the 'North-South' concept arose. It is then necessary to identify the agents and actions behind its brief flowering in the 1970s.

Following the end of the Second World War, several profound institutional changes altered the international political and economic environment. The first was the establishment of the United Nations (UN) and the 'Bretton Woods' institutions: the International Bank of Reconstruction and Development (the World Bank), the International Monetary Fund (IMF), and the General Agreement on Tariffs and Trade (GATT). This reconfiguring of global politics and economics reflected the belief of key Western states in a global liberal economy and the capacity of international institutions, the governance of which was dominated by those states, to act as 'Keynesian' managers. Woven into these institutions was also a commitment, fostered in large part by the US, to the decolonisation of the former colonies of the European powers. The tension within this system between a liberal conception of the world political economy and the tendency to dominance by the Bretton Woods institutions was never fully resolved. When in 1971, the monetary control elements of the system collapsed, instigated by the US delinking its dollar from the gold standard, it was notable that the Bretton Woods organisations did not disappear, however. Instead, they reformed themselves around different sets of politico-economic priorities. They continued the modes of their governance and the dominance of the post-war powers remained largely unchallenged. That period of reformation (in the early to mid-1970s), along with the recessions experienced by many Western countries, proved to be highly disruptive to the international political economy, however. Combined with the political volatility of the time — exemplified by the ongoing conflict in Indo-China and its impact on the US's coercive global power — the effect was to create an opening for alternative conceptions of the international political economy.

The decolonisation of Asian and African states and the push from Latin American states to free themselves from the US sphere of influence was the second key contextual factor of note. From 1945 to 1960 the number of member states in the UN General Assembly doubled from fifty-one to one hundred. By the mid-1970s it had reached one hundred and fifty. The vast bulk of the new members were developing states. The General Assembly, the Human Rights Commission, the Economic and Social Committee (ECOSOC) and, later, the UN Committee on Trade and Development (UNCTAD) became important forums in which recently decolonised countries could exercise their right to self-determination and formulate their positions on the international politico-economic issues of the day. In addition, the experience of working within a multilateral institutional framework, as well as the opportunity to engage directly with Northern, trade-based multilateral institutions (such as the growing European Economic Community [EEC]), offered developing states important models with regard to collective action.

The third contextual element was the Cold War one. This conflict was between the Soviet Union and US, and many developing countries reacted against the bipolarity it entailed. While a number of countries became 'client states' of either the US or the Soviet Union during this period, from the mid-1950s a significant portion of the developing world — at one stage involving countries that contained fifty-five percent of the global population — expressed its opposition to the established Cold War divisions via regular heads of state meetings under the auspices of the Non-Aligned Movement (NAM). This group emphasised the importance of national independence, state sovereignty, territorial integrity in the face of Cold

War security threats, and decolonisation and anti-imperialism. The NAM should be viewed as an early attempt on the part of newly decolonised developing states to cast themselves as a political bloc capable of exercising coercive power separate from the 'great powers', and as an important forerunner to the political economy debates of the 1970s.

The final factor was the changing composition of global economic relations. Running alongside a massive increase in the global oil economy, with a commensurate rise in the wealth and economic power of oil-producing states, was a gradual decline in the relative prices of other commodities against manufactured goods. This was compounded by the increasing restrictions placed on the export of agricultural goods to Europe and the US, and the early indications that structural reform would be required in a number of developing countries to ensure the labour mobility necessary to capitalise on global post-war economic growth. The overall effect on non-oil producing countries, combined with population growth, was the achievement of lower than anticipated GDP per capita growth figures (two percent as opposed to the UN target of five percent), even though these years had been designated by the UN as the 'development decade'.

Within this international political and economic setting, specific agents of change can be identified as having had a considerable influence in instigating the North-South contest. The first was the conceptualisation of the international political economy provided by the 'dependency school' of development theorists.

Critical to this endeavour was the work of the Executive Secretary of the UN Economic Commission for Latin America, Raúl Prebisch, who argued that a structural division within the global political economy existed between what would later be described as the 'centre' and the 'periphery'. Firms and labour within industrialised economies (the 'centre') were heavily focused on manufacturing and had the capacity to increase profit margins through restrictive, cartel-like practices, that were reinforced by the inflexible global supply of, and the significant demand for, manufactured goods. There were fewer opportunities, he said, for firms and labour in non-industrialised economies ('the periphery') to engage in such 'rent-seeking'. Though the supply of the commodities provided by the periphery was relatively flexible, demand was uneven and, initially at least, there was greater access to surplus labour. This enabled growth without increases in wages. Taken together, these economic realities ensured that domestic firms in developing countries continued to attain only low profit margins. They decreased the capacity that such firms had to import the capital goods they needed to improve their productivity and to shift to more profitable manufacturing sectors. It was for this reason that Prebisch initially said that developing country governments should establish trade barriers and engage in strategic import substitution in order to enable infant manufacturing industries to grow without being inhibited by direct competition with Northern firms. Furthermore, he argued that developing countries needed to act in a collective fashion to reach agreements with the North on commodity prices and to introduce remedial resource transfers between the developed and developing world that would counterbalance the inherent inequalities in international trade (Prebsich, 1950).

Prebisch's ideas were taken up and modified by a slew of development economists and activists over the 1960s and 1970s, a number of which imparted their own 'radical', often neo-marxist spin on his approach. The overall thrust of the (loosely defined) 'dependency school' was that the global capitalist political economy was, at best, preventing poor countries from improving the incomes of their citizens, and, at worst, creating poverty and 'under-development' (see Frank, 1969; Wallerstein, 1974; Higgott, 1983; Leys, 1996). The general prescription was for developing countries to either engage in import substitution, or attempt to change international economic structures by directly contesting Northern states.

A second, politically vital, factor was the rise in collective action on the part of oil-producing states to influence global oil prices. Operating through the Organisation of Petroleum Exporting Countries (OPEC), and in response to US support for Israel in the 1973 Arab-Israeli War, these states agreed in October 1973 to increase the price per barrel of crude oil from US$3 to US$5.11, to place an oil embargo on the US, and to cut production by twenty-five percent (to be followed later by another five percent). By 1974 the real price per barrel of crude oil had reached US$12, even though the embargo on the US had been lifted in May that year. Ultimately, the refusal by Saudi Arabia, which was allied to the US, to agree to further rises led to an easing of price increases by 1975 — although the fall of the Shah of Iran in 1979 led to a second 'oil crisis' several years later.

More than simply impacting on costs of production, the actions of OPEC made clear to Northern countries the degree to which the North was intimately tied to developing countries via trade in energy and commodities. It also indicated the sort of coercive power oil-rich Arab states could exert if they acted in concert with other developing countries. The next two years were to provide ample further evidence of this capacity.

The implications of the 1973 oil crisis on the North-South divide were profound. With the support of major Arab states, Houari Boumedienne, the President of Algeria and Chair of the Organisation of Non-Aligned States (ONAS) (the institutional expression of the NAM), instigated a campaign to alter the established institutions and structures of the global economy. At the Fourth Summit Conference of the ONAS in Algeria, held in December 1973, Boumedienne announced a Declaration and Plan of Action for the Establishment of a New International Economic Order (NIEO), which called for protection of the real value of commodities, the right of developing states to expropriate foreign enterprises, and the international regulation of multinational corporations. The Declaration built on the establishment of the North-South Conference on International Economic Cooperation a month earlier by the UN, which included Saudi Arabia and Algeria on its panel. The Declaration's key terms were reiterated in the Sixth Special Session of the UN General Assembly in 1974. This was given more formal expression later in the UN Charter of Economic Rights and Duties of States of the same year, proposed by Mexico (Jones, 1983).

While NIEO negotiations between developing and developed countries continued in more established fora such as the UN General Assembly, there were also concurrent negotiations occurring for several years in a number of other organisational settings. Within UNCTAD, developing countries were pushing for a Common Fund to be established that would act to stabilise commodity prices. The European Economic Community was negotiating the Lomé Convention between its members and African, Caribbean and Pacific (ACP) countries, many of which were former European colonies. This led to some agreement on preferential trade arrangements and mechanisms for stabilising commodity prices. The Jamaica Agreement was reached in 1976 on reconstituting the international monetary system following the demise of the gold standard. This included propositions for reforming the IMF to enable it to better assist developing countries with balance-of-payments difficulties. Similarly, developing countries were making concerted efforts within the Tokyo Round of GATT negotiations, and even in the early stages of the subsequent Uruguay Round, to reorient international trade structures.

In spite of extended negotiation, this intensive period of North-South debate and negotiation produced few long-term changes within the global economy. Southern countries were provided some increased access to Northern markets, and, via significant increases in capital for the World Bank and the IMF, access to relatively cheap sources of investment finance. Also, a range of international commodity agreement processes — such as on rubber, coffee, sugar, tin, jute and timber — were established within UNCTAD's Integrated Programme for Commodities, although only one price-stabilising agreement, on rubber, was ever reached. The UN General Assembly Resolution 3362 of 1975 acknowledged the historical role of Northern exploitation in creating international poverty, and attempted to entrench principles such as empowering the UN to push for agreement on better North-South terms of trade, indexing Southern commodity prices to Northern manufactured good prices, and Northern states committing 0.7% of their Gross National Products to official development assistance (Marshall, 1994; Clemens and Moss, 2005).

Against these successes, however, must be recorded the fact that the UN failed to get binding commitments with regard to resources from Northern states on the NIEO, and the final GATT agreement from the Uruguay round did not achieve beneficial trade outcomes for developing countries. The 11th Special Session of the UN General Assembly on negotiations between the North and South in 1980, and the follow-up 1981 Cancun Summit, collapsed because of a failure to get agreement on the appropriate action. The 1980 Brandt Report on international development publicised the phrase 'North-South divide' and instigated a number of academic works in the early to mid-1980s that evaluated the nature of that division, but its recommendations were not picked up by Northern governments and the political capacity of the South to push for further change was, by this time, fading fast. (Independent Commission on International Development Issues, 1980) The Third World debt crisis of the early 1980s, built in part on the ease with which Southern states could get credit from private banks that were seeking borrowers for the 'petro-dollar' deposits they had received from OPEC states, further diminished the credibility of ongoing Southern-instigated discussions in the UN regarding substantive international economic change.

The 1986 UN Declaration on the Right to Development, and the formation of the South Commission in 1987 through the efforts of Malaysia's then Prime Minister Mahathir and the former President of Tanzania, Nyerere, represented something of a last gasp of the notion of 'the South' as an international institutional concept. By the early 1990s the South Commission had ceased to function. Moreover, the Right to Development had not been explicitly referred to in any of the missions of any official aid donor, despite its reiteration in the 1993 Vienna Declaration.

The inability of the South to press home its brief political and economic advantage in the early 1970s reflected the historical contingency at the heart of the 'North-South' debate. With hindsight, this period of dominance of the 'North-South divide' in international relations looks increasingly at odds with the more pervasive post-war evolution of economic globalisation and with liberal concepts of free trade and comparative and competitive advantage.

That the contest between developed and developing countries became so politicised can be seen as a product of the turbulence in the international political economy in the early 1970s. Northern states emerging out of the era of stable, post-war growth found themselves confronted with successive oil shocks, the collapse of the Bretton Woods system of monetary regulation, global recession, regional conflicts and the continuance of the Cold War, which shifted out of a period of 'détente' over the course of the decade. These political and economic realities required considerable institutional adjustment and created an opportunity for different ontologies of international relations to bloom, even if only briefly. For Southern states, the possibility presented itself for a collective imagining of an international community different from what appeared to be on offer in Cold War *realpolitik*, international marxism, or liberal internationalism. Yet Southern solidarity, largely founded on oil-exporting countries' support of poor, non-aligned nations, proved illusory. Even during the heyday of the NIEO movement, it was apparent that the countries of 'the South' were as much divided as united. The range of domestic political systems they represented, and the variety of positions they occupied within global and economic structures, suggested that the values they shared were predominantly strategic rather than central to their political interpretation of the world. As argued by Jones (1983):

> Of any single LDC by the middle of the decade [1970s] one would wish to know whether it was a net importer or exporter of oil; rapidly industrialising or based primarily on agriculture and mining; heavily or lightly indebted, and to whom; a recipient of aid, and whether from the OECD, OPEC, or the Soviet bloc; aligned or non-aligned; restrictive or permissive in its domestic economic regime; democratic or authoritarian in constitution (p. 56).

When political allegiances changed — most notably when the alliance between the US and Saudi Arabia was reinvigorated — and commodity prices fell, Southern solidarity was shown to be ephemeral.

GLOBALISATION AND THE FADING OF THE NORTH-SOUTH DIVIDE

In the wake of the collapse of collective Southern efforts regarding the NIEO, and with large numbers of developing countries hit by the debt crisis and global recession of the early 1980s, the power of Northern governments (especially the US under Reagan and the UK under Thatcher) and international organisations (the World Bank and the IMF) to insist on Southern commitment to neoliberal international economic structures was enhanced. The results for many developing countries of the 'structural adjustment programmes' and restrictive monetary policies enforced by the North were catastrophic, earning the 1980s the moniker of the 'lost decade' of development. In Latin America, per capita incomes were nine percent lower at the end of the decade than they had been at the beginning; sub-Saharan African GDP per capita dropped sixteen percent; health spending in the world's poorest countries dropped by an average of fifty percent; meanwhile foreign debt in the 'South' doubled over the same period. By the late 1990s, in reviewing what had occurred, even the World Bank had to admit that the 'Washington Consensus' of reduced public sector activity, lowered tax burdens, reduced trade barriers, and policies that increased microeconomic competition had largely been a failure when it came to encouraging economic growth in developing countries (Rodrik, 1997).

Complicating this interpretation is the fact that a number of poor countries over the 1980s, and an even greater number over the 1990s and into the 2000s, *did* manage to grow their economies, increase gross national incomes per capita, and improve their human development ratings. Over the past two decades, with a modified form of neoliberalism remaining central to the policies and operations of key international economic institutions and aid donors, there has been a consistent decline in the percentage of the world's population living below the international absolute poverty line of US$1.25 per day. In 1981, 1.9 billion people, or approximately fifty percent of the population of the developing world at the time, lived below the international poverty line. By 2005 that figure was 1.3 billion, with some analysts (such as the Brookings Institute) suggesting it may have even fallen to below one billion. Given the rise in overall population, this means one sixth of the developing world can now be classified as being in absolute poverty.

There is, however, a picture emerging that, while many national economies might be benefitting from increasing economic integration across state boundaries — driven by capital investors seeking access to raw materials, low-cost labour, and new markets for their goods and services — not all economies have been equally well served. Significant numbers of countries, especially within sub-Saharan Africa, have gone backwards in comparative terms on economic indicators such as GDP per capita and percentage of world trade (although there have been recent signs that they are starting to recover from this reversal). This is also reflective of the manner in which the income divide between the richest and the poorest countries has been consistently increasing for more than a hundred years. According to Milanovic (2006, p. 143) in 1870 "the average (unweighted) GDI per capita of the ten richest countries was 6 times greater than the average (unweighted) GDI per capita of the ten poorest countries". By 2002, however, "the ratio was 42 to 1". More than that, the past several decades have witnessed growing income inequality at a household level both globally and *within* countries, including those countries, such as China, that have steadily increased their GDP per capita over that time. Globally, the richest five percent of individuals in the 2000s earned approximately 165 times the income of the poorest five percent. China, which has dramatically reduced over the past thirty years the number of its population who live in absolute poverty, has begun to record large increases in income inequality, with its Gini coefficient (where one equals absolute income inequality and zero equals absolute equality) currently standing at 0.47, and the wealthiest ten percent of the population earning twenty-three times the income of the bottom ten percent. Another success story in relation to reducing absolute poverty, Brazil, has a Gini coefficient of 0.55, while Sierra Leone, one of the world's poorest countries, has a coefficient of 0.63. A developed social democracy such as Norway has, by comparison, a Gini coefficient of 0.26.

From the mid-1990s on, analysts attempted to unravel how the Northern-backed push toward global convergence on neoliberal macroeconomic policy, and especially its focus on lowered trade barriers, could have created such manifestly different outcomes. They were faced with an initial problem in defining what they meant by 'globalisation'. 'Globalisation' is usually regarded as both a product of the immanent economic forces that structure the global economy and as a set of interrelated normative ideals on what 'good' domestic and international economic policy looks like. It can also be seen as a rhetorical device, an historical phenomenon, and a description of the late-twentieth century reality of intensified political, cultural and social exchanges across borders. Econometrists, attempting to decipher the relationship between globalisation and poverty, however, commonly reduce 'globalisation' to measurable trade and capital flows. Even with this simplification, the answers that have emerged from the available econometric evidence have been contradictory and influenced by measurement and data collection choices.

After canvassing the wide variety of economists' debates as to whether globalisation results in growth in developing country economies and reductions in poverty levels, Harrison (2007) draws several tentative lessons. First, the poor in countries with an abundance of unskilled labour do not always gain from trade reform, largely because of domestic structural impediments to labour mobility. Second, developing countries require complementary policies to get the full poverty alleviation benefits from trade reform, especially the provision of social safety nets to ameliorate the social impacts of sectoral change, and also access to entrepreneurial credit and productive technology. Third, where countries have experienced overall increases in exports and foreign investment inflows there has an overall positive effect on absolute poverty, although significant regional discrepancies are often found in those countries' results. Fourth, evidence gained from the impact of financial crises highlight the economic vulnerability of poor populations within developing countries, as measured by the rates at which bottom income percentiles drop below absolute poverty lines, even when those countries may have previously benefited from increased economic growth. Fifth, unrestricted capital flows are generally associated with higher levels of poverty, but foreign direct investment (which tends to be 'stickier' in that it is less likely to be withdrawn by investors when changes occur in economic conditions) is associated with lower poverty levels. Finally, the evidence suggests that increased trade and general capital flows create 'winners' and 'losers' among different economic sectors within developing countries, which is indicative of how structural impediments to labour mobility, inflexible domestic investment, and government incapacity to transfer wealth via effective tax systems helps produce bifurcated economies.

The overall story to be drawn from the economic evidence is that where developing states have been able to reform domestic financial and microeconomic structures, and implement social policies, underpinned by tax-transfer systems, that help redistribute income, the opening up of economies to global trade and capital flows has produced 'pro-poor' growth which lowers both absolute and relative poverty. As compared with the high point of the North-South debate, contemporary international politico-economic discourse attempts to account for the impact of *both* global and domestic economic structures and institutions in explaining the existence of poverty. This amalgamation of the domestic and the international, as well as the importance attached to understanding poverty as being at least partly defined by reference to domestic income inequality, has implications for the way the North-South relationship might now be reconceived in an era of mature globalisation.

THE POLITICS OF POVERTY AND 'THE NORTH-SOUTH DIVIDE'

There is some irony in the fact that, even as the use of 'the South' as a development term has diminished, the discrepancies in average incomes between the poorest and the richest nations have reached historical highs. Yet international political cohesion among developing countries has not increased as a result of the shared experience of economic inequality. Indeed, there is a growing sense that, while economic, political and social globalisation may have helped create sites of inequality and poverty, it has also helped produce wealth in enough countries to raise the question whether the notion of a North-South division may have become redundant. In line with this, the politics of development and poverty is increasingly being framed as a domestic as much as an international concern. On the one hand, this may be a global expression of late-modernism's normative focus on the devolution of risk from collective institutions to individuals (Beck, 1992). A clearer driver of change, however, is the push of human rights advocacy networks to shift the international political focus onto the rights of poor people within developing countries and away from issues of state sovereignty and self-determination that were central threads of the NIEO debate in the 1970s. This move toward the political economy of rights poses a challenge to many developing country governments. It also begins to alter normative perceptions of the appropriate goals and modes of Southern cooperation. Whether there is any capacity to even begin to conceive of such change is another issue.

On the face of it, it is clear that 'the South' has failed to regain the influence on the international political economy that it had in earlier decades. The inability of the World Trade Organisation's Doha round of trade talks to reach agreement on fair terms of agricultural trade between 'developing' and 'developed' countries, for example, is indicative of the incapacity of poor nations to form effective negotiating blocs, or to capitalise on the economic and political rise of middle income BRIC countries. While some vestiges of 'the South' as a rallying point of development activism remain, with NGOs such as the Focus on the Global South continuing to push for reform of unequal global politico-economic structures, the tendency among academics and analysts is now to view developing countries either as fitting into 'convergence' models of fast-paced development on the back of competitive advantage in wages and resources (such as China, India, Brazil), or regional blocs (such as ASEAN), or the collection of countries characterised either as Low Human Development (by the UNDP), Low Income (by the World Bank), or low on a Corruption Perceptions Index (Transparency International) or Good Governance Index (World Bank).

The 2005 Paris Declaration on Aid Effectiveness and the 2008 Accra Agenda for Action, and their emphasis on the need for development partnerships between donors and recipients, might, on the face of it, represent some recovery of the idea of 'the South' as a politically relevant term. On the other hand, both initiatives are creatures of the Organisation for Economic Cooperation and Development (OECD). They do not allow for the sort of contest over international systems envisaged in the 'original' North-South dichotomy. If that contest is to be seen anywhere, it is in the rise of the 'Beijing Consensus' (as opposed to the 'Washington Consensus') and in China's use of foreign aid in strengthening its politico-economic relationships with developing countries (Ramo, 2004).

Recent increases in trade and aid *between* developing countries may signal a new phase in the North-South conceptualisation of the international political economy. The UN's ECOSOC recently estimated that twenty percent of global trade is now South-South, and around ten to twelve billion US dollars is exchanged in foreign aid, with China (four billion US dollars), Saudi Arabia (thirty-two billion US dollars) and India (one billion US dollars) providing the lion's share. China's first foreign aid policy White Paper, released in 2011, highlighted how the government perceived its foreign aid distribution to be an integral part of 'South-South cooperation'. Critics of Chinese aid argue that, in actuality, it is delivered to countries from which China wishes to import oil and other commodities, or which offer clear security benefits. A counterpoint to this critique is the absence of conditionality placed on Chinese foreign aid and the greater openness that country has, compared with many Northern states, to providing grants and low-cost loans for developing country governments to pursue their own development plans, something that appears to place them in line with the goals of the Paris Declaration.

Chinese aid policy, and that of many other middle-income aid providers, accords with earlier South-South interaction in its focus on states as opposed to the political and economic rights of the individual citizens within those states. While the early version of the 'North-South division' embodied an economic justice narrative that only concerned states and their position within global structures, economic justice as it applied to their citizens was of less interest — as were the domestic political systems and regimes that had direct responsibility for those citizens. Key players in the NIEO debates and the Non-Aligned Movement included a number of representatives from states that were, at best, only partly democratic and protective of human rights. This emphasis on the state rather than the citizenry is at odds with more recent perspectives on the political economy of develo-pment that highlight the importance of individual rights and capacities.

Rights-based approaches to development have emphasised the power of human rights conceptual frames and 'rights language' to help uncover the power inequalities behind poverty at both domestic and international levels. As argued by Eyben (2003), there have been "myriad . . . social, cultural and political struggles and debates" where communities and individuals demand the recognition of their rights, without necessarily linking those claims to specific international human rights legislation (Eyben, 2003, p. 1). Human rights concepts and language should instead be regarded as tools for local, national and international advocacy. Slim (2002) notes that while rights-talk in Washington and London may often be no more than "rhetorical fluff", for the politically and economically marginalised it is "a political philosophy that can have deep meaning to people — meaning deep enough for them to risk their lives and die for" (Slim, 2002, pp. 3–4).

Another theme of 'rights-based approaches' is their belief in the capacity of rights-talk to alter professional vocabularies and discourses and thus change decision-makers' perceptions. This position goes further than simply expressing faith in the procedural capacity of Habermasian discourse to alter power structures. It also envisages a transformation of the individual subjects of development into citizen-like actors who are entitled to just treatment by states and the institutions of the international political economy. Justice in this case is taken to mean equity of access to the processes of, and political exchanges over, development decision making (procedural justice), as well as some level of equity in the local and national distribution of resources (distributive justice). There is also, in the rights-based literature, a common, liberalist belief that individuals are the basic unit of human rights, that no distinction should be made between individuals on this score, and that no one person's rights should be abused in order to fulfil those of others.(See Nussbaum, 2000; Nelson and Dorsey, 2003; Pettit and Wheeler, 2005). From a rights perspective states are, by contrast, duty-holders that are morally and legally obliged to promote and protect the rights of their citizens. Rights-based approaches do not entirely shift the locus of development debates from North-South at the international level to individual-state relations at the domestic. They maintain some connection to earlier, collectivist notions of the 'South'. Authors such as Pogge (2002) highlight how a rights perspective can provide a valuable reframing of the international distributive injustice created by the operation of the global capitalist system. Pogge phrases his structural critique in rights terms by arguing that industrialised nations fail to meet their 'negative' duty not to do harm when they engage in activities such as support of firms based in their jurisdictions which exploit international divisions of labour. This is conceived of as a state's duty to not reinforce an international political economy that harms individuals who have rights claims akin, if not equivalent, to citizens. The caveat with regard to this position is that there are significant impediments to claiming these rights in an international environment where only the most limited of social contracts exist.

This last point offers a potential, normative path forward for reconstituting the 'North-South' concept in a manner that responds to the current historical moment, and which also provides a useful analytical tool for explaining the dynamics of the political economy of global poverty. The approach suggested here is that the relationship between North and South has to be conceptualised in a way that takes greater account of the rights-defined duties of states to their citizens.

As part of this rethinking, 'the South' needs to be re-imagined as representing a collective response on the part of developing states to enable their citizens to claim their rights, where appropriate, against developed, Northern countries. Engaging in political negotiation and conflict, with the aim of forming an international social order capable of supporting the substantive rights of the most marginalised of citizens, provides a strong normative justification for Southern states to conceive of themselves as a collective. In short, citizens need to be 'brought in' to the new notion of the South for it to have normative validity.

This reworking also offers a more comprehensive explanation for how international politico-economic change might occur. The original concept of the 'North-South divide' represented an interpretation of international politico-economic dynamics that was relevant to a specific historical time. The division it described was not a first order ideational or structural driver of change, however, unlike, for example, rational choice, Weber's 'Protestant work ethic', nationalism, marxist 'emancipation', or, as suggested here, human rights normalisation. In order to reconstruct the North-South concept for the contemporary world, it is important to view that distinction as saying less about the inherently exploitative nature of global capitalism and more about the fact that the moral and practical responsibilities for global poverty lie with those actors who control access to, and create the margins of, that economy and the international political institutions that promote and protect it.

CONCLUSION

The lasting benefit of the North-South concept is that it alerts us to the injustice of large-scale poverty and to the political value of undertaking collective action in pursuit of economic justice. The vision of the 'North-South divide' that prevailed in the 1970s, however, only faintly reflects the politico-economic realities that pertain today. It sits uneasily with contemporary understandings of the relationship between rights and development. Global poverty remains unconscionably high and is the key failure of the capitalist international political economy. Earlier state-based conceptions of 'North' and 'South' are unable to capture how the location and nature of economic inequality have changed, and especially the degree to which the poor are now found *within* middle-income countries that also contain large numbers of wealthy individuals. Economic globalisation is, in effect, producing a multiplicity of 'Norths' and 'Souths' within developing regions, countries and provinces.

The argument put forward in this chapter is that a substantial re-conceptualisation of the 'North-South divide' is required in order to go beyond the historical specificity of the original understanding of that term and to revitalise its normative and explanatory power in the context of the new, 'domesticated' power relationships of global poverty. In order to accomplish this successfully, the normative rationale of 'the South' needs to be reworked to describe a collective need for an international social order that reflects and protects the human rights/international development nexus. This is not to say that state exclusion from the institutions of international politico-economic power is no longer a valid motivation for action; only that it should be seen as simply one element within a more all-encompassing ontology of international human rights. On an explanatory level, it also needs to be recognised that the actors who compose 'the South' are no longer just the states and their political regimes but also include civil society and private economic actors. Their capacity for individual and collective agency, significantly under-appreciated at the time of the NIEO movement, needs now to be included within a new vision of a 'South' that has a major role to play in the creation of a just international social order and, through that, of a just international political economy.

REFERENCES

Beck, U (1992). *Risk Society: Towards a New Modernity.* London: Sage.

Clemens, M and T Moss (2005). Ghost of 0.7%: Origins and Relevance of the International Aid Target, *Center for Global Development Working Paper* No. 68, September. Washington DC: Center for Global Development.

Eyben, R (2003). *The Rise of Rights: Rights-based Approaches to International Development. IDS Policy Briefing, Issue 17, May.* Brighton, Sussex: Institute of Development Studies, in partnership with the Development Research Centre on Citizenship, Participation and Accountability.

Frank, A (1969). *Latin America: Underdevelopment or Revolution; Essays on the Development of Underdevelopment and the Immediate Enemy.* New York: Monthly Review Press.

Harrison, A (ed.) (2007). *Globalisation and Poverty.* Chicago: University of Chicago Press.
Higgott, R (1983). *Political Development Theory: The Contemporary Debate.* London: Croom Helm.
Independent Commission on International Development Issues (1980). *North-South, a Programme for Survival: Report of the Independent Commission on International Development Issues.* Cambridge, Mass., MA: MIT Press.
Jones, C (1983). *The North-South Dialogue: A Brief History.* London: Frances Pinter.
Leys, C (1996). *The Rise and Fall of Development Theory.* London: James Currey Ltd.
Marshall, P (1994). Whatever happened to the NIEO? *Round Table,* 331(1), 331–339.
Milanovic, B (2006). Global income inequality: A review. *World Economics,* 7(1), 131–157.
Nelson, P and E Dorsey (2003). At the Nexus of Human Rights and Development: New Methods and Strategies of Global NGOs. *World Development,* 31(12), 2013–2026.
Nussbaum, M (2000). *Women and Human Development: The Capabilities Approach.* New York: Cambridge University Press.
Pettit, J and J Wheeler (2005). Developing rights? Relating discourse to context and practice. *IDS Bulletin,* 36(1), 1–8.
Pogge, T (2002). *World Poverty and Human Rights: Cosmopolitan Responsibilities and Reforms.* Oxford: Polity.
Prebisch, R (1950). *The Economic Development of Latin America and its Problems.* New York: The United Nations.
Ramo, J (2004). *The Beijing Consensus.* London: The Foreign Policy Centre.
Rodrik, D (1997). *Has Globalisation Gone Too Far?* Washington: Institute for International Economics.
Slim, H (2002). A response to Peter Uvin: Making moral low ground: Rights as the struggle for justice and the abolition of development. *Praxis: The Fletcher Journal of Development Studies,* XVII, 1–5.
Wallerstein, I (1974). The rise and future demise of the world capitalist system: Concepts for comparative analysis. *Comparative Studies in Society and History,* 16, 387–415.

CHAPTER 16

Corporations

John Mikler

University of Sydney

Corporations are among the most powerful institutions on the planet. We are often told that as their operations increase in size and scope, the world is increasingly 'ruled' by them. This perspective has been at the heart of debates about globalisation in IPE that revolve around the prospect of the demise of the nation state due to the 'inevitability' of global neoliberal market deregulation. This prospect is celebrated by liberalists for the triumph of free market capitalism that it heralds, while it is attacked by marxist anti-globalisers as evidence of the spread of exploitative relations of production and of the deeper embedding of a core-versus-periphery structure in the global political economy. Between these views there is a more nuanced debate that revolves around the extent to which states are being constrained to function (rather than rule) in a more passive, market-facilitating role, with the interests they serve being corporate ones rather than those of their citizens. The argument about the extent to which global markets and corporations, as the key actors in them, are now 'in charge' is therefore a central and ongoing one in contemporary IPE.

In this chapter the power of corporations is considered critically, in both theoretical and empirical terms. The key points made are that:

(i) corporations' power is multi-faceted, encompassing instrumental, structural and discursive aspects;
(ii) measuring corporations' size and influence in comparison to states is not a straightforward matter; they rival states but also share authority with them; and
(iii) it remains very much the case that corporations are not placeless entities; there is a need to re-territorialise their power in relation to that of their home states.

The conclusion reached is that both powerful states and their corporations still matter, and that it is the intersection of the interests of both, and how they reconcile their interests, that should be at the heart of any contemporary analysis of them.

THEORISING THE POWER OF CORPORATIONS

The debate about the power of corporations is inseparable from the master concept of today, namely, globalisation. Theorising globalisation has been characterised by three broad 'waves' over the past three decades: that of the globalists, the sceptics and the transformationalists. These waves suggest power relationships between the state and non-state actors such as corporations along the lines of Table 1.

In the first wave, the globalists of the late 1980s and early 1990s stressed the retreat of the state. All the other implications of globalisation — political, economic, social, cultural and so on — were seen as flowing from a belief that markets were increasingly "the masters over the governments of states" (Strange, 1996, p. 4). This is because states, regardless of what they might like to do, or what their citizens may desire, inevitably needed to attract and retain globally mobile finance and productive investment. This implied that states were becoming less able to regulate corporations effectively, having sacrificed the right to do so on the altar of globally integrated markets. Ultimately, state sovereignty was deemed to be so undermined that the only regulatory functions left for governments were those which supported markets. The globalists did not see this as a matter of opinion, nor necessarily a matter of a politically left-versus-right ideology, but as a *structural* reality. Ultimately, they saw the result as being a shift in authority from government and in the latter's a place "a yawning hole of non-authority, ungovernance it might be called" (Strange, 1996, p. 14). Multinational corporations (MNCs) that straddle the globe with the prime goal of maximising their material returns, and bearing allegiance to no one except their shareholders, were seen as stepping in to fill the void. To the extent that they 'governed' they did so undemocratically, since they represented a much narrower range of interests than states and, unlike governments, could not be voted in or out of office. States were dependent on them, however, for the economic benefits they could confer or take elsewhere.

Table 1: Locating power in the three waves of theorising globalisation.

Globalists	Sceptics	Transformationalists
Global governance/ neoliberalism; decline of the nation state; loss of national sovereignty.	Nation states remain central; regional blocs; international power and inequality; political agency is possible.	Politics is globally transformed; nation states remain important but are reconstructed; shared sovereignty.

Source: Based on Martell (2007, p. 177).

Since the 1990s, many authors have taken issue with this perspective to the point that it is now virtually on the fringes of mainstream IPE. In its place, two subsequent waves of theorising have emerged. The second wave, that of the sceptics, sees globalisation as more a discourse or an idea, in other words, it is largely what states make of it. As such, states remain key actors, with international politics still best understood as a function of political agency in terms of the relations between states. The sceptics say that it is a fallacy to suggest that all states are equally weakened by the globalisation of the world economy. Indeed, it serves the interests of powerful industrialised states to promote the notion that there are undeniable 'forces' of globalisation that are 'out there' attacking all states' sovereignty in order that their flagship corporations may more easily access cheap factors of production worldwide and sell their products in new markets. To the extent that there is something popularly termed 'globalisation' underway, it is probably more accurate to call it regionalisation, or the internationalisation of the interests of powerful states.

The third and most recent wave of theorising on globalisation belongs to the transformationalists. In many ways they may be regarded as 'fence-sitters'. They recognise the changes being wrought by globalisation and do not dismiss them as easily as the sceptics. They do not see nation states as increasingly irrelevant, however, so long as their political agency is a reconstructed one. They share the concerns of the sceptics in that they reject the 'globaloney' of the first wave globalists (Hay and Marsh, 2000, p. 6). In recognising that states remain central actors in the international political economy, however, they do not dismiss the idea of the increasing importance of non-state actors either. They see a complex picture, one key aspect of which is the recognition that states' rely on sharing their sovereignty with each other in order to retain it, as well as with private actors such as corporations. Sometimes, states may push neoliberal deregulatory reforms if this is in their interests, but this is one of a range of policy paths that states may choose to pursue. As such, the transformationalists can be seen as occupying a complex middle ground between the globalists and the sceptics.

The ongoing debate about conceptualising globalisation in IPE suggests that theorising the role, and therefore the power, of corporations in a world still very much comprised of nation states is not at all straightforward. Drawing on a wealth of literature analysing the nature of power, Fuchs (2007) suggests that there are three broad aspects of the power that corporations wield in respect of states: instrumental, structural and discursive.

Corporations possess instrumental power in respect of states in the sense that there are direct and observable relationships of power between the two. In relational terms, what one does affects the other, and as corporations have grown in size and transnationality so their instrumental power to achieve their ends has increased. Rather like the traditional perspectives on power in international relations more generally, where the relative power of states determines their position in the state system and their ability to act in their interests, so the increased resources at the disposal of the corporations that straddle the globe give them greater power over states in lobbying for their desired ends. The problem with such an approach is that it does not lend itself to an in-depth understanding of the interests and actions of corporations versus states. If it is possible to takes these as given, however, based on *a priori* assumptions (for example, that corporations desire profits while states desire power) then their ability to realise these desires depends on their relative positions.

Structural conceptions of power focus on the agenda-setting power of actors. It emphasises the "input side of policy and politics and the predetermination of behavioural options or political decision makers" (Fuchs, 2007, p. 58). In the case of corporations, their interests can truly be said to have rivalled states in the latter decades of the twentieth century through the greater transnationality of their operations and thereby their ability to influence states' policy agendas. For example, Margaret Thatcher's 'TINA' dictum of the 1980s — i.e. that There Is No Alternative to the free market — led to states handing power to corporations via deregulatory reforms and the privatisation of formerly public services in the belief that this was 'inevitable'. In particular, states came to see their fortunes as dependent on satisfying corporate interests because not giving corporations what they wanted risked them deciding to locate their operations elsewhere. This is why it is often said that the structural power of corporations in the global economy has the propensity to produce a race to the bottom, that is, a competitive bidding down of salaries, conditions and standards by states. By being in control of "pivotal networks and resources" (Fuchs, 2007, p. 59) corporations are able to influence agendas and rules that are made by states in their own interests. Their interests come to be seen as synonymous with states' national interests.

Discursive power is perhaps the most nuanced as well as the hardest to observe. Discursive approaches stress the power of ideas and the way in which "some definitions of issues are organised into politics while other definitions are organised out" (Hajer, quoted in Fuchs, 2007, p. 60). The discursive power of corporations stresses the way they shape perceptions to increase their legitimacy in the eyes of governments and the public. In so doing, they achieve their ends by influencing, shaping, or determining the wants of others and competing with states as sources of authority in their own right through "naming, framing and campaigning" (Fuchs, 2007, p.63). For example, it is striking that democratically elected governments are now judged on their ability to attain and retain credit ratings that are determined by private ratings agencies and that international standards are largely a matter for private business associations to determine (e.g. the International Organisation for

Standardisation). Corporate social responsibility is now widely believed to be as important as making profits. It is certainly the case that the instrumental and structural power of corporations has facilitated this but their discursive power has also led them to be perceived as legitimately entitled to make such claims. Rather than the more classical liberalist view of the firm as a mechanism of profit, corporations are now often seen as self-regulators and solvers of environmental and social problems, with these being cast as *business* problems. While the discursive power of corporations is therefore arguably the hardest of all to 'see', since when it works it is as if it does not exist, it does establish legitimacy and thereby private authority. It does not just rely on corporations' size *vis-a-vis* states, nor their structural ability to influence the policy-making processes of states. It manipulates and conditions society into accepting the desires and ends of corporations as *right*.

The complexity of theorising the power of corporations suggests that it is problematic to purely understand corporations' power in terms of their size, sales, and market power. One would have to believe that there is a direct link between these and political processes. In reality, one needs to see the power of corporations not just in a linear fashion but in three dimensions. For example, the discursive power of corporations enhances their instrumental and structural power and vice versa. This is worth bearing in mind as the chapter turns to empirical measures of the extent to which corporations may be said to be 'in charge'.

CORPORATIONS "IN CHARGE"

In the post-war period, the growth in the size and scope of corporations has entrenched them as powerful political actors in international affairs. Whereas official public flows of finance and investment between states had predominated, increasing private flows has meant that by 1971 the liquid assets of the top one hundred US multinational corporations (MNCs) exceeded the reserves of the largest industrialised countries. What they decided to do with these assets, in the sense of where they held them, where they decided to invest them, and the international production networks they controlled, came to be seen as at least as important as the decisions taken by the governments of nations. States, even great powers such as the US, had to be mindful of their domestic policy settings, because those seen as unfavourable by major corporations could potentially result in serious economic consequences. For example, if a handful of these major corporations decided to switch just a small proportion of their liquid assets from one currency to another they could cause an exchange rate crisis, or if they decided to move a major proportion of their manufacturing operations offshore where conditions were more conducive they could cause high unemployment and social catastrophe. By operating globally, and by raising finance and investing in multiple jurisdictions, even by the early 1970s it was the case that no one government alone could control MNCs' actions and there was no international organisation that could do this either (Panic, 1995).

Today, corporations remain outside the scope of international law and are still subjects only of national laws despite the fact that they increasingly have interests beyond national boundaries. Given this, to get a sense of corporations' potential power in respect of states, it is useful to consider their relative size. It is sobering to note that the world's fifty largest MNCs each have annual sales revenues in excess of the national incomes of one hundred and thirty-one UN member states (there are currently one hundred and ninety-two UN member states). For example, ExxonMobil and General Motors' sales are each larger than the GDP of New Zealand (Fuchs, 2007). Harrod (2006) suggests, however, that a better indicator of corporations' size, and therefore power, is to be found in comparing their sales revenue to government expenditure and the annual budgets of international organisations. This is because the sales figure of a corporation shows how much it has spent on purchasing labour, resources, investments, goods, advertising, corporate image-making, lobbying and consultants in order to produce a desired surplus. As such, a corporation's sales figure is an indicator of its organisational budget, which is analogous to a state or international organisation's budget. Seen in this light, he notes that in 2001 the French government spent two hundred and seventy billion US dollars, while Walmart spent around two hundred and ten billion US dollars and Toyota around one hundred billion US dollars. By comparison, the United Nations had a budget of around ten billion US dollars. Either way, together and individually, the world's largest corporations rival states in terms of their size and the potential relational influence they may derive from this.

It is not just that corporations are increasing in size, however, and therefore in their propensity to exercise instrumental power to achieve their desired ends. It is also that they dominate the global markets in which they operate. Contrary to the liberalist notion of free and open markets that are coordinated by competition, the liberalising agenda of the world's industrialised states, and the international organisations they largely control (such as the OECD, the WTO, the IMF and the World Bank), has produced a consolidation of global markets. Competition tends to produce winners and global competition tends to produce winners on a global scale. Today's oligopolistic 'competition' is the global norm. For example, Fuchs (2007) notes that in excess of eighty percent of the global markets in bananas, cocoa and tea are controlled by three corporations; over seventy percent of the global market in cereals and tobacco are controlled by five corporations; and in excess of seventy percent of private water supplies are controlled by three corporations. In fact, Harrod (2006) points out that almost all industrial sectors are controlled by five MNCs at most, and that twenty percent of these have one corporation that accounts for more than forty percent of the global market.

These "mega-corporations", as Braithwaite (2008) terms them, extend their power beyond the industrial sectors which they control to markets for raw materials, labour markets and global supply chains. Increasingly, international trade is intra-firm in nature so that trade data is not a reflection of national comparative advantage but of internal corporate strategies. They also have the power to determine the basis on which innovation occurs and therefore the kinds of products and services offered in global markets. For example, it is striking to note that over the last twenty years, eighty-four percent of research and development expenditure and ninety-five percent of US patents were carried out by just ten companies. In a nutshell, "the development and consolidation of sectoral concentration … has freed the corporation from the restraints of classical competition" (Harrod, 2006, p. 25). Given the size of corporations relative to states and their dominance of global markets, it is no wonder that over a decade ago Strange (1996, p. 45) declared that corporations had structurally consolidated their position as the world's 'central organisers' and 'engines of growth'.

Yet, measures of total government expenditure show that states are not shrinking as a result of the growing influence of corporate interests. Table 2 shows that over the course of a decade from 1996 to 2006, total government expenditure as a percentage of GDP remained either remarkably stable for the ten largest OECD member states, increased in seven of them, and in some is around half of GDP.

Table 2: Total government expenditure as a percentage of GDP.

	1996	2006
US	33	37
Germany	46	46
Japan	29	38
France	52	53
UK	41	45
Italy	49	50
Canada	43	39
Spain	41	39
Korea	16	28
Mexico	17*	21

Source: OECD (2000; 2007).
Note: *1999

This suggests that rather than the state becoming less relevant, it is probably more accurate to say that its role is changing. Commensurate with the view of the transformationalists in the globalisation literature, authors such as Braithwaite (2008) have pointed out that the increasing concentration evident within industrial sectors, and the growth in the size and influence of the corporations in them, has led not to the demise of the nation state but a reorientation of its role. Markets that are highly competitive and made up of many small enterprises are harder to regulate than those that are comprised of a handful of mega-corporations. Contrary to 'the neoliberal fairytale' it is therefore more efficient for states to control them in cooperation with these corporations and therefore to *re-regulate* rather than to deregulate them. Braithwaite (2008, p. 4) explains it thus:

> In the era of regulatory capitalism, more of the governance that shapes the daily lives of most citizens is corporate governance than state governance. The corporatisation of the world is both a product of regulation and the key driver of regulatory growth, indeed of state growth more generally ... The reciprocal relationship between corporatisation and regulation creates a world in which there is more governance of all kinds.

Even as they have come to rival states, or perform roles that states once unilaterally controlled, corporations are increasingly regulated by states in how they do this. This is the transformation in power relations being wrought by the processes of globalisation: neither a loss of power by states, nor an outright shift in power to corporations, but a re-negotiation and reconstitution of the relationship between the two.

It is not size alone that is a measure of power but how the will of actors involved in corporations versus states is exercised. As corporations have increased their power the role played by states has shifted to become one more of rule by regulation, particularly since states have found it irresistible to share their sovereignty with non-state actors such as corporations. This implies that a world where borders are more permeable, markets are less territorially defined, and increasing market concentration is a reality, is an opportunity for states as much as firms. States that effectively share their sovereignty with corporations in the making and implementation of regulations may even extend the *de facto* territorial jurisdiction of their regulations and in the process potentially enhance rather than diminish their sovereignty. States that have the capacity to do this reap the reward of making rules not just for themselves but for the world (see Mikler, 2008). This suggests that corporations are best not conceived as stateless entities. It also suggests that for powerful, industrialised states there is considerable scope for sharing sovereignty with corporations and mutually deriving benefits from doing so. This is the subject of the following section.

RE-TERRITORIALISING CORPORATIONS

As corporations have grown in size and become more multinational in their operations, the effect of this on states has not been felt equally. While it may seem obvious to say that they increasingly rule the world, the reality is that they rule some parts of it more than others. Despite over sixty years of the liberalisation of global markets and the multi-nationalisation of corporations, it remains the case that rich, Northern countries dominate international investment and production and are the source of seventy to ninety percent of all foreign direct investment. In fact, nearly ninety percent of the world's top five hundred corporations are headquartered in just ten countries: the US, Japan, the UK, France, Germany, Canada, the Netherlands, Switzerland, Italy and Australia. Furthermore, according to the United Nations Conference on Trade and Development (UNCTAD), the vast majority of their foreign direct investment goes to other Northern countries, rather than those in the poorer global South. The latter have rarely had more than thirty percent of global foreign direct investment stocks, a figure that disguises the fact that the South's share of foreign direct investment has tended to be concentrated in a few emerging Asian economies like China and India (Harrod, 2006, p. 26).

This is borne out by measures of corporate transnationality. One such measure is UNCTAD's Transnationality Index (TNI), a simple composite ratio of foreign assets, sales and employment to total assets, sales and employment. As shown in Table 3, considering the top five corporations of the OECD's three largest member states demonstrates that even their most global of firms' TNIs are not as high as might be expected. Their TNIs are no higher than around seventy, with the majority in the range of forty-six to sixty. Apart from the top three or four most global companies from Germany, the US, and Japan, the rest of the MNCs have at least fifty percent of their assets, employment and sales 'at home'. In nearly all cases it is more their sales, rather than the location of their assets or employment, that is the driver of their transnationality. This is changing over time, though the change is occurring quite gradually. For example, the TNI for the top one hundred MNCs grew from fifty-two to fifty-seven over 1993 to 2002 so that on average they still had around half of their operations at home and only twenty-one of them had a TNI above seventy-five (Dicken, 2007). The vast majority of MNCs are therefore more accurately viewed as national corporations with global interests, rather than being global in and of themselves.

Only the very largest corporations, or those that have their headquarters in smaller states such as Switzerland, rely more on foreign sales than sales in their

Table 3: The trans-nationality of the largest US, German and Japanese MNCs.

	TNI	Foreign assets as a proportion of total assets (%)	Foreign sales as a proportion of total sales (%)	Foreign employment as a proportion of total employment (%)
Germany				
1. BMW	67	61	73	67
2. Bertelsmann	63	56	70	64
3. Siemens	62	61	63	62
4. Volkswagen	56	49	72	48
5. BASF	54	60	59	43
Japan				
1. Honda Motor	69	73	77	56
2. Nissan Motor	61	52	70	61
3. Sony Corporation	57	41	70	60
4. Toyota Motor	49	53	60	36
5. Mitsui and Co.	46	49	43	46
US				
1. Coca Cola	71	61	69	81
2. McDonald's	66	74	66	57
3. ExxonMobil	63	69	70	50
4. Hewlett-Packard	62	60	63	62
5. Procter and Gamble	57	59	55	57

Source: UNCTAD (2006).

home market. For the vast majority "a statistical profile for the current corporation indicates that it is predominantly Anglo-American, with a greater interest in domestic markets; that it invests predominantly in rich countries…and that it is one of a small group of corporations that dominate the sectors" (Harrod, 2006, pp. 27–28). Even the most global MNCs are not as global as one might think and this is not changing as rapidly as is often popularly asserted. Perhaps most importantly, this is true of corporate ownership and control, which has long been recognised as remaining very much national rather than transnational or diffused or whatever other global descriptor happens to be used. Indeed, Wade's (1996, p.79) declaration over a decade ago that "in Japanese companies foreign directors are as rare as British sumo wrestlers" remains applicable today.

These observations are important because it is striking that the globalisation of increasingly oligopolistic world markets has led to the expansion of the North's share of global wealth while the South's has shrunk. Even if levels of absolute poverty have fallen — dramatically so in certain states such as China, India and Brazil — global inequality has increased. Global patterns of production, trade and investment that are driven by large corporations suggest that this trend will continue. Focusing on states in the North, it is especially true to say that for them globalisation is a political process mediated by national economic institutions that impact on and construct the strategic interests of their corporations. Rather than placeless entities, these are institutionally embedded in their home states so that in a world in which markets are increasingly global, the corporations that compete in them are less so. The relationship between corporations and the states within which they are headquartered also remains crucial.

This resonates with marxists because the strategies and interests of large corporations, located in a handful of Northern industrialised states whose interests are mutually reinforcing, make up the core, while other states are increasingly satellised on the periphery of politico-economic affairs. Capitalist relations of production and the centrality of corporations with regard to them are resulting in a world in which the class divide produced between those who control the means of production versus those who are dependent on them are being reproduced worldwide. The resulting inequalities are not only being reproduced in all countries but between them as well, and MNCs are arguably the emissaries.

There is another way to consider the intertwined interests of powerful, industrialised states and their nationally embedded corporations, however. Although much has been said about the inevitability of a convergence on a single neoliberalist form of the state, the evidence shows that this is not the case. Indeed, it would seem naive to assert, as both hardline liberalists and marxists do, that global capitalism must be predominantly (neo)liberalist. As Fuchs (2007, pp. 46–47) points out, it is not possible to generalise for all states the "institutionalised channels of consultation and negotiation frequently created by government and dependent on government". With this in mind, authors in the 'comparative capitalism' tradition have long pointed out that capitalism is not monolithic and that differences in capitalist relations of production between industrialised states remains the case. National institutions remain important for understanding nationally divergent forms of capitalism while global-domestic linkages are important for understanding the interplay between domestic and international factors.

The 'comparative capitalism' literature is now extensive having burgeoned since the 1990s. Of particular relevance to the study of corporations, Hall and Soskice (2001) propose a firm-centred (rather than state-centred) "varieties of capitalism (VOC)" approach. Their desire is to "to bring firms back into the centre of the analysis of comparative capitalism", thus recognising that firms are "the crucial actors in a capitalist economy" (Hall and Soskice, 2001, pp. 2 and 6).

In observing that all firms must 'solve' coordination problems to succeed, they go further than other studies of 'comparative capitalism' to categorise capitalist states as tending towards liberalist market economies (LMEs) versus coordinated market economies (CMEs). In this regard:

- the US, the UK, Australia, Canada, New Zealand and Ireland are clear LMEs;
- Germany, Japan, Switzerland, the Netherlands, Belgium, Sweden, Norway, Denmark, Finland and Austria are clear CMEs; and
- France, Italy, Spain, Portugal, Greece and Turkey are ambiguous.

Put simply, LME-based corporations prefer to coordinate their activities via market competition, whereas CME-based corporations prefer more non-market cooperative relationships to coordinate their activities, including using the state. The US is usually taken to be the archetypal LME. Others include the Anglo-Saxon countries. By contrast many European states are CMEs. Some, such as Italy and France, occupy a more ambiguous position, though the latter has long been characterised as a *dirigiste* state in the sense that the elites within its bureaucracy perform a steering function with respect to the national economy. East Asian industrialised states such as Japan are often said to possess 'Asian' forms of capitalism, but they are often seen as sharing CME attributes with continental European countries.

Although the VOC approach has been the subject of sustained attack for its dualistic categorisation of states, it has come to be a dominant starting point for studying the strategic preferences of nationally embedded corporations. The rationale for the simplifying assumptions underlying the VOC approach's categories is that states possess sub-national institutional complementarities and therefore can be considered not just as discrete cases but as belonging to coherent and enduring categories. That states in each of these two categories tend to have more in common with each other than across the categories has been borne out by multiple studies which have demonstrated that even if there has been a 'slide' towards more liberalist forms of capitalism worldwide over the last two decades, if anything the *gap* between states has widened, along with a clustering around the two categories proposed by the VOC approach (see Hall and Gingerich, 2009). This is because public and private actors 'inhabit' institutional structures — at any given point in time — that they cannot easily change. They certainly can change over time, and indeed they may act purposively to do so along the lines of the three conceptions of power outlined above, but they do so path-dependently. As such, it is easier for LMEs to become more liberalist than CMEs and it is preferable for institutional complementarities that have served states and their corporations well to be reinforced in the face of international challenges, rather than abandoned.

While it is an over-simplification to say that firms of the same nationality are identical, national characteristics nevertheless predominate such that corporations of the same nationality, as in the case of their home states, have more in common with each other than with those of different nationalities. For example:

- there are closer state-business relations in CMEs versus a preference for the separation of the state and markets in LMEs; a preference for market-based solutions in LMEs will be different, therefore, from a partnership approach and the acceptance of a greater coordinating function on the part of the state in CMEs;
- a priority for markets as organisers of economic activity is clear in LMEs in both the product and financial spheres; by contrast the market is seen as one among a variety of mechanisms for organising economic activity in CMEs, where a more relational, cooperative approach prevails and there is a greater willingness on the part of corporations to accommodate higher levels of state intervention in markets;
- LME-based firms may be conceived of as networks of contracts with significant power invested in management; they act on market signals in order to make profits in the short term and pay dividends to their shareholders; a CME-based firm is best conceived of as a collective (Germany) or a community (Japan) that acts to enhance its reputation through close relational ties with its stakeholders: there is a stronger role for senior office holders as drivers of strategic change as is the case for LME-based firms; this compares with CME-based firms where the corporate culture is not necessarily driven from the 'top'; and
- there is a preference for non-price competition via product innovation in established industries in CMEs; in LMEs radical technological change in new industries is the norm; this suggests that incremental steps in mature industries are most likely to be driven by CME-based firms in the absence of market and regulatory signals, whereas LME-based firms will resist this until new industries become materially viable.

This is neither an exhaustive list nor an unproblematic one but the key point stressed by many authors is that there are nationally differentiated constructions of corporate strategic interests. In comparing Germany and Japan with the US, for example, Dore (2000, p. 106) notes that "they remain economies in which the stock market plays a much less central role, and the state a larger one; in which the financial sector is less dominant; and manufacturing industry [is] correspondingly more important; in which engineers tend to have the edge over accountants; and the doctrine of the supremacy of shareholder value is still a much weaker element in determining company goals". In short, he found that while the US embodied a liberalist market-shareholder form of capitalism, states such as Germany and Japan exhibited a more coordinated stakeholder form.

The contemporary relevance of this is that, in the aftermath of the global financial crisis (the GFC), the inevitability of neoliberalist globalisation involving privatisation, deregulation, market-determined exchange and interest rates, minimal government spending, and the unfettered opening of borders to trade, investment and financial flows, seems more open to challenge than ever before. Indeed, France's Nikolai Sarkozy danced on the grave of neoliberalist capitalism proclaiming "*le laisser-faire, c'est fini*". Chinese Vice Premier Wang Qishan was more diplomatic, declaring that "the teachers now have some problems" (Altman, 2009, p. 11).

The World Bank has also declared the death of the 'Washington Consensus'. This seems to open the way for a re-negotiation of state-corporate relations in world affairs and for alternative, rather more state-coordinated forms of capitalist relations of production. The extent to which this may happens remains to be seen but the possibility of deeper, more embedded forms of regulated capitalism, as a result of international agreements between the world's most powerful states (such as the members of the G20), should not now be discounted. After all, corporations remain nationally embedded in states. They depend on state support for their ongoing viability, just as states themselves are in turn dependent on corporations supporting national interests. For example, in the aftermath of the global financial crisis the US government considered General Motors to be 'too big to fail'. Bailing out this flagship company was as much in the interests of the US as the company itself.

While the predominant, mainstream hope is that global markets will recover so that the long-term benefits of a global liberalist economic order may continue be realised, it may also be that greater acceptance is emerging of the idea that there is a more explicit role for states with regard to realising the benefits for all. It may be the case that alternative ways of sharing sovereignty between states and corporations come to be more widely embraced as part of the transformation of the state-corporate sharing of authority in world affairs. Moreover, these may not necessarily follow the Anglo-Saxon LME form of capitalism but more the CME forms found in other dominant and emerging states in the world political economy and their corporations.

CONCLUSION

The global political economy is not predominantly characterised by small, entrepreneurial firms adrift on a sea of competitive market forces. Rather, large corporations create and moderate market conditions in their own interests and the choices they make affect the fortunes of states. They possess instrumental, structural and discursive power and employ all three in doing so. Although they rival states, however, there is dependence between the two such that a sharing of sovereignty on the part of states, and a sharing of authority on the part of corporations, serves their mutual interests. Given that this is the case, it is striking that a handful of corporations control most of the global markets in which they operate, and that they still retain distinct national home bases. They therefore remain institutionally embedded in distinct national contexts and distinct national capitalisms.

As such, neoliberalist globalisation and the power of markets and market actors that it involves is not inevitable. If anything, debates about alternative forms of capitalism have intensified in the post-global financial crisis environment. For industrialised, powerful states and those that are emerging as new powers, there is nothing inevitable about the role played by corporations in their national economies, nor in the global economy. Today, capitalism is being questioned much as communism was three decades ago. Just as the fall of the Berlin Wall and the end of the Cold War produced an expectation of the inevitability of convergence on a neoliberalist form of the state, where markets and corporations became the dominant actors in them and were 'in charge', it seems reasonable to conclude that the first decade of the twenty-first century ended with an impetus for convergence in the opposite direction. There is even the possibility that powerful states and the international organisations to which they belong may increasingly become masters over their corporations and that this may serve the interests of both.

REFERENCES

Altman, R (2009). The great crash: A geopolitical setback for the west. *Foreign Affairs*, 88(1), 2–14.

Braithwaite, J (2008). *Regulatory Capitalism: How it Works, Ideas for Making it Work Better.* Cheltenham: Edward Elgar.

Dicken, P (2007). *Global Shift: Mapping the Changing Contours of the World Economy*, 5th ed. London: Sage Publications.

Dore, R (2000). Will global capitalism be Anglo-Saxon capitalism? *New Left Review*, 6, 101–119.

Fuchs, D (2007). *Business Power in Global Governance.* Boulder: Lynne Rienner Publishers.

Hall, P and D Soskice (2001). An Introduction to Varieties of Capitalism. In *Varieties of Capitalism: The Institutional Foundations of Comparative Advantage*, P Hall and D Soskice (eds.). Oxford: Oxford University Press.

Hall, P and D Gingerich (2009). Varieties of capitalism and institutional complementarities in the political economy. *British Journal of Political Science*, 39(3), 449–482.

Harrod, J (2006). The Century of the Corporation. In *Global Corporate Power*, C May (ed.). Boulder: Lynne Rienner Publishers.

Hay, C and D Marsh (eds.) (2000). *Demystifying Globalisation.* Basingstoke: Palgrave.
Martell, L (2007). The third wave in globalisation theory. *International Studies Review*, 9(2), 173–196.
Mikler, J (2008). Sharing sovereignty for global regulation: The cases of fuel economy and online gambling. *Regulation and Governance*, 2(4), 383–404.
OECD (2007; 2000). OECD in Figures. http://www.sourceOECD.org [23 September 2010].
Panic, M (1995). The Bretton Woods System: Concept and Practice. In *Managing the Global Economy*, J Michie and J Smith (eds.). Oxford: Oxford University Press.
Strange, S (1996). *The Retreat of the State: The Diffusion of Power in the World Economy.* Cambridge: Cambridge University Press.
UNCTAD (2006). *World Investment Report 2006.* New York and Geneva: United Nations.
Wade, R (1996). Globalisation and its Limits: Reports of the Death of the National Economy are Greatly Exaggerated. In *National Diversity and Global Capitalism*, S Berger and R Dore (eds.). Ithaca: Cornell University Press.

CHAPTER 17

The World's Workers

Verity Burgmann

University of Melbourne

In 1848 Marx and Engels famously announced in the *Communist Manifesto* that: "The proletarians have nothing to lose but their chains. They have a world to gain. Workers of the World, Unite!" They believed the continued development of capitalism would create the conditions necessary for workers within each country to unite, because capitalist development encouraged the growth of a proletariat better able to organise and mobilise as a result of being brought together in workplaces. By the same token, they believed the spreading of capitalism around the globe provided conditions for the workers of the whole world to unite across national borders and express their shared interests in challenging the capitalists who exploited workers everywhere.

Workers are those who produce the goods and services of the world, who receive wages or salaries from employers, and who do not have significant control over the circumstances of their employment. This definition excludes people in managerial roles but includes many other 'white-collar' employees, as well as most 'blue-collar' workers. Zweig (2000), in *The Working Class Majority*, estimates that sixty-two percent of adults in the USA are working class, despite the country's image as being predominantly middle class, hence the subtitle of his book: *America's Best Kept Secret*. Around the world, workers and their dependents — along with peasants, subsistence farmers, tribal peoples and unemployed people — form the bulk of those who lack wealth and power. The trajectory of capitalist development is to draw more and more people into waged work.

So, the global spread of capitalism, in marxist thought, is a necessary precondition for the workers of the world uniting to oppose the conditions of employment imposed upon them by employers. In the short term, however, globalisation has increased the power of corporations to exploit the world's workers. According to Martin and Schumann (1996, p. 8), globalisation is a strategy and a rhetoric actively pursued by capital to increase profit levels and subdue labour internationally. "Global economic integration is by no means a natural process; it is consciously driven by a single-minded policy." Those who manage the global flows of capital are intentionally driving down the wage levels of their tax-paying employees. "Wages as a share of national wealth are declining worldwide. ... Share prices and corporate profits rise in double-digit leaps, whereas wages and salaries sink" (Martin and Schuman, 1996, p. 7).

HOW GLOBALISATION HAS AFFECTED WORKERS

Since the late 1970s, the world's workers have, in the main, experienced rising unemployment, declining real wages, increased working hours, deteriorating working conditions, decreased occupational safety, and increasing casualisation and insecurity of employment. Globalisation, according to Pronk (2000, p. 42), has ensured that "macroeconomic growth continues to go hand in hand with the grossest social abuses". He notes that the ratio of the top twenty percent of the world's income earners, as against the poorest twenty percent, grew from 30:1 in 1960 to 80:1 in 2000. The most important changes brought about by globalisation have taken place at the bottom of the economy, not at the top. A union organiser for twenty years in the US and Mexico, Bacon (2004, pp. 3–4), has described how he learnt this firsthand:

> People who can't make a living as coffee farmers in Veracruz become farm laborers picking grapes in Delano, or die crossing the border's Desierto del Diablo in the attempt. Mexican workers won a nineteen-month strike at Watsonville, California, frozen food plant, only to see other Mexicans hired to fill their jobs a few years later, when the company move[d] production a thousand miles south to Irapuato.

Some sectors of the economy in developing countries have experienced dramatic growth, but the reality for workers in these instances is far from the impression conveyed in mainstream media, which imply that such workers are prosperous. Workers in these industries tell their own stories. In the Indian blog, "Developing Unrest: New Struggles in Miserable Boom-Town Gurgaon", for example, workers reveal their vulnerability to the vagaries of the global market and how they continue to be dependent on the villages from whence they have come in order to sell their labour to global capitalists.[1]

According to this blog, Gurgaon, a satellite town south of Delhi, has become the symbol of 'Shining India'. Many people are dazzled by the glass-fronts of the shopping malls and corporate towers. They fail, however, to see the development of a massive industrial working class. Together with industrial centres like the Pearl River Delta in China or the Maquiladoras in northern Mexico, the Delhi industrial

[1]See www.gurgaonworkersnews.wordpress.com; www.faridabadmajdoorsamachar.blogspot.com.

belt has become a focal point of global working-class formation. Hundreds of thousands of migrant garment workers work next to the assembly lines of India's biggest automobile hub and next to thousands of young workers sweating under the headsets of Gurgaon's call centres.

The blog reflects on how the collective workforce exists beyond factory walls or company units, along supply chains, in backyard living quarters, and in remote villages. It is shaped by local, regional and global divisions of labour. Assembly plants around the globe depend on parts manufactured in Gurgaon by companies like Rico or Delphi. Production in the huge garment factories is supplied via supervisor middlemen with piecework from working (wo)men stitching 'at home'. The majority of workers are migrant workers, going back and forth between their urban industrial lives and their villages. "Wages are too low to reproduce a nuclear family in Gurgaon, [therefore] most workers leave their family in the villages... Though disintegrating, the village still functions as the main unemployment insurance" because wages are too low to survive a period of unemployment or strike action. "Workers arrive in Gurgaon with hopes, which are in most cases disillusioned". Their desire not to be a worker anymore is usually expressed in the plan to open a shop back home.

Employers are ruthless, according to this blog. In winter 2000/2001, for example, Maruti Suzuki used a minor labour dispute to lock out the permanent workforce and replace them through compulsory 'Voluntary Retirement Schemes' with temporary workers. This was repeated in other companies to the point where seventy to eighty percent of the average factory workforce was hired through contractors. The latter were clearly less interested in resolving struggles for long-running wage agreements and company pension schemes. The remaining casual and permanent workers were often young workers with much less job security and lower wages than the old type of permanent workforce. In the garment factories the skilled tailors on piece rates producing 'full-piece' garments were increasingly put under pressure by chain-systems employing less skilled workers to produce the same garment using divisions of labour and machines. In this complex picture the majority of workers did not face a single 'company boss' but many bosses, who hired local goons as a repressive force ready to quell expressions of worker unrest.

The blog emphasises the precarious nature of the Gurgaon workforce in a globalised economy. In spring 2008 the *rupee* reached its peak in relation to the US dollar, causing bad conditions for export. The garment industry in Gurgaon dismissed thousands of workers and shifted orders to 'low currency' countries like Vietnam and Bangladesh. In autumn the *rupee* plummeted, but so too did the US and European stock markets, sending shock waves through the industrial areas of Gurgaon. There was a credit crunch for real estate, garment orders fell, and US banking services slumped. The blog concludes that workers who might otherwise have thought they had little in common but *chai* stalls — workers like the English-speaking call centre night shift ones; the migrant garment and construction ones; and the young skilled ones in the car-part plants — now faced a common situation, namely, cuts in bonuses or piece rates, the cancellation of free company meals or transport, and the threat of job cuts.

Other workers typical of those in the global 'South' (see Chapter 15 on this contested concept) are the children who stitch shoes in Indonesia's Nike factories or the adults who act as 'firm fodder' in Mexico's notorious Export Processing Zones. On the US/Mexican border, more than a million workers labour in three thousand eight hundred factories. Bacon has found a long history there not only of exploitation but also of powerful resistance struggles that mostly go unreported.

> Those movements that surge from below — workers trying to wrest survival from low-wage factory jobs, squatter communities holding on to their land even as their leaders are jailed and they are threatened with eviction — have a history as unrecorded as that of the strikes in which I was organiser. The voices of the people who understand the consequences of globalisation most directly, and who can speak with the authority of their own experience, are unheard (Bacon, 2004, pp. 4–5).

The detrimental effects of globalisation have also been experienced by workers in developed countries, who are nowadays mostly worse off than their counterparts of the 1970s. The current generation of young workers is the first in US history to face a substantially lower standard of living than that of their parents (Herbert, 2005). Between 1979 and the mid-1990s, real wages in the US declined twelve percent, despite a productivity increase of twenty-one percent over the same period (Moody, 1998, p. 60). The per capita real gross output of the US economy was fifty-four percent larger in 1994 than in 1973, however, the real hourly take-home pay was four cents lower; in 1996, average weekly earnings in constant dollars were nineteen percent lower than they had been in 1973, falling from three and fifteen dollars to two hundred and fifty-six dollars (Smith, 2006, p. 286). According to Zweig (2000), Clinton's America experienced greater poverty and lower real wages than Nixon's:

> Our society's growing inequality of income and wealth is a reflection of the increased power of capitalists and the reduced power of workers. In the last two decades the working class has experienced lower real incomes, longer hours at work, fewer protections by unions or government regulations, and inferior schools (Elliot, 2000).

By 1997 US CEOs were paying themselves two hundred and nine times more than their workers — the average CEO's pay having doubled between 1989 and

1997, while workers' real wages having fallen by 3.1 percent over the same period (Smith, 2006, p. 287). According to an August 2005 report by United for a Fair Economy and the Institute for Policy Studies:

> The ratio of average CEO pay (now $11.8 million) to worker pay (now $27,460) spiked up from 301 to 1 in 2003 to 431 to 1 in 2004. If the minimum wage had risen as fast as CEO pay since 1990, the lowest paid workers in the US would be earning $23.03 an hour today, not $5.15 an hour (as quoted in Smith, 2006, p. 306).

In 2005, the federal minimum wage, unchanged for eight years, fell to its lowest level in fifty-six years. As Economic Policy Institute economist Jared Bernstein observed in 2005:

> With hourly wages falling in real terms, the only way working families can raise their incomes is by working more hours — certainly not the path to improving living standards that we would expect in an economy posting strong productivity gains (as quoted in Smith, 2006, p. 302).

The phenomenon of the 'overworked American' was starkly documented by Schor (1991). By 1997 full-time employees in the US were working a full workday each week more than in 1969 (Henwood, 1998, p. 22). At the same time, many US workers were denied full-time employment and job security. Of the hundreds of thousands of workers who lost their jobs due to corporate downsizing between 1990 and 1992, nearly a third of these were still unemployed two years later. Of the seventy-one percent who found new jobs, thirty-one percent had to take a wage cut of twenty-five percent or more, thirty-one percent a wage cut of up to twenty-five percent, and only thirty-five percent of this seventy-one percent found new jobs at comparable wages. By 1997, almost thirty percent of all US workers had jobs that were not regular full-time jobs. Downsized or laid-off workers earned an average of thirteen percent less in their next job (Smith, 2006, pp. 285–286). A decade later the situation had deteriorated further. In Ohio two million of its eleven million people in 2002 were forced to turn to charity for food after the state lost one in six of its manufacturing jobs (Borger, 2003). And these were good days for US workers compared with the recession and the rising unemployment that occurred after the global financial crisis that struck in 2008.

WHY GLOBALISATION HAS ADVERSELY AFFECTED WORKERS

Academic studies relate the worsened circumstances of the world's workers to processes associated with globalisation. There is debate about which aspects of globalisation have proven most problematic but the ones most commonly identified are enhanced capital mobility, the transition to post-Fordist production methods in most developed countries, increasing fragmentation of the workforce along lines of race, ethnicity and gender, and marketisation as policed by transnational institutions such as the World Trade Organisation.

Capital Mobility

Enhanced capital mobility (moving or threatening to move production) has caused de-industrialisation in developed countries which has weakened workers' power and rights in myriad ways. For example, traditionally strong union enclaves in manufacturing have notably dwindled. Capital flight, or the threat of it, has also enabled corporations to intimidate workforces with the prospect of relocation should wage demands be pressed. At the same time, capital mobility has coerced nation states to enact policies that directly favour corporations against the interests of employees. To attract and retain mobile international capital, states have not only reduced the 'social wage' (public health and other free public services, welfare and social security systems) to provide low taxation regimes but have also deregulated labour markets and passed anti-union industrial relations legislation (Hyman, 1999, p. 107; Wood, 1998, p. 12). Martin and Schumann (1996, p. 7) describe some of the tactics in the arsenal of " ... new ... capital" as follows: it threatens to pull out altogether according to the circumstances of the hour, thus forcing massive tax reductions as well as massive government subsidies or the provision of cost-free infrastructure as an incentive to remain or to set up onshore; if that does not work, then it discloses its profits only in countries where the rate of taxation is relatively low. Indeed, "... [a]ll around the world, the owners of capital and wealth are contributing less and less to the financing of public expenditure... At the same time, unemployment is growing in parallel with national budget deficits".

In 2004, an audit conducted by the General Accounting Office found that sixty-one percent of American corporations paid no income tax between 1996 and 2000. At the same time, the National Labor Relations Board statistics in the US revealed that in 2004, half the companies facing union drives threatened to close their plants, and that companies illegally disciplined or fired twenty thousand workers that year for union activity (Smith, 2006, pp. 287, 303). A *New York Times* columnist named Herbert remarked on 12 May 2005:

> Workers have been so cowed by an environment in which they are so obviously dispensable that they have been afraid to ask for the raises they deserve, or for their share of the money derived from the remarkable increases in worker productivity over the past few years. And from one coast to the other, workers have swallowed draconian cuts in benefits ... (as quoted in Smith, 2006, p. 303).

In the case of workforces, it matters not whether company threats to relocate are idle. A climate of labour-force vulnerability encourages the self-policing of wage demands. According to Leisink (1999, p. 16): "Wage restraint policies by trade unions are not so much the effect of direct open threats by employers ... but rather emerge as a result and as a part of broader changes in the cultural and political environment ...". As Panitch (2001, p. 376) puts it: "the very purpose of globalisation, from the perspective of business and the capitalist state, has been to bring about competition among workers ... at a higher level".

The literature is clear that actual or threatened capital flight has been a crucial weapon for capital in its globalisation project, used to good corporate effect against both governments and workforces. Silver (2003, p. 4) notes that the most common explanation of the crisis of labour internationally is that the hyper-mobility of capital in the late twentieth century created a single labour market in which all the world's workers were forced to compete. By moving or just threatening to move production, multinational corporations brought the competitive pressure of unorganised workers to bear on the international labour movement, weakening labour's bargaining power and unleashing a 'race to the bottom' in wages and working conditions. At the same time, the indirect impact of the hyper-mobility of capital pressured states to repeal social welfare provisions and other fetters on profit maximisation within their borders in order to avoid being abandoned by investors scouring the world for the highest possible returns.

Footloose corporations are starting to be circumvented by new forms of labour organisation, however, that encourage transnational working-class cooperation. The labour movement is rapidly globalising its capacities, for example, precisely because of the challenge of globalisation. As Starr observes:

> As assembly lines have stretched across the globe and production processes [have become] sufficiently flexible to make it easy to exchange one workforce for another nearly anywhere, unions have recognised the need to build global organising capacity ... Labour's new awareness has overcome the divide that formerly positioned [F]irst [W]orld workers' standard of living as dependent on [T]hird [W]orld workers' cheap labour ... It has enabled workers to challenge the logic of 'international competitiveness', recognising that such a logic will drive all wages down ... Unions are widely recognising the need to bring the standards of all workers up in order to make all workers safe (2000, pp. 88–89).

Carty's study of transnational labour mobilisation in two Mexican *maquiladoras* reveals that, while the NAFTA strengthens the ability of those in power to impose their will on more marginalised groups, it has also enhanced the connection between workers in the North and South as they have come to recognise that they share a common enemy in their respective struggles.

> Jobs have been exported from the North to the South on an unprecedented scale. This means jobs for workers in Mexico, but under exploitative conditions. This has negative consequences for workers in both countries. To combat these forms of abuse workers are collectively focusing their anger on what they understand to be the collusion between the elite representatives of MNCs and their governments that work on behalf of business interests rather than on those of their citizens … This convergence is occurring because globalisation is creating common interests … that transcend both national and interest-group boundaries (Carty, 2004, p. 304).

Bacon's twenty-year experience as a union organiser on the US/Mexican border persuaded him that progressivist developments among workers in both countries owed their origins to NAFTA. "After all, but for the treaty, interest among US workers in their co-workers south of the border would have remained low, as it had been for decades" (Bacon, 2004, p. 16).

Smith (2006, p. 320) predicts that the living standards of the US working class will either continue to fall drastically to approximate those of the poorest workers of the world, or US workers will unite in solidarity to fight to raise the living standards of the world's poorest workers, thereby salvaging their own. International collaboration is manifestly in the interests of workers in the developed world, but workers in developing countries also have an interest in improved pay and conditions, despite corporate rhetoric that suggests they do not.

In direct response to enhanced capital mobility, then, there is increased labour transnationalism, which involves unions utilising transnational networks and organising global resistance campaigns by acting across borders (Moody, 1997, pp. 249–275; Starr, 2000, pp. 88–89; Waterman and Wills, 2001; Hurd *et al.*, 2003, p. 114; Baccaro *et al.*, 2003, p. 129; Bandy and Mendez, 2003, p. 180; Carty, 2004, p. 306; Burgmann, 2008, pp. 241–243). As Baccaro *et al.* (2003, p. 120) note: "In an age of expanded capital mobility, external support becomes essential for union survival, and unions have increasingly acted accordingly". This new internationalism is a response quite distinct from the posturing on the part of Western states about developing countries' labour standards, which were rightly seen by developing countries as protectionism expressive of varying degrees of chauvinism (Leisink, 1999, p. 23; Panitch, 2001, p. 379).

On a more formal organisational plane, in 2000 the industry-specific trade secretariats within the International Confederation of Free Trade Unions (ICFTU) adopted the name Global Union Federations. It also began to utilise computer and internet technology to facilitate international working-class cooperation.[2] Myconas (2005, p. 135) acknowledges that there is a longstanding tradition of international

[2]http://www.icftu.org/

labour collaboration, but the new century has brought with it "a far more integrated network of transnational network of transnational labour organisations", which has grown "more coherent and unified as still more interests converge". He also argues that "it is clear that organised labour's particular form of globalisation will continue apace" (Myconas, 2005, p. 157).

Post-Fordism

In the globalising period since the 1970s, there has been an identifiable change in the organisation of production and labour processes. This is known as the transition to 'post-Fordism'. Its characteristic methods involve flexible globalised networks of production, disaggregated smaller workplaces, increasing automation, and sped-up, just-in-time production. It has been accompanied by heightened employer antipathy towards unions (encouraged by neoliberal management cultures), a decline in manufacturing, and a rise in service sector industries, with fewer blue-collar and more white-collar workers and an increase in the casualisation of the workforce. Post-Fordism is strongly implicated in the decline of the density of unions and their influence in most developed countries, because its features undermine traditional forms of workplace organisation and make it more difficult for unions to attract and retain members (Freeman, 2004, p. 5; Silver, 2003, p. 5; Kaufman, 2004, pp. 84–85).

It is argued that fundamental changes in the international political economy from the 1970s on prompted firms to change from the 'Fordist' forms of mass production characteristic of the middle decades of the twentieth century to 'post-Fordist' or 'flexible specialisation' forms of production common today. This transition is both part of globalisation and one of its effects. The forces of globalisation have made the old system of mass producing identical, cheap goods uncompetitive. Corporations in an era of globalisation have found it more profitable to produce diverse product lines targeted at different groups of consumers. Instead of investing in the mass production of a single product, that is, corporations have created more flexible systems of labour and equipment that can respond to the whims of the market.

In the international automobile industry, for example, Japanese manufacturers, especially Toyota, led the way from the early 1980s in establishing 'lean production' as the standard manufacturing mode. Rinehart *et al.* (1997) describe how, in this industry, mass production was diagnosed as terminally ill. It was unmourned in both media and business circles:

> The emergent system, which carried few, if any, traces of Fordism, offered … optimum efficiency ... It featured simultaneous precision and flexibility, the

capacity to reduce costs, tight inventories, quick die changes, and low per-unit assembly hours. It was also characterised by multiskilled workers (Rinehart *et al.*, 1997, p. 1).

Material for one US plant might arrive from all over the globe — engines and transmissions from Japan, mirrors from Australia, seats, bumpers and J grills from Canada and the US. All the vendors operate on a just-in-time (JIT) basis. The plant uses automated processes for delivering components to the assembly line (Rinehart *et al.*, 1997, p. 16).

More and more workers are spending a good part of their lives in lean workplaces. Before 1981 there were no Asian automobile 'transplants' in the US. Between 1982 and 1990, seven began in the US and four in Canada. US auto manufacturers, including the Big Three, then implemented — or strived to emulate — the manufacturing methods developed in Japan. "If there is one non-debatable proposition in the early literature, it surely must be the claim that lean production will be the standard manufacturing mode of the twenty-first century"(Rinehart *et al.*, 1997, p. 2).

Some scholars argue that the post-Fordist aspect of globalisation has had an even more dramatic adverse effect on labour organisations than the impact of capital mobility. For example, Jenkins and Leicht (1997, pp. 378–379) argue that the replacement of the traditional Fordist system of standardised mass production that provided fertile ground for the development of a post-Fordist one has undermined the traditional bases of workers' bargaining power. Global competitive pressures have obliged employers across the globe to follow suit in implementing the new 'flexible production' systems. Once-stable working classes have been replaced in the process by "networks of temporary and cursory relationships with subcontractors and temporary help agencies". The result is a structurally disaggregated and disorganised working class, prone more to a politics of resentment than traditional working class unions and leftist politics (Silver, 2003, p. 5).

The post-Fordist transformation is not without its benefits for industrial militancy, however. A small-scale strike at a factory in Thailand that produces the thread for Porsche seatbelts, for example, will result in a worldwide disruption to Porsche production. As Silver (2003, p. 6) stresses, there are dangers for multinational corporations in some of the changes in the organisation of production. In some situations, just-in-time production actually *increases* the vulnerability of corporations to disruptions in the flow of production since it enhances workers' bargaining power, that is, the effectiveness of any direct action at the point of production. This is true not only of industries using just-in-time methods but also for workers in the transport and communications industries, whose reliability this production method is dependent upon (see Chapter 11 on containerisation). The more globalised the networks of production, the wider the potential geographical ramifications of disruption by workers.

Workforce Fragmentation

The workforce has become increasingly fragmented along lines of race, ethnicity, gender and hours worked. Workforces have long been heterogeneous but this tendency has been increased by the effects of globalisation, which has drawn into waged labour people previously engaged in other forms of production, such as subsistence farming. It has encouraged migration both within and between nations. Although commodification sometimes works in the direction of reducing prejudice, as Marx and Engels predicted in the *Communist Manifesto*, globalising capitalism has actually depended heavily on discrimination to establish divisions of labour and hierarchies of control (Hyman, 1999, pp. 105–107).

In 1995 the World Bank conceded, on the basis of extensive empirical evidence, that inequalities between men and women and between ethnic and racial groups were proving particularly difficult to resolve through market forces alone (World Bank, 1995, pp. 43–47; Leisink, 1999, p. 11). Precisely so. The logic of market relations, as Hyman (1999, p. 105) observes, is that competition reinforces disparities of power within as well as between classes. Heightened competition increases such disparities, even though at the same time some people from marginalised groups become upwardly mobile. Within the US, for example, notwithstanding the phenomenon of African American elites, African Americans in married-couple working families worked almost five hundred more hours per year than equivalent white families in 1996. This indicates one consequence of wage disparities between blacks and whites due to racism (Smith, 2006, p. 285). Similarly, though a small proportion of women enjoy highly paid employment, women are disproportionately employed in the lowest-paid jobs because they are handicapped by the extent of their unpaid work and by sexist assumptions about their abilities and rights to paid employment. Employers have capitalised upon women's weakened position in the labour market, especially in developing countries, to pay most women less than men who perform equivalent work. Historically this has always been the case, however, globalisation has brought dramatically higher proportions of women into paid employment, where they are now as systematically undervalued as they have been in unpaid employment. Jeffreys provides a cogent critique of international political economy from a feminist perspective in the following chapter.

The staunch commitment of neoliberals to the free market falters in relation to labour and international migration. One of the glaring hypocrisies of our time is that while capital, as was seen in the previous section, enjoys unprecedented freedom to cross national boundaries, people continue to face severe restrictions on their mobility. Corporations globetrot at the whim of profitability, while workers migrating in response to market forces are frequently obstructed and vilified. Worse still is the situation of people who leave their homeland in fear of their lives.

The obvious incentives to migrate share as their primary cause the increasing division in the world between rich and poor. This has been a hallmark of neoliberal globalisation. The problems prompting the migration of people — poverty, war, persecution and environmental degradation — are all exacerbated by unfair free trade regimes and neoliberal policies imposed on developing countries to force the repayment of debts owed to the developed nations. The rights of capital, yet again, are given precedence over the urgent needs of humanity. The contrasting constraints on the rights of people to live and work where they wish are not merely the physical ones of detention camps and the legalistic ones of quotas and court rulings. Increasingly, these constraints are also ideological ones in the form of racial and ethnic prejudice in host societies. Prejudice does not prevent migration but it greatly weakens the ability of migrants to participate in labour markets without suffering various forms of discrimination, such as non-recognition of foreign qualifications, racial stereotyping, or being denied legal status. Each makes resistance to harsh working conditions problematic.

The S11 movement, which organised the protests against the World Economic Forum (WEF) meeting in Melbourne, 11–13 September 2000, argued that capitalism, with all its pretences to universalism and globalism, continually plays people off against each other on the basis of 'the nation'. For instance, people are forever being urged to punish themselves by accepting lower incomes and living and working conditions for the sake of the 'national economy':

> In short, the kind of globalisation the WEF participants want is one on their terms. Their globalisation is one where people are confined but capital can move freely. Their globalisation is one where boundaries and divisions are used against us to keep us segmented, repressed and fighting among ourselves (S11, "Think Globally, Act Locally" leaflet, Melbourne, September 2000).

Labour movements have become more aware of the need to integrate the most vulnerable sections of workforces (Gindin, 1995, p. 268; Moody, 1997, p. 290; Bandy and Mendez, 2003, p. 174). As with the effects of capital flight, increased levels of working-class fragmentation under the impact of globalisation has produced a global working class potentially inclined and better suited to transnational solidarity. As Moody argues:

> If capitalism is now more global than ever, so too is the working class it begets. Even within most nations, the worldwide class that is still forming also crosses borders with greater regularity, is more ethnically diverse, and international in nature ... The material substance of working-class internationalism is at hand (Moody, 1997, p. 309).

At the Sixteenth World Congress of the ICFTU in Brussels in 1996, the ICFTU General Secretary reported on "[a] world of widening divisions" and stressed the importance of "[b]uilding solidarity, attacking poverty ... and strengthening the voice of working men and women through international trade union solidarity". Affiliates at the Seventeenth World Congress in Durban in 2000 revealed their commitment to a global social justice agenda in a raft of statements and resolutions on the social clause, relations with NGOs, equality for women, Third World debt, and poverty (Myconas, 2005, p. 136). Myconas argues that there has been a discernible shift in priorities across the entire ensemble of labour organisations:

> It shows a trend away from the instrumental, parochial, and functional; and to a set of interests that reflect concern for human rights, equity, and justice. We have seen through the 1990s a renewed and concerted focus on the amelioration of the most pernicious aspects of the prevailing neoliberal order. These bread-and-butter issues relate to child labour, discrimination, safety and environment, the power of multinational corporations, and labour rights. Linked to all this is the redoubling of efforts to have social clauses — in their various guises — inserted into trade agreements, and into various compacts with governments (Myconas, 2005, p. 137).

Though this tendency is still inclined towards the ameliorative and reformist, "it nevertheless represents a more contrary and oppositional ideological disposition than has been the case in recent decades" (Myconas, 2005, p. 138).

Marketisation

A hallmark of globalisation is a neoliberal policy emphasis on marketisation: privatisation, decreased public-sector spending, deregulation, and downsizing to reduce labour costs in both private and public sectors. This results in turn in deteriorating employment conditions. In a related process, the growth of the private sector at the expense of the public sector, brought about by privatisation and decreased public-sector spending, weakens unions and therefore workers' capacity to resist worsening wages and conditions, since unions have historically been stronger in the public than the private sectors. Policing them falls to transnational marketisation agencies such as the World Trade Organisation, the World Bank, the International Monetary Fund, and the World Economic Forum. The rise to prominence of the latter is an undeniably important aspect of globalisation. According to Starr (2000, p. 17), their role in promoting free market policies has undermined labour standards worldwide.

Marketisation is the essence of the Structural Adjustment Programmes (SAPs) imposed upon poorer countries. From the late 1970s, developing countries were often obliged to pursue SAPs in exchange for debt relief and loans from the World Bank and the International Monetary Fund. In return for financial assistance, governments were required to adopt neoliberal policies, which adversely affected the majority of the people in these countries. The liberalisation of trade reduced or abolished the tariffs that protected developing industries, causing lack of development and rising unemployment. The abolition of government price controls on, or subsidies for, food resulted in higher food prices and increased poverty. The cuts in public expenditure reduced spending on health, education, welfare, public sector wages and salaries. The privatisation of publicly owned utilities led to retrenchments, price rises and poorer services. The rolling back of labour market regulations to protect workers undermined wage rates and made workplaces less safe and working conditions worse. The redirection of agricultural land to develop crops for export increased rural poverty as subsistence crops were replaced by coffee plantations or mangoes, or caused deforestation as producers tried to find more opportunities to produce export crops. And the deregulation of the financial sector of the economy made it more difficult for poorer people to obtain credit and other financial services at reasonable interest rates.

Labour movements were often at the forefront of the huge protests against the SAPs that occurred in developing countries from the late 1970s on (Bacon, 2000, pp. 84–102; Uba, 2005, p. 385; Moghadam, 2009, pp. 95–96). SAPs dismantled many of the accomplishments of post-colonial regimes, reversing the nationalisation of industries, cutting anti-poverty programmes, downgrading civil services, and revoking land reforms (Starr, 2005, p. 20). Moghadam (2009, p. 95) notes that a cycle of protests "called food riots or anti-IMF riots" enveloped the Third World from the latter part of the 1970s, when the first SAPs were introduced, and continued to do so into the 1990s.

In 2001 the World Development Movement pointed out that industrial and direct action protests around the world, involving millions of people, had opposed the policies promoted by the International Monetary Fund, the World Bank and the World Trade Organisation. The protests had ranged from strikes to riots and had occurred in countries such as Brazil, Nigeria, Pakistan, South Africa, South Korea and Turkey (Mayo, 2005, p. 2). The 2002 report issued by the World Development Movement, called *States of Unrest*, observed: "the fiercest critics of IMF and World Bank policies were the people most affected by them" (as cited in Starr, 2005, p. 20).

As Bello *et al.* (1994) point out, however, the First World was also undergoing a "structural adjustment" in terms of the interests of its corporations and that this was equivalent to the processes experienced in the Third World, that is, it involved cutting social expenditure, privatisation, the rolling back of regulations and their enforcement, and the undermining of wage rates and other labour gains. Other scholars, such as Silver (2003, p. 4), Leisink (1999, p. 16) and Panitch (2001, p. 376) highlighted the veracity of this insight.

Castells (1997, p. 354) identifies marketisation as a problem for labour movements rather than an opportunity as well. Thus he argues:

The privatisation of public agencies and the demise of the welfare state, while alleviating societies from some bureaucratic burden, worsen living conditions for the majority of citizens, break the historic social contract between capital, labour, and the state, and remove much of the social safety net, the nuts and bolts of legitimate government for common people.

> The privatisation of public agencies has been hotly contested by workers around the world, especially in developing countries. Bacon (2000, p. 84) has examined two decades of worldwide workers' struggles against privatisation and other aspects of marketisation, especially in India, Mexico, Russia and China. For example, thousands of workers at India's state power company went on strike in 2000 to prevent privatisation of electricity generation and distribution in Uttar Pradesh. They were supported in ports along the subcontinent's coast by longshore workers who also stopped work. Uba (2005, p. 385) agrees that, in the Indian anti-privatisation mobilisations between 1990 and 2003, trade unions played a leading role and that two thirds of the actions were strikes involving an average of two million workers. The strikes were backed up by demonstrations of similar proportions.

The most famous example of resistance to privatisation was the 'water wars' of Cochabamba, a city of 600,000 in the Andes in Bolivia. In 1997 World Bank officials told Bolivia's president that six hundred million dollars in international debt relief was dependent on Cochabamba putting its public water system into privatised corporate hands. In September 1999, in a closed-door process with just one bidder, Bolivian officials leased off Cochabamba's water until 2039 to a subsidiary of the California engineering giant, Bechtel. After rate increases of up to two hundred percent, the Coalition for the Defence of Water and Life, *La Coordinadora*, was formed to challenge the privatisation. In January 2000 it organised a city-wide general strike which shut down Cochabamba for three days. With continuing protests and strikes, in April 2000 *Coordinadora* leaders called for a cancellation of the privatisation contract altogether and announced the Final Battle, an April general strike and highway blockade, that would not be lifted until Bechtel was gone and a new law enacted to guarantee water rights. As a result Bechtel's officials fled Bolivia, the water contract was cancelled, and a new, publicly controlled water company was installed. The Bolivian water revolt has since become an international symbol of popular resistance to neoliberal globalisation (Schultz, 2003, pp. 34–47).

CONCLUSION

As the global financial crisis unfolded, most dramatically from late 2008, public attention became focused on the neoliberal policies associated with globalisation. These policies had encouraged government withdrawal from the regulation of financial services, an upward push on corporate remuneration packages, downward pressures on employees' wages and conditions, and dangerously high levels of mortgage and credit card indebtedness.

The global politico-economic pendulum swung temporarily in the direction of confronting corporate excesses and protecting workers' employment security and living standards. Neoliberalism appeared discredited, with governments around the world pursuing Keynesian strategies, such as stimulus packages to build public infrastructure and restore consumer demand by payments to low-income people with a high marginal propensity to spend.

As soon as the 'green shoots of recovery' appeared, however, and fear of complete financial collapse had receded (thanks largely to the Keynesian 'trickle-up' strategies), governments demonstrated a clear intention to return to neoliberal policies. This was evident in their promises — or threats — to restore national budgets to surplus by huge cutbacks in public spending. This was evident most spectacularly in Greece, though, most governments had — to varying degrees — had to usher in regimes of 'austerity', or indicate that they would do so as soon as recovery was ensured.

Employees around the world, from traditional blue-collar production line workers to the skilled white-collar ones in post-industrial economies, frequently opposed the neoliberal ideologies and policies associated with globalisation in general and the new austerity regimes in particular. Indeed, interesting comparisons can be made between the riots organised by labour movements in developing countries against the SAPs of the 1980s and 1990s and the more recent anti-austerity protests in Greece, France, Britain and other more developed economies. It seems that this is a story that is likely to continue.

REFERENCES

Baccaro, L, K Hamann and L Turner (2003). The Politics of Labour Movement Revitalisation. *European Journal of Industrial Relations*, 9(1), 119–133.

Bacon, D (2000). World Labor Needs Independence and Solidarity. *Monthly Review*, 52(3), 84–102.

Bacon, D (2004). *The Children of NAFTA. Labor Wars on the U. S./Mexico Border*. Berkeley/Los Angeles/London: University of California Press.

Bandy, J and J Bickham Mendez (2003). A Place of Their Own? Women Organisers in the Maquilas of Nicaragua and Mexico. *Mobilisation*, 8(2), 173–188.

Bello, W, S Cunningham and B Rau (1994). *Dark Victory: The United States, Structural Adjustment, and Global Poverty*. London: Pluto Press.

Borger, J (2003). Special Report: Long Queue at Drive-in Soup Kitchen: George Bush's America, Wealthiest Nation in History, Faces a Growing Poverty Crisis. *The Guardian*, 3 November, p. 1–3.

Burgmann, V (2008). Striking Back Against Empire: Working-Class Responses to Globalisation. In *The Postcolonial and the Global*, J Hawley and R Krishnaswamy (eds.). Minneapolis: University of Minnesota Press.

Carty, V (2004). Transnational Labor Mobilising in Two Mexican Maquiladoras. *Mobilisation*, 9(3), 295–310.

Castells, M (1997). *The Power of Identity*. Oxford: Blackwell.

Elliott, L (2000). Gore and Bush in a Class of their Own. *Manchester Guardian Weekly*, 23 August.

Freeman, R (2004). The Road to Union Renaissance in the United States. In *The Changing Role of Unions. New Forms of Representation. Issues in Work and Human Resources*, P Wunnava (ed.). Armonk and London: M.E.Sharpe.

Gindin, S (1995). *The Canadian Auto Workers: The Birth and Transformation of a Union*. Toronto: J. Lorimer.

Henwood, D (1998). Talking About Work. In *Rising From the Ashes? Labor in the Age of "Global" Capitalism*, E Wood, P Meiksins and M Yates (eds.). New York: Monthly Review Press.

Herbert, B (2005). The Young and the Jobless. *The New York Times*, 12 May, A.27.

Hurd, R, R Milkman and L Turner (2003). Reviving the American Labour Movement. *European Journal of Industrial Relations*, 9(1), 99–118.

Hyman, R (1999). Imagined Solidarities: Can Trade Unions Resist Globalisation? In *Globalisation and Labour Relations*, P Leisink (ed.). Cheltenham UK: Edward Elgar.

Jenkins, C and K Leicht (1997). Class Analysis and Social Movements: A Critique and Reformulation. In *Reworking Class*, J Hall (ed.). Ithaca: Cornell University Press.

Kaufman, B (2004). The Two Faces of Unionism. Implications for Union Growth. In *The Changing Role of Unions. New Forms of Representation. Issues in Work and Human Resources*, P Wunnava (ed.). Armonk, New York and London, England: M.E.Sharpe.

Leisink, P (1999). Introduction. In *Globalisation and Labour Relations*, P Leisink (ed.). Northampton, Mass.: Edward Elgar.

Martin, H-P and H Schumann (1996). *The Global Trap: Globalisation and the Assault on Prosperity and Democracy.* London and New York: Pluto Press Australia/Zed Books.

Mayo, M (2005). *Global Citizens. Social Movements & The Challenge of Globalisation.* London & New York: Zed Books.

Moghadam, V (2009). *Globalisation and Social Movements. Islamism, Feminism, and the Global Justice Movement.* Plymouth UK: Rowman & Littlefield.

Moody, K (1998). American Labor: A Movement Again? In *Rising From the Ashes? Labor in the Age of "Global" Capitalism*, E Wood, P Meiksins and M Yates (eds.). New York: Monthly Review Press.

Moody, K (1997). *Workers in a Lean World: Unions in the International Economy.* London: Verso.

Myconas, G (2005). *The Globalisation(s) of Organised Labour: 1945–2005.* Basingstoke and New York: Palgrave Macmillan.

Panitch, L (2001). Reflections on Strategy for Labour. In *Socialist Register* 2001, L Panitch and C Leys (eds.). London: Merlin Press.

Pronk, J (2000). Globalisation: A Developmental Approach. In *Global Futures: Shaping Globalisation*, J Pieterse (ed.). London and New York: Zed Books.

Rinehart, J, C Huxley and D Robertson (1997). *Just Another Car Factory? Lean Production and its Discontents.* Ithaca and London: ILR Press.

Schor, J (1991). *The Overworked American.* New York: Basic Books.

Schultz, J (2003). Bolivia: the Water War Widens. *NACLA. Report on the Americas*, XXXVI (4), 34–47.

Silver, B (2003). *Forces of Labor: Workers' Movements and Globalisation since 1870.* Cambridge: Cambridge University Press.

Smith, S (2006). *Subterranean Fire. A History of Working-Class Radicalism in the United States.* Chicago: Haymarket Books.

Starr, A (2000). *Naming the Enemy: Anti-Corporate Movements Confront Globalisation.* London and New York: Zed Books.

Starr, A (2005). *Global Revolt. A Guide to the Movements against Globalisation*, London and New York: Zed Books.

Uba, K (2005). Political Protest and Policy Change. *Mobilisation*, (10)3, 383–396.

Waterman, P and J Wills (2001). *Place, Space and the New Labour Internationalisms.* Oxford: Blackwell.

Wood, E (1998). Labor, Class, and State in Global Capitalism. In *Rising From the Ashes? Labor in the Age of "Global" Capitalism*, E Wood, P Meiksins and M Yates (eds.). New York: Monthly Review Press.

World Bank (1995). *World Development Report 1995. Workers in an Integrating World.* New York: Oxford University Press.

Zweig, M (2000). *The Working Class Majority. America's Best Secret.* Ithaca and London: Cornell University Press.

Part Five

Globalisation and the Male/Female Divide

CHAPTER 18

Globalisation and the Male/Female Divide: An Overview

Sheila Jeffreys

University of Melbourne

WHO MADE ADAM SMITH'S DINNER? FEMINIST CRITIQUES AND THE INTERNATIONAL POLITICAL ECONOMY

Feminist political economists throw the basis of mainstream — the idea of 'rational economic man' — into doubt. Mainstream (liberalist) economics is based upon two main patriarchal assumptions. It is based upon the way in which men in Western societies, and in their institutions and systems of government, make their livings and create wealth. Sweetman, editor of the Oxfam journal, *Gender and Development*, puts it this way: "Homo Economicus is nominally asexual, but inhabits a very male world of paid work and priced leisure" (Sweetman, 2008). Women, it seems, do not fit in. As feminist critics have long pointed out, women's work is mostly unpaid and unrecognised "counts for nothing" in male-stream systems of accounting (Waring, 1988). Mainstream (liberalist) economics is also based on an assumption that men are 'rational' and seek to maximise self-interest, an idea severely challenged by the sort of behaviour in the finance industry which led to the global financial crisis of 2008. This chapter will present feminist criticisms of the mainstream (liberalist) concept of 'rational economic man'.

As one feminist international relations analyst (Jan Pettman) argues: "Many aspects of the IPE do not make any sense if we do not gender the account" (Pettman, 1996, p. 160). Despite three decades of feminist critique of the international political economy (Mies, 1998 [1986]; Enloe, 1989), however, even left-wing critics show no awareness that their discipline could or should be gendered. Thus the collection, *American Empire and the Political Economy of Global Finance*, republished in 2009 with an added chapter on the global financial crisis, contains one woman amongst its ten contributors and does not have 'woman/women', 'gender', or 'feminism' in its index (Panitsch and Konings, 2009). The book takes account of economic class but not sex class. In contrast to such texts this chapter will focus on sex class, and will look at the ways in which men, masculinity and male domination have constructed global capitalism and particularly finance capitalism. The global financial crisis needs to be gendered, and this chapter will offer a starting point for this task.

ECONOMIC ACCOUNTING AND WOMEN'S WORK

The main problem with mainstream male-stream interpretations of the international political economy, according to feminist analysts, is the way in which economic accounting takes place. GDP, for instance, counts only that which is in the paid economy. It does not take into account subsistence, unpaid work, or exploitation of nature as a "free" good (Bennholdt-Thomson and Mies, 1999). Bennholdt-Thomson and Mies, for instance, point out in their chapter "Iceberg Model of Capitalist Patriarchal Economics", that only a very small part of the world's work is in the "visible" economy. It is just the tip of the iceberg. The vast majority of the iceberg which is under the surface of the water contains all of the rest of the politico-economic activity taking place in the world, including that performed by housewives, home-workers, the informal sector, child labour, subsistence peasants, the exploitation of colonies (external and internal), the South, Eastern Europe, and Nature, all of which are regarded as free goods to be mined, fished and destroyed (Bennholdt-Thomson and Mies, 1999, p. 31).

The vast majority of women's work is not in the visible economy, including as it does, unpaid work in the home, domestic labour, unpaid work in the marketplace, labour in bearing and rearing children, and unpaid sexual and emotional labour. This unpaid work constitutes the unrecognised female foundation for all that which is actually counted in mainstream/male-stream economics. The very idea of 'work', as something that takes place outside the home for a set number of hours per day, is constructed from the activities of men, whose lunchboxes are packed by their wives (Pateman, 1988). Wives are a vital necessity for the male worker. Wives buy and cook food, buy sheets and place clean ones on the bed, organise clean clothes for male family members. They do much more than these tangible activities, however, since they also provide emotional sustenance or "emotional labour" (Hochschild, 1983) and contribute in the process to the wages that their husbands gain in performing market labour.

The issue of how women's unpaid domestic labour should be understood in marxist and feminist theory has been an important topic for discussion since the early 1970s. Mies says that it is the issue of women's unpaid labour that animates the debate about how capitalism and patriarchy are entwined to create "capitalist patriarchy" (Mies, 1998 [1986]). It became clear in the 1980s, she says, that "women's unpaid caring and nurturing work in the household was subsidising not only the male wage but also capital accumulation" (Mies, 1998 [1986], p. ix). The importance of this work was obscured by constructing the woman as "mother, wife and housewife", which was the "trick by which fifty percent of human labour was defined as a free good" (Mies, 1998 [1986], p. ix). Delphy and Leonard offer a useful summary of the debates and a sharp analysis of the place of domestic labour in what they call "materialist" feminist theory (Delphy and Leonard, 1992) by highlighting what they see as the main flaw in the "domestic labour" debates. These debates, they see, tend to see women's unpaid work as being performed for 'capitalism' rather than for individual men. They rework the idea of exploitation (usually understood as the appropriation of the fruits of labour by others) to explain that women are exploited "not because the factory or field in which ... [they] work belongs to someone else, but more simply because ... [their] labour belongs to someone else — because ... [they] do not own ... [their] own ability to work (... [their] own labour power)". It is the male heads of the families concerned who own women's labour, though as they explain: "... [o]wning the means of production is unnecessary if you own slaves or serfs or wives or children" (Delphy and Leonard, 1992, p. 43).

Feminist theorising of the international political economy can become extraordinarily euphemistic in order to avoid mentioning male domination and women's oppression. A 2010 article, in an issue of the key feminist journal *Signs* devoted to analysis of the IPE, uses the term "difference" rather than refer to men or women at all. Bair's account investigates the "relationship between difference and capital" (Bair, 2010, p. 224). Use of this euphemism effectively obscures the existence of male domination and the ways in which men, or any powerful groups, profit from the labour of the less powerful. Oppression, exploitation, and subordination — good, strong political terms that describe inequality — are eliminated by "difference", even though "difference" cannot explain why women perform a wide variety of tasks directly for the betterment and benefit of the men they live with.

Delphy and Leonard are critical of domestic labour theorists for concentrating on a narrow understanding of domestic labour — such matters as cleaning, cooking, and childcare — and failing to acknowledge the wide variety of unpaid work that wives perform, such as that done for "their husbands' occupations, for men's leisure activities, and for their emotional and sexual well-being" (Delphy and Leonard, 1992, p. 226). This latter form of work, they say, "gets completely lost sight of because it is so varied, so personalised and so intimate" (Delphy and Leonard, 1992, p. 226). They explain that husbands use their wives' labour for their own economic gain. Wives take bookings for husbands who are plumbers, for instance, work in the shop and on the family farm, and they "calculate, type and send out estimates and bills to clients" (Delphy and Leonard, 1992, p. 226). When men are employed, wives are often part of the deal for employers, in jobs such as the diplomatic services, the rural police force, and running a pub. In pubs, wives have the position of 'institutionalised consort' by being a hostess or cooking meals or 'looking decorative' behind a counter. Wives also help with husbands' voluntary and leisure activities. They have to clean leisure clothing and equipment, and run fundraising for Boy Scout troops. They may help husbands run for political office and provide 'hospitality' in this regard too. Wives often take over when husbands are absent, in a crisis, or when busy. The wives of academics may type up research reports and do other research and administrative tasks. Clergymen's wives have to support constituents and make appointments. Farmers' wives may have to run the farm when their husband is away. Moreover, as Delphy and Leonard say: "Most of these activities can be done even if the wife herself has paid employment" (Delphy and Leonard, p. 231). The aspect of the unpaid work of wives which directly services the man's income generating activities has gained a little more recognition from scholars since the early 1990s, when the Delphy and Leonard book was written. Lisa Philipps calls it "unpaid market labour" (Philipps, 2008), which she defines as "the involvement of family members in bread-winning activities that are the official responsibility of only one person in the household" (Philipps, 2008, p. 37). Philipps chides feminist analysis in international political economy for thinking that industrial capitalism splits "waged work in the market from unwaged work in the household" (Philipps, 2008, p. 51). She argues that unpaid and paid market labour are interdependent.

Another less well recognised aspect of the work of wives is the provision of 'moral' support to husbands and of caring for their wellbeing. Wives have the role of informal therapists, to whom husbands can 'unburden' themselves. They have an important role to play as the providers of "trouble-free sex — which is why employers may encourage men to take their wives with them on jobs abroad" (Delphy and Leonard, 1992, p. 232). Wives also "make a house a home" (Delphy and Leonard, 1992, p. 233). They smile and keep cheerful; "flatter, excuse, boost, sympathise, and pay attention to men". This in turn gives men a sense of "belonging, of empowerment, and of general well-being" (Delphy and Leonard, 1992, p. 233). The care that wives deliver to men, McMahon remarks in *Taking Care of Men*, is hidden under ideas of biological destiny or romantic love. The idea that this care might serve men's interests is often strongly refuted (McMahon, 1999), however, he considers it important to recognise the scale and significance of the caring for men that women do and the way in which it constructs men's success and achievement in the marketplace.

It is not 'rational' for women to perform any of this labour, which services the betterment of their menfolk and gives them no monetary reward. Women's unpaid labour constitutes a powerful challenge to the idea of the 'rational economic man' that underlies mainstream liberalist thinking. Feminist analyst, Lourdes Beneria, says that "[e]conomic rationality is based on the expectation that human beings behave in ... ways ... [that realise] maximum gains" (Beneria, 1999, p. 64). From this perspective, she says "the entrepreneur seeks to maximise profits, the employee seeks to attain the highest earnings possible, and the consumer to maximise his or her utility" (Beneria, 1999, p. 64). This basic idea of 'rational economic man', Beneria says, is embedded in neoclassical liberalist theory, with " ... [e]conomic rationality ... assumed to be the norm in human behaviour" (Beneria, 1999, p. 64). The fact that women engage in so much unpaid work is not clearly in their self-interest and provides a rather damning criticism of the idea of 'rational economic man'. Adam Smith, in the eighteenth century, is the analyst most usually identified as the originator of the idea that the "selfish pursuit of individual gain" was positively linked to the "wealth of nations through the invisible hand of the market" (Beneria, 1999, p. 64). Waring quotes Adam Smith, illustrating his idea of how self-interest works, in order to show the male bias it represents. He says: "It is not from the benevolence of the butcher, the brewer, or the baker that we expect our dinner, but from their regard to their own interest" (quoted in Waring, p. 19). Waring sums up the crucial flaw in this analysis as follows: Smith would not have got his dinner, in fact, without the unpaid work of his wife who was clearly not motivated by self-interest. Indeed Smith, like other men, rely on the lack of self-interest on the part of women in order for them to act in the marketplace at all:

> If Adam Smith was fed daily by Mrs Smith, he omitted to notice or to mention it. He did not, of course, pay her. What *her* interest was in feeding him we can only guess, for Adam Smith saw no "value" in what she did (Waring, 1988, p. 19).

The issue of women's unpaid labour has been crucial to feminist understandings of how the international political economy operates.

WOMEN AND GLOBALISATION

Feminist theorists have produced a considerable body of work examining the way in which women have been affected by the globalisation of the economy (Enloe, 1989). Mies explains that her analysis of the position of women in globalisation was spurred by the need to extend a feminist understanding of the importance of women's unpaid labour in the West to women in the rest of the world, where women's 'housewifized' labour, i.e. labour that was seen as secondary and easily exploitable, was a foundational component of what was coming to be called 'globalisation' (Mies, 1998 [1986]). Her work *Patriarchy and Accumulation on a World Scale* is a *tour de force* which shows how women are mobilised around the world to enable capitalist accumulation. She shows how women in the rich and poor worlds are linked. This linkage occurs through the creation of Export Processing Zones, for example, in which women constitute the overwhelming majority of workers. Women in the rich world can buy very cheap clothes and shoes because they are manufactured in cheap labour enclaves using the work of women who are paid a pittance and who suffer poor conditions in countries such as Indonesia and Vietnam. Women are attractive as workers because they are considered docile, dextrous and cheap, and because their cultural relegation to subordinate roles as housewives in the new production sites, so that paid employment can be seen as secondary, facilitates their exploitation (Bair, 2010). As companies in rich countries seek to reduce their costs in order to compete with the cheap goods allowed in by neoliberal free trade policies and the reduction of tariff barriers, women enter low paid and exploitative work in very large numbers in less developed countries (Mies, 1998 [1986]).

Wichterich explains that it was cheap women's labour that offered the main element in the "comparative advantage" that caused the shift in production from the industrial heartlands of old to poor countries in Europe and then to South East Asia (Wichterich, 2000, p. 1). This shift, she says, revolutionised world trade. There were other elements that made such a shift attractive, such as general low pay without "secondary wage-costs", weak trade unions, and fiscal and investment incentives, but women's labour power was the "most important 'natural' resource" (Wichterich, 2000, p. 1).

Wichterich, like Mies, points out that alongside this outsourcing to poor countries there were colonies in the West in which women were engaged in low paid and unprotected "homeworking" and where they produced clothing, footwear, and other goods. She explains that the role of woman in the international political economy was to augment the profits of multinational companies through outsourcing and to provide the shock absorbers for the brutal exigencies of the economic changes being forced through by neoliberal economic ideologies and practices. As countries began to be pitted against each other in "fierce undercutting", she says, "globalised woman" was "burnt up as a natural fuel"; she was the "piece-rate worker in export industries, the worker living abroad" who sent back "foreign currency, the prostitute or catalogue bride on the international body and marriage markets, and the voluntary worker" who helped to absorb the shock of "social cutbacks and structural adjustment" (Wichterich, 2000, p. 167).

Mies has developed the concept of "housewifization" to describe what she sees as the destruction of properly remunerated jobs with benefits that male workers in the West had come to expect before the ravages of globalisation in the 1980s (Mies, 1998 [1986]). Women were "housewifized", she says, during the industrial revolution when a strict division between public and private worlds was created and the women of the middle classes were removed from the public world to be imprisoned in the role of the housewife within the home.

Women were permitted "housewifized" jobs in the twentieth century, which were part-time, poorly paid, non-unionised, casual, without benefits, short-term, atomised, and without the protection of labour laws, on the grounds that their husbands were the main breadwinners and the women were not really workers but housewives. During the last decades of the twentieth century, she contends, as neoliberal globalisation took hold, more and more jobs, including those usually done by men, were housewifized, i.e. casualised to the extent that many workers — male and female — had to take more than one job and juggle them to survive financially.

A great deal of home-working is also camouflaged by concepts like 'self-employment' or 'entrepreneurship' and "... [m]uch of ... [which] is nothing but commodified housework" (Bennholdt-Thomson and Mies, 1999, p. 47). Mies is able to adapt language derived from feminist ideas to explain these broader concepts. She uses the concept of "colonies of the white man", for example, to place all parts of the "submerged 'hidden economy'...nature, women and colonised people and territories" within the context of "Colonies of White Men" where "White Men stands ... for the [W]estern industrial system" (Mies, 1996, p. 6). As such women are the shock absorbers of neoliberal economic policies and of the forces of globalisation. As a result women experience the harm of events like the global financial crisis of 2007/9 differently to men.

GENDERING THE GLOBAL FINANCIAL CRISIS

The global financial crisis is a powerful example for the feminist argument that 'economic man' is not rationalistic at all. In an Australian public television show on the global financial crisis, Coates, who has made a reputation from his work on testosterone levels among financial traders, commented, "Yeah — we have to build a model that shows how people are systematically non-rational and unfortunately non-rational at the points at which it's most dangerous". The narrator, Newby, reinforced this point: "Perhaps not extinction yet, but for Homo economicus, it is time to evolve" (Newby, 2009). Since the global financial crisis occurred in 2007 there have been a few critical articles in the media in the US and Australia pointing out that the GFC had a masculine face, and that blame for the crisis needs to be sheeted home to those who created it, that is, to men in general and elite men in particular.

Sunderland, the business editor of the UK's *Observer* newspaper, has been particularly involved in gendering this crisis by pointing out that the politico-economic deliberations involved were overwhelmingly dominated by men. Of the World Economic Forum, she states: "It's ludicrous that men ... [were able to dominate] the debate in Davos. The single biggest force for economic growth is being ignored" (Sunderland, 2009). She also points out that the crisis will have particularly devastating effects on women. The theme of the WEF was "Shaping the Post-Crisis World", however, half of the human population was excluded from the proceedings. Meanwhile the "male Davos elite" remained "mired in its own preening self-regard and complacency … [having] wrecked the world economy … [they] seem oblivious to the idea [that] they may not be the best people to rebuild it". She points out that the crisis was caused by a "macho, tooth-and-claw brand of capitalism" and that there were only five women on the abridged list of one hundred and seventy "business leaders" present. Sunderland had to trawl through twenty names of invitees before finding a woman — Her Highness the Begum Aga Khan. Sunderland comments that the news media have broadcast a "steady stream of masculine voices, to the extent that it is remarkable to see or hear a woman". She points out that the international banks that should be playing a role in resolving the crisis are almost entirely male too, for example: " … [t]he Bank for International Settlements has no female directors; the IMF has one woman executive and the World Bank has two out of 10 executive directors. It's disgraceful".

The men generally pinpointed as bearing most responsibility for the global financial crisis are those in the finance industry and banking. There is an increasing literature demonstrating the problematic ideology and practice of these men. They represent not just everyday masculinity but hyper-masculinity, super-powered by aggressive sexism. McDowell's study of the gendered nature of the banking industry in the city of London (1997) found that men overwhelmingly outnumbered women in managerial grades (eighty-eight percent), with women clustered in clerical roles. She found that the masculine culture of the workplace was represented in language used. To "lift your skirts", for example, means to reveal your position. A rising market is referred to as a "hard-on". A successful trade is greeted with cries of "bollocks out" and "to rape the cards" means to "exaggerate expenses claims …". Indeed, "[a] number or interviewees suggested that work/deals are as good as/better than orgasm" (McDowell, 1997, p. 148). Military and sporting images are common, as is talk of jungles, races and battles. She found the most extreme versions of masculine language in the inner sanctum of hyper-masculinity, that is, on the trading floors and in the dealing rooms where "a rougher, tougher type of everyday exchange … [is] more common than in the elite atmosphere of the capital markets and corporate finance divisions" (McDowell, 1997, p. 151).

McDowell was inspired by the global financial crisis to write a brief article explaining how the masculine culture she identified in 1997 was still dominant in the finance industry, and that this needed to be seen as a part of the explanation for the crisis (2010). In fact, she says, she wonders whether she had "under-estimated this masculine tendency [on the part of men] to exaggerate their own abilities" when they found themselves amongst the patriarchs of investment banking (McDowell, 2010, p. 654). In the dealing rooms, she says, a sexualised culture continues to flourish, with practices that promote hyper-masculinity and exclude women, such as, "[e]xaggerated forms of masculinised language and behaviour... Horseplay, sexualised banter, loud and aggressive talk, as well as forms of sexual harassment". In this arena "women are often forced into the position of unwilling arbiters of boundaries or less than willing participants in the sexualised banter". Women cannot be equal in this sphere of the finance industry since "[s]ocial exchanges are still commonly set in masculinised arenas, including in golf clubs or hospitality suites at major football clubs as well as ... lap dancing clubs" (McDowell, 2010, p. 653). Unfortunately, McDowell admits to being impressed by the work of Coates on the role played by testosterone in dealing rooms. This rather undermines her otherwise helpful social constructionist approach to the finance industry.

RISK TAKING IN THE FINANCE INDUSTRY?

Neither classical liberalist nor socialist or marxist analyses of the international political economy is critical of the ways in which masculinity constructs the practices of corporations, banks and the finance industry. Even within feminist approaches the necessity to highlight the socially constructed nature of masculinity with regard to the workings of the male-stream economy is little discussed.

There is, nonetheless, illuminating research on the masculinist nature of the culture of such workplaces as corporations and banks. This is despite the fact that there is no wider analytical interest in the way in which the social construction of masculinity around aggression, competition, and risk-taking underpins the whole political economy.

In relation to the global financial crisis, it is risk-taking that is most implicated in what took place in 2007. Men's studies analysts have sought to explain the ways in which risk-taking is created in boys and young men. They have also documented the harmful results for boys and young men in terms of suicide rates, the numbers of car accidents, the incidence of drug-taking, the incidence of dangerous sexual practices, and of higher mortality rates generally (Mansdotter *et al.*, 2009). They see competitive sport as playing a central role in inuring boys to be risk-takers.

Theorists such as Sabo and Messner explain how pressuring boys to engage in sports that are painful and can create lifelong injury, particularly to the head, creates a training in carelessness towards the body, and a willingness to take risks (McKay *et al.*, 2000). There are other key aspects to this training, including adventure sports such as bungee jumping, which have developed into large industries in the last two decades, and including inculcation into war cultures through toys and games. The results of the creation of risk-taking are serious physical harm, however, such as in the practice by boys of reckless driving (young men between seventeen and twenty-five in New South Wales, Australia, having four times as many serious speed-related casualty crashes as young women) (Walker *et al.*, 2000). The role of risk-taking in the construction of masculinity has also been examined in relation to HIV risk. Researchers concerned to lower the intensity of the HIV epidemic have argued that the risk-taking element in masculinity must be transformed if HIV is to be contained in Africa (Foreman, 1999). One study, related to HIV risk in the West, examines the relationship of masculinity and risk-taking amongst gay men who take part in "bareback sex", i.e. anal penetration without condoms, as being either reckless as to risk or as an activity where risk plays an important part in the pleasure and satisfaction the behaviour entails (Holmes *et al.*, 2008).

In the last decade neuroscientists have sought to explain the risk-taking behaviour of men in the finance industry. Feminist political economists are concerned about the implications of this biological essentialism, however. Bedford and Rai say, "We have seen a proliferation of reductionist biological explanations rather than rigorous analysis ..." (Bedford and Rai, 2010, p. 2). Neuroscientists use evolutionary psychology to explain behaviour in terms of biology, that is, the difference between male and female hormones. They explain the behaviour of men as being the result of natural biological differences between them and women. Neuroscientists provide the 'hard' science for the claims of evolutionary psychologists by testing hormone levels.

This form of testing is now going on apace to explain the 'irrationality' of male finance workers and why women are averse to 'risk' (and are therefore less suited to employment in the finance industry or to work in what Susan George (1986) called "casino" capitalism). A 2007 study, for example, published in the prestigious *Proceedings of the National Academy of Sciences* appeared immediately before the global financial crisis began. It studied the "endocrine system in financial risk-taking" (Coates and Herbert, 2008, p. 6167). This study, by an analyst already mentioned, examined the testosterone level in male finance industry traders at eleven in the morning and at four in the afternoon. It was designed to assess whether higher levels of testosterone were associated with greater financial success: "... [w]e predicted", said Coates, "that testosterone would rise on days when traders made an above-average gain in the markets" (Coates and Herbert, 2008, p. 6167). They found that this hypothesis was correct. They decided that "high morning testosterone predicts greater profitability for the rest of the day" (Coates and Herbert, 2008, p. 6168). If testosterone levels remained elevated, however, they thought this could have a very negative effect since it could cause traders to engage in unreasonably risky behaviour which "could cause financial markets to deviate from the predictions of rational choice theory" (Coates and Herbert, 2008, p. 6170). As Coates himself put it, "We don't think biochemistry explains what starts a bubble or a crash. We do think however that steroids can exaggerate a bull market and turn it into a bubble. A bull market can almost be seen as a market with steroid rage" (Newby, 2009). This research gives the lie to the idea that the men in charge of the finance industry are rationalistic. Rather, according to the most scientific (i.e. rationalistic) of research, the politico-economic futures of investors, governments, and pensioners are tied to men's testosterone levels.

A similar biologistic approach is employed in relation to women's "risk aversion" in the same journal. This article states: "Women are generally more risk averse than men" (Sapienza *et al.*, 2009). The research studied testosterone levels in men and women in relation to being risk-averse and in relation to the choice of a career in financial risk-taking. They found that high levels of testosterone were associated with a tendency towards risk-taking in both men and women.

The difficulty with studies of this kind is that they do not take social context into account. The construction of masculinity is not considered because, for these particular researchers, male behaviour is based upon testosterone.

They also do not take into account the possibility that anticipation may affect hormonal levels, although the study on male traders did mention that testosterone rises "in athletes preparing for a competition and rises even further in the winning athlete, while falling in the losing one" (Coates and Herbert, 2008, p. 6167). This could be seen as an argument for the effect of social context and behaviour on hormones and not the other way around, i.e. for a social constructionist rather than a biologically determinist approach.

HYPER-MASCULINITY AND SEX INDUSTRY USE IN TRADER BEHAVIOUR

The hyper-masculinity of the finance industry is illustrated by the ways in which male finance executives utilise the sex industry. Masculinity and femininity are constructed in relation to each other and make no sense on their own (Connell, 1995). Men understand themselves as masculine to the extent that they are not feminine and masculine practices are designed to achieve this understanding and self-presentation.

One of the most straightforward ways in which men can establish their difference is through the sex industry, where women are used as sexual subordinates to service the male sex right (Pateman, 1988). In this respect in particular there is copious evidence that men in the finance industry are hyper-masculine.

The men who are supposed to regulate the finance industry in the US — those in the Securities Exchange Commission (SEC) — exemplify this addiction to the construction of hyper-masculinity. When the global financial system was collapsing the SEC enforcement team was using online pornography. An investigation of porn use by the SEC discovered that a senior attorney at the SEC headquarters in Washington spent up to eight hours a day looking at and downloading porn (Harshaw, 2010). An accountant at the SEC was blocked more than sixteen thousand times a month from visiting porn websites. Seventeen of the employees found to be using a significant amount of porn were at a senior level and earning salaries up to $222,418. Pornography use escalated as the global financial crisis unfolded in 2008. One SEC employee started his own private porn business using SEC resources.

The finance industry's use of prostitution was depicted in the novel by Tetsuya Ishikawa, a top London employee of the Goldman Sachs bank, who was involved in the company's sale of toxic mortgage investments (Seamark, 2010). Eton and Oxford-educated Ishikawa regularly travelled abroad. As he subsequently admitted: "The first thing I asked on arriving was, where is the brothel?"

The book is based upon his experience of six years in the finance industry in London. He admitted in interviews publicising it that he "slept with escorts" and that he "regularly visited Spearmint Rhino, the lap-dancing club". He also tells of the "drugs, prostitutes, strippers, booze and general excessive nightlife" of city bankers in the build-up to the financial crisis.

In recent years there has been some exposure of the interrelationship between the sex industry and the finance industry in legal cases prosecuted by women employees who cite discrimination when their male colleagues use sex industry venues for work purposes. Reports from the UK feminist organisation, the Fawcett Society (founded in the nineteenth century), document these cases (Jeffreys, 2010). Feminist analysts have started to argue that this usage constitutes a serious obstacle to the equality of women in the finance industry in particular, but also in other businesses where such practice are seen as natural and normal.

FINANCIAL CRISIS IMPACT ON WOMEN

Most writing on the effects of the GFC on women are speculative at this point, and are based upon what happened to women in previous crises. As Espey, Harper and Jones say, in a recent issue of the Oxfam journal *Gender and Development* which is devoted to gendering the crisis, the effect of previous politico-economic shocks have been "poorer nutrition, declining attendance at school (most usually of girls who are considered less worthy of education), longer working hours, and increased strains on adults trying to meet their responsibilities for family care" (Espey *et al.*, 2010, p. 296). The journal issue is devoted to what is likely to take place rather than what is actually happening on the ground. Elson explains that the crisis in the global North has been transmitted to developing countries "through international markets for finance and goods" (Elson, 2010, p. 204).

The global financial crisis is likely to affect women differently from men and in many cases in more severe ways. This is ironic considering that women are the innocent victims of a crisis created by men and masculinity. Before the most recent crisis happened, van Staveren was writing of the way in which men in the finance industry take the risks, and women are forced to bear the burden of them (van Staveren, 2002). Thus she says, "[a] shift of financial risk to those who are not responsible for it is costly and unfair. This shift has a significant gender dimension. The generation of excessive financial risk is almost exclusively a male activity. Men are the main decision-makers in finance, men undertake the larger financial transactions, and men are the main speculators. Yet the persons who carry the consequences of global financial crises — especially in the care economy — are predominantly female" (van Staveren, 2002, p. 230). The care economy, she points out, is mainly female and it compensates for "(mainly male) rent-seeking in financial markets" (van Staveren, 2002, p. 230).

One most significant result of the global financial crisis, predicted but still to unfold in many countries, is that women's employment will be the greatest casualty of cutbacks in expenditure as governments seek to make good the very large debts they have run up in order to compensate for the losses caused to the finance industry by men's risk-taking. In the UK the unfairness of the cuts that the newly elected government proposes to implement is clear in research carried out by a shadow minister, Yvette Cooper (Asthana, 2010). It shows that seventy-two percent of the effect of the proposed tax and benefit cuts will be suffered by women, and that women will suffer most of the job cuts to the public sector because four in ten women are in those jobs. Indeed 85.4 percent of part-time jobs in the civil service are filled by women and these are likely to be the first affected. This spurred the Fawcett Society to mount a legal challenge to the budget in August 2010 on the grounds that the cuts will manifestly affect women more than men.

Cuts to public services do not just affect women's jobs. Women suffer doubly, since the care services that were previously state-funded still have to be provided, and this is now an extra component of women's unpaid work. Children, the elderly and the sick have to be cared for by women in the home. Women constitute the reserve army of labour which can be thrown out of work when governments face financial crises.

Up until now such policies have tended to affect women in the less developed world more than those in the West. Thus, as Sweetman says, ignoring the reality of women's unpaid work enables the international institutions that impose "structural adjustment policies" on developing countries to ignore the "true suffering of women, men and families" that follow from the "cutbacks in state provision of essential services." With their "[b]acks to the wall, women struggle — and just about succeed — in replacing these services and keeping families afloat" (Sweetman, 2008, p. 1). The present crisis, however, affects women in both rich and poor countries unequally.

Another effect of the global financial crisis that has harmed women is the increased stress that men feel as their investments go bad, or they lose jobs or contracts. Men take out their stress upon women in the form of domestic violence. There is greater sexual exploitation of women, and more girls are driven into prostitution, thus exploiting women's increased vulnerability as well as offering men stress relief in this form of greater abuse. When the 1997 East Asian financial crisis took place there was increased trafficking of women across the Northern Chinese border as well as heightened domestic violence. In South Korea, after the crisis, an estimated one in seven women were involved in prostitution.

As Sweetman argues, "Men's inability to find alternative employment which fulfils their vision of themselves as 'real men' often leads to increased violence against women and children within the home" (Sweetman, 2008, p. 2). Men who become unemployed do not generally wish to take on extra caring roles in the home should their wives shoulder the burden of earning the family income, often in lowly paid jobs. Instead, "women often end up doing a double shift while men become depressed and violent" (Sweetman, 2008, p. 2).

In May 2009 a survey of more than six hundred domestic violence shelters in the US found a seventy-five percent reported increase in women seeking help since the economic downturn in September 2008 (AWID, 2010, p. 22). In Australia, too, an increase in violence against women has been reported. According to the Australian Childhood Foundation, there has been a fifteen to twenty percent increase in cases of domestic violence, physical abuse, and neglect (Massola, 2009). In just two months, post-crisis, the number of calls spiked sharply from an average of two hundred and twenty per month to more than two hundred and fifty per month.

Men facing financial ruin can go to the lengths of murdering their families out of a sense of shame and damaged masculinity. In 2009 a businessman in Shropshire, the UK, who was facing financial ruin, killed his wife and daughter (Carter, 2009). Christopher Foster shot dead his wife and fifteen-year-old daughter in their beds, shot the family dogs, placed a horsebox in the driveway so that fire services could not get in to help, then set fire to the mansion in which the family lived. He died in the blaze. In 2010 a father in Hampshire, UK, was deeply in debt (Taylor, 2010). He killed his wife and daughters before hanging himself. Men who murder their families and then, usually, themselves, are described as family annihilators.

It is men who are usually the perpetrators in situations like these and they are usually separated from their wives. The murders are motivated by rage and revenge. There has been no systematic research on the connection between family annihilation and men's financial problems, but understanding it may require understanding how a man's 'honour' is damaged by losing his role as provider to the point where he feels he must kill his wife and family rather than have them reproach him for his improvidence.

CONCLUSION

A solution to the problems created by political economies organised around men's interests, and the exclusion of subsistence and unpaid labour, may require more than a tinkering at the edges to bring a few more women in. When measures to prevent further destabilisation in global financial markets show an awareness of the gender dimension, they are most likely to involve liberal feminist solutions such as getting more women into the finance industry. Thus a Treasury Committee report from the UK government in April recommended that there should be more women in top finance jobs to improve corporate governance (Penny, 2010). Goodhart, a former Bank of England policy maker, told the committee that the global financial crisis of 2007 would have been less likely if there had been more women at a senior level given "[t]he longer-term, more cautious tendency" of women and the "beneficial" way they behave, that is, how they act "with less of the alpha male ..." (Penny, 2010). Bringing women in as watchdogs to try to moderate the excesses of men's behaviour is not likely to offer a substantial solution to the problems caused by the gendered nature of a global financial crisis, however. There is no challenge to masculine culture here, nor an understanding that the finance industry may be based on problematic premises. Women cannot be transformed so that they acquire the same values and behaviours as men in the banking industry without losing precisely the qualities that keep the hidden political economy going, i.e. the selfless performance of unpaid labour. Tinkering is not enough when finance capitalism is founded upon risk-taking masculinity.

The critique by feminist analysts of not just the global financial crisis of 2007, but the gendered nature of market accounting and the international political economy, suggests that a more root-and-branch set of changes is required. Mies argues that unpaid work needs to be respected. Hence she asks, " ... [w]hat would an economy look like in which nature mattered, in which women mattered, in which children, in which people mattered, which would not be based on colonising and exploiting others?" (Mies and Shiva, 1993, p. 13). Her answer is to promote the revaluation of women's unpaid work. "In an alternative paradigm," she says "presently colonised and marginalised actors, activities and values ... [would] be put into the core (center), because they ... [would be] central to ensuring that life ... [could] go on in its regeneration and fullness". So long as unpaid work is unrecognised, however, national and international politico-economic policies will go on structurally adjusting and reacting to market crises with respect to men's anti-social behaviours, and women will remain the shock absorbers of the whole system.

REFERENCES

Asthana, A (2010). Thousands of Women Fear Bleak Future as they Bear the Brunt of Public Sector Cuts. *The Guardian,* 8 August. http://www.guardian.co.uk/society/2010/aug/08/women-public-sector-cuts-pay-freeze [24 December 2011].

AWID Brief 11 (2010). The Impact of the Crisis on Women: Main Trends across Regions. Toronto, Canada: Association for Women in Development.

Bair, J (2010). On difference and capital: Gender and the globalisation of production, *Signs: Journal of Women in Culture and Society*, 36(1), 204–226.

Bedford, K and S Rai (2010). Feminists theorise international political economy, *Signs: Journal of Culture and Society*, 36(1), 1–18.

Beneria, L (1999). Globalisation, gender and the Davos man, *Feminist Economics*, 5 (3), 61–83.

Bennholdt-Thomson, V and M Mies (1999). *The Subsistence Perspective. Beyond the Globalised Economy.* Melbourne: Spinifex.

Carter H (2009). Millionaire Facing Ruin Shot Wife and Daughter and then Killed Himself. *The Guardian,* 4 April. http://www.guardian.co.uk/uk/2009/apr/04/8 [24 December 2011].

Coates, J and J Herbert (2008). Endogenous steroids and financial risk taking on a London trading floor, *PNAS*, 105(16), 6167–6172.

Connell, R (1995). *Masculinities.* St Leonards: Allen and Unwin.

Delphy, C and D Leonard (1992). *Familiar Exploitation: A New Analysis of Marriage in Contemporary Western Societies.* London: Polity Press.

Elson, D (2010). Gender and the global economic crisis in developing countries: A framework for analysis, *Gender and Development*, 18(2), 201–212.

Enloe, C (1989). *Bananas, Beaches and Bases: Making Feminist Sense of International Politics.* London: Pandora.

Espey, J, C Harper and N Jones (2010). Crisis, care and childhood: The impact of economic crisis on poor households in the developing world, *Gender and Development*, 18(2), 291–307.

Foreman, M (1999). *AIDS and Men. Taking Risks or Taking Responsibility?* London: The Panos Institute and Zed Press.

George, S (1986). *Casino Capitalism.* Oxford: Blackwells.

Harshaw, T (2010). Will Wall Street Be Saved by Porn? *New York Times* Opinionator Blogs, 23 April. http://opinionator.blogs.nytimes.com/2010/04/23/will-wall-street-be-saved-by-porn/?emc=eta1 [24 December 2011].

Hochschild, A (1983). *The Managed Heart: Commercialisation of Human Feeling*. Berkeley: University of California Press.

Holmes, D, D Gastaldo, P O'Byrne and A Lombard (2008). Bareback sex: A conflation of risk and masculinity, *International Journal of Men's Health*, 7(2), 171–191.

Jeffreys, S (2010). The sex industry and business practice: An obstacle to women's equality, *Women's Studies International* Forum, 33(3), 274–282.

Mansdotter, A, A Lundin, D Falkstedt and T Hemmingsonn (2009). The association between masculinity rank and mortality patterns: A prospective study based on the Swedish 1969 conscript cohort, *Journal of Epidemiology and Community Health*, 63, 408–413.

Massola, J (2009). Financial Crisis 'Contributes to Violence, Child Abuse'. *CanberraTimes*, 1 June. http://www.canberratimes.com.au/news/national/national/general/financial-crisis-contributes-to-violence-child-abuse/1527976.aspx [24 December 2011].

McDowell, L (1997). *Capital Culture. Gender at Work in the City*. Oxford: Blackwells.

McDowell, L (2010). Capital culture revisited: Sex, testosterone and the city. *International Journal of Urban and Regional* Research, 34(3), 652–658.

McKay, J, M Messner and D Sabo (eds.). (2000). *Masculinities, Gender Relations and Sport*. Thousand Oaks: Sage Publications Inc.

McMahon, A (1999). *Taking Care of Men. Sexual Politics in the Public Mind*. Cambridge: Cambridge University Press.

Mies, M (1998, [1986]). *Patriarchy and Accumulation on a World Scale. Women in the International Division of Labour*. Melbourne: Spinifex Press.

Mies, M (1996). Globalisation of the Economy and Women's Work in a Sustainable Society. Paper at 6th International Interdisciplinary Congress on Women. Adelaide, 22–26 April.

Mies, M and V Shiva (1993). *Ecofeminism*. Melbourne: Spinifex.

Newby, J (2009). Risky Business. Catalyst. Australian Broadcasting Corporation, 26 March. http://www.abc.net.au/catalyst/stories/2525497.htm [24 December 2011].

Panitsch, L and M Konings (eds.). (2009). *American Empire and the Political Economy of Global Finance*. New York: Palgrave MacMillan.

Pateman, C (1988). *The Sexual Contract*. Cambridge: Polity Press.

Penny, T (2010). Women in Top Finance Jobs Would Reduce 'Group Think', U.K. Lawmakers Say. *Bloomberg News*, 3 April. http://www.bloomberg.com/news/2010–04–02/women-in-top-finance-jobs-would-reduce-group-think-u-k-lawmakers-say.html [24 December 2011].

Pettman, J (1996). *Worlding Women*. St. Leonards: Allen and Unwin.

Philipps, L (2008). Silent partners: The role of unpaid market labor in families. *Feminist Economics*, 14 (2), 37–57.

Sapienza, P, L Zingales and D Maestripieri (2009). Gender differences in financial risk aversion and career choices are affected by testosterone. *PNAS*, 106(36), 15268–15273.

Seamark, M (2010). Goldmans Banker always Asked: Where's the Brothel? *The Daily Mail*, 23 April. http://www.dailymail.co.uk/news/article-1268099/Goldman-Sachs-fraud-banker-Tetsuya-Ishikawa-asked-Wheres-brothel.html?ITO=1490#ixzz0lx9D5fBo [24 December 2011].

Sunderland, R (2009,). This Mess was Made by Men. Now Let the Women have their Say, The *Guardian* 1 Feb. http://www.guardian.co.uk/commentisfree/2009/feb/01/ davos-global-recession-gender [24 December 2011].

Sweetman, C (2008). Feminist Economics. From Poverty to Power, Oxfam International background paper.

Taylor, M (2010). Family Found Dead in Hampshire Home were Deeply in Debt. *The Guardian*, 27 July. http://www.guardian.co.uk/uk/2010/jul/27/debt-problems-family-killed-hampshire [24 December 2011].

van Staveren, I (2002), Global Finance and Gender. In *Civil Society and Global Finance*, J Scholte and A Schnabel (eds.). London: Routledge.

Walker, L, D Butland and R Connell (2000). Boys on the road: Masculinities, car culture, and road safety education, *The Journal of Men's Studies*, 8(2), 153–169.

Waring, M (1988). *If Women Counted: A New Feminist Economics*. San Francisco: Harper and Row.

Wichterich, C (2000). *The Globalised Woman. Reports from a Future of Inequality.* London: Zed Books; Melbourne: Spinifex.

CHAPTER 19

Production/Reproduction

Meagan Tyler

Victoria University

> *The problem with all these "approaches" is that they ultimately share the same approach — the denial that men and markets are, in some of the deepest and broadest historical senses, "of woman born."*
>
> Runyan "Of Markets and Men"

Women have traditionally been invisible in studies of the international political economy (IPE). Indeed, women continue to be invisible in most mainstream and even many critical theorisations of IPE today. The issue of reproduction illuminates central debates about the continued exclusion of women in IPE. This chapter seeks to outline the history of feminist engagement with the concept of reproduction, particularly social reproduction, and with the reproductive economy in the IPE literature and the possibilities and limitations of various approaches. Following this, it is argued that feminist analyses focusing on women's work and social reproduction challenge the fundamental basis of much politico-economic thinking rather than simply being ancillary to it. Ultimately, it is suggested that future attempts to make women's work visible must put women's experiences at the core of analytic thinking rather than attempting to make women's experiences fit pre-existing politico-economic models.

INVISIBLE WOMEN AND THE PRODUCTION/REPRODUCTION SPLIT

It is often remarked upon in critical feminist texts dealing with mainstream international politics and IPE that gender is largely absent from the foundational texts of the disciplines and continues to be absent there (Ferber and Nelson, 1993; Peterson, 2003). As a result of this exclusion, it can sometimes appear as though gender is absent from the functioning of IPE altogether. As Cook and Roberts point out in *Towards a Gendered Political Economy*, however, "[g]ender is not absent from political economy, but rather invisible" (Cook and Roberts, 2000, p. 3). Furthermore, gender is *made* invisible, that is, women clearly exist and there is no debate about whether or not women play a role in the global political economy since they clearly do. The issue is that mainstream analyses of politics and economics have marginalised women and women's work to the point that women's experiences and contributions are largely incompatible with much existing political thinking and most economic models. This thinking and these models are at best gender-blind. More commonly, however, they display an entrenched male bias which results in the grand narrative of IPE being one of "(white) men, states and markets" (Runyan, 1997, p. 79).

One of the most central dichotomies found in mainstream international political economy is the distinction between the public and the private spheres. The public sphere accounts for high politics. It was (and is) overwhelmingly male dominated. The private sphere accounts for home life and the family. It thereby encompasses what remains mostly women's work.

Feminist scholars have, for decades, pointed out that this imaginary separation between the public and private is false; that the two spheres are not separate but are rather interconnected and interwoven (Waylen, 2006). In addition, feminists have highlighted the ways in which this central concept of a public/private split operates to obscure not only the experiences of women but also the realities of the international political economy (Enloe, 1989; MacKinnon, 2006). Feminists have also recognised that this distinction operates in IPE under the guise of a split between production and reproduction (e.g. Peterson, 2003; Runyan, 1997; Waylen, 2006; Young, 2000).

As Peterson explains in her text, *A Critical Re-writing of Global Political Economy* (2003):

> Pre-occupied with 'productive' activities — waged/commodified labour and market exchange — neoclassical and most [m]arxist theories ignore the reproductive economy. Preoccupied with 'politics' and 'economics', liberal theories ignore sex/affective relations and social reproduction (p. 80).

The productive political economy is seen to be the 'real economy' in the same way that the high politics of the public sphere is taken to be 'real politics'. In Peterson's (2003) words, the productive political economy, as conventionally understood, is "the (formal) economy that is further specified by reference to primary (natural resources), secondary (manufactures) and tertiary (services) production" (p. 47). The reproductive political economy includes what is forgotten, overlooked, or intentionally left out of this conventional understanding of the productive political economy. In Peterson's terms, the reproductive political economy is "the economy of families and the private sphere — where human life is generated, daily life maintained, and socialisation reproduced" (p. 79).

It should be noted that the very concept of a political economics of the private sphere challenges much mainstream politico-economic theory. As a feminist political economist, Waylen (2000) notes: "Neoclassical economics generally sees the family and the household as a kind of 'black box' lying outside the realm of economics in the private sphere..." (p. 19). The concept of a reproductive political economy to cover the private sphere, therefore, can be seen as the politico-economic equivalent to the feminist charge that the personal is political. The personal, it turns out, is politico-economic too. Just as feminists have pointed out that the personal and the political, the public and the private, overlap and are interconnected, some feminist political economists and IPE analysts have sought to show that the distinction between the productive and reproductive political economies is a false one as well.

While a sexual division of labour is generally taken to be universal, and from a feminist perspective is implicated in women's oppression, the construction of a clear distinction between the productive and the reproductive political economies is arguably a relatively new development. Picchio (1992) — in one of the few in-depth discussions available about the history of the production/reproduction distinction in political economics — argues that the separation between production and reproduction is largely a function of capitalism and industrialisation. In particular she posits that the industrial revolution formalised and exacerbated the divide between production and reproduction and therefore between men's and women's work. She states that while women have always been involved in the processes of both production and reproduction, the industrial revolution required them to conduct different kinds of labour in different places. Reproductive work, most prominently housework and child-rearing, was to be conducted in the home, in private, while waged, 'productive' work was to be undertaken outside the home, in public.

Picchio contends that this process of separating and privatising women's labour led to an even greater undervaluing of women's work in the home and in family life. Rather than being seen as integral to the functioning of daily life, women, and in particular wives, became ever more commodified as possessions of the 'real worker': the wage earning man. Picchio also shows that the inequality of this situation has been decried by feminists and women's rights campaigners for almost one hundred years. For example, she provides the following quote from a British MP and women's rights campaigner, originally published in 1927. Rathbone critiques here the way in which 'real work' became men's work and women became largely invisible in politico-economic models:

> In the work of still more recent economists, the family sank out of sight altogether. The subsistence theory of wages was superseded by theories in which wives and children appear only occasionally, together with butchers' meat and alcohol and

> tobacco, as part of the 'comforts and decencies' which make up the British workman's standard of life and allow him to stand out against the lowering of his wage (Rathbone, quoted in Picchio, 1992, p. 82–83).

Emphasising the way in which the distinction between men's 'productive' work and women's 'reproductive' work has been enshrined in politico-economic analysis, and has served to further disadvantage women, has therefore been understandably a central feminist concern with regard to IPE. Feminists have also sought to show that the productive political economy is, in fact, reliant upon the reproductive political economy, an argument most prominently put forward by Mies (1998 [1986]; for a discussion see the previous chapter by Jeffreys).

These critical feminist insights, however, have not been widely adopted in the mainstream IPE literature, nor have they been adopted in much of the critical IPE literature either (Waylen, 2006). Indeed, the invisibility of feminism, women and the reproductive political economy remains striking. In their introduction to the collection *Beyond Economic Man* (1993), Ferber and Nelson provide evidence from Samuelson's 1948 text, *Economics*, to emphasise the historical male bias in politico-economic thinking. They state that Samuelson's text only contains "two references to 'females'...both included in a section on minorities" (p. 5). Very little has changed more than sixty years on. For example, Cohen's *International Political Economy: An Intellectual History* (2008), published by Princeton University Press, only mentions feminism once and that somewhat disparagingly in the context of critical theories including marxism and "other radical schools of thought" (p. 62). There are only two references to women in the entire volume. Rather ironically, one reference is to critique other edited volumes for their lack of female authors (p. 53). There is not a single mention of reproduction. In the collection *International Political Economy: Perspectives on global power and wealth* (Frieden & Lake, 2003) there is one mention of reproduction but not in relation to feminist IPE. Reproduction is mentioned in relation to non-capitalist, small-scale communities (p. 450). When the discussion moves on to 'more complex' societies the term reproduction falls away from the list of areas for consideration.

There is also one mention of reproduction in *Global Political Economy* (2008), a text-book style volume edited by Ravenhill and published by Oxford University Press. The reference to reproduction is actually in relation to feminist critiques of IPE and appears in a chapter by Watson entitled "Theoretical Traditions in Global Political Economy". Unfortunately, mirroring the way that feminism is so often marginalised in studies of IPE, the mention of reproduction appears is in an inset text box entitled "Feminist Political Economy". It is separated from the main text and so it is also separated from the mainstream theoretical traditions in political economy. The section amounts to less than a page in a book that is more than five hundred pages long. It is clear that women, feminism and the concept of the reproductive economy, still lie at the margins of IPE analysis here.

INCORPORATING WOMEN AND REPRODUCTION IN MAINSTREAM IPE

While the concept of the reproductive economy may still lie on the margins of IPE, this is not to say that there have not been both feminist and mainstream attempts at incorporating the work that women do. In fact, Gilman (1900) was writing about the importance of women's work in the home and the artificial nature of the gendered division of labour as early as 1898 (Walby, 2000). The issue of women's work and women's exploitation within the family noticeably fell from favour, however, with the end of the first wave of feminism in the early twentieth century. It was not until the late 1960s, with women's increasing participation in the paid workforce in the West and the beginnings of the second wave of feminism, that the organisation of the family and women's work again became a topic of serious politico-economic interest (Ferber and Nelson, 1993; Humphries, 2000). Since then there have been three prominent attempts to incorporate women and women's work/the reproductive economy into mainstream political economics. The first was the emergence of the neoclassical-based new home political economics in the late 1960s. The second was the dual systems theory promoted by marxist feminists in the 1970s and 1980s. The most recent has been the push from the 1990s onward to include notions of social reproduction to cover women's unpaid labour.

The New Home Economics (NHE)

The NHE movement certainly constitutes one of the most prominent attempts to account for women's unpaid labour in the home and was the first mainstream school of political economics to analyse household production in any formal way (Gardiner, 2000, p. 62). The doyen of NHE is widely recognised to be Becker whose work, *A Treatise on the Family* (1981), was highly influential. Becker himself received the Nobel Prize for economics in 1992. From a feminist perspective, however, Becker's attempts to understand women's work are quite troubling. Put simply, Becker and many NHE proponents naturalise the sexual division of labour in the home, relating it to a rather spurious socio-biology. They claim that the status quo — where women perform unpaid labour in the home and men work for money in the public sphere — is both a natural and an efficient allocation of labour resources. Women specialise in housework (and are therefore better at it than men) and men specialise in paid work (and are therefore better at it than women). This situation, according to Becker at least, is inescapable, as women give birth to children and are therefore more suited to child-rearing. Ignoring the social world altogether, Becker claims that the sexual division of labour is not only universal among humans but can be found among all vertebrates:

> Although the sharp sexual division of labour in all societies between the market and the household sectors is partly due to the gains from specialised investments, it is also partly due to *intrinsic differences between the sexes.* A man completes his biological contribution to the production of children when his sperm fertilises a woman's egg, after which she controls the reproductive process: she biologically houses and feeds the fetus, delivers the baby, and often feeds the infant with her own milk. *Sexual reproduction along these lines is all but universal among vertebrates...* (Becker, 1993 [1981], p. 37 [emphasis added]).

He continues by explaining that men are therefore not as committed as women to the rearing of children and subsequently spend their "time and energy on food, clothing, protection and other market activities" (p. 38). He concludes this section on the nature of men's and women's work by adding that: "[s]ince the biological natures of men and women differ, the assumption that the time of men and women are perfect substitutes ... is not realistic" (p. 39).

Feminist critics have pointed out numerous flaws in this rather extreme biological determinism (Waylen, 2000). Becker posits a world in which there are almost no social influences at all. Women's role in the home is as natural as childbirth and men's role in the market is similarly (although not as directly) biologically determined. This line of argument has persisted among NHE followers despite the concept of the social construction of gender having been firmly embedded in the social sciences for decades.

One of the most obvious general flaws in the NHE from a social science perspective is the assumption that the market is a naturally existing entity rather than a social construct. Such an assumption is required, however, in order to make the argument consistent. If the market was not natural, it could be changed, and a fairer division of labour could be negotiated. The NHE therefore completely ignores the issue of power relations, particularly between men and women (England, 1993). Rather than simply reaching the most efficient outcome, the sexual division of labour in the family "may be seen as the profoundly unequal accommodation reached between individuals who occupy very different social positions with very different degrees of power" (Elson quoted in Waylen, 2000, p. 20). Becker's above analysis also overlooks the fact that the provision of food, clothing and protection are not always market activities (especially in non-capitalist societies) and that it is women who are often responsible for these within the household. There must therefore be some crossover between the household and market spheres, but this is not how the two are conceived in the NHE. Indeed, Becker implicitly assumes that the spheres are so separate that the skills acquired in each are completely non-transferable (Gardiner, 2000).

In addition, the NHE relies on a strange internal contradiction. While the market is taken to be a sphere of perfect selfishness, the home is taken to be a sphere of perfect altruism. Indeed, the NHE proposes that all functioning family units have a male household head who acts somewhat like a benevolent dictator. That is to say, the household head should have supreme authority in the household but should use his power in the best interests of the family (Humphries, 2000). Even in terms of basic logic, the internal inconsistency of resting a theory on an absolute concept of a biologically determined 'human nature', only to state that humans can be completely altruistic or completely selfish depending on context, leaves the NHE looking very weak. From a feminist perspective, though, there are further issues with the NHE. For example, Becker ignores or omits the possibility of equal, dual heads of a household (Humphries, 2000). The NHE model essentially validates the status quo, denying the potential for equality between men and women and shackling women to lives of unpaid domestic labour, as this is their 'natural' comparative advantage. As Waylen (2000) rightly points out, the "NHE demonstrates that considering an issue (i.e. the economics of the household) is not the same as having a feminist analysis of it" (p. 20).

Dual Systems Model

The dual systems model is certainly an advance on the NHE and it does begin a new, explicitly feminist analysis of women's work. It was proposed mostly by marxist feminists and had some success in influencing the marxist IPE literature. It had less success in influencing more mainstream approaches. It is in the context of the dual systems model that the production/reproduction split was first advanced, although it arguably led to a reinforcement of the very split that it was supposed to be exposing (McLaughlin, 2002). Unlike the NHE, the dual systems model does not rely on strict biological determinism. It rather posits that the sexual division of labour is constructed and places men as responsible for production and women as responsible for reproduction. The mix of marxism and feminism replicates this split: marxism explains the relations in the public sphere of production and feminism explains the relations in the private sphere of reproduction.

The dual systems model is seen as a significant improvement on the earlier marxist treatment of 'the woman question', which subsumes all issues of women's exploitation under the greater issue of a genderless exploitation by capitalism (Hartmann, 1979). As Hartmann wrote in her widely cited "The Unhappy Marriage of Marxism and Feminism" (1979):

> Though aware of the deplorable situation of women in their time the early Marxists failed to focus on the *differences* between men's and women's experiences under capitalism. They did not focus on the feminist questions — how and why women are oppressed as women. They did not, therefore, recognise the vested interest men had in women's continued subordination...men benefited from not having to do housework, from having their wives and daughters serve them and from having the better places in the labour market. Patriarchal relations, far from being atavistic leftovers, rapidly outmoded by capitalism as the early Marxists suggested, have survived and thrived alongside it (p. 12).

The academic analyses of women's work tied to the dual systems model were heavily linked to marxist feminist activism regarding women's oppression through unpaid work and through familial structures. It was as a result of both the activism and the analysis that women's demands for paid housework began to form (Luxton, 2006). Again, there is a serious difference between the previous NHE attempts to incorporate women's work and the reproductive sphere. While the NHE did make women and the reproductive sphere subjects of analysis, it was largely written and proposed by men and it ultimately advocated the status quo. The dual systems approach, however, involved women and advocated the recognition of and remuneration for women's work. This was an immensely important step but it still relied heavily on the older marxist notions of who benefits from women's housework. In recognising women's work as 'real work', which should be waged, many marxist feminists couched the issue as one of women working (and creating surplus value) for capitalism, overlooking the fact that women also work for the benefit of individual men (Waring, 1988; see also Chapter 18). As a result, this often appears to be a replication of marxist analyses of women's work, which, in Hartmann's (1979) terms, "give no clues about why *women* are subordinate to *men* inside and outside the family and why it is not the other way around. *Marxist categories, like capital itself are sex-blind*" (p. 13).

To try and solve the apparent impasse between feminist and marxist understandings, the production/reproduction split was introduced as a basis for further analysis. In looking at issues such as housework, reproduction and child-rearing, marxist feminists suggested that there needed to be two separate systems of thought. Mitchell (1973), for example, stated that the analysis needed to be separated into "two autonomous areas: the economic mode of capitalism and the ideological mode of patriarchy" (p. 92). Hartmann (1979) herself suggested a more complex relationship of "patriarchal capitalism" or "capitalist patriarchy", but ultimately the dual systems approach continued to propose a "marriage", albeit one that by the 1980s was recognised as an unhappy one.

Despite these problems, the dual systems model is still widely used (Luxton, 2006). Luxton (2006) suggests that its continuing appeal is in the introduction and acknowledgement of the sphere of reproduction which accounts for what is seemingly "an empirical reality":

> In almost every society, at least two dominant genders, feminine and masculine, are recognised and anchored by divisions of labour in which specific work is associated with one to the exclusion of the other, where women are typically responsible for childcare and much of the work related to feeding, clothing and caring for people... (p. 26).

The acknowledgement of this common split in the division of labour between the productive and the reproductive, however, can be seen as being enshrined through dual systems theory rather than undermined by it. This issue is still debated today, some thirty years after the publication of Hartmann's paper. In "Something Old, Something New: Lingering Moments in the Unhappy Marriage of Marxism and Feminism", for example, McLaughlin (2002) writes that in the dual systems model: "Marxism takes care of the public world of economics and feminism takes care of the private world of the family, reproduction and sexuality, thus reinforcing the dominant ideological construction of the public/private dichotomy" (p. 32). It was recognition of these ongoing issues with dual systems theory that led many marxist feminists toward the more complex and inclusive concept of social reproduction.

Social Reproduction

The concept of social reproduction is more integrated and all encompassing than the earlier reproductive sphere of dual systems analysis. Rather than focusing only on the material labour involved in housework and child-rearing, social reproduction includes a greater acknowledgement of the symbolic processes that are required to reproduce human beings over time (Sen, 1996) and the intimate links and crossovers between what is seen as 'productive' and what is seen as 'reproductive'. In its earliest formations social reproduction was not an explicitly feminist concept (Dickinson and Russell, 1986), but it has been frequently amended and is now most often used by feminists in an attempt to have reproductive labour recognised in IPE and even to reorient IPE altogether. Like dual systems theory, the use of social reproduction as a concept has developed largely through marxist feminism and the concept of social reproduction is often closely associated with a particular brand of materialist feminism (Luxton, 2006).

Social reproduction is variously defined by different authors writing in the field of IPE and a precise definition remains elusive. Initially social reproduction was recognised, stemming from marxism, as processes involved in reproducing the labour force. One of the earliest references to social reproduction in the IPE literature, which reflects this initial conception, appears in the *Family Economy and State* (1986), edited by Dickinson and Russell. The authors explain that the fledgling social reproduction literature takes:

> [T]he dominant relationship of our time — the wage labour/capital relationship, as its principal object of analysis and considers the institutions, mechanisms and processes associated with the economic, social, political and ideological reproduction of this relationship (p. 1).

They suggest that consideration of social reproduction is especially important due to the 'failure' of mainstream political economy to consider issues of reproduction. They also acknowledge that feminist research had played "a critical role in redressing the limitations of both traditional political economy and the conventional sociology of the family…" (p. 4). Their definition of social reproduction was not a feminist one, however.

Writing only a few years later, feminist sociologists Laslett and Brenner (1989) provided one of the first and most thorough definitions of social reproduction from a feminist perspective. Laslett and Brenner noted that the use of the concept 'social reproduction' by (primarily marxist) feminists came about as a result of the perceived failings of marxism and the dual systems model to fully explain the enormity of women's unpaid labour and its repercussions. They gave a broad but detailed description of what social reproduction entails:

> [F]eminists use social reproduction to refer to the activities and attitudes, behaviors and emotions, responsibilities and relationships directly involved in the maintenance of life on a daily basis, and intergenerationally. Among other things, social reproduction includes how food, clothing and shelter are made available for immediate consumption, the ways in which the care and socialisation of children are provided, the care of the infirm and elderly, and the social organisation of sexuality. Social reproduction can thus be seen to include various kinds of work — mental, manual, and emotional — aimed at providing the historically and socially, as well as biologically, defined care necessary to maintain existing life and to reproduce the next generation (p. 383).

It is the focus on the reproduction and maintenance of life on both a daily and intergenerational basis that has become a mainstay of many definitions of social reproduction (Luxton, 2006). It is also the focus on the maintenance and reproduction of life that has led some scholars to believe that if social reproduction became widely used in IPE it could better account for women's politico-economic role. This is a theme, for example, in Picchio's (1992) work on social reproduction. Picchio critiques the narrowness of rationalist/liberalist economics and puts forward the inclusion of social reproduction as a possible way of recognising women's work and broadening current politico-economic analyses. She states: "My approach...permits the inclusion of the process of social reproduction in the general analytical framework of political economy: reproduction in all its aspects, is the touchstone of my criticism of the narrowness of modern economics..." (p. 1). She does also note, however, that it is not simply enough to add social reproduction to existing theories. It is also necessary to revalue women's work and the reproductive sphere.

Other scholars have taken the implications of social reproduction further and called for the complete reorientation of IPE and of orthodox rationalist/liberalist economics. Nelson (1993), for example, argues that the productive/reproductive split is a manifestation of the Cartesian split and as such has allowed the overlooking of "nature, childhood, bodily needs and human connectedness..." (p. 26) in favour of a "masculinist and separative view of the world" (p. 33). She suggests that in making the detached individual the centre of analysis, orthodox rationalist/liberalist economics overlooks the material reality of "real persons in the real world" (p. 26). Nelson puts forward instead that rationalist/liberalist economics should focus first and foremost on the provisioning of human life, not the nature of individual choice with regard to conditions of scarcity. As will be discussed in the next section, however, this radical approach is relatively rare for those advocating a social reproduction model. While there have been significant gains in recognising women's work, through incorporating reproduction into IPE, there are also significant limitations to this approach.

THE LIMITS OF (SOCIAL) REPRODUCTION

From a feminist perspective the dual systems and social reproduction models represent a significant step forward from the biologically determinist NHE. It was immensely important to put forward a social constructionist model for understanding women's work and its relationship to women's oppression. It was also important to push for the recognition of women's work in mainstream IPE. The reproductive approaches (both dual systems and social reproduction) have offered ways forward in this regard. There are, however, limitations to the reproductive approaches. These include the continuing focus on capitalism, the reduction of women's experiences to (rationalist/liberalist) economics, the disappearance of biological reproduction, and the continuation of the 'add women and stir' approach, which ultimately results in a failure to recognise the radical nature of critiques from the margins.

The Focus on Capitalism

Most proponents of the social reproduction model do not advocate a radical rewriting of IPE. For instance, Bezanson and Luxton (2006), in their introduction to one of the few feminist collections that does explicitly deal with social reproduction, claim only modest results for the concept, stating: "social reproduction builds on and deepens debate about domestic labour and women's economic role in capitalist societies" (p. 3). Unfortunately, this is a serious limitation on much of the writing that attempts to incorporate social reproduction. Firstly, the focus, as Bezanson and Luxton clearly point out, is still on capitalist societies, which is not surprising given the influence of marxist feminism on the development of the concept. While there can be little doubt that the influence of capitalism is felt in all corners of the globe, non-capitalist influences still exist (Peterson, 2003). This leaves a significant gap in understanding the sexual division of labour in non-capitalist societies and the way women's unpaid and/or unrecognised labour is exploited in non-capitalist systems. It also highlights a significant weakness in the social reproduction model as it similarly fails to recognise the similarities of women's oppression across capitalist and non-capitalist societies. Given that women's disadvantages due to the sexual division of labour are generally taken to be universal, it is problematic to provide a theory that only explains it in the capitalist context.

Moreover, some authors seem determined to ignore the possible integration of other analyses of women's oppression, such as ones that highlight patriarchy, which further limits the scope for approach. For example, in Luxton's (2006) historical overview of the concept of social reproduction, she explicitly rejects patriarchy as an analytical tool, doing away with it in a few lines by citing decades-old research which suggests that the concept often relies on notions of men's innate need for power (p. 27). This is a common misrepresentation of the concept of patriarchy, which is often used interchangeably by radical feminists with the term "male dominance" (Thompson, 2001). Radical feminism and the use of the term patriarchy are steeped in a tradition of social constructivism (Thompson, 2001) that certainly does not advocate the idea that male dominance is a result of men's innate need for power. To reject engagement with the concept of patriarchy on this basis is not only convenient but also misleading. Sweeping aside the radical feminist critiques of women's oppression leaves a much clearer path for a marxist analysis. Rather than overcoming the problems involved in the dual systems model, the social reproduction approach at times seems to replicate them. Luxton's version of a single integrated system of social reproduction looks a lot like a marxist approach that has simply added women.

There is another significant replication of the problems with the dual systems model in the social reproduction literature and that is in regard to the production/reproduction split itself. While there can be little doubt that many authors seek to value women's work, and in Picchio's words, "reverse the priorities in favour of reproduction", the concept of social reproduction does continue to split the world into two spheres: "productive" and "reproductive". It does not often fundamentally challenge their separation in the first place. Consequently, like the dual systems model, the social reproduction approach can be seen to reinforce the distinction between the two spheres rather than fundamentally undermine it. Indeed, the varied attempts to account for women's "reproductive labour" can all be seen as problematic in this way and there is a real need to continue to think through the ways in which these spheres are actually overlapping and interconnected (Peterson, 2003).

Furthermore, reinforcing the productive/reproductive split is not only an analytical issue. The continuing distinction between men's and women's work and the push for reproductive labour to be recognised as 'real work' has had unfortunate, if unintended, consequences. As Young (2001) notes, the discourse around housework changed in the 1970s. While "[t]he initial demand was to call on men to share equally the burden of housework and childcare" (p. 319), the argument became reduced to one of wages for housework. As a result there has been very little change in the gendered distribution of housework. Even as women have entered the paid workforce in greater and greater numbers, the hours men spend on unpaid work in the home "have changed very little and show little variation internationally..." (p. 319). Instead, Young argues, professional women in the West are increasingly hiring migrant women to perform domestic labour.

This shift to paid migrant labour has had two particularly illuminating consequences. Firstly, despite the fact that what was once *unpaid labour* in the home has become *paid labour* the status of the work has not risen. So while it may now be easier to show that women's labour in the home is 'work' (as it can be remunerated) it remains undervalued 'women's work'. Secondly, as a result of this trend, "[w]e are witnessing in virtually all industrial countries a new redistribution of housework and caring work which no longer counts on males to change their behaviour" (Young, 2001, p. 319). Thus recognising women's labour as 'work' has not undermined the gendered division of labour at all. It has, in some cases, simply moved the labour from being unpaid work carried out by wives to paid work carried out by female maids. Part of the problem with the reproductive approaches, then, is that they can overlook the fundamental undervaluing of women's work. Simply moving the work from the paid to the unpaid spheres does not result in greater status and does not disrupt the gendered division of labour. From a radical feminist perspective, this limitation arises because marxist approaches do not consider women's oppression as the primary problem (Waring, 1988). That is, women's work is undervalued precisely because women perform it, not because it has been historically unpaid.

IS LABOUR ALWAYS WORK?

The reduction of women's labour in the home to 'work' highlights a larger issue within the reproductive literature. While it has been an important step to recognise what women do within the family as 'real work', rather than viewing it as unproductive, this still holds the experience of labour in the home to an implicitly male standard of what work happens to be. It does not allow women's experiences to define the terms of the debate but rather argues for the recognition of women on the basis of their (our) importance to the (male defined) economic system.

This issue is particularly obvious in non-feminist attempts to recognise reproduction. For example, Seccombe in *A Millennium of Family Change* (1992) writes that marxists have overlooked the importance of "the daily rejuvenation and generational replacement" of labour power, that is, social reproduction. He states that this exclusion of reproduction in marxist theory has "made it almost impossible to see families, as labour teams, pumping the lifeblood through socioeconomic systems" (p. 11). While it is true that the reproductive sphere is often overlooked, it is very narrow to suggest that the family should instead be primarily understood as an economic unit or labour team propping up the political economy. There is an important difference between exposing the formal market economy's reliance on women's unpaid and domestic labour, as Mies (1998 [1986]) does, for example, and suggesting that because the formal market economy relies on women's unpaid and domestic labour, the best way to understand this labour is therefore is in terms of its contribution to the formal market economy. There is often more to women's unpaid labour than simply 'work' and this is particularly apparent in regard to women's emotional labour.

Women's accounts of reproductive labour in the home do not suggest that they (we) experience a feeling of being part of a 'labour team', or that they (we) necessarily conceive of themselves (ourselves) raising children just to supply labour power (Smart, 2000). The understanding of reproductive labour offered in conceptions of social reproduction is therefore only a partial one. Much like the NHE, this vision of the family as a politico-economic unit does not fully account for the significant power differentials between men and women within the institution of the family. Nor does it account for women's emotional connection to household and family members or the influence this may have on women's continued performance of unpaid labour in the home (Smart, 2000).

In the long list of labour types that are frequently given under the banner of social reproduction, emotional labour — or what is sometimes referred to as "caring work" — is often included. But reducing such caring and emotional experiences to 'work' is intensely problematic. Women do not only experience their labour in the home as 'work', they (we) often feel emotionally connected to others and honour those emotional connections though action (England, 1993; Smart, 2000). The self in this version of labour, based on women's experiences, is much more relational than the separative-self assumed in much mainstream market and IPE literature (England, 1993). The mix of women's subordination within the family and culturally constructed norms of emotional attachment mean that a purely market-centred reading of women's labour in the home distorts women's experiences. A purely market-centred reading also fails to explain why women continue performing labour which is undervalued and unremunerated. It is therefore important to make room for the idea that not all forms of labour are necessarily best understood as 'work'.

The Disappearance of Biological Reproduction

Another limitation on the reproductive approaches is the neglect of biological reproduction as an issue. This, too, relates to the reduction of labour to 'work'. While there is considerable discussion about what constitutes social reproduction and how the processes of social reproduction are carried out, there is very little discussion about how biological reproduction plays a role. Indeed, it is striking to discover how often the issue of biological reproduction is left out of feminist politico-economic work. For instance, in *Out of the Margin: Feminist Perspectives on Economics* (1995), edited by Kuiper and Sap, there is only one mention of biological reproduction and that is in relation to the NHE (p. 20). Other texts, however, do briefly acknowledge biological reproduction in the context of the reproductive approaches. They do not analyse it in any detail, however. Peterson's *A Critical Rewriting of Global Political Economy* (2003) is a good example. In her section on the reproductive political economy she states that activities previously considered "non-waged and private" are now being commodified and consequently drawn into the public sphere. The list of such activities includes: "sexual relations, biological and social reproduction, leisure activities, household maintenance..." (p. 78). There is at least a mention here of biological reproduction, though there is no explanation of how it relates to social reproduction or the consequences of it being commodified. The same gap exists in the Bezanson and Luxton collection *Social Reproduction: Feminist Political Economy Challenges Neo-liberalism* (2006). Some contributors do mention that social reproduction may include "the work involved in biological reproduction" (Braedley, 2006, p. 216) but the focus of the book, like much of the work on social reproduction, is on housework and child-rearing.

The disappearance of biological reproduction leaves a significant gap in the reproductive literature. There is a focus on the "outsourcing" of household labour and migrant women performing nanny and maid roles in the West (Young, 2001) but there appears to have been less concern regarding the "outsourcing" of pregnancy itself. This lack of discussion is especially striking given the rise in surrogacy contracts (Spar, 2006). In *The Baby Business* (2006) Spar, a Harvard Business School scholar, tracks the surge in surrogacy toward the end of the twentieth century and its boom into the new millennium. She states that by the end of the twentieth century a mix of technology, commercial enterprise, and changing norms created a "vibrant, albeit controversial, market for motherhood" (p. 74). Spar also notes that as the commercial surrogacy market was taking off in the US there were vocal feminist critics of the practice. One of the most prominent was Gena Corea. In 1987 she proclaimed that: "The rise of the surrogate industry does not take place in isolation. It is part of the industrialisation of reproduction. It is part of the opening up of the reproductive supermarket" (Corea, quoted in Spar, 2006, p. 77).

As the market for surrogate mothers has continued to grow and spread trans-nationally, the critiques have continued. In *Women as Wombs* (1994), for example, a radical feminist writes of the trafficking in women for the purposes of breeding. She states:

> Reproductive contracts and techniques, such as surrogate arrangements, have also created a *national traffic* in women exploited for their reproductive faculties and functions. Literally, this is a system in which women are moveable property, objects of exchange...Surrogate contracts...are reproductive purchase orders where women are *procured* as instruments in a system of breeding (Raymond, 1994, p. xxii).

Raymond also explains that this should not be seen as a regular form of labour for hire. To suggest that surrogacy is akin to a normal contract for labour ignores the emotional, psychological and material realities of the situation women face in giving up the inside of their body to bear a child for somebody else. These realities are difficult for the literature on social reproduction to incorporate. If reproduction is a form of labour that should be recognised as 'real work' and therefore waged, it becomes difficult to recognise the exploitation involved in commercial surrogacy. That is, with the insistence in the social reproduction literature that the problem with 'women's work' is that it is unremunerated and not recognised as work, then commercial surrogacy may look like an improvement. Commercial surrogacy, however, as Raymond and Corea point out, tends not just to be the procuring of labour but the exploitation of women's bodies.

Part of the problem is that the contention that all labour is work also tends to overlook the differences between types of labour. Surrogacy, in the all-labour-equals-work model, becomes seen as contracted labour no different from factory work or even housekeeping. Such notions tend to rely on the assumption that women 'own' their bodies and are free to sell them. The difficulty is, as philosophy and law professor Allen (1988) has argued in regard to prostitution, women's relationship to their bodies is not simply one of ownership: "Women are their bodies. They do not own them" (Allen, 1988, p. 171). This is not to say that women should be reduced to bodies, but that there needs to be an understanding that women do actually inhabit their bodies. As Pateman (1988) argues, "There is an integral relationship between the body and the self. The body and the self are not identical, but selves are inseparable from bodies" (p. 204). The reproductive literature fails to take this relationship into account. Indeed, it fails to distinguish between different kinds of work or identify activities that are not ideally classed as work in the first place. As a result the reproductive literature fails to acknowledge how fundamentally women's experiences challenge the dominant politico-economic models and the prevailing wisdom of mainstream IPE.

Women's Experiences and the Radical Critique from the Margins

It is difficult to simply add the issue of women's labour to the existing non-feminist IPE literature. This is because women's experiences challenge many of the fundamental concepts of orthodox IPE. It is now rather common for feminists to decry the 'add women and stir' approach, which categorised the early and frequently shallow attempts at making women visible in the discipline (Ferber and Nelson, 1993). Unfortunately, many of the current attempts to account for women and women's labour, including the reproductive approaches, can be seen as an extension of the 'add women' theme. Attempts to truly rewrite IPE, with underlying assumptions and critical concepts that reflect women's experiences, rather than trying to fit these into existing approaches that rely on implicit male assumptions, are few and far between. It remains critically important, however, that feminists continue to highlight how radically women's experiences from the margins undermine orthodox approaches to IPE.

The issue of distorting women's experiences to make them fit pre-existing perspectives is highlighted well in Luxton's (2006) discussion of the problematic use of the term 'domestic labour'. As she states:

> If a working class woman does certain tasks in her own home for her family, she is doing unpaid, non-market domestic labour that contributes to the production and reproduction of labour on a daily and generational basis. If she does the same tasks in someone else's home for pay, she is a paid employee or wage labourer. The distinction lies in the social relations of work, not in the tasks themselves or the physical or emotional exertions of the worker (p. 34).

Indeed, this is a central problem. The distinction here exists due to prior formulations of the nature of 'work' based on the model of the male waged labourer (McLaughlin, 2002). The distinction is not based on the actual experiences of the women involved. This makes it difficult to expose and explain the continuity of the work, regardless of whether a wife or a maid performs it. It also makes it difficult to highlight how undervalued the work continues to be, regardless of a wage. If the paid/unpaid work distinction remains primary, then such examples are a continuation of the 'add women' approach. If women's experiences were made primary then the distinction, however, would look different.

Women's experiences also challenge much more deeply held assumptions and distinctions in IPE. As England (1993) argues, focusing on making women and women's experiences visible forces analysts to question concepts such as the individual, the social contract, and personal autonomy (Pateman, 1988). For example, England states that early writers in both politics and economics did not recognise that "men are *not* entirely autonomous — that no man would have survived to adulthood but for the altruistic work of a woman..." (England, 1993, p. 40). Similarly Runyan (1997), in the epigraph to this chapter, mentions the way in which the biological reproduction of people is completely written out of mainstream IPE. She also notes that:

> In order to discount economic relations of reciprocity, (neo)classical economists and political economists have advanced a notion of human nature that discounts care and social need as motivating factors and elevates exchange and profit as the only animating forces that compel economic activity (p. 84).

A feminist approach that attempts to account for these factors is therefore very threatening to many of the closely held assumptions that underlie mainstream IPE. Moreover, as the vast majority of feminists (from all branches of feminism) are social constructionists (Ferber and Nelson, 1993), the notion that there is an over-riding or biologically determined human nature is one that is typically rejected. Trying to account for relational selves, emotional connections, and behaviour determined by context, vastly complicates and perhaps even overturns much of mainstream IPE, and especially the form it takes when articulated in rationalist/liberalist, economic/market terms.

CONCLUSION

One way forward, as mentioned earlier, is Nelson's (1993) conception of reorienting political economics to focus on "the provisioning of life, that is, on the commodities and processes necessary to human survival…" (p. 32). After all, any vision of politico-economic interaction must consider humans in relation to the social world and take into account issues such as human connectedness. Runyan (1997), however, goes further. She says that:

> The masculinist-economistic basis of IPE prevents it from acknowledging that all manner of physical, social and spiritual needs and desires cannot be reduced to nor fulfilled by the machinations of states and markets. Mutual respect, care, and welfare can only arise through struggles for non-hierarchical social relations (p. 89).

If this is the case, then acknowledging and accounting for women's experiences, while important, is not enough. There needs to be a conscious activism behind the feminist engagement with IPE that not only challenges IPE's assumptions but also pushes (in gender terms) for a more equitable world.

REFERENCES

Allen, A (1988). *Uneasy Access: Privacy for Women in a Free Society.* Totowa NJ: Rowman and Littlefield.

Bezanson, K and M Luxton (2006). Social Reproduction and Feminist Political Economy. In *Social Reproduction: Feminist Political Economy Challenges Neo-liberalism*, K Bezanson and M Luxton (eds.). Montreal: McGill-Queens University Press.

Becker, G (1993 [1981]). *A Treatise on the Family.* Cambridge MA: Harvard University Press.

Braedley, S (2006). Someone to Watch Over You: Gender, Class and Social Reproduction. In *Social Reproduction: Feminist Political Economy Challenges Neo-liberalism*, K Bezanson and M Luxton (eds.). Montreal: McGill-Queens University Press.

Cook, J and J Roberts (2000). Towards a Gendered Political Economy. In *Towards a Gendered Political Economy*, J Cook, J Roberts and G Waylen (eds.). London: MacMillan.

Cohen, B (2008). *International Political Economy: An Intellectual History.* Princeton NJ, Princeton University Press.

Dickinson, J and B Russell (eds.) (1986). *Family Economy and State: The Social Reproduction Process under Capitalism.* Beckenham, UK: Croom Helm.

England, P (1993). The Separative Self: Androcentric Bias in Neoclassical Assumptions. In *Beyond Economic Man: Feminist Theory and Economics*, M Ferber and J Nelson (eds.). London: University of Chicago Press.

Enloe, C (1989). *Bananas, Beaches and Bases: Making Feminist Sense of International Relations.* London: Pandora.

Ferber, M and J Nelson (1993). The Social Construction of Economics and the Social Construction of Gender. In *Beyond Economic Man: Feminist Theory and Economics*, M Ferber and J Nelson (eds.). London: University of Chicago Press.

Frieden, J and D Lake (eds.) (2003). *International Political Economy: Perspectives on Global Power and Wealth.* London: Taylor and Francis.

Gardiner, J (2000). Gender and the Family in the Formation of Human Capital. In *Towards a Gendered Political Economy*, J Cook, J Roberts and G Waylen (eds.). London: MacMillan.

Gilman, C (1900). *Women and Economics: A Study of the Economic Relation Between Men and Women as a Factor in Social Evolution.* Boston: Small, Maynard & Co.

Hartmann, H (1979). The Unhappy Marriage of Marxism and Feminism: Towards a More Progressive Union, *Capital and Class*, 3(2), 1–33.

Humphries, J (2000). Rational Economic Families? Economics, the Family and the Economy. In *Towards a Gendered Political Economy*, J Cook, J Roberts and G Waylen (eds.). London: MacMillan.

Kuiper, E and J Sap (eds.) (1995). *Out of the Margin: Feminist Perspectives on Economics.* London: Routledge.

Laslett, B and J Brenner (1989). Gender and Reproduction: Historical Perspectives, *Annual Review of Sociology*, 15, 381–404.

Luxton, M (2006). Feminist Political Economy in Canada and the Politics of Social Reproduction. In *Social Reproduction: Feminist Political Economy Challenges Neo-liberalism*, K Bezanson and M Luxton (eds.). Montreal: McGill-Queens University Press.

MacKinnon, C (2006). *Are Women Human? And Other International Dialogues.* London: Harvard University Press.

McLaughlin, L (2002). Something Old, Something New: Lingering Moments in the Unhappy Marriage of Marxism and Feminism. In *Sex and Money: Feminism and Political Economy in the Media*, E Meehan and E Roidan (eds.). Minneapolis, University of Minnesota Press.

Mies, M (1998 [1986]). *Patriarchy and Accumulation on a World Scale: Women in the International Division of Labour.* Melbourne: Spinifex Press.

Mitchell, J (1973). *Woman's Estate.* New York: Vintage books.

Nelson, J (1993). The Study of Choice or the Study of Provisioning? Gender and the Definition of Economics. In *Beyond Economic Man: Feminist Theory and Economics*, M Ferber and J Nelson (eds.). London: University of Chicago Press.

Pateman, C (1988). *The Sexual Contract.* Cambridge MA: Polity.

Peterson, V S (2003). *A Critical Rewriting of Global Political Economy: Integrating Reproductive, Productive, and Virtual Economies.* New York: Routledge.

Picchio, A (1992). *Social Reproduction: The Political Economy of the Labour Market.* Cambridge UK: Cambridge University Press.

Ravenhill, J (2008). *Global Political Economy*, 2nd ed. New York: Oxford University Press.

Raymond, J (1994). *Women as Wombs: Reproductive Technologies and the Battle over Women's Freedom.* Melbourne: Spinifex Press.

Runyan, A (1997). Of Markets and Men: The (Re)making(s) of IPE. In *Constituting International Political Economy*, K Butch and R Denemark (eds.). London: Lynne Rienner Publishers.

Seccombe, W (1992). *A Millennium of Family Change: Feudalism to Capitalism in North-Western Europe.* New York: Verso.

Sen, G (1996). Gender, markets and states: A selective review and research agenda. *World Development*, 24(5), 821–829.

Smart, C (2000). New Dimensions to Gendered Power Relations in Families. In *Towards a Gendered Political Economy*, J Cook, J Roberts and G Waylen (eds.). London: MacMillan.

Spar, D (2006). *The Baby Business: How Money, Science and Politics Drive the Commerce of Conception.* Boston: Harvard Business School Press.

Thompson, D. (2001). *Radical Feminism Today.* Sydney, Gorgon's Head Press.

Walby, S (2000). The Restructuring of the Gendered Political Economy: Transformations in Women's Employment. In *Towards a Gendered Political Economy*, J Cook, J Roberts and G Waylen (eds.). London: MacMillan.

Waring, M (1988). *If Women Counted: A New Feminist Economics.* San Francisco: Harper and Row.

Waylen, G (2000). Gendered Political Economy and Feminist Analysis. In *Towards a Gendered Political Economy*, J Cook, J Roberts and G Waylen (eds.). London: Macmillan.

Waylen, G (2006). You Still Don't Understand: Why Troubled Engagements Continue between Feminists and (Critical) IPE, *Review of International Studies*, 32(1), 145–164.

Young, B (2000). Globalisation and Gender: A European Perspective. In *Gender, Globalisation and Democratisation*, R M Kelly, J Bayes, M Hawkesworth and B Young (eds.). New York: Rowman and Littlefield.

Young, B (2001). The 'Mistress' and the 'Maid' in the Globalised Economy, *The Socialist Register*, 37, 315–327.

Part Six

The Global Environment

CHAPTER 20

The Global Environment: An Overview

Loren R. Cass

College of the Holy Cross

The environment arguably lies at the core of international political economy (IPE) even though the fact often goes unacknowledged in mainstream IPE scholarship. The IPE literature tends to analyse the environment through an anthropogenic lens by focusing on the services that it provides to humans. From this perspective the environment fulfils two critical functions. It is both the source of the resources that drive the modern globalised politico-economic systems as well as a sink to absorb and process much of the waste that is generated as a side effect of global production and consumption. Both aspects of the environment are critical to the functioning of local, national, and international systems of production and consumption. For example, the fossil fuels that drive the global political economy are extracted from the environment, and when they are burned the carbon dioxide, sulphur oxides and nitrogen oxides that are created are released freely into the atmosphere where they contribute to climate change, acid rain, and smog. This is but one example of the intertwined relationship between the environment's role in the creation of value and the absorption of pollution. Mineral extraction and agricultural production also involve this relationship to the environment as a source of value and a sink for pollution. It is this dual role of the environment in relationship to international political economy that will be explored in this chapter.

While there are a wide range of issues that could be addressed in a chapter such as this, four important questions at the intersection of research related to global environmental politics and international political economy will provide a framework for further investigation. The first two questions to be examined relate to the sources of environmental challenges. First, on the consumption side, can the increasing extraction of raw materials and growing agricultural production, associated with the dramatic acceleration of economic development across much of the world, be sustained without undermining the ability of future generations to meet their needs? Second, on the production side, can the dramatic increase in waste generation, associated with extraction, processing, and the use of raw materials and final goods be managed effectively to prevent substantial harm to the environment and its ability to sustain life on earth? These two questions are derived from fundamental debates about sustainability (that is, the ability to 'meet present needs without compromising the ability of future generations to meet their needs'). These debates go to the heart of the structures of global political economy (WCED, 1987).

The questions surrounding sustainable development and growth inevitably lead to questions relating to how to deal with the challenges created by potential resource depletion and environmental degradation. For example, the character of many environmental problems necessitates government intervention in some form to address them. Therefore, the third question that will be addressed is whether the existing global politico-economic system is capable of effectively addressing growing problems related to resource extraction and pollution production?

Finally, while much of the IPE literature related to the environment focuses on the services provided to humans, within the literature on global environmental political economy, there is also frequently an understanding of the environment as having intrinsic value. The environment is not only valuable in so far as it provides services to humankind, but humans are only one small part of nature. From this perspective, humans have the potential to do irreparable damage to the planet and this could ultimately lead to the destruction not only of mankind but also of the ability of the earth to support the diversity of life that is on it today. These concerns have produced a radical critique of the existing globalised capitalist system, which leads to the fourth question that will be addressed. Is the existing globalised capitalist structure of the world political economy compatible with continued sustainability, or is it necessary to fundamentally alter the politico-economic structures to create a more sustainable system?

While this chapter offers few answers to these questions, it provides a foundation to begin to explore them and to understand the current state of the debates that surround them. These issues will be taken up in greater detail in the following three chapters.

WILL THE EARTH RUN OUT OF RESOURCES?

It is an empirical observation that the natural resources available on earth are finite. In theory, with the appropriate technologies (that do not currently exist), it should be possible to quantify all of the oil, coal, iron, rare-earth minerals, copper, and so on that are available on earth at a particular moment. It would seem only logical that the continued extraction of these resources will eventually lead to their depletion. This is the foundation of the debate surrounding 'peak oil' production or the point at which oil production will reach its greatest level, followed by a likely rapid decline in oil production and thus consumption. There is a lively debate, however, surrounding the question of whether the world will inevitably run out of oil or any other natural resource. This debate pits the resource optimists or 'cornucopians', who argue that the world will never run out of resources, against the pessimists or 'neo-Malthusians', who argue that increasing population and unsustainable consumption will necessarily deplete the world's resources with devastating environmental and human consequences.

The neo-Malthusian position is based on the predictions made at the turn of the nineteenth century by Thomas Malthus (1973 [1798]), that population growth necessarily outpaces the increased production of food thus creating a check on population through famine and disease. Modern neo-Malthusians, such as Paul and Anne Ehrlich (1990), extend this logic more broadly to the relationship between global population growth and the unsustainable use of the earth's resources. The neo-Malthusian argument is that increased population growth and associated consumption must inevitably lead to over-exploitation and the depletion of resources, which will produce crises of food production and energy shortages — along with the depletion of a vast range of natural resources — and have devastating environmental consequences.

The cornucopian position, as most prominently articulated by Simon (1981; 1998), offers a counter-intuitive argument that resources will never run out. The cornucopian argument centres on two forces: those of the market and those of human ingenuity. From this perspective the resource itself is unimportant. What is important is the service that the resource provides. Oil is only important as a source of energy for transportation or electricity generation or as an input into the production of synthetic materials. It is only these services that oil provides that make it valuable. The market then becomes the critical variable in sending signals about how resources should be used. As demand increases relative to the available supply, prices rise. As prices rise, the market triggers an attempt to find ways to conserve the resource, to find more of it, or to find alternative sources of the service that that resource provides. From the cornucopian perspective, human ingenuity has throughout history always found solutions to shortages and there is no reason to expect that this will not continue. Oil will not run out because as its price increases, oil that currently is not commercially viable to extract, such as oil in sands in Canada, will become viable, or new technologies will likely be developed to extract oil more efficiently from existing sources. Alternatively, more fuel efficient vehicles will be produced and/or oil's use in transportation will be curtailed through the substitution of alternative energy sources such as ethanol or electricity or mass transportation systems. Oil will then only be used in processes where alternatives may not be available at the existing price.

Historically, cornucopian predictions have held up very well. The prices of most raw materials have largely remained constant or declined in real terms (Cashin and McDermott, 2002). Market forces and technological innovation have been sufficient to address any shortages that have arisen. Improvements in extraction, more efficient use, and recycling have largely driven down the long-term price of most commodities.

Critics of the cornucopian position, however, such as Homer-Dixon (1991), argue that the world today is fundamentally different. In the past, shortages emerged slowly and in only one or two commodities at a time. With the dramatic increase in the global population, combined with the rapid growth of China, India, Brazil and other emerging economies and the associated increases in food demand and resource consumption, however, resources are being depleted at an ever-accelerating rate. Shortages are thus likely to occur rapidly and simultaneously across a wide range of resources. Furthermore, the decline in resources and in the availability of food will impoverish vast parts of humanity, dramatically undermine the political stability of states, and foster resource competition and conflict, thus complicating the ability of markets to respond effectively to shortages.

At its core, the debate between neo-Malthusians and cornucopians is about whether the past should be viewed as a good guide to the future. Does the fact that market signals and human ingenuity have largely been able to address problems of shortages in the past mean that it is inevitable that humans will solve these problems moving into the future? Or is the world today fundamentally different from that of the past?

WILL POLLUTION OVERWHELM THE ABILITY OF THE EARTH TO ABSORB IT?

It is important to note the fundamental structure of most international environmental pollution problems which makes them difficult to resolve.

There are two basic types of international environmental problems: 'upstream/downstream' ones and 'global commons' ones. The critical distinction between the two types of problems is the degree to which those facing the consequences of environmental degradation are also the perpetrators of the problem (Mitchell, 2010, pp. 33–34).

In an 'upstream/downstream' problem, such as the discharge of pollutants into a river in one country flowing into a second country, the perpetrators of the environmental problem may not face the consequences of their actions. The upstream state can freely dump pollution into the river, while the downstream state faces the primary consequences. The same logic applies to the transboundary flow of air pollutants. The problem in such situations is that the upstream state faces few incentives to address the problem and the downstream state has little leverage to force the upstream state to alter its behaviour.

Upstream/downstream issues are typically bilateral or regional in nature. They will thus normally be addressed at this level rather than at a global level. There have been many relatively successful agreements by states to manage regional seas, riparian pollution, and trans-border flows of air pollution, but the successes are matched by an even greater number of similar environmental problems that continue to languish. The ability to deal with these types of problems largely depends upon broader regional, political and economic structures. In regions with growing political and economic integration, such as the European Union, there has been much more success in addressing regional problems like acid rain and water pollution alongside trade, financial, and migration issues. In regions with less developed regional political and economic structures, however, like East Asia, progress has been much slower. It would appear that progress on these issues is likely be achieved only when the broader politico-economic context creates greater incentives for regional cooperation across a range of issues and not just environmental ones (Mitchell, 2010, pp. 120–121).

The issues to do with the 'global commons' are slightly different (Hardin, 1968). Much of nature is held in common by all humankind. No one owns the atmosphere or international waters. It is a common space available to everyone. Because no one owns the atmosphere or the oceans, they can be utilised freely as 'sinks' for pollutants. The resources of the oceans, such as fish stocks and whales, are also available freely for appropriation by anyone with the means to gain access to them.

In principle, perpetrators and victims are the same. Those who release carbon dioxide into the atmosphere face the consequences of climate change. Those who take the fish from the oceans also face the consequences of the depletion of fish stocks.

In practice, the fates of perpetrators and victims rarely align fully. For example, the small Pacific island state of Kiribati may cease to exist within sixty years as climate change produces rising sea levels, even though the people of Kiribati have contributed an infinitesimally small amount to the problem.

The distinction between perpetrator and victim is helpful, however, in thinking about how to address issues of the 'global commons'. Their solution is often to be found in the regulation of access to the relevant resource to assure its sustainable use over time. The most important global environmental problems today, including global warming, ozone depletion, biodiversity loss, and the depletion of fish and marine mammal stocks, embody the logic of the 'global commons'.

One of the issues that has both 'upstream/downstream' and 'global commons' components, at least as they relate to the international political economy, is that market prices frequently do not capture the full environmental cost of the production, consumption, and disposal of a good. The extraction and processing of raw materials, the generation of energy, the manufacture of goods, the disposal of goods, and the production of agricultural commodities, all have negative externalities that arise whenever a politico-economic transaction adversely affects people not involved in the transaction (Mitchell, 2010, p. 58).

In the case of environmental externalities, the environmental costs associated with an activity are not fully included in the price of the good. The inevitable effect (absent intervention by a higher authority or agreement by perpetrators) is over-consumption. For example, the burning of coal to produce electricity typically produces large amounts of sulphur oxides, which are released into the atmosphere. They then return to the earth as 'acid rain'. This leads to damage to buildings and public art, the reduced productivity of agricultural lands, and broader ecological damage. The costs associated with these effects are not captured in the price of the electricity generated by coal combustion. The owners of power plants face few incentives to reduce emissions because they do not bear the full consequences of their actions.

To the extent that the perpetrators and victims reside within the same country, it is possible for a government to create a regulatory system to balance the interests of the perpetrators and victims. In those cases where the victims and perpetrators are in different countries, addressing the problems involved requires cooperation across states and the likely creation of international agreements and associated organisations to address them. In an anarchic system like the contemporary one, which has no political authority higher than the state, it is difficult to induce cooperation and to force compliance with international agreements. The structure of the global politico-economic system and the incentive structures surrounding global environmental problems create profound difficulties for managing the environment's role as a sink for pollution or as a source for resources held in common.

Despite the difficulties associated with addressing global environmental problems, there is a lively debate surrounding the question of the relationship between globalisation and the environment (Clapp and Dauvergne, 2005; Stevis and Assetto, 2001). On the one side are those who argue that globalisation and the associated creation of wealth will generate the resources and the political will to tackle some of the most pressing environmental problems (Grossman and Krueger, 1995). On the other side are some of the neo-Malthusians discussed in the prior section who argue that globalisation only facilitates and exacerbates unsustainable levels of consumption (Rees, 2002; Lipschutz, 2004). The IPE literature tends to be dominated by market liberalists who argue that maximising wealth creation is the surest way to create the resources to achieve sustainable development. The global environmental politics literature, however, tends to focus more on the creation of international structures and rules to promote sustainable development. Both approaches tend to argue that there is a need for some form of international structure to manage global environmental problems — though they differ with regard to the types of structures they advocate.

CAN EXISTING INTERNATIONAL POLITICAL STRUCTURES EFFECTIVELY ADDRESS THE CHALLENGES TO THE GLOBAL ENVIRONMENT OR BE REFORMED TO ADDRESS THESE CHALLENGES?

Following World War Two, the US and its allies established a network of international organisations to help manage the global political economy and to promote global development and integration. The International Monetary Fund, the World Trade Organisation, and the World Bank served as the foundation of the post-war globalised politico-economic system. These organisations have been very successful in promoting globalisation. They were not created with a mandate to address global environmental problems, however. As a result, environmental issues largely languished internationally until the 1970s. Since then an increasingly dense web of international environmental agreements and associated organisations has been created alongside the global politico-economic ones. The United Nations Environment Programme, for example, currently supports the following international conventions and their secretariats: the Convention on Biological Diversity; the Convention on International Trade in Endangered Species; the Montreal Protocol on Substances that Deplete the Ozone Layer; the Convention on Migratory Species of Wild Animals; the Basel Convention on the Control of Transboundary Movements of Hazardous Wastes and their Disposal; the Stockholm Convention on Persistent Organic Pollutants; the United Nations Framework Convention on Climate Change; the Convention to Combat Desertification; as well as thirteen different programmes to do with regional seas. One thousand multilateral environmental agreements and over one thousand five hundred bilateral environmental agreements have been negotiated thus far (Mitchell, 2002–2011).

The effectiveness of these agreements and organisations varies. The Montreal Protocol on Substances that Deplete the Ozone Layer is widely viewed as a successful effort to address the problem of atmospheric ozone depletion. The various protocols under the Convention on Long-Range Transboundary Air Pollution have also significantly reduced the problems posed by acid rain in Europe. Efforts to address climate change, biodiversity loss, desertification, deforestation, and many bilateral and regional environmental problems, however, have been much less successful. The evidence related to the ability of the existing system of international governance to effectively address global environmental problems is mixed at best.

There are a large number of variables that influence the ability and willingness of states to address international environmental problems. The more significant the consequences of the environmental problem, for example, the more likely states are to take action to address it. As widespread evidence of the ecological damage from acid rain in Europe increased during the 1970s, the political momentum to act increased as well. The other side of this, however, was that where the politico-economic consequences of the policies necessary to address the environmental problem increased, the more difficult it became to achieve the agreement required to address the issue involved.

Addressing climate change will likely require dramatic reductions in the burning of fossil fuels and the development of alternative energies. At the moment, this appears to be very expensive and will arguably slow economic growth in many countries dramatically, which will generate opposition among affected interests in turn. The relative power status of countries in the environmental negotiations will significantly shape the outcome. Norway and Sweden led the early efforts to address acid rain in Europe, for example, but it was not until Germany began to press for an agreement that the negotiations achieved the momentum necessary to produce a binding agreement. The level of scientific uncertainty surrounding a problem will shape the political response as will the degree of public interest and the values that they bring to the issue. No two international environmental issues are identical in the mix of forces shaping their definition as problems and the subsequent international response. In almost all of these cases, the first step in addressing an emerging environmental issue is generating sufficient political will to overcome the collective action problem (Mitchell, 2010). All states will benefit from efforts to address common environmental problems, but all states would also prefer that other states bear the larger portion of responsibility for acting.

Climate change perhaps best illustrates some of the difficulties in addressing global environmental problems. It is an issue that is truly global in scope. All countries will face consequences from climate change, but the relative impact will vary substantially. All countries contribute to the problem but a small number of major states are responsible for the vast majority of greenhouse gas emissions. Policies to address climate change are predicted to have extensive politico-economic consequences, which results in a substantial controversy surrounding how to respond. The scientific understanding of climate change has evolved to the point where most scientists agree that anthropogenic climate change is occurring, but there is still significant debate surrounding the future pace of warming and the degree and timing of adverse effects associated with rising sea levels, shifts in regional rainfall patterns, and the intensity of storm activity. There is also significant debate surrounding potential feedback mechanisms that could radically accelerate warming at some point in the future. Is climate change linear in character, in which case warming will gradually increase over time (with associated negative effects)? Or will there be some future tipping point beyond which climate change could accelerate radically with dramatic and irreversible effects? Could the thawing of the Arctic permafrost, for example, release stored methane (a powerful greenhouse gas), which would result in rapid warming, with an accelerating loss of the Greenland and Antarctic glaciers and an associated rise in the level of the seas? These are some of the areas of uncertainty that continue to influence the climate debate.

The international response to climate change has been extremely controversial and slow in developing. The debate over how to respond to climate change reflects something of the neo-Malthusian versus cornucopian logics discussed above. Two recent studies reflect this debate.

On the neo-Malthusian side is the British government's Stern Review (2006). This argues that it is essential, based upon a cost-benefit analysis of climate change, that the world begin to devote one percent of global GDP to addressing climate change now to avoid the catastrophic effects of climate change in the future.

On the cornucopian side the Copenhagen Consensus Center (CCC), led by Bjørn Lomborg, has made a cost-benefit analysis addressing the same question and has determined that political leaders should divert only relatively modest amounts towards researching new energy technologies and geo-engineering strategies for addressing climate change at a future point in time (2004; 2010).

Both studies have included prominent political economists and have used similar methodologies, and yet they arrive at very different conclusions. What explains the difference in these outcomes?

Two critical differences in the assumptions that underpin them explain the different outcomes. Firstly, they utilise different assumptions about the social discount rate. The benefits of investments today to prevent future climate change will not be fully realised until the distant future. The question is how highly to value the benefits of less climate change in fifty or one hundred years relative to the alternative benefits that could flow from using those resources to address other problems today? This is a question of intergenerational justice. What does today's generation owe to future generations?

The Stern Review (2006) utilises a discount rate of almost zero. In other words, the assumption is made to value the benefits that accrue to future generations equally with the benefits that could be realised immediately.

The Copenhagen Consensus Center (Lomborg 2004; 2010) argues that a discount rate of four percent is more consistent with empirical economic research. With this discount rate, the CCC argues that it makes no sense to devote large sums to addressing climate change today. Instead, smaller amounts devoted to research and development would make more economic sense and would be more consistent with intragenerational justice. They would also address the need to meet the requirements of the disadvantaged today. Instead of devoting one percent of global GDP to addressing climate change, those resources could be used to reduce poverty, increase education funding, improve healthcare, build infrastructure in developing economies, or address a myriad of the other problems that dog the poor today. The CCC argues that the result would be future generations made much wealthier as a result of these investments made today. According to the CCC, future generations would also have more advanced technologies and would thus be able to address climate change at a much lower cost relative to the costs of any action today. From this perspective, it makes no sense to address climate change today.

There is one additional assumption that makes a significant difference in this debate. The Stern report assumes that the effects of climate change do not proceed along a linear path. As climate change continues, that is, it will reach a tipping point beyond which it will accelerate at a pace that will be unstoppable. With this assumption, it may not be possible to wait and effectively address climate change in the future. Beyond a future tipping point, any action to stem climate change may be impossible. The CCC assumes that action today and action in the future can be equally effective in addressing climate change. Depending on the assumptions that one builds into these analyses and the values that one brings to questions of inter- and intragenerational justice, it is possible to end up in very different positions on how to respond to climate change.

This debate illustrates why achieving international agreement is so difficult among countries seeking to protect the interests of their people and their industries. On the one hand rapidly developing countries such as China, India, and Brazil argue that the problem of climate change was created by the past emissions that produced the wealth found among the most developed states of the West. It would thus be unfair to force emerging economies to stem their growth to solve a problem of the West's making. On the other hand China is now the largest emitter of greenhouse gases (GHGs) and other emerging economies are dramatically increasing their contributions. A solution that does not include these states cannot adequately address the problem. The perpetrators of the problem are thus split on how to respond. Meanwhile, the greatest victims of the effects of climate change, such as the inhabitants of small island states, low-lying coastal regions, and subsistence farmers in areas facing desertification, are already feeling the consequences. Can the international politico-economic system effectively address this problem, or similar problems such as biodiversity loss, deforestation, and desertification?

There have certainly been long-running attempts to address climate change. The United Nations Framework Convention on Climate Change was created in 1992 to launch a process to address this problem. The Kyoto Protocol was signed in 1997 and came into force in 2005. It required states to meet specific emission reduction requirements. The US refused to ratify the protocol, however, and the emerging states are not bound by any commitments under the agreement. The requirements contained in the agreement also end in 2012 and there is not currently any agreement in place to extend the commitments it contains or to replace them with something else. The 2010 failure of negotiations in Copenhagen and the subsequent stalemate among the parties to these talks does not bode well for the future of climate negotiations.

While there has been a rapid proliferation of environmental agreements, one of the problems with global environmental governance has been that there is a bifurcation between international environmental and international politico-economic organisations. While there are obvious connections between them, the two types of organisations have largely been addressed separately. The international organisations with the greatest power and influence are primarily politico-economic in nature. The International Monetary Fund (IMF) and the World Trade Organisation (WTO) have the ability to significantly affect state behaviour. The IMF can influence state actions through the conditions that it places on states who borrow from the Fund. The WTO can authorise states to retaliate against partners that refuse to implement WTO rulings against them. In contrast, international environmental organisations and associated agreements rarely possess any enforcement mechanisms or provisions to punish states that do not fulfil their agreements (Clapp and Dauvergne, 2005).

In theory, it should be possible to merge elements of the international trade regime with international environmental agreements to improve the prospects for implementing policies to address environmental problems. The problem, however, is that the basic norms and rules of the international trade system actually create obstacles to achieving environmental objectives. The WTO, for example, permits countries to create product standards to achieve domestic environmental objectives. States cannot regulate process standards used in the production of goods, however, even if they are known to be harmful to the environment. Thus a country can require that all cars sold in the domestic market have catalytic converters to reduce air pollution but a country cannot require that foreign manufactured cars sold in their market be produced with systems to capture volatile organic compounds which are released during the painting of a car, even though such emissions are dangerous to humans and can harm water quality. There are many types of international environmental problems that can be addressed through trade restrictions. These are currently banned by international trade law, however.

There are significant questions surrounding whether the web of international organisations that deal with politico-economic and environmental problems are structured in a manner that could effectively address some of the most pressing global problems. While environmental issues have become a more frequent part of discussions within the WTO, the IMF, and the World Bank, none of these institutions or their member states appears to be prepared to force action to address environmental problems on a large scale. The questionable abilities of the existing international politico-economic structures to address the most pressing global environmental problems have produced calls for the creation of stronger international organisations to address environmental problems (Bierman, 2001) as well as more radical critiques of the system and its ability to create a sustainable global politico-economic order consistent with environmental protection.

IS THE EXISTING GLOBALISED CAPITALIST SYSTEM OF INTERNATIONAL POLITICAL ECONOMY CONSISTENT WITH SUSTAINABLE DEVELOPMENT?

Perhaps the most fundamental debate at the juncture of international political economy and global environmental politics relates to the question of whether the existing politico-economic system is or can be made consistent with the preservation of the earth and the achievement of sustainable growth into the future (Clapp and Dauvergne, 2005). This is a question that cannot be easily answered and is one that generates strong views on all sides. As with the other questions that have been examined in this chapter, there are numerous optimists who argue that the existing globalised capitalist system is perfectly compatible with the sustainable use of resources and the preservation of the environment, as well as numerous pessimists who argue that it is incapable of addressing the pressing environmental problems that the world faces today.

There are varied arguments about the ability of the existing system to manage the world's environmental political economy in a sustainable manner. For example, market liberalists argue that the path to a sustainable world requires improving the prosperity of all of the world's people to create the wealth and the political will to tackle environmental problems. The focus must be on freeing up the global market and permitting supply-and-demand forces to guide it along a more sustainable path (Clapp and Dauvergne, 2005, pp. 222–226). This is a position that dominates much of the IPE literature. Alternatively, Mol (2003) argues that an emerging normative focus on 'ecological modernisation' holds the potential to align politico-economic growth with environmental protection and sustainability. Supporters of the ecological modernisation perspective view politico-economic growth and development as fully compatible with achieving environmental sustainability. Self-interested actors will come to understand that resources must be used more sustainably and that this enlightened self-interest will produce the changes in behaviour that will align politico-economic growth with environmental quality preservation. Finally, institutionalists such as Bierman and Bauer (2005) argue that it is possible to reform the existing system to create a viable system of global environmental governance. Those who believe that the existing system can be maintained or reformed offer a broad range of views on the mechanisms through which the transition to sustainability will occur. Various authors have argued that the reforms will occur through government action, grassroots changes in values, enlightened self-interest among politico-economic actors, or market driven changes in behaviour. All of the perspectives, however, share a common belief that the existing politico-economic system is consistent with achieving environmental sustainability. The focus of this research is thus on how to encourage the necessary changes in global institutional structures and consumption patterns, and the development of the new technologies that will be necessary to move the global political economy onto a sustainable path.

There is also a wide range of critical voices who argue that the current international politico-economic system is fundamentally unsustainable and that only radical change can realign the system and make it sustainable. Daly (1973; 1996), for example, argues that we must achieve a 'steady-state' system where the number of humans and their associated resource usage are reduced to environmentally sustainable levels. This requires a fundamental movement away from the existing system's focus on constant growth as defined by ever rising consumption and expanding market activity. Most thinkers in this tradition advocate some form of population control to reduce and reverse population growth rates. In addition, most advocate a fundamental shift in popular culture and norms toward a more sustainable system that involves drastically reduced consumption patterns. Lipschutz (2004), for example, argues that the existing global politico-economic structures are fundamentally flawed because they result in the unsustainable use of resources. He calls for a radical reorientation of the system. There is significant debate surrounding whether this radical reform can be achieved through top-down changes led by government action, or whether they require fundamental shifts in grassroots values and behaviour, or both. There is disagreement, too, as to the strategies that can achieve the desired outcomes. Those who share this perspective concur in their assessment that the existing system is fundamentally flawed, however, and must be radically reformed. The question is how to initiate this reform.

These debates are ongoing and are unlikely to be resolved in the near future. Fundamentally, they reflect two different visions of the current global politico-economic system and its relationship to the global environment. The answer to this final question will ultimately determine whether the global politico-economic system as it exists today can be adapted to address the major problems posed by potential resource shortages and growing pollution problems, and whether a sustainable equilibrium can be achieved between the global political economy and the global environment.

CONCLUSION

This chapter has outlined some of the most important questions at the intersection between global environmental politics and the global political economy. These questions go to the heart of the sustainability of global political economy and the preservation of the environment. While the chapter offers few answers to these questions, it does offer a starting place with regard to where to begin. The next three chapters take up some of these issues and addresses them in greater depth.

REFERENCES

Biermann, F (2001). The emerging debate on the need for a world environment organisation, *Global Environmental Politics*, 1(1), 45–55.

Biermann, F and S Bauer (eds.) (2005). *A World Environment Organisation: Solution or Threat for Effective Environmental Governance?* Aldershot: Ashgate.

Cashin, P and C McDermott (2002). The long-run behavior of commodity prices: Small trends and big variability, *IMF Staff Papers*, 49(2), 175–199.

Clapp, J and P Dauvergne (2005). *Paths to a Green World: The Political Economy of the Global Environment*. Cambridge, MA: MIT Press.

Daly, H (1996). *Beyond Growth: The Economics of Sustainable Development*. Boston: Beacon Press.

Daly, H (1973). *Toward a Steady-State Economy*. San Francisco: W.H. Freeman.

Ehrlich, P and A Ehrlich (1990). *The Population Explosion*. London: Hutchinson.

Grossman, G and A Kreuger (1995). Economic growth and the environment, *Quarterly Journal of Economics*, 110(2), 353–377.

Hardin, G (1968). The tragedy of the commons, *Science*, 162, 1228–1248.

Homer-Dixon, T (1991). On the threshold: Environmental changes as causes of acute conflict, *International Security*, 16 (2), 76–116.

Lipschutz, R (2004). *Global Environmental Politics: Power, Perspectives, and Practice*. Washington, D.C.: CQ Press.

Lomborg, B (ed.) (2010). *Smart Solutions to Climate Change: Comparing Costs and Benefits*. Cambridge: Cambridge University Press.

Lomborg B (ed.) (2004). *Global Crises, Global Solutions.* Cambridge: Cambridge University Press.

Malthus, T (1973[1798]). *An Essay on the Principle of Population.* London: J. M. Dent.

Mitchell, R (2002–2011). International Environmental Agreements Database Project (Version 2010.3). http://iea.uoregon.edu/[5 January 2011].

Mitchell, R (2010). *International Politics and the Environment.* Los Angeles: Sage.

Mol, A (2003). *Globalization and Environmental Reform: The Ecological Modernisation of the Global Economy.* Cambridge, MA: MIT Press.

Rees, W (2002). Globalisation and sustainability: Conflict or convergence? *Bulletin of Science, Technology and Society,* 22(4), 249–268.

Simon, J (1998). *The Ultimate Resource 2.* Princeton: Princeton University Press.

Simon, J (1981). *The Ultimate Resource.* Princeton: Princeton University Press.

Stern Review (2006). *The Economics of Climate Change.* Cambridge: Cambridge University Press.

Stevis, D and V Assetto (eds.) (2001). *The International Political Economy of the Environment: Critical Perspectives.* Boulder: Lynne Rienner.

WCED (1987). Report of the World Commission on Environment and Development: Our Common Future. *UN Document* A/42/427.

CHAPTER 21

Resources

Gerry Nagtzaam

Monash University

Living in a finite world means choices have to be made as to how to utilise natural resources. Are they to be taken in the short term, trusting to science to find other raw materials when these are required? Are resources to be husbanded for future generations or used primarily for this generation? How are resources to be distributed within a particular generation or for the benefit of generations as yet unborn (and how far into the future should these calculations be made)? Are certain resources to be conserved so that they may be preserved for all? How should renewable as opposed to non-renewable resources be treated? Are resources just for the use of humans or should humans consider their impact on the rights of other non-human species?

The challenge — of how best to manage the earth's resources effectively — has to date not been met by international political economy (IPE) analysts. IPE, as a subset of international relations analysis, can be defined as "...the analysis of the exchange of goods and services across national boundaries, the institutional arrangements which govern these transactions, the policies taken by governments and other actors concerning these flows and institutional arrangements, and the set of questions posed by the existence of global production, distribution and consumption (Williams, 1996, pp. 45–46; see also Stevis and Assetto, 2000, pp. 1–2). Environmental concerns have been relegated to the periphery of this discipline (Williams, 1996, p. 55). Given the way global resources have to be shared, however, the costs associated with such a relegation have become ever more apparent. This chapter will critically examine these resources and the differing methods humanity employs to highlight and to use its environment.

It is possible to discern three distinct approaches to environmental concerns: *exploitation* (sometimes referred to as 'over-exploitation'), *conservation*, and *preservation.* When describing anthropogenic environmental damage and efforts to ameliorate such destruction, other approaches have been suggested as superior to those noted above, such as Barry's legitimate-use-versus-illegitimate-abuse of nature notion (Barry, 1999, pp. 57–73). Despite the worth of such perspectives, however, the terms exploitation, conservation, and preservation remain the preferred ones for the majority of analysts. They will therefore be those employed below.

The concepts of environmental conservation and preservation are highly prominent in environmental writings. They have been debated for well over a century and provide the underlying rationale for global environmental regimes (Kellow, 2000, p. 17).

Exploitation is less prominent and more recent. As human impact on the environment has become more obvious, however, it has grown in significance.

This chapter will also look at how these three approaches apply to particular case studies. These are whaling, tropical timber production, and Antarctica.

It will conclude by examining the tension between the three approaches and how this allows for change. It will examine the factors and actors that might bring about reform in how natural resources are used. It will also outline some of the reasons why change has not yet occurred and how the exploitation of natural resources continues unabated, to the detriment of the global environment.

ENVIRONMENTAL EXPLOITATION

Fox and others argue with some cogency that until very recently the dominant approach to nature has been exploitation (Fox, 1990, pp. 152–153). Such exploitation has generally been justified as the 'inherent right to take and plunder' natural resources such as oil, gold or biodiversity. Doing so has generally been seen as beneficial, at least in the short term.

This topic is both under-analysed and essentially contested, however (Connolly, 1983, p. 11). Advocates of differing positions have also assigned negative, positive or neutral values to it.

Moreover, the failure to properly define the concept is a serious gap in the current literature. This needs to be addressed first since it quickly gives rise to conceptual confusion and policy errors.

The idea of environmental exploitation has many antecedents. It is prefigured by Sismondi's idea of "spoliation" and Veblen's concept of the "vested interest", which veblen considered to be the right to "something for nothing" (Gouldner, 1960, p. 165). Bacon maintained that humanity's dominion of the planet gave it the right to use nature for its exclusive benefit (Attfiled, 2003, p. 105). Such arguments were commonly justified by reference to the Christian Bible where in Genesis 1:28, God was alleged to have given dominion of the planet to human beings by saying: "Be fruitful and increase in number, fill the earth and subdue it" (Brown, 2000, p. 44). Genesis 2:26 puts forward the proposition that, in God's eyes, the earth's resources are for human use stating: "And God said…and let them have dominion over the fish of the sea, and over the fowl of the air, and over the cattle, and over all the earth…"(Carroll and Prickett, 1998, p. 2).

Environmentalists are critical of these antecedents. They argue that they show an ingrained disposition by the Christian belief system to regard the natural environment as a system of resources to be exploited by humans as quickly as possible (Godden and Peel, 2010, p. 19).

The modern understanding of the concept of exploitation (as opposed to environmental exploitation) can be traced back to Marx's theory of labour. While Marx discussed both politico-economic and environmental exploitation his focus was on *homo economicus*. From his perspective, capitalist exploitation invariably arose from free market transactions (Carling, 1987, p. 175). Such exploitation happened, he said, when "…the amount of dead labour the worker can command through purchasing commodities with his income is less than the amount of labour he expends in production". It occurs, that is, through the "private ownership of the means of production" (Roemer, 1982, p. 281) and as such it is closely related to the labour theory of value. Labourers yield a significant percentage of their work to capitalists for no return for themselves (Carling, 1987, p. 174). Marx's work was built on assumption of a number of other analysts who had argued that a society can be considered exploitative when its social structure is organised in such a way that "unpaid labour" is systematically forced "out of one class and put at the disposal of another"(Reiman, 1987, p. 3).

When it came to how humanity has exploited the environment, Marx and his protagonists were woefully deficient, however. They were unable to account coherently for the concept of nature's exploitation. Marxists tended to reject the exploitation of nature as a subject of study (unless undertaken by capitalists), since the "great workshop nature" was generally accorded no value until remade into something useful by the efforts of workers (Smith and Greens, 2000, p. 1). For Marx, nature merely comprised raw material or energy to be integrated into the industrial process (Vaillancourt, 1996, p. 60).

This is surprising given Marx's knowledge of soil analysis and the connection between nature and exploitation. In his writings he chose not to make such links explicit, however. He focused on the perceived failings of the capitalist system instead and the capital law of accumulation, which inexorably "push[ed] society…to the limits of its natural resource base…" (Benton, 2002, p. 409). As Redclift and Woodgate point out, marxists to date have not adequately considered the implications of the carrying capacity of the planet and the consequences of an understanding of environmental exploitation (Redclift and Woodgate, 1994, p. 53).

Some researchers have attempted to remedy this deficiency by infusing marxism with an environmental consciousness. The most prominent has been Marcuse whose work seeks to make explicit the links between marxist thought and radical ecology using a concept he calls "liberatory dominion" (Marcuse, 1991). Marcuse argues that the domination of humanity is inextricably linked to the domination of nature and that ecological protection is critical if the radical project he espouses is to succeed. He argues that societal transformation can only occur through a process of radical psychology that alters humanity's perception of the environment (Marcuse, 1964, pp. 166–167). Again, however, like many marxists, Marcuse undercuts his argument by focusing on conventional marxist accounts of exploitation and the flaws of the capitalist system. He does not examine environmental exploitation as a whole (Clancy, 1999, p. 256; Marcuse and Kellner, 2005, p. 162).

If marxist analysts cannot adequately define environmental exploitation, how should it be understood? Gouldner starts with the dictionary definition as "an unfair or unjust utilisation of another" (Gouldner, 1960, p. 165). O'Riordan and Jordan, on the other hand, say that "any action likely to result in serious environmental harm is morally wrong ... [It] should be excluded as an option against which other options should be compared" (O'Riordan and Jordan, 1995, p. 194). Frederick believes that exploitation incorporates a non-sustainable component but, problematically, he does not consider the time frame as relevant (Frederick, 1999, p. 102). Wertheimer, in his magisterial discussion of exploitation, argues that — at the most basic level — it occurs when "A takes *unfair* [italics added] advantage of B", thus connoting a wrongful action (Werthemier, 1996, pp. 5, 10). Wertheimer neglects to apply this insight to environmental exploitation, however (Wertheimer, 1996, pp. 10–12). Carter takes this a step further by arguing that a "central tenet of green thinking is the belief that the current ecological crisis is caused by human arrogance towards the natural world which legitimates its exploitation in order to satisfy human interests" (Carter, 2007, p. 15). Taylor believes that humans sometimes adopt an *exploitative attitude* whenever nature is considered merely instrumentally, that is, as nothing more than a vast repository of resources to satisfy human appetites (Taylor, 1989, p. 95), though Cutter and Renwick disagree with this approach, arguing that exploitation should be under stood in more neutral terms as the "complete or maximum use of a resource for individual profit or societal gain" (Cutter and Renwick, 2004, p. 9).

Exploitation can be understood as a 'good', however, if it is in the service of a better quality of life for the citizens of a society. Thus Taylor argues that for Western civilisation to have developed, it was necessary to exploit nature to create a better quality of life for the majority of humanity (Taylor, 1989, p. 95). Such an argument is often made by developing states, too, to justify ongoing exploitationist practices (see the example of tropical timber forestry in a subsequent section). Taylor maintains that there is nothing *morally* wrong with choosing an exploitative attitude towards nature since the environment is "rightly controlled, transformed and consumed in the service of human interests alone" and since aside from its "actual or potential usefulness to humans" it "lack[s] all worth" (Taylor, 1989, pp. 51–52) Such an approach presupposes that nature has no intrinsic worth, however. It assumes that it has no value except for its instrumental value to human beings.

Market economists such as Inozemtsev assert that exploitation can be a positive in that "...while a social evil, ... [it] has nonetheless played a positive role, enabling people to concentrate their material resources and efforts where they were necessary, and developing advanced forms of production that became the springboard for further progress" (Inozemtsev, 1998, p. 69). Heilbroner also promotes such a position arguing that "...[e]xploitation is not only the dark, other side of civilisation; it is also a necessary condition of, if not all its achievements, at least a considerable number of its material triumphs" (Heilbroner, 1988, p. 87; Inozemstev, 1998, p. 69). While these are arguably valid points, neither accounts for the cost to individuals or ecosystems inherent in an exploitationist approach, however.

Historically, states have pursued the exploitation of their domestic (and global) natural resources by maintaining that state sovereignty allows them to do so in order to improve the lot of their peoples (or in some cases their elites) (Sucharitikul, 1996, p. 837). Principle 21 of the Stockholm Declaration (1972) entrenches this right: "States have the sovereign right", it says, "to exploit their own resources pursuant to their own environmental policies ..." (United Nations, 1972). Twenty years later the right to exploit sovereign resources was reiterated in Principle 2 of the Rio Declaration. The rights of sovereign states to 'exploit' their domestic resources is thus deeply enshrined as a key international legal principle. Legal writings to date on this right do not dwell, however, on the negative side of it. Rather, there appears to be an implicit assumption that the use of resources is an internal domestic matter limited to the state and a necessary and inevitable by-product of state development.

Defining Environmental Exploitation

Given the confusion noted above, how should exploitation be defined and distinguished from conservation and preservation? Given that, for many environmentalists, the term is weighed down with negative connotations, it cannot be said to be 'neutral' or 'good', as is maintained by some international lawyers and political economists (Gouldner, 1960, p. 167). Rather, to promote definitional clarity it needs to be made explicit that some environmental practices are short-sighted and detrimental to both society and ecosystems. There needs to be a way of depicting the idea that such resource use is unsustainable ('over-exploitation') if no consideration is given to resource replenishment or the integrity of the overall ecosystem from which resources are drawn.

If nature is considered merely a repository (drawing on exploitation's marxist roots) to be drawn upon or considered only from an anthropocentric (human) perspective, no consideration need be given to other species' right to thrive. This incorporates an element of irresponsibility in that it is also uncaring of the consequences for other humans and the biosphere in both the short and long terms. Environmental exploitation can be carried out by collective entities (for example, a state) or individuals acting alone or in small groups. The question is not the numbers of people involved but rather the scale and effect of the environmental harm done. This suggests that environmental exploitation should be understood as occurring where humanity treats environmental resources as merely instrumental, to be consumed in the short term, without consideration for the survivability of the resource, the overall ecosystem, or of future generations of humans.

Such a definition provides a starting point to examine what might be considered to be unjust behaviour by humans towards the environment. This would potentially allow for a better understanding of how to conserve and preserve the environment while ameliorating the damage done by exploitationist practices.

Whaling

Examining whaling in the twentieth century, it is possible to see how this works in practice. States focus on short-term economic gains that lead to excessive hunting without any thought for the future of the resource or the right of future generations to enjoy access to whales. States also kill whales in large numbers to prevent other whaling nations from gaining access to this resource — a classic instance of the "tragedy of the commons" (Hardin, 1968, pp. 1, 244). Each new state that undertakes whaling must pass through a phase of "fierce competition and ruthless exploitation" with "improving techniques" that can only end in "diminishing resources, exhaustion and failure" (Ommanney, 1971, p. 69). A short-term advantage is given to those with the most rapacious technologies, particularly with regard to open access resources such as fish or whales (Boyce, 2002, p. 6). Just prior to World War Two, for example, some species of whale were threatened with extinction (International Whaling Statistics, 1953, p. 13). The situation after World War Two did not improve. In 1937 there were approximately one hundred thousand blue whales in the world's oceans. By 1967 there were around one thousand, in part due to superior technology such as faster ships, explosive harpoons, and radar (Nineteenth Report of the Commission, 1969, p. 15).

Birnie maintains that this decline occurred for many other reasons as well, including the inadequacy of the scope of regulations, inadequate scientific data, non-cooperation by some major whaling nations, poor enforcement of agreements, no international supervision or control and lack of global interest (Birnie, 1985, pp. 129–130). More importantly, it was in the politico-economic interest of whalers to continue harvesting what was perceived by many to be a 'free' resource, to be taken as quickly as technology allowed.

Tropical Timber

Similarly with the case of tropical forests and timber extraction, here, too, is a case of ongoing exploitation of a natural resource. While humanity has always utilised tropical forests, we reached a point in the twentieth century where the increased scale and rate of exploitative activity threatened tropical forests globally. At the beginning of the nineteenth century, it was estimated that there was about 3.5 billion hectares of forests in tropical states (Smouts, 2003, p. 1). Throughout the nineteenth century global forests were cut down either for fuel or building material to feed growing industrial needs (Abramovitz and Mattoon, 1999, p. 61). Even in the 1920s and 1930s, the exploitation of forests was not considered an issue since it was assumed that the forests were so large and plentiful that humans could draw on them for centuries (Switzer, 2004, p. 227). This has not proven to be the case. Increased demand coupled with better technology has seen the large-scale felling of tropical forests in the 1950s and 1960s (Poore, 2003, p. 277). Global logging has accelerated to the point of unsustainability, particularly in South East Asia where little effort has been made to conserve forests for intergenerational needs (Poore, 2003, p. 14). This is due to forests being perceived as valuable for their timber and carbon, leading to a disincentive being placed on sustainable practices (Poore, 2003, p. 23).

Exploitation has become so severe that it is estimated that in the period between 1964 and 1984, one half of every tree ever harvested by humanity was cut down (Barbier *et al.*, 1994, p. 5; Smouts, 2003, p. 29). Deforestation in the new millennium has not slowed down. The UN Food and Agriculture Organisation has estimated that tropical deforestation rates increased 8.5% from 2000 to 2005 when compared with figures from the 1990s. By now at least eighty thousand acres of forest are cut down each day and another eighty thousand acres of forest are degraded, with the irreplaceable biodiversity lost in the process (Mongabay, 2010). While there may be a debate over the exact numbers, it is clear that tropical forest degradation is ongoing and a serious problem (Colchester, 1995, pp. 1–2).

In 1995 Dudley, Jeanrenaud and Sullivan, in *Bad Harvest: The International Tropical Timber Trade and the Degradation of the World's Forests*, argued that the major cause of deforestation is the continued exploitation of forests to satisfy the wants of consumers and the desire of producer states to earn export dollars (Kibel, 1999, pp. 127–128). Vested politico-economic interests (corporations, producer and consumer states) privilege tropical timber extraction to the detriment of other forest values (Poore, 2003, p. 24). The problem of 'crony capitalism', with its emphasis on short-term profits for political elites at the expense of sustainable practices, holds sway. For producer countries the loss of export revenue is too great a price to pay in the short term, while consumer states want a steady supply of tropical timber for their markets.

States, particularly producer states, constantly seek to dilute even the weak environmental constraints suggested by the global body charged with putting in place sustainable practices: the International Tropical Timber Organisation (ITTO). The prominent placing of a draft section in the 2006 Successor Agreement to the International Tropical Timber Agreement (ITTA) 1983, allowing states unfettered exploitation of their sovereign resources, is just one indicator of the relative strength of the principle of exploitation. Problematically, on the ITTO's watch, the global logging industry actually expanded. Exploitationist practices became further entrenched, to the detriment of global forests and the ability of future generations to access this resource.

Antarctica

Even the most pristine wilderness areas on the face of the planet are not immune from environmental exploitation. In contemporary times the interest in Antarctica by states, for example, was initially dominated by the desire to exploit living resources like seals and non-living resources like minerals. In the late nineteenth and early twentieth centuries, the possibility of Antarctic mineral deposits served as a spur to Antarctic exploration (Sahurie, 1992, p. 433). In 1905, for example, the British Government granted a mining exploration licence for South Georgia Island (Fridtjof Nansen Foundation, 1973, reprinted in Bush, 1982, p. 288). While there is evidence of mineral traces in the region including copper, gold, silver, cobalt, chromium, nickel and platinum, very few actual mineral deposits have been located (Larminie, 1991, p. 83). An alternative view to the prevailing one is that there are vast resources waiting to be exploited but that they have not yet been located. Some estimate that there is enough iron ore in the Prince Charles Mountains to meet the global demand for two hundred years. Natural gas reserves under the Ross, Weddell and Bellinghausen Seas are estimated to be in the range of tens of billions of barrels (Buck, 1998, p. 62). Given the current knowledge of

Antarctica, and the present level of technology, it will be a long time before exploring and exploiting mineral resources there will be cost effective. This has not stopped states from seeing the region in terms of its politico-economic potential, however, and wanting to tap its riches in the short to near term (Larminie, 1991, p. 83).

ENVIRONMENTAL CONSERVATION

The principle of environmental conservation is often described as an attempt to correct the 'negative' environmental practices of the past. Eckersley argues that resource conservation can be seen as the first step away from the unrestrained development associated with exploitation (Eckersley, 1992, p. 35). Smith maintains that conservationism has tended to act as a brake "...to moderate the pressures for an exploitative 'free for all' inherent in the drives which propel actions in economic markets" — thus ameliorating the damaging practices of the past (Smith, 1998, p. 11). Rodman supports this position, arguing that resource conservation can potentially replace the "reckless exploitation of forests, wildlife, soils etc." with an "ethical and legal requirement that 'natural resources' be used 'wisely', in the interests of humanity at large rather than in the interests of a mere few, and considered over the 'long run' rather than the short term" (Hay, 2002, p. 31). Problematically, while it is the most closely scrutinised of the environmental principles (whether in the form of conservationism, sustainable development, or ecological modernisation) conservationist practices are rarely clearly defined. Moreover, they seem to be applied on a case-by-case basis.

Both political economists and conservationists are concerned about the future, in particular the future use of natural resources (Ciriacy-Wantrup, 1985, p. 207). For political economists, resources need to be utilised or allocated efficiently. How to measure efficiency is open to debate, but efficiency is generally considered to occur when resource allocation maximises the overall benefit to a given society. Mainstream market economics attaches no moral opprobrium, therefore, to activities that cause environmental damage or pollution, if the allocation of resources is otherwise efficient. In some cases the most efficient allocation of a particular resource might afford greater protection to the environment. In other situations, higher levels of pollution might be considered acceptable since a reduction in pollution might not be considered as advantageous as politico-economic development (Godden and Peel, 2010, p. 28).

Human understanding of the need to conserve or wisely use natural resources is an ancient one. It is discussed in the Bible and the writings of Cicero, Plato and Mencius. (Eckersley, 1992, p. 35) Leviticus 25: 2–4, for example, argues that farmers should adopt a conservationist ethos: "keep a Sabbath unto the Lord...But in the seventh year shall be a Sabbath of rest unto the land…thou shalt neither sow thy field, nor prune thy vineyard…for it is a year of rest unto the land" (Carroll and Pricket, 1998, p. 153). Some Biblical scholars have argued that the proper interpretation of the Bible's view of natural resources says that humans are stewards of the planet. Thus, two contrasting views of the Christian religious attitude to natural resources are discernable. One sees humans as rulers over nature. The other sees humans as the guardians of the earth for this and future generations. As Godden and Peel argue, "At various points in history, approaches along the spectrum between these two extremes have played an important role in framing our understandings of the environment" (Godden and Peel, 2010, p. 19).

Non-religious philosophers have also grappled with these issues. Cicero said humans were the "absolute master of what the earth produces" and that they should seek to produce "another nature" (Wall, 1994, p. 32). The writings of Plato contained observations on the costs of ecological damage. They described, for example, the soil erosion that results from overgrazing by goats (Walker, 1994, pp. 2–3). These writings alluded to the ongoing tension between the oft-competing concepts of stewardship and dominance of the world's natural resources that even today leads to confused interpretations about what constitutes (or should constitute) conservationist practices.

Modern ideas of conservation were initially popularised by the first Chief of the US Forest Service, Gifford Pinchot (Eckersley, 1992, p. 5–6). Pinchot considered conservation "the ownership, control, development, processing, distribution, and use of the natural resources for the benefit of the people" (Pinchot, 1998, p. 506). He also observed that:

> The first great fact about conservation is that it stands for development. There has been a fundamental misconception that conservation means nothing but the husbanding of resources for future generation. There could be no more serious mistake. Conservation does mean provision for the future, but it means also and first of all the right of the present generation to the fullest necessary use of all the resources … Conservationism demands the welfare of this generation first, and afterward the welfare of the generations to follow (Pinchot, 2004, p. 15).

For Pinchot, the second limb of his conception of conservation was the elimination of waste. In his eyes it was a vital component of the industrial infrastructure and it was necessary for people to develop an abhorrence of waste (Pinchot, 2004, p. 16). His solution was to promote the idea of "sustainable yields" when it came to utilising resources (Hay, 2002, p. 14). Pinchot was willing to preserve parts of nature but only if they could be considered useful as a resource to humankind

(Pinchot, 2004, p. 17). Thus, conservation was only to apply for the benefit of humans and utilitarian in the sense of trying to be the "greatest good to the greatest number" for the "longest time" (Pinchot, 2004, p. 16).

Initially, conservation was perceived merely to mean "planned and efficient progress" (Switzer, 2004, p. 15). The principle has evolved since then, though it retains its roots in the need for efficient design. Prior to World War Two, conservationists' goals were to manage efficiency and prevent over-exploitation. The two main natural resources focused upon were water and forests. (See the creation of the Tennessee Valley Authority, for example, that melded an engineering approach with an integrated approach to environmental resource management, Irwin, 2000, p. 19).

Osborn's book, *Our Plundered Planet*, says that conservationists are right to say that each generation is responsible for its natural assets. Political economists are also correct, it says, when conservationists want resources used for the benefit of all humanity (that is, when no non-human species are included in such a calculus) (Osborn, 1968, pp. 157–162).

The traditional view of governments (and in some ways this is still the dominant position) is to regard market policy as critical to societal development and to regard environmental protection as a peripheral issue. Thus, politico-economic development and environmental protection are seen as competing and sometimes mutually antagonistic goals. Policy makers treat the issue as a zero sum game. With greater politico-economic development there is less environmental protection, and vice versa. From this perspective the role of government is to find an acceptable balance between these two competing aims. The 1972 United Nations Conference on the Human Environment (Stockholm Conference) brought the concepts of development and the environment together (Stevis and Assetto, 2000, p. 1). Similarly, in the early 1980s, the *World Conservation Strategy* was released which emphasised the integration of conservation activities and politico-economic development (Godden and Peel, 2010, p. 135).

The Brundtland Report and Ecologically Sustainable Development

In 1983 the World Commission on Environment and Development (the Brundtland Commission) was tasked by the UN General Assembly to investigate the environment and development debates and to create long-term environmental strategies for what became known as Ecologically Sustainable Development (ESD). This encapsulated many of the ideas inherent in conservation. The goal of the Commission was to enhance global environmental co-operation and find a way past the environment/development dichotomy. The Commission examined many problematic global environmental issues, including population, food security, species and ecosystems, energy, urban development, and international cooperation (including peace and security) (The World Commission on Environment and Development, 1990, pp. 139–140).

The key conclusion of the Brundtland Report was that governments no longer needed to regard politico-economic development and environmental protection as mutually exclusive. It saw the two as integrated. Creating a synergistic relationship, it argued, would mutually benefit both. ESD proponents and the Brundtland Report claimed that the global political economy could be sustained without having to worry about the "limits to growth" argument propounded by the Club of Rome, which concluded that given current trends there would be global resource shortages as the earth's carrying capacity limited its politico-economic development. The "limits to growth" analysis was explicitly rejected by participants at the Stockholm conference and implicitly rejected by the analysis put forth by the Brundtland Commission (Irwin, 2000, pp. 33–34).

The Commission argued that ESD did imply limits but that they were not absolute. Any current limits were created by such factors as the state of technology, social organisation, and the ability of the planet's biosphere to cope with humanity's activities (The World Commission on Environment and Development, 1990, p. 8). By adding the idea of 'sustainability' to development it introduced the element of time to the equation. It demanded that a higher value be placed on every ecosystem's overall health, since continued human well-being required that this be the case (Harris and Goodwin, 2001, p. 1).

The Brundtland Commission also sought to link ESD with the alleviation of existing poverty. It sought to do this through the principles of intra- and intergenerational equity. Intragenerational equity means "meeting the basic needs of all and extending to all the opportunity to fulfil their aspirations for a better life" (The World Commission on Environment and Development, 1990, p. 8). Intergenerational equity allows the "present generation" to ensure that the "health, diversity and productivity of the environment is maintained or enhanced for the benefit of future generations (although this is not taken as a prohibition on growth, since the need to develop a strong, growing and diversified economy is also recognised in order to enhance the capacity for environmental protection)" (Godden and Peel, 2010, p. 136).

A broad conception of ESD allows for the embrace of new responsibilities (for example, responsibilities towards future generations) and a potentially more integrative environmental approach (for example, one that includes indigenous traditions) (Godden and Peel, 2010, p. 136). Problematically, no one yet appears to have been able to work out how best to incorporate future generations' interests into these calculations. As Boyce points out, future generations cannot defend their interests and so they tend to lose out (Boyce, 2003, p. 4).

Also underpinning ESD is the precautionary principle which maintains that "where there are threats of serious or irreversible environmental damage, lack of full scientific certainty should not be used as a reason for postponing measures to prevent environmental degradation". Together, the principles of intra- and intergenerational equity, and the precautionary principle, allow decision-makers to take a more holistic approach to natural resource allocation. This allows for both scientific uncertainty and a long-term focus (Godden and Peel, 2010, p. 137).

The take-up of the concept of ESD by the global community was startlingly quick. By the beginning of 1990 the Brundtland Report had been endorsed by a majority of the world's governments, by major international organisations like the World Bank, and by numerous environmental non-governmental organisations. At the United Nations Conference on Environment and Development (Earth Summit), in Rio De Janeiro in 1992, it was officially enshrined as a core goal of the global community. The UN Commission on Sustainable Development (CSD) was created in December 1992 to ensure effective follow-up to the conference and to monitor and report on the execution of the Earth Summit agreements at the local, national, regional and international levels (UN Commission on Sustainable Development, 2010).

The reasons that ESD was so well received are varied. For example, the ideas underpinning ESD meshed well with both traditional and contemporary understandings drawn from philosophical, scientific and politico-economic traditions. ESD also shared with ecology a holistic focus and with political economics a desire to ensure the wise use of scarce natural resources (Godden and Peel, 2010, p. 135). Moreover, the ESD — as envisaged by the Brundtland Commission — was "appealingly ambiguous". Since the definitions used were not proscriptive, the Commission's rather vague formulations enabled all parties to agree to abide by its principles (while continuing not to take the hard decisions required in practice).

In the annex to his book, *Blueprint for a Green Economy,* Pearce identifies twenty-three different formulations of the principle of ESD as used by various stakeholders (Pearce, 1989, pp. 173–185). Like 'freedom' or 'justice', ESD has become both a 'motherhood statement' and an essentially contested concept. It is not one but many ideas. Stakeholders may agree with its aims but not with how to achieve them. How to implement ESD is open to multiple interpretations while all agree that ESD is critical.

Furthermore, the Brundtland Commission's formulations of ESD (and current definitions of conservation) do not answer many key questions inherent in the term. Which aim should come first, a sustainable economy or a sustainable ecology? What is meant by intergenerational equity? Do obligations to the next generation apply to them as a group or do they apply to each individual of the next generation? How many generations should be factored into calculations of natural capital stock usage? If intra- and intergenerational equity is allowed for, why not promote for inter-species equity as well rather than focus on an anthropocentric perspective that denies other species as having any intrinsic worth, that is, any worth over and above their use value to humanity? To date none of these questions has been answered satisfactorily. As a result ESD has not moved beyond an aspirational target to that of an agreed upon approach.

Ecological Modernisation

A variant of ESD is Ecological Modernisation (EM). This focuses on Pinchot's admonition regarding waste elimination. Like ESD, EM argues that economic growth and environmental deterioration can be "decoupled" by promoting "greener growth". This is generally accepted as being economic growth that uses less energy and resources and produces less waste per unit of gross domestic product (GDP). To achieve this goal, advocates promote technological innovation, and less material-energy intensive methods of production, with the eventual aim of "closed-loop production" where nothing is wasted (save the dissipation of heat as per the second law of thermodynamics) (Christoff, 1996, p. 483).

Christoff is critical of this approach, arguing that it is concerned with mere "technological adjustments" at the level of the firm and that it is relatively ignorant of the globalised nature of resource use (Christoff, 1996, pp. 486–487). Christoff points out that many claims by EM advocates should be treated cautiously since many of the supposed reductions are achieved by the relocation of dirty or energy-intensive industries to less developed states and that this cannot continue forever (Christoff, 1996, p. 487). Furthermore, concepts such as preservationism and wilderness are not easily reduced to mere monetary considerations and they are marginalised or ignored completely by EM-style policy considerations (Christoff, 1996, p. 485).

The biggest issue with EM is that, while a useful approach with regard to becoming more efficient, it still promotes growth in absolute terms. As Jacobs concedes, absolute growth in global environmental degradation far exceeds any of the improvements in environmental productivity that EM offers (Jacobs, 1999, pp. 22–23). Thus, overall environmental degradation inevitably continues (albeit at a potentially diminished rate).

Both ESD and EM can be considered modern variants of conservationism. The current idea of environmental conservation is integrally bound up with a production process that understands the non-human world only in terms of a resource to be used (Eckersley, 1992, p. 36). Such an approach treats nature as merely a well of matter-energy to be transmuted by technology for exclusive human use. This perspective

> ...mirrors Christian traditions, especially in its anthropocentric outlook. Nature and natural entities are not sacred, have no end or justification in and of themselves, and exist solely as means in terms of which human ends might be fulfilled (Oelschlager, 1993, p. 287).

This idea of conservation can utilise both renewable and non-renewable resources providing there is a husbanding of resources for future use. Unlike Pinchot's definition, such an approach maintains that retaining resources for future generations is just as important as providing them for the present generation (Taylor, 1989, p. 289). Mirroring Pinchot's approach, Rodman argues that modern conservationism is an "unconstrained total-use approach, whose upshot is to leave nothing in its natural condition (for that would be a kind of 'waste' and waste should be eliminated)" (Rodman, 1983, p. 83).

Environmental conservation also embodies a rhetoric of restraint which also suits the interests of states seeking better politico-economic returns from their resources. Thus modern environmental conservationism

> concedes that nature is not inexhaustible: accordingly, that there are limits to material growth and that husbandry must therefore be practised because it becomes necessary to consider the interests of human generations as yet unborn when determining courses of action (Hay, 2002, p. 33).

At its heart, environmental conservation seeks to put limits on or moderate the impact of the behaviour of humans towards the environment. Conservationists can be distinguished from exploitationists, therefore, by decreeing that conservationist practices benefit both present and future generations of humans and work to ensure the survivability of natural resources or ecosystems into the future. Conservationists are cognizant that natural resources are finite and thus should be husbanded or put to 'wise' use, with an emphasis on eliminating wastage and inefficiency for the good of all humans. Markets should focus on integrating sustainable practices at all levels. While conservationist practices may privilege a minority of humans, the driving principle of conservationism is that it benefits human society as a whole (but not necessarily the health of the planet). Further, conservationists do not consider non-human species worthy of consideration when it comes to making decisions on how resources should be allocated.

Humans have sought and sometimes succeeded in putting in place conservationist practices at both the domestic and global levels. The principle of conservation (and sustainable development) is present in dozens of conventions, agreements, national briefings and policy documents, particularly those related to biodiversity.

Whaling Again

In the early 1930s, the killing of blue whales hit such heights that it depressed whale oil prices (International Whaling Statistics, 1935, p. 4). D'Amato and Chopra argue that it was at this point that whaling nations began to recognise the need to regulate the taking of whales to prevent the extinction of the major whale species, and that they were acting out of their own self-interest to maintain profits (D'Amato and Chopra, 1991, p. 29). The whalers themselves had realised that the national controls proposed by states such as Norway and Iceland were not sufficient and that a global regulatory system aimed at stabilising prices was required (Stoett, 1997, p. 57).

After four years of negotiations between the states attached to the League of Nations, the first Convention for the Regulation of Whaling was created in 1931 in Geneva, Switzerland (the Geneva Convention). The Convention covered all waters (Article 9), including states' territorial waters (Article 1), and enforced the licensing of whaling vessels (Article 8) (D'Amato and Chopra, 1991, p. 31). It also exempted coastal aboriginal peoples providing they used "canoes, pirogues or other exclusively native craft propelled by oars or sails" and did not use firearms or employ non-aboriginals in their whaling activities (Gillepsie, 2005, p. 194; Firestone and Lilley, 2005, p. 194; Reeves, 2002, p. 72). For the first time, conservation as a concept was applied globally to whaling, in other words, though D'Amato and Chopra argue that the principle was limited to merely protecting the long-term viability of the whaling *industry* rather than the welfare of whales themselves (D'Amato and Chopra, 1991, p. 31).

The 1931 treaty was eventually superseded by the current convention, the International Convention for the Regulation of Whaling (ICRW). This was created in 1946 and came into force on 10 November 1948. It created the International Whaling Commission (IWC) as the pre-eminent body for regulating the global whaling industry (First Report of the Commission, 1950, p. 3; Reeves, 2002, p. 72). It further introduced maximum catch quotas for the total season for Antarctic pelagic whaling. It initially encompassed only the great whales. It was later expanded to other cetaceans (D'Amato and Chopra, 1991, p. 32; Vogler, 2000, p. 53).

The Preamble's language incorporated the more conservationist goals of intergenerational equity and the safeguarding of endangered species. This was particularly apparent when it spoke of

> ...(1) recognising the interest of the nations of the world to safeguard for future generations the great natural resource represented by the whale stocks; ...
>
> (4) [and the] establishment of a system of international regulation for the whale fisheries to ensure proper and effective conservation and development of whale stocks ... (International Convention for the Regulation of Whaling, 1946, p. 9).

Antarctica Again

In the case of Antarctica, the Consultative Parties to the Antarctic Treaty (1959) sought to address the issue of mining without damaging the fragile ecosystem of Antarctica in the long term by attempting to put in place a Convention on the Regulation of Antarctic Mineral Resource Activities (CRAMRA). While CRAMRA was not designed to promote sustainable mining, it was intended to balance resource extraction and damage to the Antarctic environment in order to conserve the region for other uses and for future generations (US Department Handbook for the Antarctic Treaty System, 2002, p. 434).

Another example is the Convention on Biological Diversity (CBD) which in its Preamble notes the key role to be played by conservation:

> Aware that conservation and sustainable use of biological diversity is of critical importance for meeting the food, health and other needs of the growing world population, for which purpose access to and sharing of both genetic resources and technologies are essential; Noting that, ultimately, the conservation and sustainable use of biological diversity will strengthen friendly relations among States and contribute to peace for humankind; Desiring to enhance and complement existing international arrangements for the conservation of biological diversity and sustainable use of its components, and; Determined to conserve and sustainably use biological diversity for the benefit of present and future generations... (Convention on Biological Diversity, 1992).

Tropical Timber Again

Likewise, the International Tropical Timber Agreement 1983, Article 1(h) includes the following aim:

> To encourage the development of national policies aimed at sustainable utilisation and conservation of tropical forests and their genetic resources, and at maintaining the ecological balance in the regions concerned (International Tropical Timber Agreement, 1983).

Chasek believes that the aim of the ITTA is "to promote [the] sustainable development of tropical forests by encouraging and assisting the tropical timber industry and trade and thus ... [conserving] the resource base upon which they depend" (Chasek, 2001, p.102). Kolk points out that while the ITTA was originally envisaged as being yet another commodity agreement, the attempted melding of conservation with the promotion of trade and increasing producer states' revenues made it an exceptional agreement (Kolk, 1996, p. 137).

Urban Development and Forestry

Emphasis is now placed on conservation and sustainability in urban development with the aim of reducing key inputs such as energy and water and minimising waste generation. For example, the city of Vitoria-Gasteiz in Spain has implemented a policy of mixed land use and high-density development along its major transport routes, combined with green belts that provide habitats for wildlife and recreational areas for its people. Business has also recognised the need for conservation within the product life cycle. The US company Interface Inc., for example, a major carpet tile producer, has greatly reduced its ecological footprint in a variety of ways. It now uses recycled and more environmentally friendly products combined with a more efficient manufacturing process. This has led to reduced energy and water consumption and reductions in waste (Examples of Sustainable Development, 1987).

Forest areas that used to be exploited only for their timber are now being reassessed with conservationist principles in mind. Market economists have concluded that the harvesting of forest products without destroying the forest can be more profitable in the long term than logging, particularly for any inhabitants of the forest. One study in the Peruvian Amazon, for example, found that logging a one-hectare patch of forest generated one thousand dollars. The annual net yield of the sustainable harvest of fruit and rubber on the same hectare, however, was estimated to be four hundred and twenty-two dollars, for a net present value of six thousand three hundred and thirty dollars per hectare (Butler, 2010). Virtually every country now keeps records of how sustainable their practices are in conserving national resources. (For example, see the Australian Department of the Environment and Heritage Report, 2002).

ENVIRONMENTAL PRESERVATION

The last of the approaches to the earth's natural resources is that of preservation. To speak of saving a resource *from* use rather than using it *for* some human goal is to speak about 'environmental preservation'. Preservationists focus on the importance of natural resources and of non-market activities, including non-income related activities. They believe that in the absence of strict controls the negative impact of human activities will overwhelm ecosystems and destroy them (Boyce, 2003, pp. 2–3). John Passmore defines this as

> ...the attempt to maintain in their present condition such areas of the earth's surface as do not yet bear the obvious marks of man's handiwork and to protect from the risk of extinction those species of living beings which man has not yet destroyed (Passmore, 1980, p. 101).

Preservationists perceive that nature is not merely a resource to be utilised. They tend to focus on promoting wilderness values and protecting biodiversity from humanity's ever encroaching needs (Paehlke, 1997, p. 78). Preservationism is seen as an alternative, therefore, to conservation. The environment is to be considered valuable in itself rather than a politico-economic problem (Irwin, 2000, p. 20).

The idea of 'wilderness' (derived from the Celtic term for 'outside of man', or an absence of human presence) was a major influence on early environmental preservation laws in the US, Australia, and other Western nations (Godden and Peel, 2010, p. 33). There are numerous examples. In 1626 Plymouth colony leaders in the US regulated the cutting of timber on colony land. In 1681 William Penn, proprietor of Pennsylvania, ruled that for every five acres of land cleared, one should be left untouched. In 1691 Massachusetts Bay leaders decreed that forest reservations be created leading to an entrenched domestic norm that forests should be preserved (Switzer, 2004, pp. 12–13).

The preservationist wilderness ideal has historical resonance with nineteenth century British Romanticism and with recreational values (Irwin, 2000, p. 20). A pastoral vision of nature that celebrates the need for a simpler lifestyle, more in tune with nature, for example, was argued by some as a necessary antidote to the ongoing excesses of progress. In the early twentieth century, advocates of the preservation of nature were heavily influenced by fervent anti-urban and anti-technology attitudes (Godden and Peel, 2010, p. 33). The influence of these wilderness ideals found concrete expression in the creation of national parks, Ramsar sites (globally significant wetland sites), biosphere reserves, and world heritage areas (Godden and Peel, 2010, p. 34).

Preservation of nature was pursued by a variety of actors. In 1870 in the US a group of explorers argued that portions of Yellowstone should be preserved in perpetuity because of its unique features (Switzer, 2004, p. 14). One of the key investors was John Muir of the North American Sierra Club. His quest was to create a system of national park wilderness areas preserved in perpetuity. This system was to limit human intervention to a recreational or educational one. His first major success was the designation of the two million acre Yellowstone National Park in Wyoming in 1872 (Eckersley, 1992, p. 39). The public embraced the concept and soon a host of areas considered pristine or unique were set aside. Interest in preserving fast disappearing forests and trees in the US led to the first Arbor Day on April 10, 1872 (Switzer, 2004, p. 14).

This period of American history saw an ideological clash between the conservationist Pinchot and the preservationist Muir as to how best to protect and use particular areas, a debate that resonates to this day (Hay, 2002, p. 16). Preservationist-inspired movements quickly spread to the UK, Canada, NZ and Australia. The global National Parks movement inspired the preservation of flora and fauna in 'pristine' sanctuaries. It transcended state borders and became global (Irwin, 2000, p. 24). In some ways the movement has become too successful, however. There are so many people wanting to use these set-aside areas that the latter are being killed with kindness. For example, Yellowstone National Park had 3,295,187 visitors in 2009, a number so large that it threatens the ecological fragility of this area (National Park Service Public Use Statistics Office, 2010). Another by-product of the obsession with creating national parks was the way preservationism focused on the setting aside of wilderness reserves rather than on critiquing the impact of politico-economic forces on nature (Irwin, 2000, p. 24).

Preserving a natural resource can be argued a 'good' on both intrinsic and instrumental grounds. An instrumental approach would argue that deriving value from the natural world is enhanced if the resources are allowed to exist untrammelled (Hay, 2002, p. 33). Even in the most exploitative periods of Western civilisation, some have seen the need to preserve nature (Godden and Peel, 2010, p. 33). This includes perceiving and using nature as a retreat (an asylum), a place of recreation (a gymnasium), and a place of worship (a cathedral), as well as a laboratory, an art gallery, a silo of genetic diversity, a monument, or simply somewhere to marvel and to wonder (Sessions, 1992, p. 97). Fox maintains that preservationist approaches tend to be better accepted by the community if argued in instrumental terms (Fox, 1990, p. 5). Consequently, preservationist proponents tend to frame their arguments in these terms.

The most powerful arguments for preserving forest biodiversity, for example, appeal to their value to humans as a source of medicines. It downplays any argument based on the intrinsic value of forests (Sessions, 1992, p. 96). Such an approach says that humanity "...should preserve as wide as possible a range of genetic diversity because there is no way of anticipating what our *future* needs might happen to be" (Godfrey-Smith, 1980, p. 31).

Nelson argues that these instrumental arguments can be supported by others including: the environment's use as a teaching tool; its ontological significance ("we are what we are because of our environment"); its cultural diversity ("the diversity of cultures depends on a variety of different ecosystems"); its relevance to national character ("designated wilderness areas can symbolically encapsulate national character"); its role in allowing self-realisation as per the philosophical principle of deep ecology; and its role in disease sequestration ("viruses in non-protected or damaged ecosystems are under extreme selective pressure"). Further instrumental reasons for preserving natural resources are said to be the role they play in the salvation of freedom (as a "potential sanctuary from oppressive governments") and their mythopoetic role (as a "perfect location for viewing the history of myth") (Nelson, 2003, pp. 423–428). Sessions further proposes that preservation as an argument can be justified in terms of the "minding animals argument" whereby humanity needs wild animals in a pristine ecosystem so humans can prosper since human intelligence is "bound to the presence of animals" (Sessions, 1992, p. 98).

For some green theorists, an instrumental approach to preservation is a morally bankrupt approach because:

> ...to categorise and quantify the benefits of what they take...is a flawed approach to ...preservation. It is, in effect, to play the game of your opponent by trying to bolster your side by including on your team bigger, better, and more players (or, in this case, more human benefits arguments), while the question of whether or not the correct game is being played in the first place goes unanswered and unasked (Nelson, 2003, p. 423).

The Ehrlichs argue, for example, that at its heart preservationism accords an *intrinsic* or non-instrumental value to the world, even if it conflicts with human interests (Godfrey-Smith, 1980, p. 31). Passmore's work assumes as a given that 'true' preservationist arguments *must* rely on the concept of intrinsic value (Godfrey-Smith, 1979, p. 310; Norton, 1986, p. 196). This philosophical position is at odds with some green thinkers, however, who also include instrumental arguments to support the preservation of nature (Godfrey-Smith, 1979, p. 310; Norton, 1986, p. 196). Eckersley is critical of the attempt to marry the two approaches, arguing that while one can mount preservationist positions based on instrumental grounds, doing so does a disservice to the intentions of many global actors who, for instance, argue that whales or other creatures deserve not to be culled because they have an intrinsic right to exist (Eckersley, 2004, p. 32).

Preservationism is about acknowledging the role and vitality of the 'other' both at the individual level and that of the biosphere. Conservationists and preservationists can, in some circumstances, agree to implement the same policy for different reasons (for example, zero quotas on endangered species). Because their underlying principles are so radically different, however, they cannot form a secure alliance in the longer term.

Whaling Yet Again

There are many examples of proponents arguing the need for a preservationist approach on intrinsic or instrumental grounds. During the 1980s, after it was clear that conservationist measures were failing to stem the ongoing extinction of whales, for example, a coalition comprising states and environmental non-governmental organisations (ENGOs) espoused a preservationist creed. They wanted to ban "all whaling, irrespective of whether a particular species is stable or endangered" (D'Amato and Chopra, 1991, p. 37). ENGOs like Greenpeace, the World Wildlife Fund, the International Fund for Animal Welfare, and the Environmental Investigation Agency were able to highlight the brutality of whaling and its impact on whaling species in their efforts to persuade the global populace to end whale hunting and to reframe the debate away from one about exploitation or conservation towards one about preserving all whales in perpetuity (Stoett, 1997, p. 95). At the 1982 International Whaling Commission Meeting in Brighton, the UK, the Seychelles argued for a phasing out of commercial whaling because such an approach would

> ... facilitate the adjustment that whaling nations will have to make if the whale is to be saved from extinction, and at the same time [would] safeguard the future work of the Commission as a growing alliance of nations committed to *preserving* [my italics] all cetaceans for posterity (D'Amato and Chopra, 1991, p. 37).

The amendment was eventually passed. Given the overwhelming numbers voting for the ban, it is arguable that a "critical mass" of states had agreed to be bound by the preservationist principle (Bailey, 2008, p. 298). Paragraph 10 was amended so that the catch-limit for the 1985/86 season would be zero (Annual Report of the International Whaling Commission 33, 1983, p. 40). Some states (for example, Australia, the US and the Netherlands) had come to accept that whales had an intrinsic right to live. For these states and most of the ENGOs, whaling was a barbaric practice and the taking of even one whale was anathema due to their intrinsic uniqueness, intelligence, and beauty, and the way such creatures were worthy of fair treatment (Wapner, 2002, p. 48).

Tropical Forests Yet Again

Similarly with tropical forests: the most common solution espoused in developed states to save the tropical rainforests was a preservationist one. It said that states should designate large swathes of forested land as forest reserves not to be logged. This method sought to protect "...internationally recognised forest resources by setting standards of harvesting and control ... [and designated] forest areas ... for inclusion in the international list of protected areas" (Kasimbazi, 1996).

Antarctica Yet Again

In the case of Antarctica, the region has now been designated as a 'natural reserve' with no mineral exploitation allowed. The only exceptions are light tourism and scientific activities (which are activities consistent with preservationist goals).

This came about because of the efforts of preservationist actors such as Australia and France, and ENGOs such as Greenpeace, which were determined to preserve the fragile continent from exploitation and which worked together to defeat the introduction of CRAMRA. When CRAMRA failed, the preservationist coalition framed the issue as a choice between unrestrained exploitation or the preservation of a unique, fragile wilderness that was in danger of being despoiled by mining. They successfully appealed to 'higher values', such as wilderness, that resonated with a global populace that had an ideational affinity with the concept of maintaining ever-shrinking pristine areas (Clark, 1994, p. 180; Cordonnery, 1997, pp. 4–5; Elliott, 1993, pp. 58–59; Eliott, 1994, p. 195; Joyner, 1991, p. 167, 175; Sahurie, 1992, p. 425; Vidas, 2000, p. 3; Vogler, 2000, p. 82).

In 1991 they were successful in passing the Protocol on Environmental Protection to the Antarctic Treaty (Madrid Protocol, 1991). Article 2 of the Protocol stipulates that member states agree to the "comprehensive protection of the Antarctic environment and dependent and associated ecosystems" and to designating the region as a "natural reserve, devoted to peace and science" (The Madrid Protocol, 1991). Article 3(1) includes language that explicitly refers to the preservation of the Antarctic environment, that is:

> … [t]he protection of the Antarctic environment and dependent and associated ecosystems and the *intrinsic* [my italics] value of Antarctica, including its wilderness and aesthetic values and its value as an area for the conduct of scientific research, in particular research essential to understanding the global environment … [These] shall be fundamental considerations in the planning and conduct of all activities in the Antarctic Treaty area (The Madrid Protocol, 1991).

ENVIRONMENTAL NORMATIVE TRANSFORMATION

Three different environmental norms — exploitation, conservation and preservation — underpin environmental regimes. Like tectonic plates, however, they are fluid and often changing. It is critical, therefore, to understand how change is brought about and the role played by various actors in trying to initiate environmental change. It is also important to understand what factors forestall necessary environmental change.

Whaling and Change

Returning to whaling, for example, it can be seen that the principles involved are changing. In the twentieth century, as noted above, whales were exploited

---

http://antarctica.gov.au/antarctica-law-and-treaty/the-madrid-protocol [accessed 8 January 2011]. Madrid Protocol (1991).

to the point where species were in danger of extinction. With the failure of conservationist measures to reduce the ongoing extermination, some states (in particular the US and Australia), in part influenced by ENGOs, came to accept that preserving whales was the correct approach. They argued that whales were worthy of such consideration due to their instrinsic intelligence and beauty and their uniqueness. Many states (and individuals) internalised this approach as part of their state identity and as a consequence became powerful proponents for an end to whaling (DeSombre, 2002, p. 141). In a speech by the UK delegate to the fiftieth IWC meeting, for example, the delegate said, "We do not believe that any whaling is justified" and that only the introduction of a "permanent, comprehensive moratorium on all whaling other than aboriginal subsistence whaling" was acceptable (DeSombre, 2002, p. 141).

While preservationist advocates have not yet brought about a universal shift sufficient to end the debate regarding whaling, they have been remarkably successful, in a relatively short period of time, in changing the way whale-hunting is perceived globally (Stoett, 1997, p. 134). The issue is still in flux, though. Whaling advocates led by Japan seek to reverse the preservationist position and to allow commercial whaling (banned since 1986) to flourish again. There has also been a change in the arguments put forward by such groups in support of whaling.

Exploitative whaling states like Japan, Norway and Iceland are now required to put forth their arguments in conservationist rather than exploitationist language and there are signs that these arguments are no longer merely rhetorical. ENGOs have forced whalers to adopt a conservationist approach (in terms of the scientific management of whaling stocks) to justify their commercial whaling practices (Fletcher, 2001, p. 224). (The case of tropical timber is similar where the arguments by all parties are couched in the language of conservation or sustainable development regardless of whether such a principle is the one being adopted on the forest floor.)

In the case of whaling, what brought about the change whereby preservationist principles triumphed? In part it was because states were not able to stop their exploitationist practices, seeing it as in their short-term interests to harvest whales before other states did. Another factor was that scientists were not able to convince states of the need to abandon their ongoing exploitationist practices and to adopt conservationist principles without risking the extinction of whale species.

The failure to adopt conservationist principles and the ongoing threat to whale stocks opened the door for ENGOs and some states to advocate a preservationist position that emphasised whales' uniqueness, intelligence and intrinsic beauty. They also successfully combined such arguments with evidence of the barbarity of whaling as an activity (Wapner, 2002, p. 48). This approach resonated with the global populace, leading to a domestic outcry in key states, including the US, calling for an end to the slaughter. In this case ENGOs and preservationist states were able to argue successfully that whales were both in danger of extinction and worthy of fair treatment.

In both the Antarctic and whaling case studies, ENGO arguments on the fragility and beauty of Antarctica and the uniqueness and intelligence of whales were highly persuasive and led to normative changes. They pegged their arguments to values such as wilderness or uniqueness thus giving them 'moral authority'. While persuasion of the type utilised by ENGOs sometimes works, it rarely works on its own, however. To achieve their goals, ENGOs used both persuasion and strategic means (such as entering into strategic alliances). They looked to influence regime development, that is, they used persuasion as but one component of a 'toolkit' of approaches.

In the case of Antarctica, ENGOs prepared policy documents to influence proceedings. They were seconded to state delegations where they used fears that the UN would seize control of the region. They also fostered concerns by lesser developed states that technologically advanced states would have the edge in exploiting Antarctic mineral resources.

In the case of whaling, ENGOs used the Seychelles as a stalking horse to participate at the IWC and advance its agenda. It allowed ENGOs to directly debate with other IWC delegates, to obtain voting rights, to gather information, and to form voting blocs dedicated to preserving whales.

Tropical Timber and the Lack of Change

There are significant limits to the power of persuasion, however, as is manifest in the tropical timber case study. ENGOs have not been able to reframe the issue of tropical forest protection to incorporate values such as wilderness. The entrenched economic interests of logging companies, and a coalition of producer and consumer states, have been able to negate the ENGOs' arguments about the need for wilderness protection or the negative impact of deforestation. More particularly, they have been able to exclude them from the key negotiating forum — the ITTO.

Despite the role played by ENGOs, states are still the main actors in bringing about changes in principles, both at the domestic and global levels. The roles played by France and Australia in rejecting the CRAMRA, that would have allowed the mining of Antarctica, and the role played by the US in pressuring states to stop whaling or face politico-economic sanctions, were critical to the adoption of environmentalist principles. The failure of any of the main producer and consumer states involved in the tropical timber regime to promote environmentalist norms is one reason that the tropical timber regime has not changed. The case studies reveal that states have been both powerful advocates for change (the US, Australia and France in the case of whaling and Antarctica) and powerful vetoers (the US, Japan and Malaysia in the case of tropical timber).

CONCLUSION

What is the 'correct' environmental approach to a particular natural resource, or to the world as a whole in this regard? How should precious natural resources be distributed and to whose benefit? The answer to these questions define what human beings are as a species. Answering these vital questions should be one of the key tasks for IPE analysts in the future. This chapter is merely meant to be a starting point for a discussion about how humans should interact with natural resources and a snapshot of the 'toolkit' of the varying choices currently available.

The exploitationist practices, as defined in this chapter, continue to be a major factor in human development. They cannot continue indefinitely, though a rapprochment between humans and nature would arguably require a "transformation of human nature" in relation to the environment. There would arguably need to be a greater understanding of how development and the biosphere interact and coexist (Kellner, 2008). Already some states and ENGOs are leading the way but more needs to be done. If humans as a species are ever to transcend exploitative practices, something all researchers can agree is a worthy goal, IPE needs to play a part. The case studies in this chapter, particularly that of tropical timber, illustrate that if the focus is on politico-economic growth, then this will invariably come at the expense of the environment.

Political economists and policy makers arguably need to be more aware of the three competing approaches outlined above. They should arguably incorporate them into their various analyses. If political economists only perceive nature as a capital asset to be exploited as efficiently as possible, as quickly as possible, the consequences will be devastating in terms of lost species and a blighted biosphere.

IPE arguably needs to put more of a focus on accounting for environmental damage and ways to avoid destructive exploitationist practices while supporting conservationist or preservationist practices where appropriate. Natural resources can no longer be considered mere 'free goods'. Any depletion must arguably be treated as a cost that should be properly accounted for (Boyce, 2003, p. 21).

Further, there arguably needs to be an end to relegating environmental matters to the periphery of IPE debate and policy-making (Williams, 1996, p. 55). This is something both conservationists and preservationists can agree on. Change is possible, as was seen in both the whaling and Antarctica case studies, where an understanding that something irreplaceable was being threatened led to transformation.

If a robust world is to be left for future generations or a biosphere preserved that contains more species than just humanity, this is fundamental. A paradigm shift will arguably have to occur.

REFERENCES

Abramovitz, J and A Mattoon (1999). Reorienting the Forest Products Economy. In *State of the World 1999: A Worldwatch Institute Report on Progress Towards a Sustainable Society*, L Starke (ed.). New York: W.W. Norton & Company.

Annual Report of the International Whaling Commission (1983). No. 33. Cambridge: International Whaling Commission.

Australian Department of the Environment and Heritage Report (2002). *Are We Sustaining Australia? Report against Sustainability Indicators*, Department of Sustainability, Environment, Water, Population and Communities.

Attfield, R (2003). Christianity. In *A Companion to Environmental Philosophy*, D. Jamieson (ed.). Oxford: Blackwell Publishing.

Bailey, J (2008). Arrested development: The fight to end commercial whaling as a case of failed norm change, *European Journal of International Relations*, 14(2), 289–318.

Barbier, E, J Burgess, J Bishop and B Aylward (1994). Deforestation: The Role of the International Trade in Tropical Timber. In *The Causes of Tropical Deforestation: The Economic and Statistical Analysis of Factors Giving Rise to the Loss of the Tropical Forests*, K Brown and D Pearce (eds.). London: UCL Press Limited.

Barry, J (1999). *Rethinking Green Politics: Nature, Virtue and Progress*. London: Sage Publications.

Benton, T (2002). Animal Rights and Social Relations. In *Environmentalism: Critical Concepts*, D Pepper, F Webster and G Revill (eds.). London: Routledge.

Birnie, P (1985). *International Regulation of Whaling: From Conservation of Whaling to Conservation of Whales and Regulation of Whale-Watching*. New York: Oceana Publications.

Boyce, J (2003). From Natural Resources to Natural Assets. In *Natural Assets: Democratizing Environmental Ownership*, J Boyce and B Shelley (eds.). London: Island Press.

Boyce, J (2002). *The Political Economy of the Environment*. Cheltenham. UK: Edward Elgar.

Brown, P (2000). *Ethics, Economics and International Relations: Transparent Sovereignty in the Commonwealth of Life*. Edinburgh: Edinburgh University Press.

Buck, S (1998). *The Global Commons: An Introduction*. Washington, DC: Island Press.

Butler, R (2010). The Harvest of Sustainable Forest Products. http://rainforests.mongabay.com/1003.htm [1 January 2012].

Carling, A (1987). Exploitation, Extortion and Oppression, *Political Studies*, XXXV, 173–188.

Carroll, R and S Prickett (1998). *The Bible: Authorised King James' Version*. Oxford: Oxford University Press.

Carter, N (2007). *The Politics of the Environment: Ideas, Activism, Policy* 2nd ed. Cambridge: Cambridge University Press.

Chasek, P (2001). *Earth Negotiations: Analyzing Thirty Years of Environmental Diplomacy.* Tokyo and New York: United Nations University Press.

Christoff, P (1996). Ecological modernisation, ecological modernities, *Environmental Politics*, 5(3), 476–500.

Ciriacy-Wantrup, S (1985). *Natural Resource Economics: Selected Papers.* London: Westview Press.

Clancy, J (1999). *The Old Dispensation: Loyalty in Business.* Madison, NJ: Fairleigh Dickenson University Press.

Clark, M (1994). The Antarctic Environmental Protocol: NGOs in the Protection of Antarctica. In *Environmental NGOs in World Politics: Linking the Local and the Global*, T Princen and M Finger (eds.). London: Routledge.

Colchester, M (1995). Colonising the Rainforests: The Agents and Causes of Deforestation. In *The Struggle for Land and the Fate of the Forests*, M Colchester and L Lohmann (eds.). London: Zed Books.

Connolly, W (1983). *The Terms of Political Discourse* 2nd ed. Princeton: Princeton University Press.

Convention on Biological Diversity (1992). http://www.cbd.int/convention/text/ [1 January 2012].

Cordonnery, L (1997). *The Implementation of the Protocol on Environmental Protection to the Antarctic Treaty: The Interplay between Law and Environmental Management.* Hobart: University of Tasmania.

Cutter, S and W Renwick (2004). *Exploitation, Conservation, Preservation: A Geographic Perspective on Natural Resource Use 4th ed.* Hoboken NJ: John Wiley & Sons Inc.

D'Amato, A and S Chopra (1991). Whales: Their emerging right to life, *The American Journal of International Law*, 85, 21–62.

DeSombre, E (2002). *The Global Environment and World Politics, International Relations for the 21st Century.* London: Continuum.

Eckersley, R (2004). Soft Law, Hard Politics, and the Climate Change Treaty. In *The Politics of International Law*, C Reus-Smit (ed.). Cambridge: Cambridge University Press.

Eckersley, R (1992). *Environmentalism and Political Theory: Toward an Ecocentric Approach.* London: UCL Press.

Elliott, L (1994). *International Environmental Politics: Protecting the Antarctic.* New York: St. Martin's Press.

Elliott, L (1993). *Protecting the Antarctic Environment: Australia and the Minerals Convention*, Australian Foreign Policy Papers. Canberra, ACT: Australian Foreign Policy Publications Programme Dept. of International Relations, Research School of Pacific Studies, Australian National University.

Examples of Sustainable Development (1987). http://www.fwrgroup.com.au/sustainable-development-examples.html [1 January 2012].

Firestone, J and J Lilley (2005). Aboriginal subsistence whaling and the right to practice and revitalise cultural traditions and customs, *Journal of International Wildlife Law and Policy*, 8(2), 177–219.

Fletcher, K (2001). The International Whaling Regime and U.S. Foreign Policy. In *The Environment, International Relations, and U.S. Foreign Policy*, P Harris (ed.). Washington. DC: Georgetown University Press.

Fox, W (1990). *Toward a Transpersonal Ecology: Developing New Foundations for Environmentalism.* Boston: Shambhala.

Frederick, M (1999). A Realist's Conceptual Definition of Environmental Security. In *Contested Grounds: Security and Conflict in the New Environmental Politics*, R Matthew and D Deudney (eds.). New York: State University of New York Press.

Fridtjof Nansen Foundation (1973). Report of a Meeting of Experts Organised by the Fridtjof Nansen Foundation on Existing Law Relevant to the Authorisation or Prohibition of Mineral Exploration for Commercial Purposes in the Antarctic Treaty Area, 30 May–10 June. Reprinted in Bush, W (1982). *Antarctica and International Law: A Collection of Inter-state and National Documents*, Vols. 1–3. London: Oceana Publications Inc.

Gillespie, A (2005). *Whaling Diplomacy: Defining Issues in International Environmental Law.* Cheltenham: Edward Elgar.

Godden L and J Peel (2010). *Environmental Law: Scientific, Policy and Regulatory Dimensions.* Oxford: Oxford University Press.

Godfrey-Smith, W (1980). The Rights of Non-Humans and Intrinsic Values. In *Environmental Philosophy*, D Mannison, M McRobbie and R Routley (eds.). Canberra: Department of Philosophy, Research School of Social Science, Australian National University.

Godfrey-Smith, W (1979). The value of wilderness, *Environmental Ethics*, 1, 309–319.

Gouldner, A (1960). The norm of reciprocity: A preliminary statement. *American Sociological Review*, 25(2), 161–178.

Hardin, G (1968). The tragedy of the commons, *Science*, 13(162), 1243–1248.

Harris, J and N Goodwin (2001). Volume Introduction. In *A Survey of Sustainable Development: Social and Economic Dimensions*, N Goodwin (ed.). Washington: Island Press.

Hay, P (2002). *Main Currents in Western Environmental Thought.* Sydney: UNSW Press.

Heilbroner, R (1988). *Beyond the Veil of Economics: Essays in the Worldly Philosophy.* Markham, Ontario: Penguin Books Canada Ltd.

Inozemtsev, V (1998). Exploitation: A phenomenon of consciousness and social conflict, *Sociological Research*, 37(6), 67–86.

International Convention for the Regulation of Whaling (1946). http://iwcoffice.org/commission/convention.htm [1 January 2012].

International Tropical Timber Agreement (1983). http://sedac.ciesin.org/entri/texts/tropical.timber.1983.html [1 January 2012].

International Whaling Statistics 1953 (1953). Oslo: The Committee for Whaling Statistics.

International Whaling Statistics 1935 (1935). Oslo: The Committee for Whaling Statistics.

Irwin, R (2000). Posing Global Environmental Problems from Conservation to Sustainable Development. In *The International Political Economy of the Environment: Critical Perspectives*, D Stevis and V Assetto (eds.). London: Lynne Rienner.

Jacobs, M (1999). *Environmental Modernisation: The New Labour Agenda.* London: The Fabian Society.

Joyner, C (1991). Cramra: The Ugly Duckling of the Antarctic Treaty System? In *The Antarctic Treaty System in World Politics*, A Jorgensen-Dahl and W Orstreng (eds.). New York: St. Martin's Press.

Kasimbazi, E (1996). Sustainable development in International Tropical Timber Agreements, *Journal of Energy & Natural Resources Law*, 14(2), 137–160.

Kellner, D (2008). Marcuse, liberation and radical ecology. *Illuminations*. http://www.uta.edu/huma/illuminations/kell11.htm [6 January 2012].

Kellow, A (2000). Norms, interests and environmental NGOs: The limits of cosmopolitanism, *Environmental Politics*, 9(9), 1–22.

Kibel, P (1999). *The Earth on Trial: Environmental Law on the International Stage*. New York: Routledge.

Kolk, A (1996). *Forests in International Environmental Politics: International Organisations, NGOs and the Brazilian Amazon*. Utrecht, Netherlands: International Books.

Larminie, G (1991). The Mineral Potential of Antarctica: The State of the Art. In *The Antarctic Treaty System in World Politics*, A Jorgensen-Dahl and W Ostreng (eds.). New York: St. Martin's Press.

Madrid Protocol (1991). Protocol on Environmental Protection to the Antarctic Treaty. http://www.antarctica.gov.au/antarctic-law-and-treaty/the-madrid-protocol [1 January 2012].

Marcuse, H and D Kellner (2005). *The New Left and the 1960s*. Abingdon, Oxon: Psychology Press.

Marcuse, H (1991). One-Dimensional Man: *Studies in the Ideology of Advanced Industrial Society*. Boston: Beacon Press.

National Park Service Public Use Statistics Office (2010). Yellowstone National Park, http://www.nature.nps.gov/stats/viewReport.cfm [1 January 2012].

Nelson, M (2003). An Amalgamation of Wilderness Preservation Arguments. In *Environmental Ethics: An Anthology*, A Light and H Rolston (eds.). Malden, MA: Blackwell Publishing.

Nineteenth Report of the Commission (1969). London: International Whaling Commission.

Norton, B (1986). Conservation and preservation: A conceptual rehabilitation, *Environmental Ethics*, 8, 195–220.

O'Riordan, T and A Jordan (1995). The precautionary principle in contemporary environmental politics, *Environmental Values*, 4, 191–212.

Oelschlaeger, M (1993). *Idea of Wilderness: From Prehistory to the Age of Ecology*. New ed. New Haven: Yale University Press.

Ommanney, F (1971). *Lost Leviathan*. London: Hutchinson.

Osborn, F (1968). *Our Plundered Planet*. New York: Pyramid Books.

Paehlke, R (1997). Environmental Values and Public Policy. In *Environmental Policy in the 1990s: Reform or Reaction*, N Vig and M Kraft (eds.). Washington: Congressional Quarterly Inc.

Passmore, J (1980). *Man's Responsibility for Nature: Ecological Problems and Western Traditions*. London: Duckworth.

Pearce, D (1989). Annex. In *Blueprint for a Green Economy,* D Pearce, A Markandya and E Barbier (eds.). London: Earthscan Publications.

Pinchot, G (2004). *The Fight for Conservation.* Whitefish, Montana: Kessinger Publications.

Pinchot, G (1998). *Breaking New Ground.* Washington: Island Press.

Poore, D (2003). *Changing Landscapes: The Development of the International Tropical Timber Organisation and Its Influence on Tropical Forest Management.* London; Sterling, VA: Earthscan Publications.

Redclift, M and G Woodgate (1994). Sociology and the Environment: Discordant Discourse. In *Social Theory and the Global Environment,* T Benton and M Redclift (eds.). London: Routledge.

Reeves, R (2002). The origins and character of 'aboriginal subsistence' whaling: A global review, *Mammal Review,* 32, 71–106.

Reiman, J (1987). Exploitation, Force and the Moral Assessment of Capitalism: Thoughts on Roemer and Cohen, *Philosophy & Public Affairs,* 16(1), 3–41.

Rodman, J (1983). Four Forms of Ecological Consciousness Reconsidered. In *Ethics and the Environment,* D Scherer and T Attig (eds.). Englewood Cliffs, NJ: Prentice Hall.

Roemer, J (1982). Property relations vs surplus value in marxian exploitation, *Philosophy & Public Affairs,* 11(4), 281–313.

Sahurie, E (1992). *The International Law of Antarctica,* New Haven Studies in International Law and World Public Order, Vol. 6. New Haven: New Haven Press.

Sessions, G (1992). Ecocentrism, Wilderness, and Global Ecosystem Protection. In *The Wilderness Condition: Essays on Environment and Civilisation,* M Oelschlager (ed.). San Francisco: Island Press.

Smith, M (1998) *Ecologism: Towards Ecological Citizenship,* Concepts in the Social Sciences. Buckingham: Open University Press.

Smith, T and P Greens (2000). Review: James Bellamy Foster's Marx ecology; Paul Burkett's Marx and nature, *Synthesis/Regeneration,* Fall.

Smouts, M (2003). *Tropical Forests, International Jungle: The Underside of Global Ecopolitics.* New York: Palgrave Macmillan.

Stevis, D and V Assetto (2000). Introduction: Problems and Solutions in the International Political Economy of the Environment. In *The International Political Economy of the Environment: Critical Perspectives,* D Stevis and V Assetto (eds.). London: Lynne Rienner.

Stoett, P (1997). *The International Politics of Whaling.* Vancouver, BC: UBC Press.

Sucharitikul, S (1996). State Responsibility and International Liability under International Law, *Loyola of Los Angeles International and Comparative Law Journal,* 18(3), 821–839.

Switzer, J (2004). *Environmental Politics: Domestic and Global Dimensions* 4th ed. Bemont, CA: Thomson Wadsworth.

Taylor, P (1989). *Respect for Nature: A Theory of Environmental Ethics.* Princeton, NJ: Princeton University Press.

The World Commission on Environment and Development (1990). *Our Common Future.* Melbourne: Oxford University Press.

United Nations (1972). Declaration of the United Nations Conference on the Human Environment ("Stockholm Declaration"). http://www.unep.org/Documents.Multilingual/Default.asp?documentid=97&articleid=1503 [1 January 2012].

UN Commission on Sustainable Development (2010). http://www.un.org/esa/dsd/csd/csd_aboucsd.shtml [1 January 2012].

US State Department Handbook of the Antarctic Treaty System 2002 (2002). Washington, DC: US State Department.

Vaillancourt, J (1996). Marxism and Ecology: More Benedictine Than Franciscan. In *The Greening of Marxism*, T Benton (ed.). New York: The Guilford Press.

Vidas, D (2000). Entry into Force of the Environmental Protocol and Implementation Issues: An Overview. In *Implementing the Environmental Protection Regime for the Antarctic*, D Vidas (ed.). Boston, MA: Kluwer Academic Publishers.

Vogler, J (2000). *The Global Commons: Environmental and Technological Governance* 2nd ed. Chichester: John Wiley.

Wall, D (1994). Ecology and Early Urban Civilisation. In *Green History: A Reader in Environmental Literature, Philosophy and* Politics, D Wall (ed.). New York: Routledge.

Walker, A (1994). Nobody Was Supposed to Survive. In *Green History: A Reader in Environmental Literature, Philosophy and Politics*, D Wall (ed.). New York: Routledge.

Wapner, P (2002). Horizontal politics: Transnational environmental activism and global cultural change, *Global Environmental Politics*, 2(2), 37–62.

Wertheimer, A (1996). *Exploitation.* Princeton, NJ: Princeton University Press.

Williams, M (1996). International Political Economy and Global Environmental Change. In *The Environment and International Relations*, J Vogler and M. Imber (eds.). London: Routledge.

CHAPTER 22

Pollution

José Pablo Zambrano Ramírez

University of Melbourne

During the 1980s several Beluga whales were found dead in the waters off the coast of the Quebec Province, Canada. In their blubber was found a high concentration of DDT (i.e. dichlorodiphenyltrichloroethane, a very powerful insecticide used for agriculture that was banned throughout the world during the 1960s and 1970s because of its harmful effects on the environment and human health); plus PCBs (polychlorinated biphenyls, a long-lived industrial compound used mainly in the manufacture of electronic goods); and Mirex (a chlorinated hydrocarbon that is used mainly as an insecticide for agricultural purposes and that was subsequently banned because of its bio-accumulative effects). All of these compounds degrade slowly. They linger in the environment, floating in the air and water, permeating the soil, and accumulating in animal fats. For this reason they are banned in most developed countries and for this reason the whales cited above were disposed of as toxic waste. Furthermore, the Quebec authorities label living whales as "toxic waste" too (Prins, 1991, p. 16). (This incident motivated Prins to write a book entitled *Top Guns and Toxic Whales* in which she highlighted the tensions between the dominant narrative of security and the world's politico-economic system.)

A few years later the political economist Easterbrook declared: "In the Western world, the Age of Pollution is nearly over"(Dryzek, 2005, p. 55), despite the fact that a Canadian research team that measures toxicity levels in the free-ranging Pacific killer-whales ('orcas') that swim in the waters of British Columbia, Canada, Washington and Alaska found blubber levels of PBCs of over one hundred and forty-six parts per million(Ross *et al.*, 2000). In humans the average is less than one part per million, which means that these killer-whales were about four to five hundred times more polluted than humans.

These reports about toxic whales, along with Easterbrook's statement, represent the extreme ends of the spectrum from which pollution problems are articulated in the Western world. When pollution issues first began to gain public attention, they were seen as local, specific problems, which were only related to dirty production processes and energy inefficiencies. They were seen as the consequence of a lack of knowledge, of technological limits, and of a lack of proper regulation. The neoclassical economic approach to these problems was to prescribe more market-based growth, since this was seen as facilitating the development of new technologies, a more rationalistic use of energy, and cleaner production processes. This claim was ostensibly credible because high-income countries seemed to manifest better environmental profiles than low-income ones. It was also argued that wealthier societies demand stronger environmental policies.

What underpinned Easterbrook's prediction of an end to the "Age of Pollution" was the belief that progress, that is, Western progress, had the capacity to overcome all the shortcomings that industrial progress causes, and is thus able to restore lost biological balances. The blubber of the free-ranging Pacific killer-whales, however, was a reminder that pollution had not been overcome. Indeed, critics of neoliberalist economics argued that capitalism had increased local and international inequalities and pollution was one of the areas where these inequalities were to be found. World-systems theory, dependency theory, and globalisation scholars (among others) emphasised the way the structure of the world's politico-economic systems in general and terms of trade in particular were unequal. The distribution of the gains and the burdens of global growth were therefore uneven. Some parties were gaining at the expense of others and this included the environmental expense (Greenhalgh, 2005; Hornborg *et al.*, 2007; Jorgenson *et al.*, 2007; Pollock, 1995).

Contemporary environmental problems, like climate change, biodiversity decline, and desertification, are complex global interactive transformations governed by uncertainty. The debate over pollution stresses the tension between neoclassical liberal economics and its critics. For the former they are externalities that have not been properly internalised in the market price of goods and services. For the latter they involve issues of intergenerational fairness (Howarth and Norgaard, 1995) and North-South equity (Giljum and Eisenmenger, 2003) that require a broader, more systemic approach than the one standard market analysis adopts.

Production and consumption are the driving forces of contemporary capitalism. Producers, commodities, and consumer demands determine the supply of goods and services. To fully conceptualise the environmental impact of the dominant politico-economic system it is important to understand the driving forces behind contemporary capitalism and the contemporary global market.

An example of these issues can be found in the research done on 'carbon footprints'. As stated by the World Bank (2010), in 2009, high-income countries earned almost the seventy percent of the world's gross domestic product (GDP). The twenty richest economies — including developing nations like China and Brazil — earned almost eighty percent of the world's wealth. At the same time, in

2006, the OECD and a few rapidly developing countries were responsible for over seventy percent of the carbon dioxide emissions from fossil-fuel combustion (World Bank, 2009). China and the US alone were responsible for forty percent of the world's carbon dioxide. Measured on a per capita basis, the top per capita emitter released ten times the global average (World Bank, 2009). The average carbon dioxide emission around the world is 4.3 tonnes per person.

Moving from the production to the consumption of carbon, the picture changes, for example, a study by Davis and Caldeira (2010) shows that approximately twenty-three percent of all carbon dioxide emissions from the burning of fossil fuels were emitted during the production of goods that were ultimately consumed in a different country. On a per capita basis, the net export of the emissions of the US, Japan and Western Europe are the equivalent to each individual consuming between 2.4 to 10.3 tons of carbon dioxide, while the net export of emissions from China, Russia and the Middle East range on average from 0.9 to 2.0 tons.

> Interpreted as an indicator of the global equity of emissions in trade, these figures suggest that individual consumers in the most affluent and least populous countries of Western Europe, for example, are importing the same mass of emissions as are exported by 5–10 people in China (Davis and Caldeira, 2010, p. 5689).

This chapter seeks to highlight the environmental consequences of the current global production/consumption system and the uneven distribution of both the environmental and politico-economic benefits and burdens of trade. It is organised as follows: firstly, it provides an overview of how the modernist narrative articulates pollution problems and the discourses that critique it. Secondly, it reviews part of the research that uses bio-physical indicators to illustrate the uneven/unequal distribution of the benefits and burdens of international trade. Thirdly, it stresses the ambiguous consequences of the Western development model. It concludes with some final reflections.

THE MODERNIST ARTICULATION OF POLLUTION

From a neoclassical liberalist perspective, pollution is market failure. It is a negative externality that has not been properly accounted for in the price of goods and or services.

In an ostensibly free market economy, with a symmetric distribution of information, the price mechanism is seen as the most efficient way to allocate resources which are by definition always scarce. Consumers' competing demands shape the supply of services and goods, while firms compete to provide — at the lowest cost possible — what consumers demand.

At its optimal equilibrium point, consumer demand and producer surplus is maximised. In this way the price mechanism is able to maximise social welfare.

There are circumstances, however, where prices do not fully reflect the total benefits and/or costs of market transactions. Market failures can lead to outcomes that are not socially optimal, that is, since the costs of the transactions involved fall on third parties who did not directly incur them. From this perspective, pollution and environmental problems are a by-product of market activity — a negative externality or a dis-economy resulting from the poorly executed exploitation of natural resources and the mis-production and mis-consumption of industrial goods.

As the International Monetary Fund (IMF) argues, there are numerous reasons for market failure. These range from a lack of the appropriate property rights, inadequate environmental standards, a lack of governmental enforcement capacities, and/or poverty and overpopulation. From a neoclassical liberalist perspective, however, pollution problems need to be addressed because "[u]ninternalised externalities not only lead to environmental degradation, but also threaten market failures that ... diminish the efficiency of international economic exchanges, reduce gains from trade, and lower social welfare" (Esty, 2001, p. 116).

The most common approach to correcting such failure is by direct government intervention in the form of regulation, that is, by introducing monitoring and enforcement systems like standards, permits, licences, and controls over water and land use. These are known in neoclassical liberalist terms as command-and-control (CAC) methods (Bernstein, 1993). There are also market-based instruments (MBIs) and economic incentives (EIs) which use price, plus any other politico-economic variable, to encourage polluters to reduce harmful emissions or make their products less polluting. These can include taxes, subsidies, tradable permits, deposit-refund systems, eco-labelling, and liability for harm (Field and Field, 2002).

Ecological modernisation theory acknowledges that politico-economic development has resulted in environmental problems but it places great emphasis on the role of human agency, not only with regard to the cause of these problems but also with regard to potential solutions to them. To tackle pollution it focuses on the industrial mode of production and consumption (and how this might be modified by innovation), the diffusion of new technologies, and the most appropriate management techniques. In line with neoclassical liberalism, the ecological modernisation approach believes that further politico-economic growth is sufficient to tackle environmental issues.

Regardless of how immobile institutions and social structures might seem, they are shaped by human agents and can therefore be reshaped (Spaargaren, 2010). In the same way that cost-benefit analysis is supposed to lead to market efficiency, developmental progress makes firms and governments weigh the costs of ecological disruption and become more ecologically rationalistic. It is precisely the linkages between politico-economic growth, trade, the environment, and the consequences of the different attempts to correct 'market failures' that lead to the differences between neoclassical liberalists and their critics.

POLLUTION, POLITICO-ECONOMIC GROWTH AND THE ENVIRONMENTAL KUTZNETS CURVE

Standard neoclassical/liberalist analysis sees the impact of trade on a country's political economy and environment in three dimensional terms. It refers, that is, to 'scale' effects (whereby the expansion generated by market access increases pollution); 'technological' effects (whereby trade and wealth increase, giving a country access to more advanced, greener technologies and resulting in stronger environmental regulation because of the social demand for it); and 'composition' effects (whereby changes in the structure of the political economy are induced by specialisation in those activities where a country has a comparative advantage) (Grossman and Krueger, 1993).

One of the arguments used to support the claim that politico-economic growth improves the quality of the environment is based on the observation that at earlier stages of development, when a country industrialises, some pollutants appear to increase until wealth reaches a particular point. After this, emissions appear to decrease. This is known as the Environmental Kutznets Curve (EKC). Grossman and Krueger first observed this phenomenon after studying the concentration of air pollutants in a cross-section of urban areas in different countries. There is a substantial literature that expands upon these initial findings, applying them to other pollutants like carbon, lead, automobile emissions, toxic waste, and indoor air pollution (for a more detailed review see also Levinson, 2000; Rothman, 1998; WTO, 1999).

In general terms, the Kutznets-curve hypothesis can be re-formulated as an argument about per capita income and how above a certain level, 'technique' and 'composition' effects outweigh 'scale' ones (Esty, 2001). This modernisation and 'industrialisation greening' process is not automatic, however, since it only happens if developing countries substitute cleaner technologies for dirty ones and if stringent environmental policies are enacted and enforced. As stated by Grossman and Krueger (1995, p. 372):

> Richer countries, which tend to have relatively cleaner urban air and relatively cleaner river basins, also have relatively more stringent environmental standards and stricter enforcement of their environmental laws than middle-income and poorer countries.

Underpinning the neoclassical liberalist perspective are two inter-related assumptions. These are that the majority of environmental pressures will stay within the geographical boundaries of nation states and that with the proper mixture of environmental policies and market incentives, these pressures can be overcome. Is this the case, however?

WORLD-SYSTEMS THEORY AND THE UNEQUAL TERMS OF GLOBAL TRADE

Neoclassical liberalist economists see in 'technique' and 'composition' effects, ways of overcoming the negative consequences of 'scale' effects. Their approach sees in 'technique' effects the force that drives global power relations. Coupled with 'composition' effects, they see this force as transferring environmental burdens from the North to South. They see it as deepening the pervasive consequences that 'scale' effects have as a source of politico-economic growth.

World-systems theory seeks to explain the dynamics of the 'capitalist world economy' as a 'total social system', integrated in terms of the world market. The core and the periphery are two different regions, the former oriented towards capital-intensive production, the latter towards labour-intensive production. They are both parts of a power hierarchy, however, where semi-peripheral states act as a buffer zone (Hornborg *et al.*, 2007; Martinez-Vela, 2001).

Technology is a central factor in the positioning of a nation state in the world system. Developed countries are in the core and less-developed countries are on the periphery. The notion of unequal exchange is central to this positioning. This is defined as "asymmetrical power relationships between industrialised and non-industrialised countries wherein the former gain disproportionate advantages at the expense of the latter through political-economic relations" (Rice, 2009, p. 219).

In its ecological articulation, world-systems analysis assumes that core countries preserve their own ecological capital through the appropriation of biomass and energy and the usurpation of the sink-capacity and waste assimilation properties of ecological systems. They are able to import resources from and export waste to the periphery. Politico-economic growth, in other words, makes it possible for prosperous states to reallocate their environmental burdens to less affluent countries. Moreover, this pattern of practices is highly dynamic. The constant expansion of production, with its asymmetric distribution of gains and burdens (both environmental and politico-economic) is what Schnaiberg (1980) and Schnaiberg and Gould (1994) call the treadmill-of-production.

Andersson and Lindroth (2001, p. 120) complement this perspective with what they call the rich-country-illusion effect. This effect means that the inhabitants of high-income countries have the illusion of a sustainable lifestyle because their environments seem not to be eroding. The *Environment Report* of the World Trade Organisation (1999) states that an inverted U-shaped pollution path (EKC) has been found for some indicators which are related to certain types of local — primarily urban — air pollution, and some types of freshwater pollutants. In contrast, pollutants of a more global nature do not support the predictions of the EKC hypothesis, particularly carbon dioxide emissions. These show a tendency towards constant growth (WTO, 1999).

BIOPHYSICAL INDICATORS: TRACING UNEQUAL EXCHANGE

Using bio-physical indicators, critics of the above approach have shown the limitations of a classical, neoliberalist analysis when it comes to unpacking the environmental pressures built into such a model. They expose the environmental consequences of international politico-economic specialisation for specific countries and global regions, and the implications for both the abuse of natural resources and of the generation of waste and emissions (Giljum and Eisenmenger, 2003).

Several accounting concepts and indicators have been used, for example, to understand environmental impacts and the effects of international trade. These include the carbon footprint (the CF; see Hertwich and Peters, 2009; Prew, 2010); material flow accounting and analysis (Giljum and Eisenmenger, 2003); and energy-related concepts (Odum, 1984).

Since the most extensively used indicator is the first one — the carbon footprint (Jorgenson, 2005; Jorgenson and Rice, 2005; Özler and Obach, 2009; Wackernagel and Rees, 1996) — what follows reviews CF. It looks at some of the large body of research this now entails.

THE CARBON FOOTPRINT

For example, Hertwich and Peters (2009) have studied the emission of greenhouse gases (GHG), such as carbon dioxide, methane, nitrous oxide and fluoride, that are part of the production of the goods and services consumed in seventy-three nations and fourteen global regions. They have also analysed the resulting CF using eight categories: construction, shelter, food, clothing, mobility, manufactured products, services and trade.

They have found that rising income causes a substantial degree of systematic change in consumption patterns. There is a strong correlation, in other words, between carbon footprint and per capita consumption expenditure as nations. In brief the CF increases by fifty-seven percent for each doubling of consumption (Hertwich and Peters, 2009).

At a global level, seventy-two percent of the CF is related to household consumption. Nutrition is one of the most relevant categories, accounting for almost twenty percent of GHG emissions. This is followed by shelter — the operation and maintenance of houses — which is responsible for nearly nineteen percent of global GHG emissions (Hertwich and Peters, 2009). There is also a significant correlation between geographic location and energy consumption for heating. For countries like Russia, forty percent of their CF is connected to their shelter-related expenditure. This is consistent with the conclusions of York *et al.* (2003), who found a strong correlation between countries' geographical distance from the equator and their ecological footprint. Countries in arctic regions have a forty percent greater CF than those in the tropics.

The impact of politico-economic growth in developing countries can be seen in the construction sector as well. In terms of the global average this sector accounts for ten percent of a country's GHG emissions. For developing countries, however, like China or Vietnam, it represents up to twenty-five percent and twenty percent respectively. This reflects a general trend as countries develop (Hertwich and Peters, 2009).

Private household mobility also accounts for seventeen percent of GHG emissions. Half of this is fuel combustion by private motorists, and as might be expected, this category is more relevant for rich countries.

The CF and the gross domestic product can also be correlated. In the period 2007 to 2009, for example, with the world's economy contracting due to the global financial crisis (the GFC), there was a decrease in global carbon emissions that paralleled the decline in the global gross domestic product (Davis and Caldeira, 2010).

One of the ways to measure the environmental impact of world affairs is through expenditure on defence. Military spending is a 'luxury' that can be strictly afforded only by developed countries or ones that aspire to a vigilant strategic position in the world system.

The US has the largest and most modern armed forces in the world. Not coincidentally the Department of Defence is "the world's leading consumer of petroleum" (Klare, 2007, as quoted in Jorgenson *et al.*, 2010, p. 11). Military power assists in the reproduction of unequal international ecological exchanges through direct and symbolic geo-political threats (Jorgenson, 2005; Jorgenson *et al.*, 2010). The "treadmill-of-destruction" (Hooks and Smith, 2004; 2005), for example, says that the dynamics of military technological development and militarism (derived in part from the politico-economic system) have their own expansionary logic and their own unique environmental impacts that are not limited to periods of war. Jorgenson *et al.* (2010) have found that military expenditure per soldier, and military participation, positively affect both total and per capita carbon dioxide emissions. Subsequently, states with more high-tech and labour-intensive militaries emit relatively higher overall carbon dioxide emissions.

THE ECOLOGICAL FOOTPRINT

The ecological footprint (EF) is an accounting tool that aggregates human demand with respect to ecosystems and compares it with nature's capacity to regenerate. For any given political economy or population, CF analysis measures how much nature (expressed in global hectares) would be required on a continuous basis to provide all the energy/material resources consumed and how much would be required to absorb all the wastes discharged by a particular population with its prevailing technology (wherever on earth those hectares are located) (Wackernagel and Rees, 1996, pp. 51–52). Because this accounting approach quantifies the overall amount of biomass and the waste absorption required to satisfy human consumption, it has the advantage of measuring anthropogenic pressure on the environment regardless of where the resources come from. It does not require the analyst to know specifically what use the consumed resources will be put to (Hooks and Smith, 2005; York *et al.*, 2003).

As with any other aggregate indicator, this has its limits, however. The most common critique is to do with 'current technology'. It is said that this indicator neither incorporates 'technique' effects (Costanza, 2000) nor distinguishes between what is sustainable and fair (Andersson and Lindroth, 2001; Costanza, 2000). Another critique is that accounts of consumption, regardless of the form of extraction, cannot measure environmental quality in any specific geographical region (Özler and Obach, 2009).

Despite these caveats, the EF is very useful for estimating the ecological impact of the lifestyle of a given population, because it is a measure of how much a certain population consumes, not a measure of how much the natural capital of a certain territory is exploited (Andersson and Lindroth, 2001). This allows it to overcome the "rich country illusion effect" because it captures the indirect consequences of consumption that are otherwise difficult to measure (Jorgenson and Rice, 2005).

A growing body of work in the social sciences uses CF accounting to understand the environmental impact of politico-economic growth. The analysis of the per capita EF is a good indicator of global inequalities (York *et al.*, 2003) since a country's level of per capita consumption is largely a function of its relative position in the core/periphery hierarchy of the world system, its urbanisation level, its domestic income inequality, and the amount of human capital it commands (Jorgenson, 2003; 2005). Trying to unravel the causes of environmental degradation, York *et al.* (2003) have found that the EF of nations is strongly related to GDP per capita and population size.

The EF is also a good indicator of the link between a country's position in the world system and its environmental impact. Consistent with the findings of Jorgenson *et al.* (2010), who have studied the relationship between the CF and the "treadmill-of-destruction", Jorgenson (2003; 2005) finds that the EF of a country is positively affected by military expenditure per soldier. This is due to an increase in the consumption of natural resources, in addition to other driving forces behind the EF: "Countries with greater military technological power, [which are] part and parcel of the treadmill-of-destruction, have pernicious environmental impacts independent of capital intensity and the treadmill-of-production" (Jorgenson, 2005, p. 392).

As CF analysis demonstrates, high-income countries present large ecological footprints but generally experience lower domestic levels of particular forms of environmental degradation, like air and organic water pollution, or deforestation (Jorgenson, 2003; 2005; Jorgenson and Burns, 2007; Jorgenson *et al.*, 2007). This is consistent with the findings of Hertwich and Peters (2009) and with the WTO *Trade and the Environment* report (1999).

On the contrary, export dependence can have a negative effect on natural resource consumption (Jorgenson, 2003). Less-developed countries, with higher levels of exports, can present low ecological footprints (Jorgenson and Rice, 2005) but can still suffer from severe environmental problems (Hornborg *et al.*, 2007). This is known as the consumption/degradation paradox (Jorgenson, 2010).

THE ECOLOGICAL FOOTPRINT OF CAPITALISM AS SUCH

As noted above, several research efforts have tried to unpack the environmental consequences of trade, growth, and a country's position in the world political-economic hierarchy. Very few researchers have examined the effects of capitalism itself, however. One such study uses the Economic Freedom Index (EFI) indicator (Özler and Obach, 2009), developed by the Heritage Foundation, to assess the environmental impact of capitalism as such. The EFI has nine measures that represent what the Foundation defines as essential 'economic freedoms'. The most remarkable result of this study is the finding that the more a state's policies tend towards *laissez-faire*, the greater its CF is likely to be. In almost all categories, free-market capitalism, if unchecked by government action, increases environmental degradation. Controlling for urbanisation, exports, per capita GDP, and climate, a one-point increase in the EF measure is associated with a 1.2 percent increase in per capita EF. Other factors like trade, monetary policy, financial policy and property rights, have a positive effect on the EF of nations as well.

When controlling for environmental regulation, this study shows that the stronger they are the weaker the per capita EF. Thus, state action has the capacity to effectively control environmental degradation. At the same time, government spending and taxation have been found to increase EF. This ambiguous result requires further research if the impact of state policy is to be fully understood.

CAPITALISM, POLLUTION AND CONSUMPTION

Ecological and CF analysis show that environmental degradation is driven by factors usually associated with modernisation and development, factors like urbanisation, capital intensity, export dependence patterns, high GDP per capita, and a core position in the world system. On the one hand, this directly contradicts the EKC hypothesis, because if progress were not harmful for the environment then developed countries would have reduced carbon and ecological footprints. On the other hand, bio-physical analyses tend to give support to the treadmill-of-production approach, that is, high-income countries externalise the environmental burdens of their consumption-based lifestyles by importing biomass and sink-capacity from less-developed countries.

Andersson and Lindroth (2001) warn that "the rich-country-illusion effect" can have two mutually enforcing consequences. It can prescribe unsustainable politico-economic growth for less-developed countries since it can be seen as the solution to all their pollution problems. Meanwhile the citizens of rich countries can assume that their environmental issues can be solved by ecologically unsustainable/uneven consumption patterns and can promote such patterns accordingly.

As explained earlier, ecological modernisation theory acknowledges that environmental problems are associated with politico-economic development. It also predicts that through innovation, the diffusion of new technologies, and the transfer of knowledge from high-income to less-developed countries, these problems can be solved. A key issue remains, however. Even if developing countries adopt greener technologies and enact more sophisticated environmental policies that reduce their emission of pollutants, this does not necessarily mean that their concerns are dealt with. In a study evaluating ecological modernisation theory in Brazil, for example, Milanez and Bührs (2008) demonstrate the ambiguous consequences of technological transfer. Until the 1990s the pulp and paper industry in Brazil mostly supplied its local demand. When it began to expand and oriented its production towards the international markets — mainly the European Union — most firms implemented ECF ('elemental chlorine free') and TCF ('totally chlorine free') bleaching technologies in order to comply with EU regulations. This triggered a change from reactive to preventative strategies. It also improved efficiency in terms of energy and water consumption and reduced overall costs. While these new technologies helped lower pollution levels wherever pulp and paper projects were established in Brazil, they faced strong opposition from local communities, for two key reasons: firstly, they involved the expropriation of land and, secondly, they caused the loss of native forests and the advent of a eucalyptus monoculture that allegedly harmed soil quality, reduced flora and fauna diversity, and decreased the water table. As Milanez and Bührs (2008, p. 797) argue:

> The pressure exerted by international actors for ECF/TCF bleaching has drawn attention (and resources) away from the land access issue that is of foremost importance to millions of Brazilian peasants, whilst giving the industry a green image.

A similar situation related to the lives of local communities can be found with regard to so-called 'super-seeds'. In order to 'produce' greater yields, to withstand pesticide, and to achieve higher growth rates, seeds of various grains and species have been genetically modified (GMO) to make them more productive and less dependent on the seasons. This has been the case with regard to rice in many Asian villages and communities where different aid programmes, aimed at fighting famine, have replaced 'traditional' seeds with new modified 'super-seeds'. This said, "[l] ocal knowledge ... focuses on [the] multiple-use of diversity. Rice is not just a grain; it provides straw for thatching and mat-making, fodder for livestock, bran for fish ponds, husks for fuel" (Shiva, 1995, p. 48). 'Super-seeds', by contrast, are water intensive and hence dry the soil. They are also genetically manipulated to prevent them from producing their own seeds. The consequence is that now local communities not only cannot use the rice in comprehensive ways but also have to depend on seed producers for their subsistence.

In short, local communities in less-developed countries have had their lives disrupted by the ambiguous consequences of this technological development. GMO seeds have dramatically changed the agricultural market in the US too. In 1970 the Monsanto Company, a US-based multinational agricultural biotechnology corporation developed 'Roundup', a non-selective herbicide capable of killing almost all plants. Because it was non-selective it was used for weed control along roadsides and in tree plantations. Nowadays it is the world's best-selling herbicide (Bloomberg, 2010). In 1996 Monsanto started to commercialise 'Roundup Ready' soybean seeds, a 'Roundup' tolerant seed that can grow even in the presence of the herbicide. Since then, it has also developed several GMO corn varieties that result in crops able to fight pests and resist weed-killing treatments. Currently in the US, through its branded products and licensing, Monsanto has ninety-eight percent of the soybean market and seventy-nine percent of the corn market (Reuters, 2010).

As noted in a study by Moshini *et al.* (2000), these seeds have the potential to cut production costs relative to standard varieties because 'Roundup Ready' technology involves lower herbicide expenses. It also makes crops less dependent on weather conditions for weed control. 'Roundup Ready' technology entails higher seed costs, however, and very restrictive contractual terms. Farmers can use the seed exclusively for planting but cannot resell it and cannot use harvested beans as seeds for next year's crop (Moshini *et al.*, 2000). Furthermore, Monsanto actively pursues, in order to take to court and sue, farmers who attempt to save seeds for the next year's crop[1] (see also the documentary *Food, Inc.*, Kenner, 2008). 'Roundup Ready' soybeans seeds have increased the overall efficiency of the soybean market and consumers benefit from this efficiency, however, an example like this does raise the question: who is really enjoying the benefits of such a technological innovation?

> In the long run, the major benefits of innovation flow through into lower production costs in user industries, lower prices and higher quality products, all of which ultimately benefit final consumers. The temporary profits earned by innovative firms will accrue to shareholders, who tend to be concentrated in higher income groups ... this direct income addition from innovation is accompanied by a further concentration of gains to rich final consumers (Greenhalgh, 2005, p. 1099).

THE TRAGEDY OF THE MODERN CONSUMER

Politico-economic growth, international trade, and globalisation have undoubtedly changed the composition of state markets as well as of the global system (Rothman, 1998, p. 185). Contemporary transport and production processes have widened the distance — geographical and symbolic — between producers and consumers, a distance that has been mediated in turn by a blurry web of market agents and 'middlemen'.

The treadmill-of-production concept is a powerful analytical image to apply to the dynamics of the capitalist narrative implicit above. Given that, from a neoclassical/liberalist perspective, supply and production processes are driven by consumption patterns, acknowledging them as such highlights an understanding of the capitalist system.

If, as neoclassical liberalists assume, the demand for goods and services determines production patterns, and resources are always scarce and cannot satisfy all market demands, then the follow-up question is: whose demands does the market satisfy? Or, alternatively, how and where are resources been allocated?

Neoclassical liberalists assume that the market is neutral in meeting demands, that is, that it does not prioritise any particular demands because resources are allocated by the price mechanism. Smith's 'invisible hand' concept underpins the

---

[1]http://www.monsanto.com/newsviews/Pages/why-does-monsanto-sue-farmers-who-save-seeds.aspx.

assumption that individual self-interest promotes aggregate welfare. Most politico-economic analysis is based on models of individual utility and absolute consumption of this kind. However, the ostensible neutrality of the market can also be seen as biased against equity and fairness. Demand denotes the willingness to pay, though demands that are met by supply are not necessarily the ones that are most needed. If they were:

> ... [w]hy after so many years of economic growth do we observe simultaneously unmet needs of the poor and seemingly inexhaustible demand from the rich? Why are the rich not yet satisfied, so that entrepreneurs in the market could turn their inventive activities to better supplying the basic needs of the poor today and harboring resources for supplying basic needs tomorrow (Greenhalgh, 2005, p. 1100)?

Higher income equals access to a wider variety of services and goods. Because context and evaluation are relevant factors in consumption patterns, as income rises and basic needs are satisfied, consumption reorients itself towards 'positional' goods. The demand for 'positional' goods and services is constantly adapting to changes in the social and material context. Frank *et al.* (2010) show how changes in a group's spending shifts the frame of reference defining consumption standards. The authors define this phenomenon in terms of "expenditure cascades".

Friedman's "permanent income" concept states that a family — rich or poor — saves and spends a constant proportion of its income (Friedman, 1957; as quoted in Frank *et al.*, 2010). Two findings contradict this statement. On the one hand, in the US since the 1970s, the aggregate personal savings rate has fallen from an average of roughly ten percent to below zero in the years immediately before the economic downturn of 2007. On the other hand, in 1980, the median size of a newly constructed house was approximately sixteen hundred square feet. By 2001 it had grown to over twenty-one hundred square feet — more than twice the corresponding growth in the median family (Frank *et al.*, 2010, pp. 4–5). This suggests that inequality can lead to financial distress — aggregate and personal. Those trying to catch up either increase their debts or exhaust their savings, while rich people simply buy bigger houses.

It is worth mentioning that this consumption pattern is not just a blind race towards the latest technological gadget, a bigger residence, or dinner in a more fashionable restaurant. As exemplified by Frank *et al.* (2010), good quality schools are usually located in wealthy — or not poor — neighbourhoods. Investing in a better house can also entail investing in intangible assets that might be the key to a better standard of living. Thus a job seeker who wants to be successful in an interview might buy a suit, which in turn might make a significant difference in terms of achieving not just a social but a personal goal, namely, a meaningful job.

Hardin's (1968) germinal essay *The Tragedy of the Commons* describes the dilemma whereby multiple individuals demand a common resource until each of their expected benefits are matched by the expected costs. Because each user ignores the costs imposed on others, this ultimately ends in the depletion of the resource, despite this not being in anyone's long-term interest. With all the caveats that this narrative requires, the tragedy of the contemporary consumer is that he or she is trapped in a system that both overtly and covertly encourages him or her to demand goods and services, and that these consumption decisions are the fuel of the treadmill-of-production that increases inequalities and enlarges environmental distress, including the distress of global pollution.

THE TRAGEDY IN TERMS OF THE RESULTANT POLLUTION

Most of the goods and services offered in the market involve ecological footprints — extraction, production, labelling, transport and marketing — that are not properly factored into their price. The modern consumer may or may not be aware of the embedded environmental impact of her or his decisions. The consumer needs a basic amount to satisfy essential needs, like food or shelter, and often the least environmentally friendly goods and services are the most accessible ones, that is, the least expensive ones. Even worse, they may be the least healthy as well. As shown by Kenner (2008) in his documentary *Food, Inc.*, poor families in developed countries may have to choose between "a dollar meal" in a junk food restaurant where a family of four can be "fed" for less than five dollars, or pay over a dollar for a kilo of vegetables.

It can also be the case that the contemporary consumer consciously and deliberately chooses goods and services that are socially and/or environmentally friendly, like coffee beans from the Fair Trade alliance. When a Chilean tourist enjoys a coffee in a café in Australia, made with Fair Trade beans from Colombia, packed in a Tetra Pak bag produced in Argentina, prepared in a machine made of stainless steel from China but engineered in Italy; and when that tourist pays three Australian dollars for that coffee in a recycled-paper cup, he or she might be helping the Colombian farmer who belongs to the Fair Trade alliance, but the ecological footprint of that coffee is far more problematic.

To help reduce the size of embodied EFs, organic products are presented as a better alternative to non-organic ones because they do not involve pesticides and are locally produced. Both are deemed more environmentally friendly. Because there are no chemicals involved, nor GMO seeds, they are supposed to be healthier as well. Most of the time organic products are more expensive, however, than polluted fruits and vegetables because they are 'positional' goods. Moreover, if everyone consumed just local products the Colombian farmer would not have a market wide enough or deep enough to commercialise his or her harvest.

Usually critics of capitalism remark on the 'perverse' logic of the system, with all the inequalities and unfairness associated with it. But consumers in high-income countries do not choose goods and services to preserve in a perverse fashion their privileges over citizens in less affluent states. Consumers just try to satisfy their needs and live meaningful lives. This said, while the systemic forces behind capitalism can be held responsible for the inequalities in the distribution of the benefits and burdens of economic activity and trade, it is consumers who are the driving force behind politico-economic expansion and who are the ones ultimately responsible for the impact of their decisions — including the environmental impact.

CONCLUSION

Production and consumption are the driving forces of the global politico-economic system. One begets the other in a market dialectic that neoclassical liberalists, marxists, feminists and the like see in very different terms.

While acknowledging that Western 'progress' has its shortcomings, neoclassical liberalists see the market as intrinsically cornucopian, being predicated in principle upon boundless growth. They see it as being bolstered by technological developments potentially without end and as able, by using resources efficiently, to solve any of the problems that result from such growth.

In practice such an approach is not so simple. Western needs are typically met, for example, at the expense of those of local communities, while research done with bio-physical indicators shows that the 'composition' (comparative advantage) effects of politico-economic growth, in most cases, perpetuate or exacerbate the hierarchic distribution of power in the world system.

The ecological consequences of this are that developed countries are able to preserve their environmental capital by appropriating the sink-capacity of less-developed countries. In the process, however, they 'overuse' resources held in common like the quality of the world's air and the quality of the world's water.

In addition to these issues of North-South equity, one of the most complex aspects of global pollution is the way 'modern' waste can linger in the environment for long periods of time. The two paradigmatic examples in this regard are nuclear waste and plastic waste.

Enriched uranium (U-238) has a half-life of four and a half billion years. Although the production and use of nuclear material today is highly regulated and controlled, especially in the Western world, this was not always so. The *Yablokov Commision Report* (Yablokov *et al.*, 1993) found that the former USSR disposed of medium- and low-level radioactive waste in international waters without providing the International Maritime Organisation with any word that they had done so.

Despite its best efforts, the *Report* could not determine the exact amount of radionuclides that was dumped into the marine environment at this time.

Plastic is an artificial polymer that does not bio-degrade. Rather, it breaks down into infinitesimally small particles. This creates problems for wildlife which die from ingesting these particles, if they have not already become entangled in a cruder form of this material. More relevant from a human perspective is that plastic debris in the marine environment has been shown to contain organic contaminants, such as the DDT and PCBs found in the Beluga whales. There is a growing debate regarding the consequences of these contaminants for the food chain and what their bio-accumulative effects might be.

These two examples show how intergenerational fairness is not just a matter of the aesthetic value of nature. It presents potentially unprecedented and unpredictable problems for global health, including global human health.

So: Western 'progress' rests on a self-reinforcing, hegemonic logic whereby the shortcomings of politico-economic expansion are ostensibly overcome with more (neoclassical/liberalist/marketeering) expansion. For many pollution-related problems, however, there are no technical solutions — at least given current technology — to those that 'progress' presents.

Scientific advances can be very successful catalysts for change, but long-term solutions involve close consideration of the values that underpin scientific detachment itself. In this regard the current Western consumption-based lifestyle is arguably neither ecologically sustainable nor socially fair. Indeed, it may not be surmountable by 'technological' (new technologies) or 'compositional' (comparative advantage) means at all. It may require, in short, a radical change in lifestyle.

Nowhere is this arguably more so than in the fight against global pollution. In no way is the environment arguably more stressed.

REFERENCES

Andersson, J and M Lindroth (2001). Ecologically unsustainable trade, *Ecological Economics*, 37, 113–122.

Bernstein, J (1993). *Alternative Approaches to Pollution Control and Waste Management: Regulatory and Economic Instruments*. UNDP/ UNCHS/ World Bank.

Costanza, R (2000). The dynamics of the ecological footprint, *Ecological Economics*, 32, 341–345.

Davis, S and K Caldeira (2010). Consumption-based accounting of CO_2 emissions, *Proceedings of the National Academy of Sciences*, 107(12): 5687–5692. www.pnas.org/cgi/doi/10.1073/pnas.0906974107 [24 December 2011].

Dryzek, J (2005). *The Politics of the Earth: Environmental Discourses*. New York: Oxford University Press.

Esty, D (2001). Bridging the Trade-Environment Divide, *Journal of Economic Perspectives*, 15(3), 113–130.

Field, B and M Field (2002). *Environmental Economics: An Introduction.* New York: McGray-Hill/Irwin.

Frank, R, A Levine and O Dijk (2010). Expenditure Cascades. http://ssrn.com/abstract=1690612 [24 December 2011].

Gillam, C (2010). UPDATE 1-DuPont urges U.S. to curb Monsanto seed monopoly. *Reuters*, 8 January.

Giljum, S and N Eisenmenger (2003). North-South Trade and the Distribution of Environmental Goods and Burdens. *Sustainable Europe Research Institute (SERI), Working Paper* No. 2 (June).

Greenhalgh, C (2005). Why does market capitalism fail to deliver a sustainable environment and greater equality of incomes? *Cambridge Journal of Economics*, 29, 1091–1109.

Grossman, G and A Krueger (1995). Economic Growth and the Environment, *The Quarterly Journal of Economics*, 110(2), 353–377.

Grossman, G and A Krueger (1993). Environmental Impacts of a North American Free Trade Agreement. In *The Mexico-US Free Trade Agreement*, P Garber (ed.). Cambridge, MA.: MIT Press.

Hardin, G (1968). The tragedy of the commons, *Science*, 13(162), 1243–1248.

Hertwich, E and G Peters (2009). Carbon footprint of nations: A global, trade-linked analysis, *Environmental Science & Technology*, 43, 6414–6420.

Hooks, G and C Smith (2005). Treadmills of production and destruction: Threats to the environment posed by militarism, *Organisation and Environment*, 18(1), 19–37.

Hooks, G and C Smith (2004). The treadmill of destruction: National sacrifice areas and native Americans, *American Sociologial Review*, 69, 558–575.

Hornborg, A, J McNeill and J Martinez-Alier (2007). *Rethinking Environmental History: World-system History and Global Environmental Change.* Plymouth: AltaMira Press.

Howarth, R and R Norgaard (1995). Intergenerational Choices under Global Environmental Change. In *The Handbook of Environmental Economics*, D Bromley (ed.). Cambridge, MA.: Blackwell Publishers.

Jorgenson, A (2010). World-economic integration, supply depots, and environmental degradation: A study of ecologically unequal exchange, foreign investment dependence, and deforestation in less developed countries, *Critical Sociology*, 36(3), 453–477.

Jorgenson, A (2005). Unpacking international power and the ecological footprints of nations: A quantitative cross-national study, *Sociological Perspectives*, 48(3), 383–402.

Jorgenson, A (2003). Consumption and environmental degradation: A cross-national analysis of the ecological footprint, *Social Problems*, 50(3) 374–394.

Jorgenson, A and T Burns (2007). The political-economic causes of change in the ecological footprints of nations, 1991–2001. A quantitative investigation, *Social Science Research*, 36, 834–853.

Jorgenson, A, B Clark and J Kentor (2010). Militarisation and the environment: A panel study of carbon dioxide emissions and the ecologial footprints of nations, 1970–2000, *Global Environmental Politics*, 10(1), 7–29.

Jorgenson, A, C Dick and M Mahutga (2007). Foreign investment dependence and the environment: An ecostructural approach, *Social Problems*, 54(3), 371–394.

Jorgenson, A and J Rice (2005). Structural dynamics of international trade and material consumption: A cross-national study of the ecological footprints of less-developed countries, *Journal of World-Systems Research*, 11(1), 57–77.

Kaskey, J (2010). DuPont Gains on Monsanto as Farmers Question High-Tech Seeds. *Bloomberg*, 24 August.

Kenner, R (2008). *Food, Inc.*, Magnolia Pictures, Participant Media, River Road Entertainment.

Kojima, M and R Bacon (2009). Changes in CO_2 Emissions from Energy Use. *Extractive Industries for Development Series #11*, World Bank.

Levinson, A (2000). The Ups and Downs of the Environmental Kutznets Curve. Prepared for the UCF/Center Conference on the Environment. Orlando, FL, 20 November–2 December.

Lyke, M (1999). Killer Whales are Full of Toxic Chemicals, New Study Says. *Seattle Post*, 25 October.

Martinez-Vela, C (2001). *World Systems Theory*. http://web.mit.edu/~vinayak/MacData/afs.course/other/esd.83/OldFiles/www/notebook/WorldSystem.pdf [24 December 2011].

Milanez, B and T Bührs (2008). Ecological modernisation beyond Western Europe: The case of Brazil, *Environmental Politics*, 17(5), 784–803.

Moshini, G, H Lapan and A Sobolevsky (2000). Roundup Ready® soybeans and welfare effects in the soybean complex, *Agribusiness*, 16(1), 33–55.

Odum, H (1984). Embodied Energy, Foreign Trade, and Welfare of Nations. In *Integration of Economy and Ecology — An Outlook for the Eighties*, A Jansson (ed.). Stockholm: Stockholm University Press.

Özler, I and B Obach (2009). Capitalism, state economic policy and ecological footprint: An international comparative analysis, *Global Environmental Politics*, 9(1), 79–108.

Pollock, M (1995). *Who Bears the Burdens of Environmental Pollution? Race, Ethnicity, and Environmental Equity in Florida*. Malden, MA: Blackwell.

Prew, P (2010). World-economy centrality and carbon dioxide emissions: A new look at the position in the capitalist world-system and environmental pollution, *American Sociologial Review*, 16(2), 162–191.

Prins, G (1991). *Top Guns and Toxic Whales: The Environment and Global Security*. London: Earthscan Publications.

Rice, J (2009). The transnational organisation of production and uneven environmental degradation and change in the world economy, *International Journal of Comparative Sociology*, 50(3–4), 215–236.

Ross, P, G Ellis, M Ikonomou, L Barrett-Lennard and R Addison (2000). High PCB concentrations in free-ranging pacific killer whales, *Marine Pollution Bulletin*, 40(6), 504–515.

Rothman, D (1998). Environmental Kutznets curve — a Areal progress or passing the buck? A case for consumption-based approaches, *Ecological Economics*, 25, 177–194.

Schnaiberg, A (1980). *The Environment: From Surplus to Scarcity*. New York: Oxford University Press.

Schnaiberg, A and K Gould (1994). *Environment and Society: The Enduring Conflict.* New York: St. Martin's Press.

Shiva, V (1995). *Monocultures of the Mind.* London: Zed Books.

Spaargaren, G (2010). Ecological modernisation theory and domestic consumption, *Journal of Environmental Policy & Planning*, 2(4), 323–335.

Wackernagel, M and W Rees (1996). *Our Ecological Footprint.* Canada: New Society Publishers.

World Bank (2010). Gross Domestic Product 2009. *World Development Indicators Database.*

WTO (1999). *Trade and the Environment.* Geneva: WTO Publications.

Yablokov, A, V Karasev, V Rumyantsev, M Kokeyev, O Petrov, V Lystsov, A Emelyanenkov and P Rubtsov (1993). *Facts and Problems Related to the Dumping of Radioactive Waste in the Seas Surrounding the Territory of the Russian Federation.* Tokyo: Greenpeace.

York, R, E Rosa and T Dietz (2003). Footprints on the earth: The environmental consequences of modernity, *American Sociologial Review*, 68(2), 279–300.

CHAPTER 23

Global Capitalism and Climate Change

Hans A. Baer

University of Melbourne

Humans have been emitting greenhouse gases for eons but it was the industrial revolution, with its heavy reliance on fossil fuels and the capitalist system of production and consumption, that contributed most clearly to a new type of climate change — one not generated by natural events so much as by human-induced or anthropogenic activities. As archaeologists like Fagan (2008, p. xvii) say, "[W]e've entered a time of sustained warming, which dates back to at least 1860s, propelled in large part by humanity — by the greenhouse gases from fossil fuels".

While climate scientists have debated for some time whether recent changes in the global climate are primarily a natural phenomenon or an anthropogenic one, the vast majority now agree that it has largely been created by the emission of various greenhouse gases, and in particular by carbon dioxide, which increased from two hundred and eighty parts per million (ppm) at the time of the industrial revolution to three hundred and ninety ppm today. In short, anthropogenic climate change is inducing (and will continue to induce) severe politico-economic and parallel consequences as the twenty-first century unfolds.

The Australian Academy of Sciences (2010, p. 3), for example, reports that climate change models estimate that "by 2100, the average global temperature will be between two and seven degrees centigrade higher than pre-industrial temperatures, depending on future greenhouse gas emissions and the ways that models represent the sensitivity of climate to small disturbances". Given that humanity has been on earth for some five to six million years, ongoing global warming raises the question as to how long humanity can thrive, at least in its present numbers and occupying its present-day planetary niches, in the face of climate change.

Environmental sociologists like Foster (2009) also acknowledge the way climate change constitutes the most serious ecological threat impinging upon both humanity and the planet. He views this as a manifestation of a larger global environmental crisis that has interrelated components. These include the extinction of species, the destruction of rain forests, the contamination of the oceans, the decline of fresh water, the pollution of lakes and streams, desertification, toxic wastes, acid rain, the depletion of the ozone layer, acid rain, world hunger and overpopulation.

Moreover, the more critical of the world's social scientists have increasingly come to acknowledge that human-induced climate change, or global warming, may constitute yet another contradiction within global capitalism, or the capitalist world system. As an increasingly globalised form of political economy, the capitalist drive to expand markets to maximise profits results in a perpetual treadmill of production and consumption. This treadmill is heavily reliant in turn on fossil fuels and other substances which then emit greenhouse gases — including nitrous oxide, methane, ozone, and chlorofluorocarbons.

THE IMPACT OF CLIMATE CHANGE ON THE ENVIRONMENT AND HUMAN SOCIETIES

The mean temperature of the earth increased 0.76 °C between 1850 and 1999 and 2001 and 2005 (IPCC, 2007, p. 5). Various studies indicate that the Earth experienced a rapid warming trend around 1910, a levelling off between the early 1940s and early 1970s, and another rapid rise beginning in the late 1970s. The twentieth century was the warmest century in the past millennium. The period from 1990 to 2000 was the warmest decade of the past millennium.

The *Copenhagen Diagnosis*, a report that seeks to synthesise most policy-related climate science published since the 2007 IPCC report, indicates that every single year of the twenty-first century has been among the top ten warmest years since instrumental records began, with winters warming faster than summers (Alison *et al.*, 2009, p. 15). Despite cold weather and heavy snowfalls in Europe and North America in late 2010, the World Meteorological Organisation reported that 2010 was the warmest year on record and NASA reported that 2010 tied with 2005 as the warmest year on record. The *Copenhagen Diagnosis* says that the mean global temperature is expected to increase four to seven degrees centigrade by 2100 (Alison *et al.*, 2009, p. 49). This said, temperature rises vary considerably around the planet. For example, a global temperature rise of three degrees centigrade would translate into only a one to two degree centigrade increase over most of the oceans but a rise of 7.1 to eight degrees centigrade in the Arctic (Paskal, 2010, p. 68).

The IPCC (2007) report indicated that sea levels around the world rose an average of 1.8 mm per year between 1961 and 2003. It projects a sea level rise of another 18 to 59 cm over the course of the present century. Sea levels are rising in a warming world not only because of the addition of water previously locked up in ice sheets and glaciers but also because water expands when it is warmed.

The oceans absorb perhaps forty percent of carbon dioxide emissions from the burning of fossil fuels (Hossay, 2006, p. 8). A NASA study in late 2002 found that the ice pack covering the Arctic Ocean is vanishing at the rate of about nine percent per decade (Gelbspan, 2004, p. 21). Is this good news in atmospheric terms? Not necessarily, since as glaciers melt and retreat around the world, the Arctic tundra also melts, releasing massive amounts of methane into the atmosphere. Rising temperature contributes to the thawing of peatbogs, which are wetlands located in cold, temperate areas primarily in the Northern Hemisphere. This is what results in the release of the methane.

Climate change may also contribute to the intensification of droughts, hurricanes, cyclones, precipitation, and flooding. It may cause stronger and more frequent El Nino events. Due to climate change, plants and animals are already moving into regions closer to the poles.

Climate change is already having an impact upon human societies. South Pacific Islanders in particular face threats to their traditional horticultural lifestyle due to rising sea levels and storm surges. These inundate their fields and freshwater supplies and threaten to submerge their islands. The Inuit of Arctic Canada and Alaska are experiencing a significant reduction in the number of polar bears that they have traditionally hunted. They are unable to access seals either, because pack ice is freezing later in the autumn than it once did. Andean peoples face the possibility of the eradication of their way of life as glaciers from which they have drawn water for themselves, their fields, and their animals continue to retreat. Peoples living in coastal areas around the world face the possibility of increasing flooding and hurricanes due to the rise of the oceans. Meanwhile many climate scientists contend that the droughts that people in many parts of sub-Saharan Africa as well as the American Southwest and Australia have been facing are related to climate change.

Climate change appears also to be the primary impetus behind the spread of infectious diseases to environments north and south of the equator and the heat waves that threaten the lives and health of vulnerable populations, such as the elderly and the sick. Given the health consequences of climate change, it is possible to speak of the diseases of climate change or global warming (Baer and Singer, 2009). These are not necessarily new diseases, although they might include 'tropical diseases' (e.g. malaria and dengue fever) that have spread to new places and peoples because of climate change as well as the detrimental health effects of failing food security due to the desertification of pastoral areas and the flooding of agricultural lands.

THE CAPITALIST TREADMILL OF PRODUCTION AND CONSUMPTION AS A SOURCE OF GREENHOUSE GAS EMISSIONS AND CLIMATE CHANGE

Capitalism is a global politico-economic system that in its drive for profits requires ongoing accumulation and expansion and puts people on a treadmill of production and consumption. It systematically exploits human beings and the natural environment, despite capitalist rhetoric to the effect that it contributes to the prosperity and well-being of all human beings (albeit some more than others). In reality, global capitalism results in a widening gap between rich and poor nation states and within nation states. Furthermore, ongoing poverty tends to stimulate population growth. Finally, various governments, particularly those of the US and the UK, do the bidding of capitalist multinational corporations in resource wars (Klare, 2008).

Global capitalism, which relies heavily upon fossil fuels, plays a significant role in the emission of greenhouse gases into the atmosphere. Grimes and Kentor (2003, p. 264) maintain that "world system research on CO_2 production to date has found that the volume of energy consumption and thus CO_2 production continues to track [the] world-system position [of nations and regions], being greatest in the core [the advanced capitalist nations], intermediate in the semi-periphery [the better off developing countries], and lowest in the periphery [the poorest of the developing countries]".

Core or developed countries tend to shift toward service/information economies. They have the financial resources to invest in more energy-efficient technologies which over the long run can cut costs. Multinational corporations in the core often export polluting industries to developing countries. Table 1 indicates that while the total carbon dioxide emissions in the high-income countries greatly exceeds the total carbon dioxide emissions in the high to middle, middle-income, and low-income countries combined, the production efficiency in all of these countries is worse than that for the high-income countries. As Roberts *et al.* (2003, p. 288) observe, developing countries have "enough fossil-fuel dependent technology to compete in the world market, but not enough sophisticated infrastructure to do so efficiently".

While production efficiency improves in developed countries, there is also a tendency for total carbon dioxide emissions and per capita emissions to increase.

Table 1: Average total CO_2 emissions and CO_2/unit GDP for income groups of countries, 2000.

Category of countries	Average total emissions (million tons CO_2)	Average cumulative CO_2/unit GDP
High-Income Countries (24)	120,162	0.1479
High-Middle Income (20)	5,917	0.2710
Middle Income (33)	18,161	0.2960
Low-Income (54)	20,155	0.5262
Low-Income (61)	28,834	0.4066

Source: Adapted from Roberts and Parks (2007, p. 147).

This occurred in the US, the Netherlands, Japan, and Austria between 1975 and 1996 (Clark and York, 2005, p. 412) and is consistent with global capitalism's need to continually grow. Roberts *et al.* (2003, p. 277–278) apply world-systems analysis to highlight the social factors underlying carbon dioxide intensity within countries, as defined by the quantity of carbon dioxide released per unit of market output. They found that some countries are more efficient than others in generating wealth when considered in the light of the environmental costs incurred. Elsewhere, Metz (2010, p. 39) reports that Japan as well as European countries are the most efficient economies, being about twenty-five percent more efficient than the US and more than three times as efficient as economies-in-transition (Metz, 2010, p. 39). While the West German economy grew at an average annual rate of 2.1 percent during the 1980s, its carbon dioxide emissions declined at an average rate of 1.2 percent per annum. Core countries are both economically able to and politically pressured by the environmental movement to reduce pollution (Roberts *et al.*, 2003, p. 285).

In 2005 the top ten emitters of greenhouse gasses were either specific developed countries (such as the US, Japan, and Canada) along with the EU or the "large emerging market economies" (such as China, Russia, India, Brazil, Mexico and Indonesia) (Barbier, 2010, p. 35). Altogether they accounted for over seventy percent of the world's greenhouse gas emissions.

Jevons once identified an important paradox, namely, that increasing efficiency of coal use was correlated with increasing coal consumption (York *et al.*, 2009, p. 137). It seems that the most 'eco-efficient' businesses, industries, or political economies may be the ones consuming the largest quantities of resources and producing the most pollution. While China, for example, has undergone a significant improvement in energy efficiency, it has undergone a marked increase in its total ecological footprint (York *et al.*, 2009, p. 140).

This trend challenges the basic assumption underpinning ecological modernisation theory, which says that technological transformations will be paramount in solving environmental problems. Efficiency may increase but consumption (and pollution) may increase overall. It is worth noting in this regard that four countries declined in ecological footprint intensity between 1961 and 2003 but increased in terms of their total ecological footprint (York *et al.*, 2009, p. 142). In terms of historical responsibility with regard to global carbon emissions between 1750 and 2006, the US accounted for twenty-eight percent, the UK six percent, Japan four percent, Russia eight percent, Germany seven percent, the remainder of Europe eighteen percent, and China eight percent (Schor, 2010, p. 175).

Table 2 indicates that carbon dioxide emissions from fuel combustion overall have continued to rise around the world, although there are specific regions, particularly former Soviet-bloc 'economies in transition', where it has dropped.

Table 2: World CO_2 emissions in gigatons from fuel combustion, selected countries and regions.

	1990	2008	% change 1990–2008
United States	4,868.7	5,923.6	15.7
Europe	3,153.6	3,222.9	2.2
Pacific	1,346.4	1,582.0	17.5
Economies in Transition	3,852.9	2,624.3	−31.9
Africa	545.6	889.9	61.1
Middle East	592.5	1,492.3	151.8
Non-OECD Europe	106.1	92.2	−13.1
Latin America	869.5	1,476.5	69.8
Asia (excluding China)	1,510.1	3,524.1	133.4
China	2,244.4	6,550.5	191.9
World	20,964.8	29,381.4	40.1

Source: International Energy Agency (2010, p. 13).

Much of the economic growth in developing countries, including China and India but also the oil-producing countries, results from the production of luxury goods for the wealthy and the new middle classes in these places. In China many of these people can be found in the eastern provinces where individual purchasing power exceeds seven thousand US dollars annually (Harris, 2010, p. 126). The Netherlands Environment Assessment Agency says that in 2006 China surpassed the United States in total carbon dioxide emissions (Camilleri and Falk, 2010, p. 279). China builds a new coal power plant approximately every four days and appears to have surpassed the US to become single largest emitter of carbon dioxide in the world due to the rapid growth in its fossil-fuel consumption and cement manufacturing.

Hence the argument that affluent nations need to reduce the demands they place on the environment and to transform their politico-economic systems to meet people's needs without unsustainably devouring the planet's natural resources (York *et al.*, 2009, p. 143). Hence the parallel argument that says less affluent nations need to shift their development strategies away from relentless politico-economic expansion in order to focus not only on escalating material consumption but also on strategies that improve people's quality of life.

Roberts and Parks (2007) delineate four factors they see as contributing to differences in state responsibility for climate change: (1) a country's wealth (per capita GDP or total GDP); (2) carbon dioxide emissions per unit of GDP (carbon intensity); (3) per capita carbon dioxide emissions; and (4) cumulative emissions over the fifty years that started in 1950. China and India combined have contributed only nine percent of the total quantity of accumulated anthropogenic GHGs. The US has contributed over thirty percent.

Various studies indicate a curvilinear relationship in which the intensity of this responsibility first rises as states move from being poorer to wealthier and subsequently declines when it joins the wealthiest nations. It is important here to highlight again how international trade and globalisation are used by developed states to shunt off the greatest ecological impacts of production to the developing ones (Roberts and Bradley, 2007, p. 161).

The components of global capitalism that contribute to greenhouse gas emissions and ultimately climate change are seemingly endless. In 2004 global greenhouse gas emissions, measured in carbon dioxide equivalent terms, came to 56.6 percent from fossil-fuel use, 17.3 percent from land-use changes (deforestation, biomass decay), 14.3 percent from methane, 7.9 percent from nitrous oxide, and 1.1 percent from various other highly actively sources (Pittock, 2009, p. 157). Table 3 depicts the major sources of carbon dioxide emissions worldwide.

This chapter subsequently focuses on several of these principal sources: (1) the heavy reliance on fossil fuels; (2) steel, aluminium, and concrete production; (3) transport; (4) buildings, dwelling units, and consumer items; (5) industrial agriculture and logging and (6) militarism and war.

Table 3: Total CO_2 emissions (in gigatons and percentage of total), 2007.

Source	Gigatons	Percentage
Fossil fuels	29	81
electricity	11.5	32
industry	8	22
transportation	6.5	18
residential	2	6
commercial	1	3
Deforestation	7	19
Total	36	100

Source: Adapted from Sachs (2008, p. 96).
Note: These figures are based on fossil-fuel estimates for 2005 as compiled by the International Energy Association. They assume that all categories increased by 2.3 per annum between 2005 and 2007.

The Heavy Reliance of Global Capitalism on Fossil Fuels

Capitalist and post-revolutionary societies have historically relied and continue to rely very heavily upon coal. Not only does coal contribute to air and water pollution, it is a major source of carbon dioxide and contributor to climate change. The Global Carbon Project (2010, p. 2) reported that coal constitutes the largest source of fossil-fuel carbon dioxide emissions. Ninety-two percent of the growth in coal emissions during 2007 to 2009 came from the increased use of coal in China and India. China is said to be building two coal-fired power plants every week (Li, 2008, p. 64).

Although the discovery of oil preceded the advent of the automobile era by about a half a decade, the rise of the petroleum and automobile industries were intricately interwoven. Aside from motor vehicles, it goes without saying that oil has been the principal source of market growth during most of the twentieth century and that it continues to be so in the twenty-first century. Indeed, oil replaced coal as the primary fossil fuel in the 1950s. Oil also became an essential ingredient in the production of plastics that in large part replaced packing materials such as paper, wood, glass and metal. Oil in many instances replaced coal in the heating of dwellings, offices and factories. Oil supplies about forty percent of the world's energy and ninety-six percent of its transport energy (Forest and Sousa, 2006, p. 1).

Of all the countries in the world, as none other than George W. Bush noted, "America is most addicted to oil." Klare provides a more serious elaboration:

> Addressing the energy crisis was seen by Bush and his advisors as a critical matter for several reasons. To begin with, energy abundance is essential to the health and profitability of many of America's leading industries, including automobiles, airlines, construction, petrochemicals and agriculture, and so many shortages of energy can have severe and pervasive economic repercussions. Petroleum is especially critical to the US economy because it it is the source of two-fifths of America's total energy supply — more than any other source — and because it provides most of the nation's transportation fuel. In addition to this petroleum is absolutely essential to US national security, in that it powers the vast array of tanks, planes, helicopters, and ships that constitute the backbone of the American war machine (Klare, 2003, p. 16).

Oil serves as an important energy source in transportation, the production of asphalt, the heating of houses and a wide array of other types of buildings, and in industrial agriculture as a fuel for mechanised farm equipment and the production of pesticides.

It is estimated that nearly half of global oil consumption is devoted to the products of the global auto industry. Despite much discussion of the world approaching 'peak oil', the oil industry continues to seek new sources, regardless of the environmental consequences. It is exuberant, for example, about the possibility of discovering new oil supplies in the Arctic as the polar ice cap contracts.

As peak oil quickly approaches, many parties view natural gas as a cleaner energy resource because it produces lower emissions than either oil or coal. Reliance upon it may serve to deter the development of renewable energy sources, however, which do not emit greenhouse gas emissions, since natural gas can be converted into many other products like liquid fuels, artificial fertilisers, and hydrogen for use in fuel cells.

Steel, Aluminium, and Cement Production

The manufacture of products obviously too numerous to list contributes to greenhouse gases, particularly carbon dioxide. Steel and aluminium are the most common metals that are used in the manufacture of numerous products, including motor vehicles, trains, aeroplanes and ships, not to speak of factories, office and residential buildings. In 2006, China was the leading steel producer, producing four hundred and nineteen million tons or over one third of the world total (Liu, 2008, p. 56). The number two and three steel producers in 2006 was Japan, with one hundred and sixteen million tons, and the US, with ninety-nine million tons. In 2006 China accounted for twenty-six percent of primary global aluminium production and China, Russia, Canada, the US, and Australia for fifty-nine percent of primary global production (Gardner, 2008 p. 58).

Cement and concrete are important components of many building materials and road construction materials and result in large amounts of carbon dioxide emission. As Goodal says:

> Nobody is quite sure, but most estimates suggest that the world cement industry is responsible for about five percent of global emissions. This surprisingly large figure arises because the world is now producing about 2.5 billion tonnes of cement a year, almost a third of a tonne per person on the planet. Much of this arises because of the pace of construction in China and other newly industrialising countries. But, to be blunt, Westerners bear some responsibility for this because we are buying the Chinese products made in the new buildings that are using so much cement and concrete (Goodall, 2010, pp. 229–230).

Transport

Metz reports that transport accounted for twenty percent of total energy use in 2006, almost all of it in the form of oil products (Metz, 2010, p. 153). Of this, motor vehicles accounted for more than seventy-five percent, with automobiles accounting for forty-five percent, trucks twenty-five percent, and buses eight percent. Aeroplanes, shipping, and rail transport accounted for twenty percent of transport energy consumption. According to Metz (2010, p. 153), the greenhouse gas emissions from the transport sector accounted for about thirteen percent of total global emissions in 2004.

Mees presents an even grimmer picture of the impact of transport on emissions and on climate change:

> Transport is a critical element of the climate challenge, since it is the second-largest source of energy-related greenhouse gas emissions after electricity generation, accounting for around a quarter of the world total. Transport is also the fastest-growing source of emissions, the rate of increase having overtaken that for electricity generation in the last decade. Three-quarters of transport-related emissions comes from road vehicles. OECD countries currently account for two-thirds of global transport emissions, but developing nations are fast catching up (Mees, 2010, p. 38).

Table 4 depicts changes in greenhouse gas emissions for selected countries from transport and from all sources (except land use and forests) between 1990 and 2004.

The number of cars in the world at the moment is about eight hundred million, though it continues to grow rapidly as developing societies like China and India imitate developed societies in their adoption of a culture of automobility (Montgomery, 2010, p. 9). The US is the largest producer of motor vehicles, as exemplified by the fact that in 2004 alone it manufactured nearly twelve million of them (Rutledge, 2006, p. xi). It is also the mostly highly motorised country in the world with eight hundred and thirty-four registered vehicles per one thousand people, which is over fifty percent higher than Western Europe (Rutledge, 2006, p. 13).

China is the most dramatic example of the growth in motorisation in the developing world. In 2003 it had around twenty-four million motor vehicles as opposed to the US which had about two hundred and fifty million motor vehicles. According to Sachs (2008, p. 76), "China's annual production is now soaring, up to around 7 million per year as of 2006 compared with just 2 million in the year 2000." In 2002, 1.2 million passenger vehicles were sold in China and by the following year this figure had grown by forty percent (Rutledge, 2006, p. 135). Vehicle production declined during the last eight months of 2008 as a result of the global financial crisis, but then "rose steeply enough to … exceed the pre-2008 trend" (Gilbert and Perl, 2010, p. 303).

Table 4: Changes in greenhouse gas emission for selected countries, 1900–2004, from transport and from all sources (except land use and forests).

	Change in GHG emissions from	
Country	**All sources (%)**	**Transport (%)**
Australia	25.1	23.4
Bulgaria	−49.0	−32.1
Denmark	−1.1	26.8
France	−0.8	20.8
Germany	−17.2	5.1
Ireland	23.1	143.8
Italy	12.1	27.6
Japan	6.5	19.8
New Zealand	21.3	61.6
Spain	49.0	77.3
Sweden	−3.5	9.0
UK	−14.3	12.5
USA	15.8	28.1

Source: Adapted from Gilbert and Perl (2010, p. 174).

While motor vehicles are a major contributor to greenhouse gas emissions, various sources indicate that air travel may contribute three to eight percent (Spence, 2005, p. 148). Unfortunately, the Kyoto Protocol exempts emissions from aviation and marine shipping. Aeroplane travel presently represents twelve percent of carbon dioxide emissions from transport (Gautier, 2008, p. 118). Aeroplanes also emit nitrous oxide and other contrail or exhaust fumes meaning that a "factor between two and three is normally applied to the CO_2 emissions from aviation to account for the additional warming impact" (Tickell, 2008, p. 41).

Dwelling Units and Buildings and a Seemingly Endless Array of Consumer Items

According to Little (2009, p. 319), "[b]uildings alone account for nearly 40 percent of all energy use and contribute nearly 40 percent of the world's annual greenhouse gas emissions". Dwelling units in developed societies, particularly in North America, Australia, and New Zealand, have become larger and larger. Needless to say, these larger dwelling units generally require more and more energy to heat or cool and their occupants purchase more and more consumer items, such as widescreen televisions and computers.

Consumer capitalism began to take off in the 1950s when households in developed societies began to be flooded with energy-intensive appliances and devices such as electric cookers, washing and drying machines, refrigerators, toasters, electric irons, electric toothbrushes, electric razors, televisions sets, record players, cassette players, videorecorders, electric tools, lawnmowers, hedge-cutters, leaf blowers, and elaborate lighting systems. Capitalism, with its predilection for inbuilt obsolescence, encouraged people to update older models with new ones, such as plasma televisions, CD and DVD players, and to buy new products like MP3 players, mobile phones and portable computing devices.

While developed societies constitute the leading cultures of domestic consumption, various developing countries, such as China and India, are quickly joining the pack. While many of the refrigerators, air-conditioners, washing machines, televisions and computers manufactured in China are exported, many of them are sold to members of the new Chinese middle class, as well as its elites.

Industrial Agriculture and Logging

The Green Revolution and industrial agriculture have been reliant upon fossil fuels in the form of fertilisers, farm machinery fuels, fuels for other modes of transport, and for the storage of agricultural products. An estimated three calories of fossil fuel energy are required to produce one calorie of food energy (Bello, 2009, p. 36). Reportedly the equivalent of four hundred gallons of oil was needed in 1994 to feed each American (Ruppert, 2009, p. 86). Deforestation, especially in the tropics, contributes around twenty percent of annual GHG emissions. Deforestation, intensive tillage, and overgrazing release carbon dioxide from living or recently living plants and organic matter from the soil. Growing plants can sequester large amounts of carbon dioxide from the atmosphere and store it in the form of vegetation and in the soil. Conversely, as Table 5 indicates, land changes contribute to the release of carbon dioxide, nitrous oxide and methane.

Semi-peripheral countries like Brazil and Indonesia are the sites of the most intense logging activities or deforestation that the capitalist world system promotes. In the mid-1990s, Japan received up to fifty percent of its log imports and ninety-eight percent of its plywood imports from Southeast Asia (Bartley and Bergesen, 1997, p. 369). Over half of the world's paper is consumed by the wealthiest twenty percent of its people, yet much of the deforestation that produces this paper is concentrated in the semi-periphery and periphery (Synott, 2004, p. 224).

Table 5: Greenhouse gas emissions from land use.

Land use	Annual emissions (million tons CO_{2e})	Greenhouse gas emitted
Agriculture	6,500	
Soil fertilisation (inorganic fertilisers and applied manure)	2,100	N_2O
Gases from food digestion in cattle (enteric fermentation in rumens)	1,800	CH_4
Biomass burning	700	CH_4, N_2O
Paddy (flooded) rice production (aneorobic decomposition)	600	CH_4
Livestock manure	900	CO_2, N_2O
Deforestation (including peat)	8,500	
For agriculture and livestock	5,900	
Total	15,000	

Source: Adapted from Scherr and Sthapit (2009, p. 32).

Militarism and Wars

The contribution of military operations to global warming remains an under-researched topic. The Pentagon's activities, however, reportedly resulted in about forty-six million tons or 3.5 percent of US carbon dioxide emissions in 1988 (Renner, 1997, p. 121). More recent figures indicate that carbon dioxide emissions came to sixty million tons from US military operations in 2005 and five million tons from UK military operations in the same year (Parkinson, 2007, p. 4).

Militaries, with their heavy reliance on airplanes (ranging from jet fighters to planes carrying troops and cargo to Air Force One), battleships and aircraft carriers, tanks and other military equipment, need oil. The 2007 *Energy Bulletin* reported that the Pentagon is the single largest consumer of oil in the world, with an official figure of three hundred and twenty thousand barrels of oil per day for vehicle transport and facility maintenance usage. The official figure does not include "energy for the manufacture of vehicles, energy for building and dismantling military facilities, energy for construction of roads, and energy consumed while rebuilding whatever the military blows up", however (Fitz, 2007, p. 1).

Klare (2007) maintains that the Pentagon consumed one hundred and thirty-four million barrels of oil in 2005, as much as the entire country of Sweden. Moreover, one third or more of US military oil consumption reportedly occurs outside of the US (Smith, 1990–1991, p. 1). Thus McQuaig (2004, p. 3) says, "Even as the competition over dwindling reserves heats up and threatens to cause international conflict, we are faced with a still more devastating consequence of our addiction to oil — global warming." While war contributes to climate change in the form of greenhouse emissions, the latter in turn may already be contributing to conflicts in drought-stricken regions of sub-Saharan Africa and threatening to promote larger-scale conflict as the twenty-first century unfolds.

It is difficult to determine the amount of greenhouse gas emissions that are released during actual wars themselves. During the first Gulf War, Iraq allowed over six hundred oil wells to burn, thus emitting an undetermined amount of carbon dioxide into the atmosphere.

Existing Climate Regimes and Green Capitalism as Insufficient to Mitigate Climate Change

It is self-evident that human societies will have to adapt to the reality of climate change in a variety of ways, though the crucial issue in this regard is mitigation. How will human societies stem and reverse the tide of global warming and associated climatic changes?

There is much debate on how to mitigate climate change. They range from the conscious attempt to turn to alternative energy sources (such as wind, solar, geothermal, bio-fuel and even nuclear sources), the planting of trees, the development of environmentally friendly or appropriate technologies, the development and use of energy-saving devices and the retrofitting of buildings and dwelling units with them, improvements in public transport and inducements to transition away from private vehicles, and geo-engineering.

Many of the specific proposals, albeit not all of them, would be steps toward mitigation. While numerous strategies, including emissions trading schemes, emissions taxes, and carbon capture sequestration, have been proposed as ways of coping with climate change, the vast majority of them are framed within the existing parameters of global capitalism, either under the dictates of climate regimes, such as the Kyoto Protocol and the EU's Emissions Trading Scheme (ETS), or under the rubric of 'green capitalism'. As such they will be insufficient to contain climate change in the long run.

Mueller and Passadakis (2010, pp. 562–564) delineate eight arguments against green capitalism. In the interests of space, only the first four will be considered here:

- Green capitalism will not challenge the power of those who actually produce most greenhouse gases.
- All types of green capitalism fail to acknowledge that the expansive nature of capitalism — its need to grow — will undermine any attempt to reduce its constant imperial demand for more resources.

- [I]n a green capitalist setup, wages will probably stagnate or even decline, to offset the rising costs of 'ecological modernisation'.
- The 'green capitalist state' will be an authoritarian one.

Ultimately, Mueller and Passadakis (2010, p. 563) insist that governments and corporations will not provide adequate solutions to the climate crisis but rather that solutions will have to emerge from "globally networked social movements for climate justice" around the world.

AN ALTERNATIVE WORLD SYSTEM: DEMOCRATIC ECO-SOCIALISM

Anthropologists have long recognised that social systems, whether local, regional, or global, do not last forever. Global capitalism has been extant for some five hundred years but it has many inherent contradictions. These suggest that it will ultimately be transcended and, indeed, that it must be if humanity and the planet are to survive.

It seems that there is a need to start thinking about alternative world systems, one committed to meeting people's basic needs, to social parity and justice, to democracy, and last but not least, to environmental sustainability. One scenario, that presents an alternative to an eco-fascist or at least an eco-authoritarian vision, juxtaposes environmental sustainability and climate change mitigation with ongoing social inequality, authoritarian statism, and a smaller global population. Achieving such a world would not be easy, especially given the fate of earlier efforts to create ostensibly more equitable and just social systems. Despite all of the baggage associated with the term 'socialism' and the desire of various progressivist thinkers to substitute terms such as 'radical democracy,' 'economic democracy', 'Earth democracy', and 'global democracy', such a term does make it possible to grapple with scenarios variously given this label, both reformist and revolutionist. And though scenarios like these remain very much visions still, they are ones that various individuals and groups continue to promote. They represent, in Amin's words, "a future to be invented, a project of civilisation, open to the creativity of the imagination" (Amin, 2009, p. 22).

In the nineteenth century, various reformists and revolutionaries sought to develop alternatives to a globalising capitalist world system. Unfortunately, as Wright (2010, p. 106) observes, "[t]hese attempts at ruptural transformation ... have never been able to sustain an extended process of democratic experimentalist institution-building".

Scholars have attempted to understand whether these societies constituted examples of 'state socialism', 'actually existing socialism', 'transitions between capitalism and socialism that required further democratisation', 'state capitalism', or 'new class societies'. Some have advocated eschewing 'socialism' altogether and replacing it with a less loaded concept (Aronowitz, 1994).

According to Miliband (1994, p. 51), three core propositions define socialism: (1) democracy, (2) egalitarianism, and (3) socialisation or public ownership of a predominant part of the means of production. Although some areas of a socialist society — and ultimately a socialist world system — would require centralised planning, coordination and governance, democratic socialists recognise the need for widespread decentralised economic, political, and social structures that would permit the greatest amount of popular participation in decision making possible.

Wallis (2006, p. 42) says that socialism is not synonymous with state ownership. It entails "several forms of property — collective, cooperative and small private or individual property", and even space for small businesses (Lorimier, 1997, p. 22).

Over the past two decades or so, analysts of this ilk have become more sensitive to the environmental travesties that have occurred, not only in developed and developing capitalist societies but in post-revolutionary societies as well. As a result they have sought to develop eco-socialism (Resistance Books, 1999; Foster, 2009):

> Where there was no inherent impulsion within first-epoch socialism to look beyond human welfare, ecosocialism entails a radical shift away from the anthropocentric attitude that holds humanity over nature. Plainly, if life is under threat by capital, then the threat applies to all lives. . . The option for an ecocentric perspective [entails] a decentering from our narrow species interest toward a more universal perspective that encompasses the ecosphere: the plenum of ecosystems, and all creatures, which constitutes and frames human existence (Kovel, 2008, p. 8).

The same concept has been used as the basis for a critical medical anthropology, an approach that espouses the following principles (Baer *et al.*, 2003, pp. 356–359):

- an economy oriented to meeting basic social needs, namely adequate food, clothing, shelter, and healthcare;
- a high degree of social equality;
- public ownership of means of production;
- representative and participatory democracy; and
- environmental sustainability.

Democratic eco-socialism rejects a statist, growth-centred or productivist ethic, therefore. It recognises that human beings live on an ecologically fragile planet with limited resources that must be sustained and renewed as much as possible for future generations. It resembles what world-systems theorists Boswell and Chase-Dunn (2000) call "global democracy", that is: (1) increasing public ownership of productive forces at the local, regional, national, and international levels; (2) development of an economy oriented towards meeting social needs such as food, clothing, shelter, and healthcare; (3) the blending of both representative and participatory democratic processes; (4) the eradication of health and social disparities and the redistribution of human resources between developed and developing societies and within societies in general; (5) the curtailment of population growth that in large part would follow from the previously mentioned; (6) the conservation of finite resources and the development of renewable energy resources such as wind, solar, and geothermal energy; (7) the redesign of settlement and transportation systems to reduce energy demands and greenhouse gas emissions, and (8) the reduction of waste through recycling and a revision of the reigning culture of consumption.

While the notion of a democratic eco-socialism may seem far-fetched, history suggests that social changes can occur quite quickly once economic, political, and social conditions reach a tipping point. What is more, the vision of a democratic eco-socialism able to provide an alternative to the existing capitalist world system as (or whenever) it self-destructs would have to be part of a global process. It could not be created in 'one country'. The struggle for a safe climate would need to be part of a larger struggle for environmental sustainability. It is noteworthy, therefore as Magdoff and Foster observe (2010, p. 25), that "[e]verywhere radical … strategies are emerging, based on other ethics and forms of organisation, rather than the profit motive: ecovillages; … new urban environment[s] …; experiments in permaculture, and community-supported agriculture, farming and industrial cooperatives …".

CONCLUSION

The transition to a democratic eco-socialist world system is not guaranteed. While awaiting the requisite change, however, transitional reforms are conceivable.

These are likely to draw on a broad-based alliance of anti-systemic movements, including the labour movement, the global justice or anti-corporate globalisation movements, radical political groups, indigenous and ethnic rights movements, the women's movement, and the environmental movement. As Foster (2009) says, " … there is little real prospect for the needed global ecological revolution, unless these attempts to revolutionise social relations in the struggle for a just and sustainable society, now emerging in the periphery, are somehow mirrored in movements for ecological and social revolution in the advanced capitalist world" (p. 276).

Lists of the reforms such a transition would entail are also available, though none of these lists is exhaustive. All invite dialogue as to what is necessary to create a safer climate (Wright, 2010). Not for nothing do Camilleri and Falk conclude

(2000, p. 176) that any effective response to climate change requires the involvement of "many institutions", at "many levels of spatial organisation", across "many societies, and over the long term".

REFERENCES

Alison, I *et al.* (2009). *The Copenhagen Diagnosis: Updating the World on the Latest Climate Science.* Climate Change Research Centre, University of New South Wales.

Amin, S (2009). Capitalism and the ecological footprint, Monthly Review, November, 19–22.

Aronowitz, S (1994). The situation of the left in the United States, *Socialist Review*, 23(3), 5–79.

Australian Academy of Sciences (2010). *The Science of Climate Change: Questions and Answers.* August.

Baer, H and M Singer (2009). *Global Warming and the Political Ecology of Health: Emerging Crises and Systemic Solutions.* Walnut Creek, CA: Left Coast Press.

Baer, H, M Singer and I Susser (2003). *Medical Anthropology and the World System: A Critical Perspective* 2nd ed. Westport, CT: Praeger.

Barbier, E (2010). *A Global Green New Deal: Rethinking the Economic Recovery.* Cambridge, UK: Cambridge University Press.

Bartley, T and A Bergesen (1997). World-system studies of the environment, *Journal of World System Research*, 3, 369–380.

Bello, W (2009). *The Food Wars.* London: Verso.

Boswell, T and C Chase-Dunn (2000). *The Spiral of Capitalism and Socialism.* Boulder: Lynne Rienner.

Camilleri, J and J Falk (2010). *Worlds in Transition: Evolving Governance Across a Stressed Planet.* Cheltenham, UK: Edward Elgar.

Clark, B and R York (2005). Carbon metabolism: Global capitalism, climate change, and biospheric rift, *Theory and Society*, 34, 391–428.

Fagan, B (2008). *The Great Warming: Climate Change and the Rise and Fall of Civilisations.* New York: Bloomsbury Press.

Fitz, D (2007). What's possible in the military sector? Greater than 100% reduction in greenhouse gases. *ZNet* (www.zmag.org), 30 April.

Forest, J and M Sousa (2006). *Oil and Terrorism in the New Gulf: Framing U.S. Energy and Security Policies for the Gulf of Guinea.* Lanham: MD: Lexington Books.

Foster, J (2009). *The Ecological Revolution: Making Peace with the Planet.* New York: Monthly Review Press.

Gardner, G (2008). Aluminium Production Continues Upwards. In *Vital Signs 2007–2008: The Trends That Are Shaping Our Future*, L Starke (ed.). New York: W.W. Norton and Company.

Gautier, C (2008). *Oil, Water, and Climate: An Introduction.* Cambridge: Cambridge University Press.

Gelbspan, R (2004). *Burning Point: How Politicians, Big Oil and Coal, Journalists, and Activists Are Fueling the Climate Crisis — and What We Can Do to Avert Disaster.* New York: Basic Books.

Gilbert, R and A Perl (2010). *Transport Revolutions: Moving People and Freight without Oil* (revised ed.). London: Earthscan.

Global Carbon Project (2010), Carbon Budget Highlights, released 21 November 2010, www.globalcarbonproject.org [24 December 2011].

Goodall, C (2010). *How to Live a Low-Carbon Life: The Individual's Guide to Stopping Climate Change.* London: Earthscan.

Grimes, P and J Kentor (2003). Exporting the greenhouse: Foreign capital penetration and CO_2 emissions 1980–1996, *Journal of World-Systems Research*, 9(2), 261–275.

Harris, P (2010). *World Ethics and Climate Change: From International to Global Justice.* Edinburgh: Edinburgh University Press.

Hossay, P (2006). *Unsustainable: A Primer for Global Environmental and Social Justice.* London: Zed Books.

Intergovernmental Panel on Climate Change (IPCC) (2007). *A Report of Working Group I of the Intergovernmental Panel on Climate Change: Summary for Policymakers.* United Nations: IPCC.

International Energy Agency (2010). *CO_2 Emissions from Fuel Combustion Highlights.* Paris: IEA.

Klare, M (2008). *Rising Powers, Shrinking Planet: The New Geopolitics of Energy.* New York: Metropolitan Books.

Klare, M (2007). Iraq and Climate Change, *Foreign Policy in Focus* (www.fpif.org), 7 December.

Klare, M (2003). Blood for Oil: The Bush-Cheney Strategy. In *Socialist Register 2004 — The New Imperial Challenge*, L Panitch and C Leys (eds.). London: Merlin Press.

Kovel, J (2008). Ecosocialism, Global Justice, and Climate Change, *Capitalism Nature Socialism*, 19, 4–14.

Li, M (2008). Climate change, limits to growth and the imperative for socialism. *Monthly Review*, July-August, 51–67.

Liu, Y (2008). Steel Production Soars. In *Vital Signs 2007–2008: The Trends that are Shaping Our Future*, L. Starke (ed.), 56–57. New York: W.W. Norton.

Little, A (2009). *Power Trip: From Oil Wells to Solar Cells — Our Ride to the Renewable Future.* London: Harper Press.

Lorimer, D (1997). *The Collapse of 'Communism' in the USSR: Its Causes and Significance.* Chippendale NSW: Resistance Books.

Magdoff, F and J Foster (2010). What every environmentalist needs to know about Capitalism, *Monthly Review*, March, 1–30.

McQuaig, L (2004). *Crude, Dude: War, Big Oil and the Fight for the Planet.* Toronto: Doubleday Canada.

Mees, P (2010). *Transport for Suburbia: Beyond the Automobile Age.* London: Earthscan.

Metz, B (2010). *Controlling Climate Change.* Cambridge, UK: Cambridge UP.

Miliband, R (1994). *Socialism for a Skeptical Age.* London: Courage Press, Verso.

Montgomery, S (2010). *The Powers That Be: Global Energy for the Twenty-First Century and Beyond.* Chicago: Chicago UP.

Mueller, T and A Passadakis (2010). Another Capitalism Possible? From World Economic Crisis to Green Capitalism. In *Sparking a Worldwide Energy Revolution: Social Struggles in the Transition to a Post-Petrol World,* K Abramsky (ed.). Oakland, CA: AK Press.

Parkinson, S (2007). Guns and Global Warming: War, Peace and the Environment. Web version of presentation given at the Network for Peace AGM, Scientists for Global Responsibility (ww.sgr.uk), February.

Paskal, C (2010). *Global Warring: How Environmental, Economic, and Political Crises Will Redraw the World Map.* New York: Palgrave Macmillan.

Pittock, A (2009). *Climate Change: The Science, Impacts and Solutions* 2nd ed. Melbourne: CSIRO Publishing.

Renner, M (1997). Environmental and Health Effects of Weapons Production, Testing, and Maintenance. In *War and Public Health,* B Levy and V Sidel (eds.). New York: Oxford University Press.

Resistance (1999). *Environment, Capitalism & Socialism.* Chippendale NSW: Resistance Books.

Roberts, J, P Grimes and J Manale (2003). Social roots of global environmental change: A world-systems analysis of carbon dioxide emissions, *Journal of World Systems Research,* 9(2), 277–315.

Roberts, J and B Parks (2007). *A Climate of Injustice: Global Inequality, North-South Politics, and Climate Policy.* Cambridge, Mass: MIT Press.

Ruppert, M (2009). *Confronting Collapse: The Crisis of Energy and Money in a Post Peak Oil World — A 25-Point Program for Action.* White River Junction, VT: Chelsea Green Publishing.

Rutledge, I (2006). *Addicted to Oil: America's Relentless Drive for Energy.* New York: I. B. Tauris and Company.

Sachs, J (2008). *Common Wealth: Economics for a Crowded Planet.* New York: Allen Lane.

Scherr, S and S Sthapit (2009). Farming and Land Use to Cool the Planet. In *State of the World 2009,* L Starke (ed.). London: Earthscan.

Schor, J (2010). Plenitude: *The New Economics of True Wealth.* New York: Penguin.

Smith, G (1990–1991). How fuel-efficient is the Pentagon? Military's oil addiction, *Earth Island Journal* (Winter). http://www.envirosagagainstwar.org [12 June 2008].

Spence, C (2005). *Global Warming: Personal Solutions for a Healthy Planet.* New York: Palgrave.

Synott, J (2004). *Global and International Studies: Transdisciplinary Perspectives.* Melbourne: Social Science Press Australia.

Tickell, O (2008). *Kyoto2: How to Manage the Global Greenhouse.* London: Zed Books.

Wallis, V (2006). Vision and strategy: Questioning the subsistence perspective, *Capitalism Nature Socialism,* 17(4), 38–43.

Wright, E (2010). *Envisioning Real Utopias.* London: Verso.

York, R, E Rosa and T Dietz (2009). A tale of contrasting trends: Three measures of the ecological footprint in China, India, Japan, and the United States, 1961–2003, *Journal of World Systems Research,* 15(2), 134–146.

CONCLUSION

The Cycle-of-Knowing

Ralph Pettman

University of Melbourne

As argued in the Introduction, international political economy (IPE) is described and explained in one or another of the analytical languages used to articulate the meta-discourse of modernism or 'Enlightenment rationalism'. These languages promote the assumptions modernist/rationalists make despite the fact that, as detached social scientists, they are not supposed to make any. Since only someone divine or insane could be completely detached, and since social scientists are neither, they can be seen as making assumptions regardless. It is with these that they contend in the meta-realm of the mind where rationalism makes possible the pursuit of science — be it natural or social.

What are these analytical languages? This depends in principle on the particular assumptions about human nature and nurturing practices that analysts and leaders make. In practice they include the assumption that people are competitive (this underpins economic nationalism); that they are calculating (this underpins economic liberalism); that they are cooperative (this underpins economic socialism); that there is a material nature to human nurturing practices (this underpins marxism); that there is a mental nature to human nurturing practices (this underpins constructivism); and that there is a mixed material-and-mental nature to human nurturing practices (this underpins meta-marxism). More radically, modernist detachment means marginalising those human beings deemed sub-optimal in rationalistic terms. This prompts variously outraged responses from those peripheralised as to their centrality to IPE, responses that include those of diverse feminists, environmentalists, indigenous peoples, post-colonials and the poor. Most radical of all is the way modernist/rationalists now see their attempt at detachment as being limiting and distorting in itself. This has resulted in a range of auto-critiques since modernist/rationalists are now wont to turn their objectifying mental perspective back on itself to ask what the reasons might be for looking at IPE in rationalistic terms. They are no longer convinced that modernist/rationalism as a way to know illuminates and liberates without reservation. They suspect that it might blind and incarcerate as well. Modernist/rationalists look likewise at the issues presented by language and identity (post-structuralism), the subconscious (psycho-pathology), human emotions (romanticism), human intuitions (phenomenology) and the spiritual insights that modernist/rationalism was set up to transcend in the first place (sacralism).

Despite the arguments between modernist/rationalists about what is the best way to articulate their perspective; despite how as a meta-discourse modernist/rationalism marginalises those deemed inadequate in rationalist terms; and despite the limitations and distortions of the meta-discourse of modernist/rationalism itself; standing back to look at IPE from a mental distance is still a fruitful way to start since standing back to look does make it easier to see the patterns that human practices present. Standing back to look can be likened to climbing the tower of a cathedral. In climbing such a tower, little casement windows appear that open out onto views of the surrounding town and even the countryside (IPE), views not available at street level. These windows provide constrained perspectives, hence the desire to keep climbing in the hope that the top of the tower will be reached where there will be a room with windows all around that can provide the ultimate view of IPE, since it will encompass every possible perspective at once.

This is a telling metaphor. The knowledge gleaned by objectifying ('tower climbing') has, indeed, been highly successful in that it has augmented the human capacity to describe and explain global production, consumption and market mechanics. It has also made it possible to provide a range of seemingly detached policy prescriptions.

There is a parallel here with the story of the doctor and his or her patient. The patient complains of pain. The patient says, "I push here. I push there. Everywhere I push it hurts." The doctor examines the patient, that is, he or she adopts an 'objectifying' perspective. The doctor then says that nothing appears to be wrong. However, the patient does have a broken finger.

In short, detachment can and does work. This is why it is a helpful perspective with which to begin, and why there are chapters like those provided above.

This said, privileging the tower metaphor obscures the way particular windows constrain what is seen. It obscures how specific assumptions determine the approaches that IPE analysts and practitioners take and how part truths are promoted and protected as the whole truth. Liberalism, for example, is seen as the only perspective of objectified worth and hence superior to marxism or mercantilism or feminism or postmodernism.

Is a combination of these part truths able to provide the whole truth, then? Is it possible to be a protectionist/liberalist/socialist/marxist/constructivist/meta-marxist/feminist/environmentalist/post-colonialist/developmentalist/postmodernist/poststructuralist/psychopathologist/romantic/phenomenologist/sacralist?

Not really, given the diversity of assumptions these part truths involve. This conclusion is clearly illustrated by the famous parable of the blind people and the elephant. A group of blind people, introduced to an elephant, feel the part that each one is standing near. One feels the trunk and says it is a fire hose. One feels the ear and says it is a large fan. One feels the side and says it is a wall. One feels a leg and says it is a tree. One feels the tusk and says it is a spear. One feels the tail and says it is a rope. Added together and the part views these people provide does not constitute a recognisable elephant, however. The result is a very strange animal indeed.

Modernist knowledge-making not only does not have a summit where everything is visible in every direction (the perspective the blind people above do not possess) but it obscures the fact that the metaphorical tower being climbed may not have very solid foundations. It may be built on sand or even in the sea.

Thus while detachment may seem to provide a superior perspective, this may be distorted by the assumptions that make detachment possible. Consider Horace Miner's essay on "Body ritual among the Nacirema". This seemingly objective anthropologist describes a group with a "highly developed market economy". This group also has distinctive rituals that express their belief that the human body is ugly and naturally tends towards "debility and disease" (Pettman, 2000, p. 96). The Nacirema are the Americans (spelt backwards). Miner's account shows how much is lost by talking about them in objectifying terms. Everything that Miner says is technically accurate. It is distorted and distorting, however. It radically fails to represent the Americans as those familiar with them know them to be.

THE CYCLE-OF-KNOWING

Observations like these suggest that it may be necessary not only to stand back to look but also to stand close to listen to those whose behaviour IPE is supposed to describe and explain (and prescribe policy for). Standing close to listen can compensate for the way detachment limits and distorts human understanding, firstly in terms of the competing analytic approaches that articulate the modernist/rationalist project itself, secondly in terms of those the modernist/rationalist project marginalises, and thirdly in terms of the auto-critiques of the modernist/rationalist project.

In the Introduction, various works by key IPE thinkers were cited since this allowed the reader to stand close to listen. It allowed the reader to hear what different modernist/rationalists have to say about IPE as well as how those ostensibly incapable of talking in modernist/rationalist terms speak, and how those who doubt the certainties of modernist/rationalism express their doubts.

The problem with getting close to listen is that those doing the speaking can lie, or at least they can mislead, not necessarily intentionally but because of their own false consciousness. Those listening can also be misled because of their own false consciousness.

The next step, therefore, is not only to stand close to listen but to take part. This is to actively subjectify. As such it is to suffer the shortcomings of a lack of detachment. It is to reintroduce the limits and distortions that involvement entails. Hence the need to stand back and look from a mental distance once more. This sets up a cycle-of-knowing that by right should not stop, since standing back to look from a mental distance is to reintroduce the limits and distortions of the objectifying perspective and to reactivate the need to stand close to listen and take part once again. This in turn is to reintroduce the limits and distortions of subjectifying involvement, and so on.

In standing back to look a second time, a cycle-of-knowing is established that has much to teach since the second attempt to be detached is informed by all that has taken place in-between, that is, in standing close to listen and taking part. What is seen from a mental distance the first time, in other words, is usually not the same after an attempt is made to compensate for its limits and distortions, and objectifying occurs a second time. The latter is informed by everything that is heard and done in-between.

The shortcomings of every part of the cycle-of-knowing invites those who seek to understand IPE to keep pursuing what they would like to know in terms of the spiral described above. Such a spiral might lead upwards or downwards. It might expand to encompass more and more or it might dissipate for lack of consequence.

What seems self-evident, however, is that the modernist/rationalist approach adopted by all of the contributors of the preceding chapters falls short of what can be done to understand IPE. The contributions above do conform to contemporary scholarly dictates with regard to the preferred way to know. That is their strength. Their weakness is that this is all that they do.

The key shortcoming of the preceding contributions points to the need, in conclusion, to draw attention to the cycle-of-knowing. It points to the need to demonstrate how such a cycle might be used to augment the objectifying approaches taken in this *Handbook* so far by reintroducing subjectifying ones and by returning to objectifying ones again.

Standing Close to Listen and Taking Part

What does it mean: standing close to listen and taking part? How might this augment standing back to look at IPE, which is the contemporary modernist/rationalist meta-discourse?

To stand close to listen it is necessary to allow those who talk about IPE to have their say even though there is no guarantee that they are telling the 'truth' and that they are not saying what they want their audience to hear. It is necessary to let those involved speak with a minimum of analytical inhibition.

To take part is more difficult since it can only be done vicariously here. Evoking an experience in print is a secondary practice. As such it cannot do justice to what primary experience involves. It can only ever be a lesser rendering of sensory events. For example, words on a page do not smell; nor do they bleed; nor do they weep with fatigue or cry out in pain. They may describe these events, literally or metaphorically, but they are not these events.

With limits like these in mind, what are some instances of standing close to listen to IPE and taking part? And how does this discipline look in detached terms a second time, having stood close to listen and having taken part?

Consider Bensusan-Butt, for example, who talks about what it means to stand close to the modernist/rationalist study of international political economy *per se*, and to take part. He does this in the words of a young man (clearly not one aware of his masculinist proclivities) who is about to enter university. The young man is addressing those who teach economics there. "I am told," he says, "that two views of the scope of the subject persist ... Some following the older tradition take it to cover men's lives [sic] in which money and markets play an important role, and also public policies of all kinds that impinge upon those activities. Others, in a more recent tradition, regard it as the scientific study of the rationale of intelligent choice when means are scarce and ends numerous ... [T]he proponents of Scientific Economics ... [assert] it as an axiom, not to be debated, that all behaviour is rational, though sometimes ill-informed ... [but this is to] construct a fake psychology ... [and] apply it to any topic for which a supply of statistics can be concocted ... I [on the other hand] wish to learn about economic psychology ... [so I will turn to] the older traditions of the subject ... [In so turning] I must have a great deal of *economic history*. In my little scramble from the cradle to the grave the world will change about me, for good or ill. I cannot begin to understand the trends of events ... unless I see them in the context of a long evolution ... Needless to say I must have much about *contemporary affairs* also ... [Indeed] what I want especially will be an account of the larger social framework, the aggregates and the structure too large to see for myself, and information about parts of my own country's economy and about other economies that I am unlikely ever to see at close quarters ... When I say information naturally I do not mean only statistics ... What I especially seek is a knowledge of the range and variety of the ways men [sic] take economic decisions, individually and within organisations. I must get, too, some appreciation of the place economic affairs have *vis-à-vis* the non-economic in the lives of my contemporaries near and far in space and time ... And may I, please, see as much as I can for myself. Visit factories, stay with families outside my circle, be helped to take temporary vacation jobs outside the likely scope of my adult life, share in surveys, attend board meetings, sit in parliamentary galleries ... [As to] economic theory ... [it seems that] scholastic fantasies are ... regarded as the apogee of two centuries of theoretical endeavour ... [Economics is] a great web of abstract reasoning with the grandest pretensions ... [Of course] I *must* have theory. The world is too complex for unaided common-sense. That theory must be spun out of simplifications I grant in advance. But they must be good simplifications, not leaving many big things out, and I must be taught what it is that they leave out ... [In short] I want ... the politics of political economy ..." (Pettman, 1996, pp. 1–7).

Bensusan-Butt uses this young man to express his own scepticism with regard to the benefits of studying economics rather than political economy. He provides in the process a seemingly naïve discourse that is anything but. He provides a well-informed articulation of what economics does not do that political economics does. By inviting the reader to listen to a piece of ostensibly innocent rhetoric he is taking the reader closer to his own account (and that of others like him) of what the subject involves and what policy prescriptions in this domain should therefore include.

Bensusan-Butt has his own agenda, which is to promote a concept of economy as other than a natural science. The subject is not one, he believes, that is amenable to the hypothetico-deductive method. It is one that deals with the "feelings and aspirations of ordinary mortals", he says, "in one large tract of their daily lives, one indissolubly linked and only arbitrarily distinguishable from the rest ...". This is not to say that "measurable objective entities" are not to be found there. "It gives its students an *occasional* opportunity," he says, "to retreat into ... the natural sciences, and *occasional* relief from the task of human sympathy ...". Lingering too long in these "little corners of the subject ...", however, "[is] disastrous ...," he concludes. "They have their place — [but only] in the corners"(Pettman, 1996, p. 7).

Bensusan-Butt takes us close to listen to his account of why political economy should be preferred to an objectifying, scientised study of the subject because he wants a meaningful engagement with this discipline. He suggests that such an engagement involves standing close to listen and taking part. It involves spending time on farms and in factories, on the trading floors of financial firms, interviewing people, listening to boardroom discussions and legislative debates, while visiting other countries and living in unfamiliar social environments. Experiences like these provide information of a kind that libraries and lecture theatres cannot, he says. They are directly relevant to knowledge about the political economy, even though it will still be necessary to put that knowledge into a detached context again.

Bensusan-Butt is advocating, in short, a form of the cycle-of-knowing. It is not one as explicit as the one articulated here but his intention is clear. The context is one where standing back to look is taken for granted. Bensusan-Butt seeks to complement this kind of knowing with understanding that can only be gleaned by standing close to listen and taking part, however. Only pursuing knowledge around the whole cycle, he suggests, can approximate what is 'true'.

Economic Nationalism

The first of the mainstream analytical languages used to articulate the modernist/rationalist approach to IPE is economic nationalism. This is otherwise known as economic protectionism, or in more historical terms, mercantilism.

What can be done to invoke a sense of the experience of this discourse? Consider Frederic Bastiat, who wrote a satirical petition to French legislators as to what they should do to assist the French lighting industry. Bastiat is not a protectionist. Instead, he tries to show that such an approach is ultimately ridiculous. In the process, however, he does make a memorable case for what protectionism ostensibly entails and why a liberalist approach might be preferred.

Firstly, Bastiat praises French politicians for being on the "right road". He says they clearly have "little consideration for cheapness and plenty"; that they place the interests of the producers first; that they desire, in other words, to protect producers from "foreign competition"; and that they reserve the "*national market for national industry*" (Pettman, 2006, p. 31).

Secondly, he identifies "intolerable" competition from a "foreign rival" who is in a position "so far superior" with regard to the "production of light" that he is able to "absolutely *inundate[]* our *national market* with it at a price fabulously reduced. The moment he shows himself our trade leaves us — all consumers apply to him; and a branch of native industry … is … at once rendered completely stagnant. This rival, who is no other than the sun, wages war to the knife against us …"(Pettman, 1996, p. 31).

Thirdly, he petitions the members of the Chambers of Deputies to pass a law ordering the "shutting up of all windows, sky-lights … outside and inside shutters, curtains, blinds … in a word, of all openings, holes, chinks, clefts, and fissures, by or through which the light of the sun has been in use to enter houses, to the prejudice of the meritorious manufactures with which we flatter ourselves we have accommodated our country — a country which, in gratitude, ought not to abandon us now to a strife so unequal"(Pettman, 1996, p. 31).

In short, he argues for restricting access to natural light to create a demand for all artificial alternatives and that this would benefit all related industries in turn. For example, the need for more lamp tallow would mean the need for more oxen, sheep and meadows, and hence more meat, wool, hides and manure for the fields. The need for more lamp oil would mean the need for more oil-bearing crops that would exploit fertilised fields. A much greater navy would be needed to go in search of whale oil, ultimately resulting in one that was capable of maintaining the "honour of France". *Resiniers* and coal miners alike would rejoice in "higher wages and increased prosperity". No Frenchman, he concludes, would not be benefited by the legislation he proposes (Pettman, 1996, p. 32).

Bastiat maintains that his petition is not a satire. In saying this he is seeking to bring the reader closer to the discourse he wishes to highlight. In saying this he is making clear why the ostensibly "effete works of the partisans of Free Trade" might not be a more advantageous alternative (Pettman, 1996, p. 32).

The extreme nature of the case he makes is highly effective not only in bringing readers closer to what economic nationalists say but also in providing an image of what it might be like to take part. Being obliged to admit no sunlight into the home (and to go outside it having to wear smoked-lens glasses and carrying a torch) would mean being denied a free good for the benefit of the national lighting industry and its associated producers. The inconvenience of this would be manifest at once, as would the limitations of the discourse of economic nationalism. In the real world these limitations may not be so evident. In the exaggerated example Bastiat provides they are evident at once.

Standing back to look at protectionism from a detached perspective again is made more meaningful by such an account. Even one ultimately critical of economic nationalism helps complement understanding of what it entails.

Economic Liberalism

The second of the mainstream analytical languages used to articulate the modernist/rationalist approach to political economy is economic liberalism. This is otherwise known as economics, or as marxists would call it, bourgeois economics.

In turning to those who talk about what this particular analytical language involves, this conclusion will highlight a short story by David Lodge (1980, pp. 4–17).[1] This story is a seemingly autobiographical account of Lodge's first job.

Between finishing high school and beginning at university Lodge sold newspapers and magazines from a steep-sided wooden barrow at Waterloo Station in London. The main bookstall was managed out of a "cramped and stuffy … office" by a Mr. Hoskyns, a "harassed, irascible little man who had evidently suffered a stroke or some kind of palsy, since the right-hand side of his face was paralysed and the corner of his mouth was held up by a little gold hook and chain suspended from his spectacles"(Pettman, 1996, p. 38).

[1] David Lodge is an English author and academic. He earned a PhD from the University of Birmingham where he taught English literature. He subsequently left the academy to become a full-time writer.

Lodge had two workmates, Ray and Mitch. They had trolleys of their own and the three of them serviced the "[w]aves of office workers arriving on suburban trains ..." together (Pettman, 1996, p. 38). Ray wore an Army Surplus windbreaker and heavy boots that protruded from frayed trousers. Mitch wore a collarless shirt and the jacket and trousers of two different striped suits. Lodge wore his grey flannels and grammar school blazer.

> "Watcher wanner dead-end job like this for then?' was Ray's first utterance.
> 'I'm only doing it for a month,' I said. 'Just while I'm waiting to go to University.'
> 'University? Yer mean, like Oxford and Cambridge? The Boat race and that?'
> (It should be remembered that going to University was a rarer phenomenon [then] ... than it is now.)
> 'No, London University. The London School of Economics.'
> 'Whaffor?'
> 'To get a degree.'
> 'What use is that to yer?'
> I pondered a short, simple answer to this question. 'You get a better job in life afterwards,' I said at length ...
> Mitch, nibbling his fingers, stared at me intently, like a savage pigmy surprised by the appearance of a white explorer in the jungle.'
>
> (Pettman, 1996, pp. 38–39)

The job was roaming the platform in search of customers. If stocks ran low Lodge retired to the bookstall to get more. To begin with he earned less than the others. Gradually he caught up, however, and soon it became a contest as Lodge sought to exceed the record amount taken in one day. Having achieved this goal his workmates responded in kind. "Suddenly," Lodge says, "we were locked in fierce competition. Economically, it was quite absurd, for we were paid no commission on sales ... The old record ... soon seemed a negligible sum [however] — something any one of us could achieve effortlessly on a wet Monday or Tuesday" (Pettman, 1996, p. 41).

Lodge's last day was particularly intense. He managed to make the most money of all three boys. Mr. Hoskyns subsequently turned this against Ray and Mitch calling them "idle little sods" and threatening them with dire consequences if they failed to sustain the high returns they had achieved in the competition (Pettman, 1996, p. 42).

Lodge was appalled. His mother thought he was in love. His father thought he was constipated. His riposte was to tell them he was not moody but that he had seen how capitalism exploits workers by setting one against another and expropriating the profits.

His short term feeling was one of anger. In the long term he was inspired to become a sociologist. As he says, "the faces of Ray and Mitch still haunt me, as I last saw them, with the realisation slowly sinking in that they were committed to maintaining that punishing tempo of work, that extraordinary volume of sales, indefinitely, and to no personal advantage, or else be subject to constant complaint and abuse ..."(Pettman, 1996, p. 43).

Lodge uses his story to talk about economic liberalism in real world terms. He mines it to depict calculative competitiveness in all its ugly ferocity.

He also uses it to provide a sense of the market experience. The reader is not only taken close and told about the mechanics of the liberalist market as manifest in the microcosm of a paper-selling business but he or she is also given a vicarious sense of what it means to take part in these mechanics.

Standing back to look at this cycle from a mental distance once more was enough, for Lodge, to make him a marxist. It was enough to cause him to denounce capitalism as radically exploitative. He was permanently racked with guilt, he says, for the way he had inadvertently contributed to his co-workers' plight.

Not accidently his life's work became that of an academic. He did not consider academia real work. After all, as he said in conclusion, "reading books and talking about them to a captive audience; I would do it if they weren't paying me" (Pettman, 1996, p. 42). He could easily have gone into business since his father wanted him to inherit the family dressmaking firm. After his brief brush with liberalist capitalism, however, he came to the conclusion that academic life does "less harm to one's fellow men" (Pettman, 1996, pp. 52–53). He was made permanently contrite and the reader gets the feeling that he offers this story to them as a salutary lesson from which they might also learn.

Something of the story of liberalist commerce can be found in Wriston's work. Wriston (1992, pp. 57–61, 66–67)[2] highlights the particular role played by money.

"Until recently," he says, "what we call money, whether a piece of paper, a book-keeping entry, or a physical object ... [was] linked to a physical commodity ... The old discipline of physical commodities has now been replaced [however] by a new kind of commodity: information ... For the first time in history, countless investors, merchants, and ordinary citizens can know almost instantly of breaking events all over the earth. And depending on how they interpret these events, their desire to hold more or less of a given currency will be inescapably translated into a rise or fall in its exchange value ... Minutes after any official announcement, the Reuters screens light up in the trading rooms of the world. Scores of traders make their judgments about the effects of the new politics on the value of a currency, and

[2]Walter Wriston (1919–2005) was a banker and a former chairman of Citibank/Citicorp. He was also chairman of President Ronald Reagan's Economic Policy Advisory Board.

then they buy or sell. These buy and sell orders drive the price up or down in minutes. The entire process does not take much more time than it took … [seventeenth century] Dutch bankers to adjust their scales …" (Pettman, 2000, p. 199).

More radically, there are the personal accounts of financial traders. In one of these accounts Leeson tells how he made millions of dollars on the Singapore Futures Market for his employer, Barings Bank. He subsequently began to lose money and to disguise the losses. "I was very, very surprised that nobody stopped me," he says. "The numbers weren't real …" (Leeson, 2000, p. 38). A little later he recounts a dream he had at the time; one where he was "in the middle of the … trading floor. The traders had the heads of wild dogs. Then I was looking down on myself. My body was in the middle of the floor. The dogs were eating me alive" (Leeson, 2000, p. 43). Leeson's poor judgment and Barings Bank's poor supervision of his trading activities eventually brought down the whole institution and landed Leeson himself in gaol.

Stories like these help supplement the detached discussions of economic liberalism and market finance that IPE typically provides. It gives a sense not only of what economic liberalism says but also of what it does. This makes more meaningful the understanding of economic liberalism when a detached perspective is adopted once again.

Economic Socialism

The third of the mainstream analytical languages used to articulate the modernist approach to IPE is economic socialism. This perspective is otherwise known as economic collectivism.

In turning to those who talk about what this particular analytical language involves, this conclusion will highlight a short work by David Stutsman (1972, p. 1). In this work an ironic account is given of economic liberalism and of an economic socialist alternative to economic liberalism.

"There was once a pig farm," says Stutsman, "that was operated by an old farmer, his son, and a hired man. The farmyard was filled with hundreds of pigs of all sizes, and they all ate their swill from a huge trough … One day some of the biggest hogs jumped into the trough, and the swill spilled over the sides. Some of the little pigs did not get enough to eat … [and t]he farmers … were greatly upset.

The old farmer had learned his agricultural theory in the old Classical School, and he knew that when swill overflowed a trough there was too much swill in the trough. He did not see the big hogs in the trough and he did not notice that some of the little pigs were hungry, because he had been taught that hogs do not jump into troughs and that little pigs do not go hungry (unless they are just too lazy to eat).

The farmer's son had been educated in the new Keynesian School of agricultural theory, but he saw the problem much as his father did, for he too had learned that spilling swill means too much swill, and, like his father, he did not see the big hogs in the trough, for he too had been taught that hogs do not jump into troughs. But unlike his father, he knew that little pigs sometimes were forced to go hungry ...

The simple hired man had never been to school and was completely innocent of agricultural theory. He had great respect for both father and son ... but sometimes he wondered quietly why they did not pull the big hogs out of the trough" (Pettman, 2001, p. 145).

Stutsman's brief parable is a way of talking about economic liberalism. It highlights disparities in wealth (big pigs versus little pigs) and the negative consequences these disparities have.

It is also a way of taking part. The act of pulling big pigs out of a trough so that all can eat is extremely graphic. So is a sense of what having big greedy pigs in a trough can do to little starving ones.

Standing back to look from a detached distance once again is to suggest that free markets may not be the most efficient and effective way of exchanging goods and services. The commonweal may not reach those who need it most unless there is active intervention (pulling out the big pigs). The 'trickle down' effect that economic liberalists exalt as providing for all — albeit some more than others — may in practice be a 'gush up' effect that provides for some only and not others. In which case, unless distribution is planned and resources are moved around to the advantage of the resource-poor, disparities will inevitably prevail.

Marxism

The fourth of the mainstream analytical languages used to articulate the modernist/rationalist approach to IPE is marxism. This is otherwise known as historical materialism.

In turning to those who talk about what this particular analytical language involves, this conclusion will highlight a work by Mary Atterbury (1964) on depression hitting Robinson Crusoe's island.

> 'Friday,' said Robinson Crusoe, 'I'm sorry, I fear I must lay you off.'
> 'What do you mean, Master?'
> 'Why, you know there's a big surplus of last year's crop. I don't need you to plant another this year ... When I need you I will send for you. You needn't wait around here.'
> 'That's all right, Master, I'll plant my own crop ... I'll get along fine.'
> 'Where will you do all this, Friday?'

'Here on this island.'
'This island belongs to me, you know. I can't allow you to do that.' ...
'What shall I do, Master?'
'That's your problem, Friday. You're a free man, and you know about rugged individualism being maintained here.'
'I guess I'll starve, Master. May I stay here until I do?...'
'I've thought of something, Friday. I don't like to carry my garbage down to the shore each day. You may stay and do that. Then whatever is left of it, after my dog and cat have fed, you may eat. You're in luck.'
'Thank you, Master. That is true charity ...'

(Pettman, 1996, p. 183)

The story of Crusoe and his man Friday, as Atterbury tells it, is meant to demonstrate the exploitative nature of the relationship between someone who owns the means of production and someone who has to provide their labour in a non-waged way. It is a relationship that could only end if Friday overturned Robinson's regime. In pictures of the pair, however, Robinson is typically armed while Friday is not. This would make overthrowing Robinson problematic. No wonder Robinson says to Friday, "... keep a lookout and let no one land here to settle ... You must be protected ..." (Pettman, 1996, pp. 183–184). What Robinson means of course is that he himself must be protected.

The story of Crusoe and his man Friday also lets Atterbury give the reader a vicarious sense of the experience of exploitation. Crusoe seems to be behaving in a ridiculous manner but the arrogance of the ruling class under capitalism is similar to such behaviour, if not identical. The story may seem ironic but in marxist terms it is highly salutary.

Class struggle of the kind that marxists describe is also exemplified by a brief dialogue between King Arthur, a feudal aristocrat, and Dennis, a modernist peasant. This dialogue takes place in the movie *Monty Python and the Holy Grail*. The absurdity of the one talking to (or rather past) the other, and the contradiction built into having a modernist rather than a feudal peasant (and particularly one expressing himself in marxist terms), is what allows the Monty Python writing team to take the reader close to political issues of considerable note. It also allows them to provide a sense of the feudal experience and of the modernist/rationalist alternative to this experience (Pettman, 1996, pp. 235–237).

For example:

Arthur: Well ... I *am* King.
Dennis: Oh, very nice. King, eh! I expect you've got a palace and fine clothes and courtiers and plenty of food. And how d'you get that? By exploiting the workers! By hanging onto outdated imperialistic dogma, which perpetuates the social

and economic differences in our society! … We're living in a dictatorship, a self-perpetuating autocracy in which the working classes …
Old woman: There you are, bringing class into it again …
Dennis: That's what it's all about …

(Pettman, 1996, p. 235–236)

Or:

Arthur: … who is your lord?
Old woman: We don't have a lord.
Arthur: What?
Dennis: … we're an anarcho-syndicalist commune …
Old woman: … how did you become king …?
Arthur: The Lady of the Lake, her arm clad in purest shimmering samite, held Excalibur aloft from the bosom of the waters to signify that by Divine Providence …
I, Arthur, was to carry Excalibur … that is why I am your King. …
Dennis: Look, strange women lying on their backs in ponds handing over swords … that's no basis for a system of government. Supreme executive power derives from a mandate from the masses not from some farcical aquatic ceremony … I mean, if I went round saying I was an Emperor because some moistened bint had lobbed a scimitar at *me*, people would put me away.
Arthur: (Grabbing him by the collar) Shut up, will you. Shut up!
Dennis: Ah! *Now* … we see the violence inherent in the system.

(Pettman, 1996, pp. 236–237)

The viewer of this film is told here about two important dichotomies. One dichotomy is between pre-modernity and modernity. The other is between feudal aristocrats who cannot conceive of an alternative to their dominance and workers who want a radical form of collective self-rule (anarcho-syndicalists).

The viewer is also provided with a sense of the radical difference in awareness that these two dichotomies involve. An invitation is extended, as it were, to take part in what makes differences like these so compelling.

When a detached perspective is adopted once more it is informed by what was learned standing close to listen and taking part via the film experience. This is not the same as standing back to look at these dichotomies in intellectual terms alone. There is a further dimension to viewer understanding which can only be added, firstly, by listening to the conversation between Arthur, Dennis and the old woman and, secondly, by experiencing something first-hand, as it were, of what an aristocratic mien entails and what a peasant/non-peasant form of class consciousness entails.

Constructivism

The fifth of the mainstream analytical languages used to articulate the modernist approach to IPE is constructivism. This is otherwise known, as the Introduction says, as mentalism or neo-hegelianism.

In turning to those who talk about what this particular analytical language involves, this conclusion will highlight verbatim comments from a television documentary on New Zealand. This particular documentary detailed the policy changes made after 1984 when a Labour government came to power determined to make the country more open and more prosperous. The government had a clear mental picture of what it wanted to do. Its 'norm entrepreneurs' were Labour politicians and senior public servants who had trained in the US, but they were neoliberalistic Labour politicians and public servants. As such they were determined to impose neoliberalism on the whole country. If enough people could be persuaded to accept the same ideals, then the whole country could be radically changed. It could be spun on the spot like a tug-boat, and this, indeed, is what took place.

> *Rt. Hon. David Lange* (Prime Minister 1984–1989):
> It was a revolution ... And because it all happened so quickly you got a lot of bewilderment ...
>
> *Jim Davis* (farmer):
> I don't know what we'll do ... That's me and my kids and my bloody grandkids and everybody. They can get stuffed ... [T]hey've sucked us dry ... with their bloody interest rates and now they're going to send their bastard people down here to live on our farms. Well, I'll tell you what, someone will die before we're finished. Bugger them.
>
> (Pettman, 2000, pp. 193–194)

Getting close to listen to those involved — both those in power and those on the political periphery — brings a degree of immediacy to accounts of how neoliberalism was constructed that detached analysis does not. A vicarious version of what it means to take part may still be verbal but it is still more than what objectifying allows.

The return to a detached perspective again includes the experience that immediacy provides. As a consequence it is not the same as the detachment that preceded the attempt to embark on the cycle-of-knowing. It is informed by the understanding that standing close to listen and taking part entails.

Meta-marxism

The sixth of the mainstream analytical languages used to articulate IPE is a combination of marxism and constructivism. Here the whole advertising industry could be cited as an example of what standing close to listen and taking part involves. Western societies are steeped in this industry's products. Those who own and manage secondary and tertiary modes of production vie to promote their various commodities by making the need for them seem natural and normal; by making them seem highly desirable. The television and film industries also provide a plethora of examples of what it means to have capitalist exploitation obscured by those who profit from the process by which such obscurantism is created.

The Margins

Modernist rationalists, as noted in the Introduction, marginalise the accounts of IPE by those they deem insufficiently rationalistic. This includes women, environmentalists, post-colonials, indigenous peoples, and the poor.

The Margins: Feminism

There are many feminist accounts of IPE since feminists are free to enter debates about the discipline wherever they think it tactically or strategically most advantageous to do so. Pura Velasco[3] talks in marxist terms, for example, of how she was a "global commodity" (Pettman, 1996, pp. 217–219). Thus she says, "... My background was middle class and I see it as a privilege being educated. But going to another country and servicing other people, it really crystallised my consciousness of who I am, of being a worker ... [Indeed w]hen I first applied ... as a domestic worker for an ambassador, he asked me not to sit at the table in the kitchen to eat ...". Velasco also says, apropos the global implications of women's work, "... it is important ... to link the remittances of women who are sending money to their family back home ... with the money [for example] that is going out from the Philippines which is being used to service the debts to the IMF and World Bank ..." (Pettman, 1996, pp. 218–219).

---

[3] Pura Velasco was born in the Philippines and has worked internationally as a domestic and a caregiver. She is a now a leader in the movement to further 'nanny power', that is, to organise support services for caregivers worldwide.

In these two sentences there is a wealth of insight that analytical description does not provide. Getting close to listen to Velasco is to hear the voice of female labour-made-cheap on a global basis. There are many other such voices — from industrialised zones and farms, for example, or from the heart of the global sex trade. They all help counter the reductionist character of a detached analysis of the world's women and complement it with a more engaged analysis. Taking part in the commodification of female labour on a global scale is an antidote to the analytical reification of what is involved. Velasco lived this life. She knows what happens because it happened to her. This makes her account notably more authentic than those provided by analysts who never leave the library or the lecture hall.

Analytical descriptions that seek out such proximal accounts are also more comprehensive. Distal accounts alone cannot capture the nuances and insights that standing close to listen and taking part provide.

The Margins: Environmentalism

There are also many environmentalist accounts of IPE now. Environmentalists, like feminists, are able to engage in debates from any of the mainstream perspectives as well as from non-mainstream ones.

James Lovelock[4], for example, talks in postmodernist terms of the earth as alive in that it is able to metabolise, evolve, keep its temperature and chemical balance constant, heal itself, and even, should humans manage to render another planet habitable, reproduce (Pettman, 2004, p. 153). He talks about nature in terms of organised complexity. To listen to him is to understand the world in a different way. It is to invite a very different experience of the dynamic equilibrium that makes life on earth sustainable (Pettman, 2004, pp. 145–156).

Placing what Lovelock says and the experiences it invokes at a detached distance again is not to dismiss the significance of what he says or the implications of what he feels. It is to be detached in a better informed and more nuanced way.

The Margins: Post-colonialism and Fourth Worldism

Post-colonialists and indigenous ('Fourth World') peoples provide their own first-hand accounts of what it means to be marginalised. These accounts range from Nigerian novels to reports to the government of the Solomon Islands to Maori

[4] James Lovelock is an English biologist and environmentalist. He is best known for his promotion of the Gaia hypothesis. This sees the planetary biosphere as self-regulating.

critiques of modernist epistemology. Francis Bugotu[5], for example, was the first Solomon Islands graduate. He says that "... [t]he challenge for ... Pacific Islanders is not to stand wide-eyed at one side of the arena ... [but] to find a design for a future which serves ... [their] interests ... [: a] pattern of communal land rights [for example] ... [that] could form the basis for cooperative work ... decision making by consensus [that] could be ... [adapted] ... for modern parliamentary procedures ... shared responsibility for the young, the sick and the elderly, [that] could become embraced in modern social welfare programmes; ... classless and non-elitist society forms [that] could be brought into newly planned educational structures ..." (1976, p. 616–619, in Pettman, 2001, p. 90).

To listen to Bugotu and to ask what taking part in village life was like for him is to gain access to a completely different dimension to IPE, one that modernist detachment no longer sees. It is to add to the objectifying perspective the benefit of the insights that subjectifying provides. Standing back to look again is to take that understanding along.

The Margins: Developmentalism

So what of the poor? "When I visit[ ] Bagh Nanak Chand, he and his two teenage sons and orphaned nephew... [are] handmaking black, wedge-heeled women's sandals ... The shoes are neat and workmanlike ... [b]ut ... will sell on the lower, bazaar end of the home market and command low prices ... At around 5:30 p.m. Chand collects the day's sandals into a large flat wicker basket ... and goes to the main road to hail a cycle rickshaw. He gets out at Hing Ki Mand, Agra's shoe market ... Chand stops at the premises of a white-haired merchant ... in Western dress ... He passes over the sandals, pair by pair ... A short haggle with few words ensues ... Chand is paid — but not in cash. The middleman reaches down a pad of printed promissory notes ... and fills it in ... postdated for payment three months later. This means that Chand is giving the dealer three months' credit. As Chand's family lives and works from hand to mouth, he has no choice but to seek out a special dealer ... But he will deduct a discount ..." (Pettman, 1996, p. 208).

Chand's pre-capitalist workshop has probably been replaced by now because of cheap products from capitalist China. Chand and his family have probably been forced to find paid work doing something else. This is the reality of the

[5] Francis Bugotu was the leading Solomon Islands education analyst and political statesman of his generation. He was secretary-general of the South Pacific Commission and Solomon Islands ambassador to the United Nations.

globalisation of capitalism. It has a human face and it can only ultimately be described in terms of millions of stories and experiential accounts like that of Chand's. To seek out these stories and experiences and to incorporate them into the detached account of IPE that standing back to look at the discipline entails, is to gain a significantly more nuanced understanding of that account.

Postmodernism and Other Auto-critiques of Modernity

At this point we move even further away from mainstream analytical languages to acknowledge the auto-critiques of modernist rationalism. These auto-critiques include postmodernism, poststructuralism, psychopathology, romanticism, phenomenology, and sacralism.

The reflexivity that postmodernism involves calls into question the certainty of every grand narrative that the mainstream accounts of IPE provide. Poststructuralist ideas about the contingency of language and identity do likewise. Psychopathologists question how reliable any account of IPE can be that articulates only conscious motives and not unconscious ones as well. Romantics prefer to render IPE in emotivist terms, for example, by making movies like *Wall Street.* Phenomenologists look at IPE as things-in-themselves, for example, in such intuitionist terms as 'caring'. Sacralists look at IPE in the meditative or spiritually inspired terms that modernist/rationalism was designed expressly to eschew (Islamic finance and banking or Buddhist economics).

All of these approaches invite specific experiences. The return to a detached perspective in the light of these experiences is to return to a perspective informed by these experiences. It is to return to a secondary form of detachment that is not the same as the primary form that standing back to look initially entailed. It is to return to a secondary form of detachment that is arguably a more understanding one. This again is the cycle-of-knowing in practice and not just principle.

CONCLUSION

Returning to mainstream IPE after getting close to listen to alternative accounts of it, and taking part in the alternative experiences that these alternative approaches entail, is to return to IPE changed. It is to see the discipline with more comprehensive eyes and a more understanding mind.

In short, a Conclusion like this takes the reader back to the Introduction, albeit with an added invitation. It takes the reader back to the start with the incentive to 'see' IPE in both analytic and non-analytic ways.

REFERENCES

Atterbury, M (1964). Depression Hits Robinson Crusoe's Island". In *Rebel Voices, an I.W.W. anthology*, J. Kornbluh (ed.). Ann Arbor: University of Michigan.

Bugotu, F (1976). Decolonizing and Recolonizing: The Case of the Solomon Islands. In *The Indigenous Voice: Visions and Realities*, 2nd ed. (1988), R Moody (ed.), Utrecht: International Books.

Leeson, N (2000). *Rogue Trader*. Harlow: Pearson Education.

Lodge, D (1980). My First Job, *London Review of Books*, September, 4–17.

Pettman, R (2004). *Reason, Culture, Religion: The Metaphysics of World Politics*. Houndmills: Palgrave.

Pettman, R (2001). *World Politics: Rationalism and Beyond*. Houndmills: Palgrave.

Pettman, R (2000). *Commonsense Constructivism or the Making of World Affairs*. Armonk: M.E. Sharpe.

Pettman, R (1996). *Understanding International Political Economy, With Readings for the Fatigued*. Boulder: Lynne Rienner Publishers.

Stutsman, D (1972). A parable of pigs (the inflation/unemployment dilemma), *Review of Radical Political Economics*, 4(4), 1.

Wriston W (1992). *The Twilight of Sovereignty: How the Information Revolution Is Transforming Our World*. New York: Charles Scribner's Sons.

Index